A
DESKTOP
REFERENCE
OF
HIP
VINTAGE
GUITAR
AMPS

Kendrick Books
P.O. Box 160
Pflugerville, Texas
78660-0160
© 1994 Gerald Weber

ISBN: 0-9641060-0-0

Editor: Jeanne M. Schmitt
Art direction and production: R.K. Watkins
Scans and typesetting: Artistic Group
Printed in the United States of America

Disclaimer: Tube amplifiers contain high voltages which may be lethal, even if the amplifier has been off for some time. We do not recommend that you open your amplifier or try to perform any repair operations, unless you are properly trained in electronic servicing. Gerald Weber, and Kendrick Books, accept no responsibility for accidents resulting in personal injury or destruction of property. Again, there are large voltages present in your amplifier that can kill, even with your amplifier unplugged from the wall.

DEDICATION

I dedicate this book to my father
Gerald John Weber Sr.

ACKNOWLEDGEMENTS

In no particular order:

Jill Kendrick Weber, my wife/soulmate, best friend, and greatest fan whose inspiration has been a constant source of motivation, joy, and growth.

Ken Fischer, mentor, tube guru, and friend whose knowledge and support have made the difference in my life.

Alan and Cleo Greenwood for giving me the opportunity to contribute these articles to *Vintage Guitar Magazine*.

All the dedicated employees at Kendrick who allowed me the opportunity to spend time on this project.

Robert Watkins, whose enthusiasm for this book made it possible for you to have it now.

Everyone who contributed schematics to this book.

Anyone that I forgot to acknowledge.

PREFACE

When I began writing articles for *Vintage Guitar Magazine* several years ago, my original intention was to share my knowledge with those who care as much about tube guitar amps as I do. At the time, I had no idea that this book would eventually write itself. This book is actually a compilation of those articles and a compilation of the "Ask Gerald" question and answer column with the addition of some schematics and a reprint of the "Trainwreck Pages" and some other reprints.

This book is written for the guitarist or collector who desires a common sense approach to understanding the essence of vintage tube amps and vintage tube tone. Not written for engineers, it does not contain engineering formulas, polar mathematic equations, or abbreviations that are assumed you should know. In fact, when a term is used for the first time, a definition of that term will appear at the end of the chapter in a mini-glossary.

When you come across a word that is unfamiliar, you should look at the mini-glossary at the end of the chapter and clarify the word *before proceeding*. This will keep everything clear for you.

DISCLAIMER: Tube amplifiers contain potentially lethal high voltages even after they are unplugged, that may cause personal injury or death. Do not attempt to repair or modify any amplifier unless you are absolutely certain that you know what you are doing.

FOREWORD

About the author...

Gerald Weber, a native Texan, gave up a lucrative business to pursue a lifelong dream to work in the field of music. As a player he was never quite satisfied with his tone until he plugged into an old Fender tweed 4X10 Bassman. Since this amp was out of production for about thirty years and hard to obtain in good working condition, Gerald knew what direction his life had to take.

In 1989 he started Kendrick Amplifiers in Pflugerville, Texas. Originally dedicated to reproducing the classic Fender tweeds in exact detail, Kendrick has grown to include their own unique designs. Gerald also joined a network of hand-built amplifier designers that shared an interest in helping musicians gain a knowledge of the workings their favorite guitar amps.

This book is about sharing knowledge. It has many contributors who deserve thanks for their input, but I must say thanks most of all to Gerald Weber for getting this knowledge to the musicians that until now had no source from which to obtain it.

Thanks Mr. Weber.

Ken Fischer
Trainwreck Amplifiers

Kendricks

AMPS OF OUR TIMES - VINTAGE VS. MODERN

Have you ever wondered why a vintage amp sounds the way it sounds? Or why modern amplifiers don't get the raw tone a vintage amp used to get? These are the kind of questions that have been on my mind for many years. Another way of putting it might be something like: "What allows for vintage tone that is missing in modern amps?" Living in the center of those questions as a part of my regular daily life, I invite you to consider these facts.

Early tube guitar amps were all copies of simple, example circuits that were developed and published by the vacuum tube companies. If you ever get a chance to look at an old R.C.A. tube manual, look in the back at the example circuits. Early Fender, Gibson, Rickenbacker, National, Supro, Danelectro, and Ampeg circuits can be found in tube manual examples. The tube companies wanted to sell their tubes and knew that showing example circuits would help sales.

Early tube companies never dreamed that someone would play an amplifier turned up to the point of distortion; therefore, all vintage style amps were built with relatively low gain and low output compared to modern amps. Designed with low gain and low power by today's standards, these early amps had relatively **lower plate voltage** operating the tubes. This has a major effect on the tone. Here's how:

1. Tubes in general that are operated at lower voltages will not pass highs as easily as the same tube operating at relatively high voltages. This results in a browner, more midrangey tone since the highs are rolled off by the tube. This effect happens throughout the amp in a vintage amp, but since modern tube amps use relatively higher voltages, they are generally brighter, with high end harshness.

2. Power tubes that are operated at lower voltages will distort more

easily and at lower volumes than power tubes operating at higher voltages. This results in power tube distortion that is smooth, musical and very sweet.

While virtually all modern tube amps have complicated themselves with dozens of whistles and bells on them that remove tone, dynamics and harmonics, early amps were simple with almost no loss. Consider this: you give me a copy of a tape recording and I make a copy of that copy for a friend who in turn makes a copy for his sister. What do you think his sister's copy would sound like in relationship to the original? This is the same type of loss phenomena that occurs in a modern style tube amplifier when the signal (guitar sound) goes through the first gain stage, then is sent to a gain control. From there it goes to the next gain stage, then to a volume control, then to a tone circuit, then to an effects loop send stage, then to a return gain stage, then to an E.Q. stage, then to a reverb send stage, now a reverb return stage, then a master volume control, then a phase inverter and finally the output section. How do these modern "Swiss Army knife" amps exact these tonal losses?

There is no easy, perfect way to couple one stage of an amp to another. Direct coupling, impedance coupling, transformer coupling all have major drawbacks; therefore, almost all guitar amplifiers are RC coupled. RC stands for resistor capacitor. RC coupling uses two resistors and a capacitor and is basically a high pass pi-type network. In a vintage amp, you may find only one or two stages of gain, a phase inverter and a power section. This keeps coupling losses to a minimum. Modern amps could employ a dozen or more of these RC networks. Also, to allow for tremendous gain, many modern amps use voltage divider circuits between stages. These circuits use resistors and kill many natural harmonics and rich overtones. When signal is passed through a resistor, the first thing to go is the higher harmonics. You may have noticed this on your guitar when you turn the volume down. The higher harmonics disappear resulting in bad tone. Sometimes a small compensating cap is installed on guitar volume controls to help the highs get through, but it still is not the same as not having to compensate for loss in the first place.

While we are on the subject of tonal losses, there are other losses that occur in modern amplifiers that are not obvious by looking at the schematic. One of these losses occurs in the audio transformer. In times of old, virtually all transformers were wound directly on a laminated core with only paper insulating the windings from the core; modern transformers are wound on plastic or nylon bobbins, much thicker than paper, resulting in greater loss and consequently less fidelity. Try this: hook up your guitar and play it and listen to how it sounds. Now take a small screwdriver and adjust the pickups so they are a quarter of an inch further away from the strings. Now how does it sound? From this experiment, you can see for yourself that the further a magnetic source (your guitar strings) is away from an inductive coil (your pickups), the less efficient the signal transfer. This is exactly the same phenomenon occurring in a plastic bobbin transformer. The extra distance of a plastic bobbin kills tone that would have been captured by the closer, paper-insulated vintage style transformers. Also many vintage transformers were interleaved, a practice not common in modern amps. Any audio transformer generally has two coils wound on the same core. Interleaving means winding a little bit of the first winding, then a little bit of the second winding, then a little of the first, then a little of the second, etc., until both windings have the correct number of turns. Modern transformers are usually wound by winding all the turns of one winding, and then all the turns of the other winding. Obviously the interleaved transformer will sound better because it is more efficient and better at producing low end, with richer harmonics.

In the 50s and 60s, coupling capacitors were typically made by placing two small sheets of paper (called the dielectric) between two small pieces of foil. A lead was attached to each piece of foil, and the paper and foil sandwich (double decker) was rolled up like a cigarette. Often, the finished cap was encased in plastic, wax, or epoxy. These caps had a very rich sound with nice low end. Nowadays however, technology and automation have taken us to a new level in capacitor manufacture. Polystyrene, mylar, polyester, and anything but paper are commonly used as the dielectric but do not have the same sound as paper dielectrics. Although audiophiles will tell you that polystyrene caps have the best sound (and maybe they do for stereo systems), I prefer the polyester tubular foil capacitors as the ones sounding the most like vintage for guitar amps. These caps are the Mallory 150 series caps and are made by spraying two sheets of foil with a polyester film, then making the two sheets of foil into a sandwich, and then rolling them up like a cigarette. They have a very similar sound to the vintage style paper caps.

Remember that in the 50s and 60s, semiconductors were very expensive to make and the technology was very new. All amps in the 50s and many amps of the 60s used tube rectifiers. However with today's semiconductor technology, solid-state rectifiers can be manufactured at a cost of less than a dime, with no chassis space required and almost no labor cost. Tube rectifiers, on the other hand, are very expensive to manufacture because they require an extra winding on the power transformer, a tube socket, a rectifier tube, chassis space with a mounting hole, and increased labor cost (there are only three amp companies in America that I know of that still use tube rectifiers). But how does this affect tone?

Generally speaking, tubes will distort easier and have more midrange when operated at lower voltages. They will also draw more current when they are driven hard as opposed to just idling. In a vintage amp, when it is idling, the tubes see the full voltage of the power supply. As soon as a note is struck, the tubes begin to draw more current. Since this current must pass through the rectifier tube, a voltage drop appears across the rectifier tube. And since the rectifier tube is in series with the power tubes and the power supply, the voltage drop across the rectifier tube is actually subtracted from the full voltage that was originally on the power tubes. This is sometimes referred to as sag or envelope. In other words the power tubes are now operating at a lower voltage. This means they distort easier, lose a little bit of power, and sound more compressed. They sound more compressed because as the string begins to decay in volume, the power tubes draw less current which ultimately results in more voltage, thus increasing volume of the power tubes. In other words, the power tubes increase in volume as the strings begin to die out resulting in a compressed sustain sound.

Almost all modern amps use solid-state rectifiers which do not have this sag. Generally the power tubes are run at higher voltages which give more headroom and less power tube distortion. Brighter tone with tighter low end would be the best way I know to describe the solid-state rectifier tone. Many modern amps try to compensate with preamp distortion which does not sound the same as power tube distortion. To me, preamp distortion sounds somewhat buzzy, while power tube distortion is warm, thick and brown.

To further add to the compressed tone of the tube rectifier, almost all amps made in the early 50s and some amps in the 60s used cathode-bias output tubes (a.k.a. self-bias). Today, almost all modern amps are fixed-bias output tubes. Cathode-bias is when a resistor is between the cathode and ground to set the operating level of the power tube. Fixed-bias is when the cathode is connected directly to ground and a constant negative voltage is placed on the grid. But how does this relate to tone?

In a cathode-bias amp, current is drawn through the cathode resistor in order to get through the tube. The voltage drop across that resistor is what determines the operating level of the tube. As soon as a signal is passed through the tube, the tube begins to draw more current, causing a larger voltage to appear across the resistor. This actually changes the operating level of the tube so that it has less output; however, as the note begins to decay, less current is drawn through the cathode resistor causing less voltage drop across the cathode resistor and ultimately more volume output. In other words, as the volume of the string decays, the tube has more output which results in a singing, sustained quality.

In a fixed-bias amp, the cathodes of the power tubes are connected directly to ground and a fixed amount of negative voltage is permanently placed on the grids to set the operating level. Since there is no change in the operating level of the tube while it is being played, the singing sustain characteristics of the cathode-bias amp simply will not happen.

Another major difference between vintage amps and modern amps can be found in cabinet design. In the 50s and 60s, solid pine was the cheapest wood around. As luck would have it, pine happened to be the perfect sounding wood for guitar amps. Nowadays however, solid pine is expensive and not very plentiful. Plywood is cheap and plentiful and for those reasons, it is the wood of choice for almost all modern amp manufacturers. I have done research on this subject, and I know from personal experience that solid pine has a certain richness that sounds to me as though it has high and low resonances, both at the same time, whereas plywood has a bright resonance with almost no low end richness.

Try this experiment. Find something made out of solid pine and something made of plywood. Go to a quiet room and set both articles in front of you. Knock on the pine and listen. Now knock on the plywood and listen. What you are likely to notice is that the pine sounds lively while the plywood sounds dead. You may also notice that the pine has a low and high pitched resonance all at the same time, while the plywood seems to have only one resonance that is rather high pitched. This experiment works best with uncovered wood because it is easier to hear with nothing to dampen the sound.

Amps in the old days were just not that powerful in terms of watts compared to today's amplifiers. Five to forty watts was about the range in vintage amps with little exception. Today, however, sixty to a hundred watts seems to be the rule rather than the exception. It is important to note this because it is the reason that virtually all speakers today are made differently than they were in the 50s and 60s. In lower powered amps smaller voice coils can be used (generally speaking). This results in greater efficiency. Also the standard for papercone construction of yesteryear was 3KSP paper as used in all vintage Jensens and most other speakers. This paper is very thin and would physically distort when driven hard resulting in a smooth break up. In high powered modern amps, voice coils must be made larger to handle the high wattage and paper is generally much thicker. Obviously with less cone distortion, the speakers will not sound the same. Speakers are the final link between your amp and your ears.

Lastly we must look at the actual construction of amplifiers. Virtually all vintage amps were wired in a point to point style with no printed circuit boards. Virtually all modern amps are wired using printed circuit boards. Is there a difference in tone? You bet there is.

Printed circuit boards are co-planar which means the printed traces are all on the same plane. Hand wired point to point amps are not co-planar which means the wires run in many different directions but not on the same plane. How does this affect tone?

When two conductors are separated by a nonconductor and the conductors are co-planar, what you have is a capacitor. This is easily proven by taking two lengths of wire and laying them side by side and parallel. Now measure them with a capacitance meter. What did you get? Ten to twenty picofarads? Now take the same two wires and set them where they are no longer co-planar or parallel, and measure the capacitance. What did you get? This experiment proves conclusively that printed circuit board construction has the circuit see small capacitances between traces even though the small capacitors are not in the schematic diagram! What happens is that high frequencies (harmonics and overtones) leak out of the signal path resulting in bad dry tone! If this is so, why do almost all modern amplifiers use printed circuit boards? They are expedient. With printed boards amplifiers can be built in a matter of minutes instead of a matter of days.

In vintage amps that are hand wired point to point, this capacitance leakage simply does not happen—nothing gets lost. Rich harmonics and overtones make it through the amp's circuitry and come out of the speaker for the listener's enjoyment.

A printed circuit board is never the same because of all the hidden capacitances that occur all over the board. I am certain that printed circuit board technology was available as early as 1953 and I give early amp builders credit for being hip enough to know that capacitive leakage destroys rich tone.

GLOSSARY
BIAS-*verb*-To adjust the operating level of a vacuum tube, much the same you would adjust the idle on your car. *Noun*-The negative voltage relationship comparing the grid to the cathode.
CATHODE-*noun*-This is the part of the tube or semiconductor diode where the electrical current flow enters.
CATHODE-BIASED-*adjective*-One of several ways a tube could be biased. This design uses a resistor between the cathode and ground to set the biasing. This cathode-biased design is almost always used on preamp tubes and sometimes used on output tubes. Though not as efficient as fixed-bias, cathode-biased output tubes generally sing more.
CATHODE RESISTOR-*noun*-This is the resistor that goes from the cathode to ground in a cathode-biased circuit.
CAPACITOR-*noun*-A device made from two conductors separated by a nonconductor. Whatever is between these conductors is called a dielectric. These devices store electricity. They will block D.C. current but pass A.C. current.
DIELECTRIC-*noun*-The non-conductor substance that separates the two

conductors of a capacitor. Paper, air, electrolyte, mica, mylar, polyester, and ceramic are some of the dielectrics that are used.

DISTORTION-*noun*-The difference between what goes into an electronic device and what comes out.

DYNAMICS-*noun*-The loud/soft quality of music that gives it character.

ENVELOPE-*noun*-The changing dynamics of a vacuum tube circuit that can be heard as an attack, decay and sustain volume level when a note or a chord is played through the amp.

E.Q.-*noun*-Abbreviation for "equalizer."

FIXED-BIAS-*adjective*-A way to achieve bias in a vacuum tube in which a fixed amount of negative voltage is placed on the grid of a tube. This is almost always done on output tubes and almost never done on preamp tubes.

GAIN-*noun*-The amount of voltage amplification in the preamp section of an amplifier. This voltage amplification ultimately drives the power tubes which do not add any more gain. The power tubes add current (power).

GRID-*noun*-One of the internal parts of a vacuum tube. This is usually where the input signal connects.

HARMONICS-*noun*-The frequencies that are related to the fundamental frequency by being multiples of the fundamental frequency.

HEADROOM-*noun*-The volume level that is attainable before clipping occurs.

IMPEDANCE-*noun*-Sum of all resistance, capacitive reactance, and inductive reactance.

INTERLEAVED-*adjective*-A way of winding a transformer in which a little bit of the primary is wound, then a little of the secondary is wound, then a little primary, then a little secondary, etc. until the transformer is wound. The more interleaves, the better the efficiency.

PHASE INVERTER-*noun*-The circuit in a push pull amplifier that feeds the power tubes signal. It feeds one power tube an in phase signal and the other power tube an out of phase signal. The tube for this circuit is always located next to the power tubes.

PICOFARAD-*noun*-A very small amount of capacitance that is equal to a trillionth of a farad (.000,000,000,001 farads). Sometimes also called "micro micro farads."

PLATE-*noun*-The part of a vacuum tube that has high voltage on it. Except in a cathode follower circuit, the output is always taken from this part of the tube.

PLATE VOLTAGE-*noun*-The voltage that is applied to the plate of a vacuum tube. Higher voltages give more headroom and high end, lower voltages give more breakup and a browner tone. All tweed amps had relatively lower plate voltages.

PREAMP-*noun*-The section of an amplifier whose function is to add gain. Preamps are always before the output stage.

RECTIFIER TUBE-*noun*-A vacuum tube with no grid, whose purpose is to change alternating current to direct current. Current flows from the cathode to whichever of the two plates that happens to be positive at the time.

RESISTOR-*noun*-A device used to add resistance to a circuit. This device is always used to either create a voltage drop or to limit current.

REVERB-*noun*-A sound in which sound waves are reverberated. This is done by passing sound through two or more long springs of different lengths and amplifying the resultant sound. The springs are in a small enclosure that is called a "reverb tank."

SAG-*noun*-The amount of decay in the envelope before a played note is sustained at a constant volume level. It is caused by the resistance of the power supply and that resistance would include the rectifier tube resistance as well as the internal resistance of the power transformer.

SELF-BIAS-*noun*-A type of biasing arrangement in which a resistor is used to create a positive voltage on the cathode; this now makes the grid negative with respect to the cathode.

SOCKET-*noun*-The female connector that a vacuum tube inserts into.

TRANSFORMER-*noun*-An electrical device made from two or more windings of wire wrapped around an iron core. These devices are primarily used to create power supplies and to match impedances between output tubes and speaker.

VACUUM TUBE-*noun*-A device whose major components would include an anode and a cathode in an evacuated envelope. It performs as an amplifier, oscillator, or rectifier in audio circuits.

Kendricks

THE TWEED CHAMP

Perhaps the most affordable vintage Fender tweed amp and certainly the most abundant is the tweed Champ amp. Although the circuitry changed somewhat over the years, all tweed Champs were single channel without tone controls and put out between 3 to 5 watts depending on the model. All of them used 6V6 output tubes and a 5Y3 rectifier tube. All Champs were single ended which means that they all operated in class "A." All were cathode-biased amps, which is why they had a spongy feel to the attack and decay envelope.

DIFFERENT TYPES

The first of the tweed Champs were the "Champion 600" and the "Champion 800." The only difference was that the "600" had a 6" speaker and the "800" had a 8" speaker, the "600" being the most popular. With only three watts output, these amps lacked volume and punch. Peculiar to the "Champion 600" and "800" was a circuit not to be found on many amps, a pentode first gain stage. Many people like the tone of the pentode, but only at lower volumes. Manufacturers of tubes always published example circuits in the back of their tube manuals in much the same spirit that a pancake recipe appears on a bag of flour. My guess is that Fender simply copied a suggested circuit.

The second basic type of Champ was the 5D1 and 5E1 models that were sold from 1954 and 1958. These amps changed to a triode preamp tube and used a pi filter between the output transformer and the rectifier. These amps had a very nice envelope of attack and decay qualities; however, they were still not very loud. At this time, Fender added a negative feedback loop which remained on all later Champs. If you own one of these amps, I suggest that you add a screen resistor because the original design has the screen at a higher potential than the plate. This is poor design that a simple 470 ohm 1 watt resistor could correct. The advantages would include improved tube life and output stage efficiency.

The last type of Champ was the 5F1, in my opinion the very best sounding tweed Champ ever made. This amp kept the triode preamp but went to a capacitive input filter power supply. This gave stronger low end with a punchier attack.

Tweed Champs were covered with black Tolex during the early 60s.

RESTORATION CAUTIONS

If you are restoring the electronics of a Champ, do not put larger value filter caps into the amp as this will adversely affect the tone and envelope of attack. Do not use an 8 ohm speaker as this will result in an impedance mismatch that will cut the power in half. Fender always described the speaker impedance as 3.2 ohms. This is not impedance, it is the speaker's D.C. resistance. If you measure a 4 ohm speaker on a multimeter, it will read 3.2 ohms D.C. resistance. To convert D.C. resistance to (A.C.) impedance, the factor is 1.25 (approximately). (Example : 3.2 ohms D.C. times 1.25 equals 4 ohms.)

BEST SOUNDING CHAMP

The very best sounding tweed Champ I ever heard is owned by Bobby Nathan at Unique Recording Studio in New York City. I went through it and replaced the filter caps, did a three way cleanup (pots, sockets, chassis), and hunted through about ten R.C.A. 6V6s to find which tube the amp liked best. This particular amp could have easily been the definition of good tone. With the volume on 12 and using the bridge pickup with the tone about half rolled back, the tone was reminiscent of Billy Gibbons at the Town House in Groves, Texas (1970, very, very early pre-record deal Z. Z. Top). The amp's personality responded to pick attack and left hand fingering as if it were part of my central nervous system. Come to think of it, I had replaced the 5Y3 rectifier tube in that amp to a 5V4. All Champs generally sound better using the 5V4 because it has a somewhat lower internal impedance. This makes the amp louder, with more note definition, and punchier attack with stronger low end.

GLOSSARY

A.C.-*noun*-Abbreviation for "alternating current." This is electricity that goes one direction and then reverses and goes the other direction. Your guitar signal is A.C. and so are the 120 volt wall outlets you plug your amp into.

ATTACK AND DECAY ENVELOPE-*noun*-The rise and fall of volume levels that occur inherently in an amplifier when a note is played. This shapes the overall sound and is what gives the "breathing effect" of certain amps.

D.C.-*noun*-Abbreviation for "direct current." This is electricity that goes one direction only. The tubes in an amplifier use "direct current." All batteries are D.C.

NEGATIVE FEEDBACK-*noun*-A small portion of signal that is taken from the output of an amplification stage and then reinserted to a previous stage at a point that is 180 degrees out of phase. This would phase cancel some of the louder frequencies and there would be little effect on the not-so-loud frequencies, thus the frequency response would become more even. Leaving a cathode resistor unbypassed can achieve the same effect.

NEGATIVE FEEDBACK LOOP-*noun*-A circuit in which a small portion of the amplified signal is feedback to an earlier part of the circuit in which it is 180 degrees out of phase. This has the tendency of flattening out the frequency response.

OHM-*noun*-Unit of measure of resistance.

PENTODE-*noun*-A vacuum tube that has five electrical components. They are: cathode, grid, screen grid, suppressor grid, and plate. The heater doesn't count.

PI FILTER-*noun*-A filter, called the pi filter because of its resemblance to the Greek letter pi, is a combination of the simple capacitor input filter and the choke input filter.

POTS-*noun*-Slang for potentiometer which is a variable voltage divider used in volume controls, tone controls, etc.

RESISTANCE-*noun*-That which impedes the flow of electrons is said to have resistance. Resistance accounts for the fact that different conductors will allow more or less current to pass, given the same voltage present.

SCREEN RESISTOR-*noun*-The resistor that is placed in series with the screen of a vacuum tube. It is used to limit screen current.

TRIODE-*noun*-A vacuum tube with three internal components not counting the heater. The three components are cathode, grid, and plate.

FENDER "CHAMP-AMP"
MODEL 5C1

F-DH

FENDER MUSICAL INSTRUMENTS
A DIVISION OF COLUMBIA RECORDS DISTRIBUTION CORP.
SANTA ANA, CALIFORNIA
U.S.A.

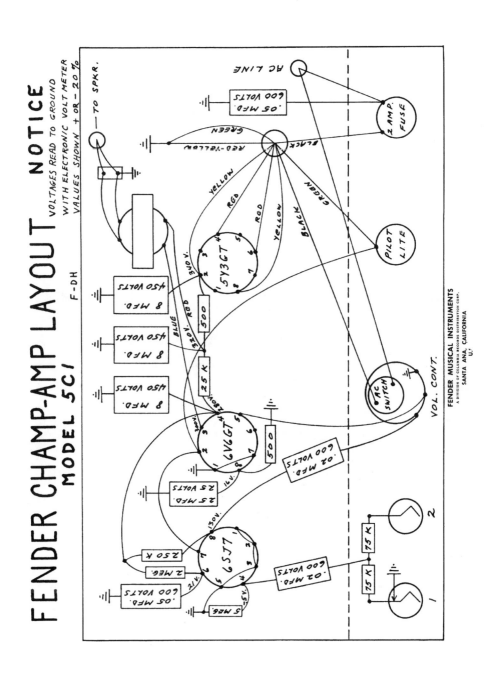

FENDER CHAMP-AMP LAYOUT
MODEL 5C1

NOTICE
VOLTAGES READ TO GROUND
WITH ELECTRONIC VOLT METER
VALUES SHOWN + OR − 20%

F-DH

FENDER MUSICAL INSTRUMENTS
A DIVISION OF COLUMBIA RECORDS DISTRIBUTION CORP.
SANTA ANA, CALIFORNIA
U.'

FENDER "CHAMP-AMP" SCHEMATIC
MODEL 5E1

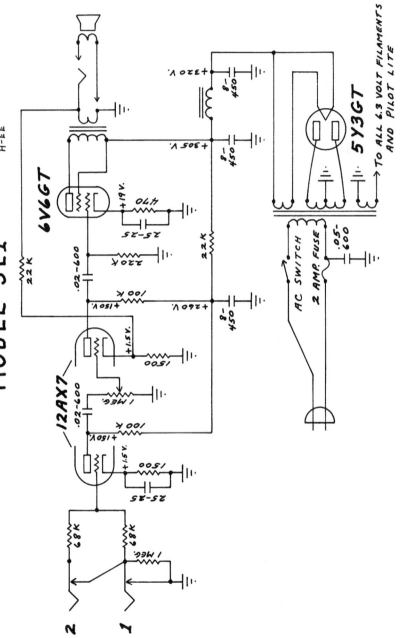

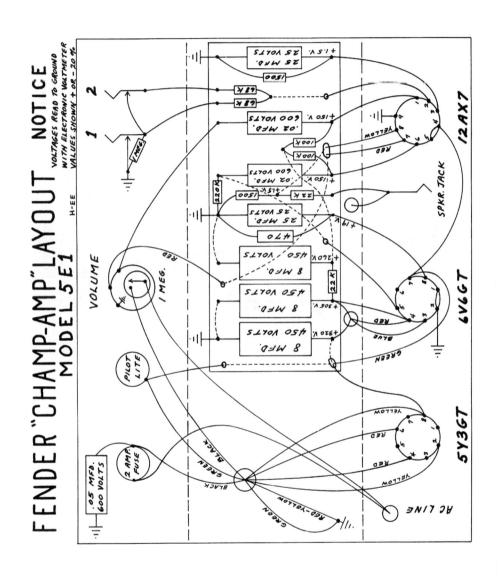

FENDER "CHAMP-AMP" LAYOUT
MODEL 5E1

NOTICE
VOLTAGES READ TO GROUND
WITH ELECTRONIC VOLTMETER
VALUES SHOWN + OR - 20%

H-EE

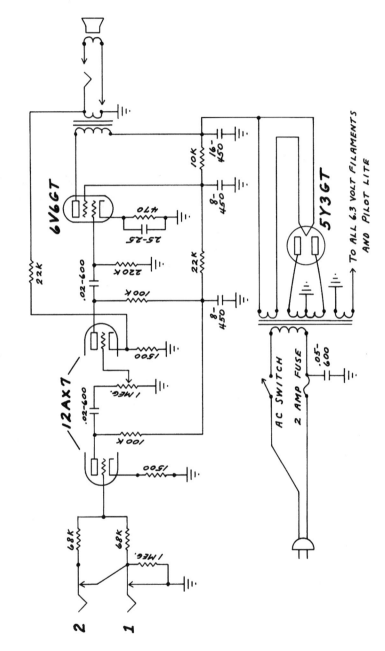

FENDER "CHAMP-AMP" SCHEMATIC
MODEL 5F1
K-EE

Kendricks

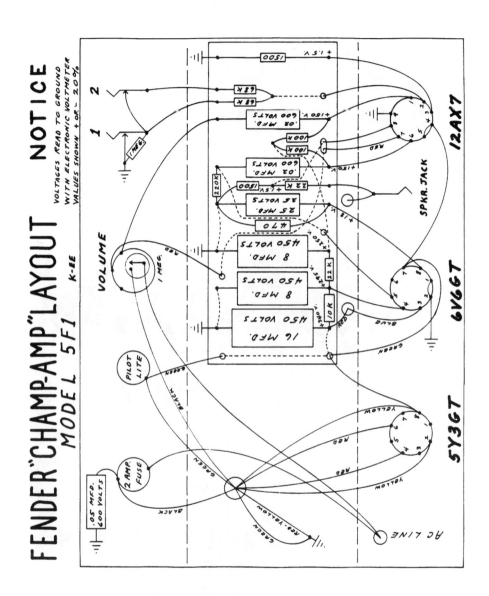

FENDER "CHAMP-AMP" LAYOUT
MODEL 5F1   K-EE

NOTICE

VOLTAGES READ TO GROUND
WITH ELECTRONIC VOLTMETER
VALUES SHOWN + OR - 20%

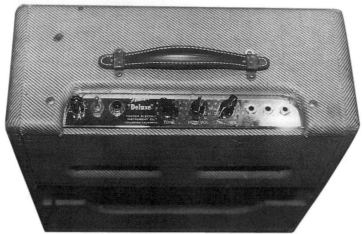

THE TWEED DELUXE

Probably the most popular tweed Fender amp is the tweed Deluxe. I suspect that Fender built more of these amps than any other, because it is the amp I see most often coming into our restoration shop for electronic tweaking and recovering. The chronological order, earliest to the latest, is as follows: 5B3, 5C3, 5D3, 5E3, 5F3. Each one is different from the others, the point of this chapter being to distinguish the actual differences.

The 5B3 and the 5C3 were nearly identical. Cosmetically they both had a wide top panel on the front. Each had three inputs. Two of the inputs were for the musical instrument channel and one input was for the microphone channel. Both units had one tone control that worked best on the microphone channel. (It was almost ineffective if used on the instrument channel, particularly while the microphone channel volume was turned up.)

Typical of both amps were the metal 6SC7 preamp tubes and 6V6 output tubes. 6SC7 tubes have lower gain than a 12AX7 and use a socket that is the size of an output tube (8 pin). I think the 6SC7 is a better sounding tube. Also typical of the 6SC7 is that even though the tube is a twin triode like the 12AX7, the tube has only one cathode that feeds both sides of the twin triode.

Unique to the 5B3 and 5C3 was the grid leak bias first gain stage. This is one way to bias a preamp tube in which there is no cathode resistor, but instead a capacitor and large value resistor (5 meg) are in series with the grid signal circuit. Grid current leaks out through the input circuit causing a negative voltage to appear on the grid, thus biasing the tube. The capacitor and large value resistor are used to keep the negative voltage fairly stable. Of course this arrangement has its disadvantages, the main one being that it cannot handle a very large input signal. Grid leak bias circuits are pretty much obsolete and have not been used since the mid 50s. Be careful using a tube driver or any other high gain device on these amps.

Both the 5B3 and 5C3 used the primitive paraphase inverter. This style inverter has one side of the preamp tube driving one power tube and some of the signal is routed through a voltage divider and sent back through the other side of the tube. Of course when it comes out of this side, it comes out 180 degrees out of phase and it then drives the other power tube. A feature of this style inverter is that any distortion caused by the first tube side is introduced to the other side and amplified. Balancing the two sides so that each power tube has the same input amplitude can be tricky. This balance will also change when a new tube is installed. If the balance is too far off, the amp will sound like it has a bad output transformer.

Somewhere around 1955 came the 5D3 Deluxe. This was nearly identical to the earlier models except that, even though it used the paraphase inverter, it was the self-balancing style while the earlier types were the conventional style. Some of the 5D3 Deluxes had 6SC7 preamp tubes, but others had the chassis punched for the large octal size socket with an adapter covering the chassis hole and a 12AY7 and a 12AX7 in place of the two 6SC7s. The 12AY7 has less gain than the 6SC7 and was used in the first position while the 12AX7, which has more gain than a 6SC7, was used in the phase inverter position. I have seen some 5C3 Deluxes with this same setup. 5D3 Deluxes had another distinguishing characteristic—the grid leak bias first gain stage was changed to the cathode-bias style circuit, a change that has remained ever since.

The 5E3 Deluxes were made from 1956 to late 1957. These amps had a new design. The cabinet had a thin top panel and four inputs appeared on the amp chassis. The paraphase inverter was dropped in favor of the cathodyne style inverter. Cathodyne style inverters (also called distributed load phase inverters) use only a single triode section instead of two triodes. The plate circuit feeds one power tube while the cathode feeds the other. Since the cathode is 180 degrees out of phase with the plate, phase inversion is achieved. Critical to this circuit is the plate load resistor and the cathode resistor. These resistors must be matched in order for the signals to be balanced. Most of the amps used 56K ohm resistors for this circuit; however, I have seen a few amps with 47K ohm resistors. Though the circuit gain can only approach a gain of one, the 56K ohm has less loss than the 47K ohm circuit. If you own one of these amps, there is a 90% chance that your resistors do not match and the sound can be improved by installing a matched set. 5E3 Deluxes were the first Deluxes that did not have a negative feedback loop.

From 1958 to sometime in 1960 the 5F3 Deluxes were produced. This circuit was almost identical to the 5E3. Voltages were somewhat higher, giving more gain. Cosmetically it looked the same. Both the 5E3 and 5F3 had more gain than all previous model Deluxes.

All tweed Deluxes had solid pine cabinets with Jensen speakers. Some of them came stock with the P12R Jensen and some had the P12Q. The P12Q sounded better. When buying an old Deluxe don't assume that the speaker is original just because it happens to be a Jensen. Jensen made many models of 12" speakers, some of which were no good. For instance, both the P12S and the P12T are Jensen but are non-original with hardly any power. The P12P and the P12N, though not original, actually sound better than stock speakers. In fact, the P12N is worth major bucks, if you can ever find one.

Triad made the transformers for all tweed Deluxes. If the output transformer has end-bells, it is non-original. Original transformers were wound with paper and had no end-bells.

One problem with all tweed Deluxes is that there is very little headroom. The amp breaks up quite a bit when the controls are about half way up and there are varying degrees of more breakup as the volume is advanced. Although this is great for recording and practice, it leaves something to be desired in a gig situation. If you would like to use your Deluxe to gig with, but it is not loud enough, here is a simple mod that you can do that will not take anything away from the amp as far as collectible value and will allow you as much volume as you like. This mod can be done with any tweed Deluxe, using the existing extra speaker jack.

Take off the back panel that covers the chassis. Notice the extra speaker jack. It has only one wire on it. That wire goes to the regular speaker jack. Replace this wire with a 2.2K ohm resistor (½ watt). Now place a 100 ohm resistor (½ watt) across both terminals of the extra speaker jack. That's all there is to it. Replace the back panel and you are done. You must leave the stock speaker plugged into the regular speaker jack. The extra speaker jack is now a line out. Plug it into the P.A. or into another amplifier or a tape recorder. Use the volume control on the Deluxe to get the amount of breakup and harmonics you desire and then adjust your P.A. or other auxiliary amp for the desired volume. I have shared this mod with many people, all of whom were completely amazed. You can always put the amp back to stock if you like, but no one ever uses the extra speaker jack anyway.

All tweed Deluxes have a cathode-bias output stage. This gives them their singing quality. As with all cathode-bias amps, the exact set of output tubes (6V6s) must be carefully chosen for punch, tone and volume. I measure the current (pin 8 on the rectifier to pin three on either power tube) to select the best set. I select a set that measures 30 to 40 mA. Less than 30 mA and the amp will have no volume and the tone will be thin. The higher current tubes (40 mA) give more midrange and quicker breakup with much more volume.

All tweed Deluxes have a 5Y3GT rectifier tube. Personally I prefer a 5V4GT rectifier tube in the tweed Deluxe. It is a little louder, more punchy, and can handle more current. Regardless of what type tweed Deluxe you own, they are all very cool. My personal favorite is the 5E3, if it is set up right.

GLOSSARY

CATHODYNE STYLE INVERTER-*noun*-Also called distributive load phase inverter, this is the only style phase inverter that uses a single triode.

END-BELLS-*noun*-The sheet metal covers that fit on the side of some transformers. Not all transformers use these.

GRID LEAK BIAS-*noun*-A way to achieve bias on a preamp tube in which a capacitor is charged by the input signal and is not allowed to completely discharge, thus placing a negative charge on the grid.

mA-*noun*-Abbreviation for milliamps which is .001 amps or one thousandth of an amp.

MEG-*noun*-One million ohms or 1000K.

OUT OF PHASE-*adjective*-If you consider that a vibration such as a guitar note changes from positive to negative in its vibrations, then a signal is said to be 180 degrees out of phase if it is going positive at the same time that the original signal is going negative and of course it will be going negative when the original is going positive. This is also referred to as an inverted signal.

PARAPHASE INVERTER-*noun*-A particular type of phase inverter in which two triodes are used. The signal goes through the first tube and is amplified enough to drive an output tube. A very small part of that signal is also sent to another triode, the output of which would drive the other output tube. Since the second triode inverts the signal by 180 degrees, phase inversion is achieved.

TWEAKING-*verb*-Adjustment of an amplifier to its best sound.

TWIN TRIODE-*noun*-A vacuum tube that has two triodes within the same glass tube.

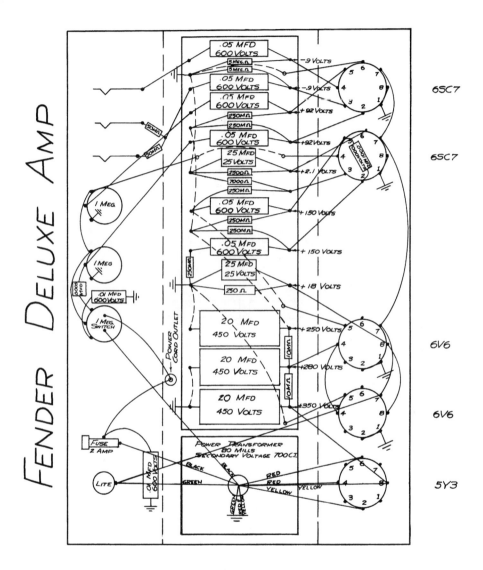

FENDER "DELUXE" SCHEMATIC
MODEL 5C3

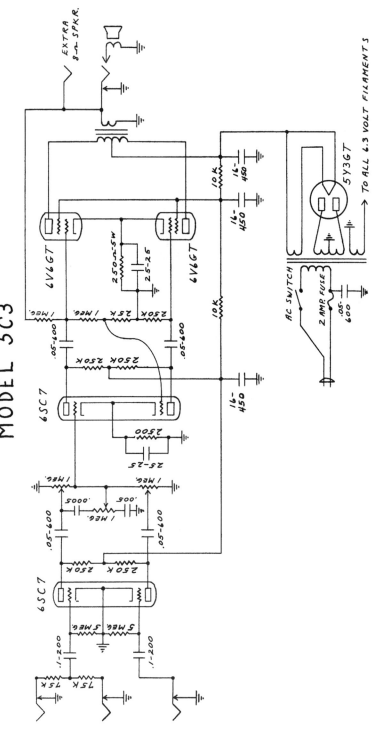

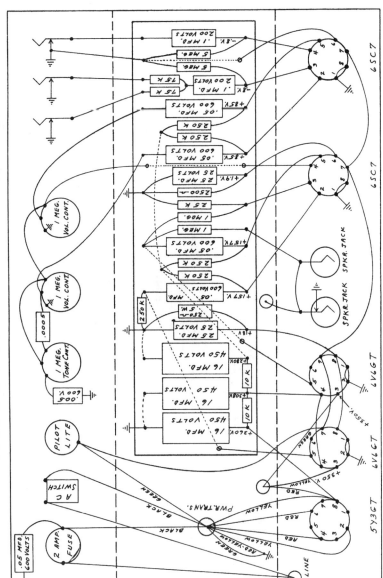

FENDER "DELUXE" LAYOUT

MODEL 5C3

NOTICE

VOLTAGES READ TO GROUND
WITH ELECTRONIC VOLTMETER.
VALUES SHOWN + OR – 20%

FENDER DELUXE SCHEMATIC
MODEL 5D3

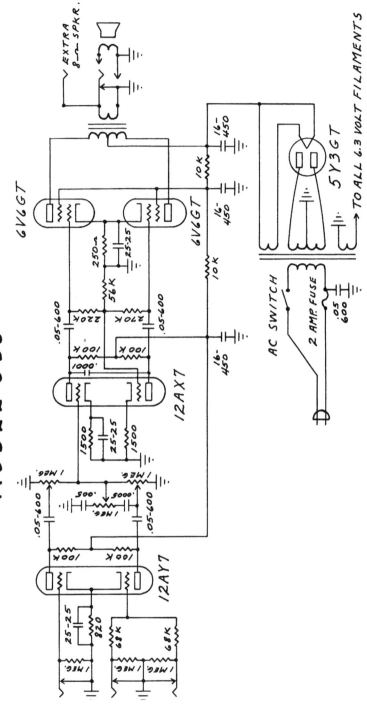

Kendricks

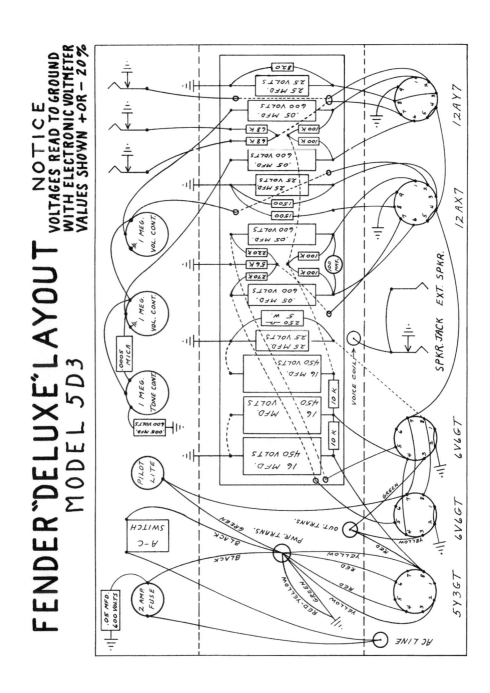

FENDER "DELUXE" SCHEMATIC
MODEL 5E3
F-EE

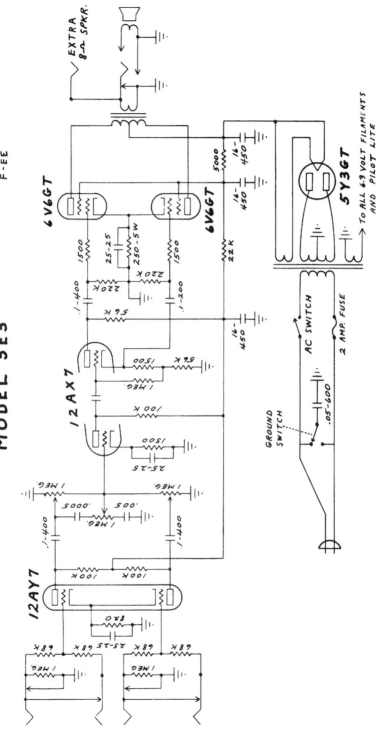

Kendricks

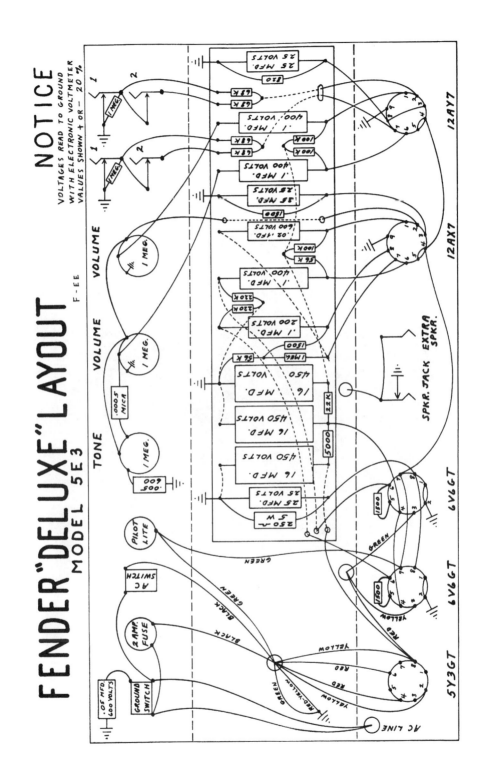

FENDER "DELUXE" LAYOUT
MODEL 5E3

NOTICE

VOLTAGES READ TO GROUND
WITH ELECTRONIC VOLTMETER
VALUES SHOWN + OR − 20 %

THE DEFINITIVE
4X10 BASSMAN

4X10 Bassmans come in many varieties because the circuit was changed several times over a period of a few years. Model numbers from earliest to latest are 5D6, 5E6, 5E6A, 5F6, 5F6A. Certain component values were changed from unit to unit. These differences and similarities, and the way they related to tone, will be the subject of this chapter.

The first 4X10 Bassmans showed up in 1954 when Fender changed the Bassman design from one 15" speaker to four 10" Jensen speakers. Fender was still experimenting on their bass amp and were looking for more low end. Because four 10" speakers move a larger wavefront of air than one 15" speaker (314.2856 inches for the four 10" speakers as opposed to 176.7857 inches for the 15" speakers), they reasoned that this would dramatically increase bass response on the lower bass notes. Remember, they were dealing with an open back enclosure, and needed something new to better reproduce that open low E. This model was the 5D6, a.k.a. the two hole Bassman. (It had two inputs, one for bright and one for normal channels.) Not many of these amps were produced and I have only seen a few. The cabinet was about an inch smaller in width than the more familiar 5F6 Bassmans. I have never seen a Fender schematic of a 5D6 and I suspect that Fender never printed one. The 5D6s I did see had circuitry identical to the 5E6 Bassman except that the 5D6 had the bass and treble controls share a common tone cap, whereas the 5E6 had separate caps for the treble and bass controls. 5D6s and 5E6s had fairly low power (30 watts) and fairly low gain in the preamp. Two 12AY7s (less gain than 12AX7s) were used in the preamp with negative feedback (reduced gain, but more even frequency response) over the second tube. Other than this second 12AY7 and a larger bypass cap on the first gain stage (to increase low end), the amp was virtually identical to the 3X10 Bandmaster. However, the Bandmaster had a 12AX7 in the second position (more gain). 5D6 and 5E6 Bassmans had another difference from the 5E7 Bandmasters—the Bassman had an extra rectifier tube and an extra filter cap. This extra rectifier tube and filter cap were put there to reduce sag (envelope) when driving the amp hard and to tighten the low end (headroom). Most guitarist today would take out one of the rectifier tubes to induce sag. Both tubes are not needed because the amp idles at about 80-85 mA and either one of the 5U4GAs can easily handle 250 mA. In fact a single 5V4 works just fine in this socket and gives even more sag (envelope).

Let's talk some more about rectifier tubes, what they do, and how they contribute to the tone. All amplifiers work on D.C. Your wall outlet supplies A.C. The rectifier tube changes the A.C. (which alternates back and forth) to pulsating D.C. (which all goes the same way). Filter caps act like batteries that smooth out the valleys between the pulses making pure D.C. from pulses of D.C.

When any current moves through any resistance, a voltage drop appears across that resistance. A rectifier tube is a resistance to the flow of current; therefore, if a little current flows through the tube, only a little voltage appears across the tube. If, on the other hand, a large current flows, then a large voltage will appear across the tube. Since the power tubes are in series with the rectifier tube, whatever voltage appears across the rectifier tube **is subtracted from the plate voltage of the power tubes** thus changing the operating characteristics of the power tubes. Power tubes operating at lower voltages tend to distort more easily, and also have a browner more midrange tone. Read the next two sentences slowly and think about it. To calculate any voltage drop, simply multiply resistance times current (Ohm's Law: E=RI, where E=voltage drop, R=resistance, and I=current). From this equation you can see that if the current increases, the voltage drop increases. Stop and look at the equation. As you push the amp harder (more current) the voltage drop across the rectifier increases leaving **less voltage on the plates of the power tubes** (5881, 6L6G, etc.) With less voltage on the plates of the power tubes, the tubes distort easier, volume drops slightly, midrange increases, low end loosens and sustain is increased. This sounds like there is an envelope around the attack that imparts both a compressed and a singing quality to guitar amps, a sound most sought after by blues players. Fender was striving for less sag. In other words, they wanted to keep the plate voltages high on the power tubes so that the tubes would not distort easily and not sag. To accomplish this they used two rectifiers wired in parallel. This cut the sag voltage in half because half of the current went through each tube. Or said another way, the current was split into two paths instead of only one. Ultimately the sag voltage was cut in half. The extra filter cap stored more energy which further reduced sag on initial attack.

6L6G power tubes (not 6L6GCs) were standard for the 5D6 and the 5E6. These tubes were an early audio tube capable of 19 watts per tube (38 watts max per pair) although the 5E6 actually put out about 30 watts total.

Characteristic of the 5D6 and 5E6 were the absence of screen grid resistors—the screens were tied directly to the center tap of the audio transformer. Also, the smoothing choke was located electronically in series between the power tubes and the rectifier tube. For a design that is obviously trying to reduce sag, this is the worst place, because the choke has a resistance that will cause a voltage drop as more current passes through it, thus increasing sag. This is an unusual design for any Fender amp. All Fender amps made later have the choke between the screen grids and the center tap of the audio transformer.

The 5D6 was the first Fender Bassman to ever use a cathodyne style (distributed load) phase inverter. 5E6 Bassmans also used this circuit. This style inverter requires use of only one half of a 12AX7, but the paraphase inverters used on earlier amps and the long-tailed pair phase inverters used on later Fenders each required use of both sides of the 12AX7. The phase inverter tube is the preamp tube located nearest the power tubes and it is what feeds signal to the power tubes. Taking advantage of the fact that the cathode is 180 degrees out of phase with the plate, the cathodyne style phase inverter feeds one power tube with its plate and the other power tube is fed by its cathode. This style inverter was used only on the 5D6, 5E6, and 5E6A and never used on any other Bassmans.

Two hole Bassmans have a presence control, but no middle control. Like all 4X10 Bassmans, the tone controls are driven by a relatively lower impedance cathode follower circuit. This circuit increases odd order harmonics thus giving a crunchy tone. This is the same crunch that you hear in all early Marshalls. Originally, this circuit was used so that the tone controls would not load down the signal. Later blackface Fenders did not use this circuit and that is why blackface amps will have no volume if all the tone controls are turned to the lowest setting. (The signal is loaded down to the point that nothing is left to amplify.)

Shortly after the 5E6 came out, Fender changed the design slightly to a 5E6A. This amp was identical to the 5E6 except that the bias voltage was increased somewhat. (They were probably having problems with power tubes blowing and increasing the bias would have the tubes run cooler.) Also the tone cap values were slightly different on the 5E6A.

In 1958, the 5F6 became the next evolution of the 4X10 Bassman. Sometimes referred to as a four hole Bassman (it had two inputs for bright and two inputs for normal-each channel having a high and low gain input), this model had quite a few design changes, although cosmetically it looks like they simply added two inputs and a middle control. There is much more to it than that. For instance, the negative feedback across the second stage was removed, thus increasing gain. Although the 12AY7 was still used on the first gain stage, the second tube was changed to a 12AX7 increasing gain even further. The tone control design was changed to what would become a classic design later used by Marshall, Vox, and many others. A cathodyne style phase inverter was dropped in favor of the familiar long-tail pair style phase inverter that has remained a characteristic of virtually all Fender tube amps to date. The choke was moved between the screens and center tap of the audio transformer—a place it has been ever since in all Fender amps. 100 ohm screen grid resistors were added and the output tubes were changed to the higher fidelity 5881s. The wattage increased to about 40 watts because the plate voltage was increased from 405 volts on the 5E6A to 427 volts on the 5F6 and the preamp gain was increased considerably.

5881 power tubes are different from the 6L6Gs in several ways. First the 5881 has always been considered a high fidelity version of the 6L6G which is considered an industrial public address tube. 5881s are rated at 23 watts per tube compared to the 6L6G's 19 watts. Being a military version, the inside of the 5881 has gold in the metal alloy whereas the 6L6G uses silver. Obviously, gold is the better conductor. The 5881 was developed by Tung-Sol (a company in New Jersey) in 1953. Almost all 4X10 Bassmans came with Tung-Sol Brand tubes.

Also characteristic of the 5F6 was the 83 rectifier tube. This tube is unusual because it is filled with mercury vapor and has no sag. Here's how it works. As the current increases, the mercury vapor is ionized thus decreasing the resistance of the tube. Since the voltage drop equals resistance times current, (E=RI) you can imagine what happens if the resistance (R) decreases as current (I) increases. You are right, the voltage (E) remains constant. (E=RI, if R decreases at the same rate that I increases, then E remains constant.) This has the effect of maintaining the plate voltage high, regardless of how hard the amp is being driven. Of course the power tubes will not sound as singing or compressed, but the tube looks cool because it glows purple to the tempo of the playing as the mercury vapor ionizes with more current.

If you own a 5F6 and would like to change the amp to take a more popular style rectifier (5Y3, 5AR4, 5V4, or 5U4) instead of the 83 mercury vapor rectifier, simply rewire the rectifier socket as follows: move the red wire on pin 2 to pin 4, move the yellow wire on pin 1 to pin 2, move both the yellow wire and the cloth wire on pin 4 to pin 8, move the red wire on pin 3 to pin 6. When you are finished, you should have a red wire on pin 4, a red wire on pin 6, a yellow wire on pin 2 and a yellow wire on pin 8, and a wire going from pin 8 to the standby switch. Your 5F6 is now ready to use any of the four rectifier tubes mentioned earlier. I suggest that you try them all and see what gives you the tone, color and envelope shape that you like best.

Shortly after the 5F6 was introduced, the design was altered to the 5F6A. This is the model that almost all players generally agree has the best sound. It differed from the 5F6 in that the second gain stage was unbypassed, smoothing out the frequency response but reducing the gain slightly. Another important change was in the negative feed-back loop/presence control. This is the circuit that takes a small signal from the speaker output and injects it back into the amp at the point that is 180 degrees out of phase with the speaker jack. It has the effect of evening out the frequency response, reducing volume a little and canceling distortion produced by the output transformer. The presence control is like another treble control that keeps certain frequencies from being fed back, thus increasing the volume of those particular frequencies. In the 5F6, the negative feedback went to the bottom of the tone controls, but in the 5F6A, the loop went to the bottom of the phase inverter. Incidentally, if you own a 5F6 and you want to convert to the 5F6A circuit, or if you own a 5F6A and want to convert to the 5F6 circuit, you must also reverse the brown with the blue wire on pin 3 of each power tube (5881) when changing the feedback loop from one model to the other or your amp will howl (positive feedback) uncontrollably. Also on the 5F6A, 470 ohm screen grid resistors were used. This became a standard for virtually all Fender amps to come.

You never know what you will see in a 5F6 or a 5F6A for tone caps. The treble cap was always a silver mica 250 picofarad; however, I know of three different sets of values used for the middle and bass caps and the slope resistor. Fender's schematic shows two caps (.02 mfd) and a 56K slope resistor in the schematic; however, a .1 mfd bass cap and the .02 middle cap with a 100K slope resistor were very common. Though I have never seen one, there are a few 5F6 series Bassmans that used a .1 mfd bass cap and a .047 middle cap with a 100K ohm slope resistor for the tone circuit. Two .02s for the bass and middle cap with the 56K ohm slope resistor are the values generally regarded as the best sounding because the bass is clearer.

The volume pots used back then were listed on the layout as audio taper; however, they appear to be a much faster taper (get louder faster) than today's audio taper. Perhaps that is why Fender used a linear taper on the recent Bassman reissue. The way the volume controls on each channel are connected, the one that you are not using actually affects the tone and volume of the one you are using. Actually the one you are not using both increases the grid resistance of the second gain stage as you turn it up and grounds out some highs. You get maximum gain and bottom when it is about one third to one half all the way up, depending on the taper of the individual pot.

A 5AR4/GZ34 rectifier tube on the 5F6A replaced the 83 rectifier on the 5F6. It's hard to find a real 5AR4 these days because many companies take a 5Y3 and label it 5AR4. You can tell by the glass bottle if it is really a 5AR4. The 5AR4 will have a bottle the same diameter or slightly larger than the base of the tube, while the 5Y3 will have a bottle diameter slightly smaller than the base. A 5Y3 is usually preferred for recording because it will sag at a lower volume; however it will not last very long if used in a nightly gig situation. Drive it hard and it will blow in a few months. But if you really like the tone, use it like you do strings and replace the rectifier every month or two.

All 4X10 Bassmans I have ever seen used Jensen P10R speakers. Because they were painted blue, they were sometimes referred to as Jensen blue frame speakers. I have also heard them referred to as Blue-Bells. On a Bassman, the bell that normally covers the magnet (strictly cosmetic) was always removed from the top two speakers. (The bottom two speakers had their bells left on.) This was because the chassis would not clear the speaker any other way. With only a fraction of an inch clearance between the cap pan on the chassis and the uncovered magnet, you are likely to find many Bassmans that rub here. I have known many people who have wedged cardboard in this space to keep these components from rattling. A better way to fix this would be to remove the cap pan (you may have to take the chassis out of the cabinet first), and dent the rubbing edge slightly with a hammer. If it rubbed at all, it would have rubbed only on the edge. So, a small dent with a hammer will cure that problem. You must remove the cap pan first to avoid smashing any of the caps that are under it.

At that time, there was no established standard concerning marking the speaker terminals plus and minus. Jensen chose to label them exactly opposite of what has become today's standard. What is today's standard? Hook a flashlight battery to a speaker and look to see if the cone moves forward. If it does not move forward, reverse the leads going to the speaker terminals. The cone will now move forward. Now look at the speaker terminals. The one going to the positive side of the battery is positive and the one going to the negative side of the battery is negative. If you do this with an original (not reconed) Jensen P10R, you will notice it is marked backwards.

Stay with me on this. The 4X10 Bassman inverts the signal. That means that the part of the input signal that goes in positive will come out of the speaker jack negative and the part of the input signal that goes in negative will come out of the speaker jack positive. Since the speakers are marked backwards, the signal is re-inverted to make the amp **play** forward. (180 degrees plus 180 degrees equals 360 degrees; now that wasn't so hard, was it?) Does this affect the sound? Forward playing amps have more apparent low end. If you own a Bassman, I suggest that you check the phase of all speakers using the battery method previously described. Often a speaker will be reconed and will be reinstalled backwards. If one speaker is moving out while the other speakers are moving in, the speakers are actually working against each other. The amp will lack punch and projection, and low end will suffer. Also, if you own a Fender re-issue, you will want to reverse the speaker wires on each speaker so that the amp plays forward like an original. I would still check them with a battery, just to make certain. When you find the positive terminal by today's standards, it should go to the sleeve of the plug and the negative terminal should go to the pin in the middle of the plug.

Almost all P10R Jensens have dropped voice coils. This means that the voice coil becomes partially unglued and either rubs or has low efficiency or both. Reconing may help, but the speaker will never sound the same because the original cones are simply not available separately. Kendrick Amplifiers has the exact cones made with the original dies and cone ingredients, but the cones are not sold separately for recone purposes.

Another distinction of the 4X10 Bassmans are the seven winding interleaved audio transformers made by Triad. When Fender quit producing the tweed Bassmans and started the piggy-back design, they changed to Schumacher transformers which are not interleaved and of course do not sound the same. Interleaved transformers are hotter (and more expensive to make) because only a few turns of the primary are wound, then a few turns of the secondary, then a few turns of the primary, then a few turns of the secondary, etc. until you end up with three windings of secondary sandwiched in between four wirings of primary. This is a more efficient design and of course sounds better. Also of note, the transformers on tweed Bassmans are wound with the turns of wire wound directly onto the core with only a thickness of paper insulation separating the turns from the core. This is significant because almost all transformers today are wound on a plastic or nylon bobbin and the core is inserted later. Modern transformers have more distance between the core and the winding. What happens when a coil of wire such as a guitar pickup or a trans-

54   Kendricks

former coil is closer to a magnetic field? You know the answer to that one from adjusting your pickups. Correct, it has more gain and clearer harmonics. That is what the wound on paper transformers sound like compared to modern cheap transformers.

All 4X10 Bassmans were wired point to point. The chassis face was scrubbed with Pepsodent tooth powder to clean it before the epoxy ink labeling was silk screened. All cabinets were constructed from yellow pine with finger-jointed corners. Pine was used because it was cheap. My guess is that, at that time, Fender was probably unaware of the superior sound quality of pine for guitar amps. With the amp standing in its normal upright position, the tweed stripes always run from 4 o'clock to 11 o'clock (and not from 7 o'clock to 2 o'clock) no matter which way you look at the amplifier.

Contrary to popular belief, Leo Fender did not design the Bassman circuit. The circuit was actually patented by AT&T and Western Electric in 1948 and later licensed to Fender Electric Instrument company.

How old is your Bassman? Look for the two letter date code rubber stamped on the tube configuration label, or it may be stamped on the inside of the chassis. The first letter tells you the year, while the second letter tells you the month. Here is the code:

1st Letter	2nd Letter	
1954 D	January A	July G
1955 E	February B	August H
1956 F	March C	September I
1957 G	April D	October J
1958 H	May E	November K
1959 I	June F	December L
1960 J		

How much is your Bassman worth? It really depends on four questions. What does it look like? What does it sound like? How much do you want to sell it? How much does your buyer want it? I have seen Bassmans go for as little as $100.00 (trash condition) and as much as $3800.00 (mint condition, motivated buyer). Don't expect a lot of money for it if it doesn't sound good or looks like hell. Some of the best amps cosmetically are the worst electronically. If you are lucky enough to own a 4X10 Bassman, have it serviced and keep good tubes in it. I always use new American old stock or Russian military grade tubes. Stay away from any of the tubes that come in fancy marketing hype packaging. The pricey designer tube companies use cheap Chinese tubes and spend more on the labeling and marketing hype than they do on the tube. You are not likely to be satisfied with such poor quality and high prices.

5F6As were sold with two different phase inverter setups. One setup used a 10K ohm resistor in the cathode circuit tied to the presence control in series, while the other setup used a 6800 ohm resistor in the cathode circuit with a 4700 ohm resistor to ground and in parallel with the presence control. There are obviously differing opinions about which one sounds better.

I have never seen a Bassman, no matter how trashed, that could not be repaired and set up to play perfectly. It might take a little time and money to get it maxed out, but any amp of this caliber is worth whatever it takes to bring out the magical tone that is the 4X10 Bassman.

GLOSSARY

BYPASS CAP-*noun*-The capacitor that is wired in parallel with the cathode resistor. This cap increases gain of certain frequencies depending on its value in microfarads. If it is large enough, it will increase gain of all frequencies.

CATHODE FOLLOWER CIRCUIT-*noun*-A vacuum tube circuit whose voltage gain is less than unity and the output is taken from the cathode. There is no phase change between the cathode-ground output signal and the grid-ground input signal. The cathode output "follows" the grid input. The circuit is usually used to match a higher impedance source to a lower impedance load.

PRESENCE-*noun*-Another type of high end, similar to treble, that gives a biting edge to the sound. On Fender and Marshall amps and many others, the presence control is actually a tone control on the negative feedback loop.

SCREEN GRID-*noun*-The part of a power tube that is between the plate and the grid. A high voltage on this component encourages electrons to be attracted to the plate thus increasing efficiency of the tube. Also it provides a shield to minimize internal capacitance between the grid and plate, thus helping low end.

SLOPE RESISTOR-*noun*-The resistor in the tone circuit that determines how fast the treble will roll off when the treble control is turned.

UNBYPASSED-*adjective*-When a cathode resistor has no capacitor in parallel with it , it is said to be unbypassed. This is actually a form of negative feedback.

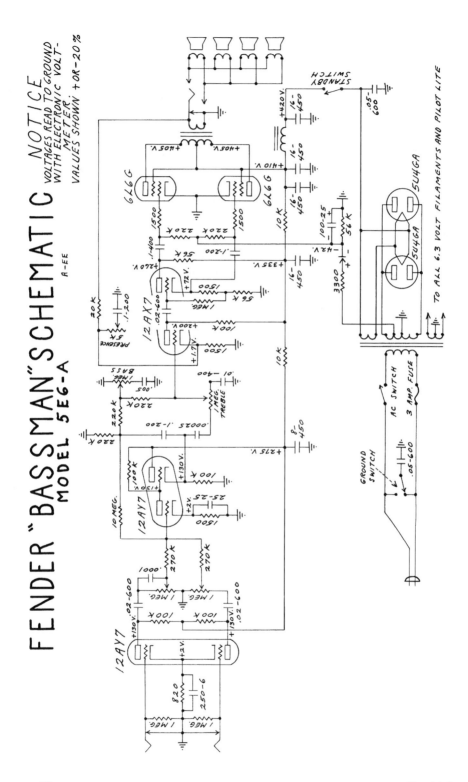

FENDER "BASSMAN" SCHEMATIC
MODEL 5E6-A
A-EE

NOTICE
VOLTAGES READ TO GROUND
WITH ELECTRONIC VOLT-
METER.
VALUES SHOWN + OR - 20%

Kendricks

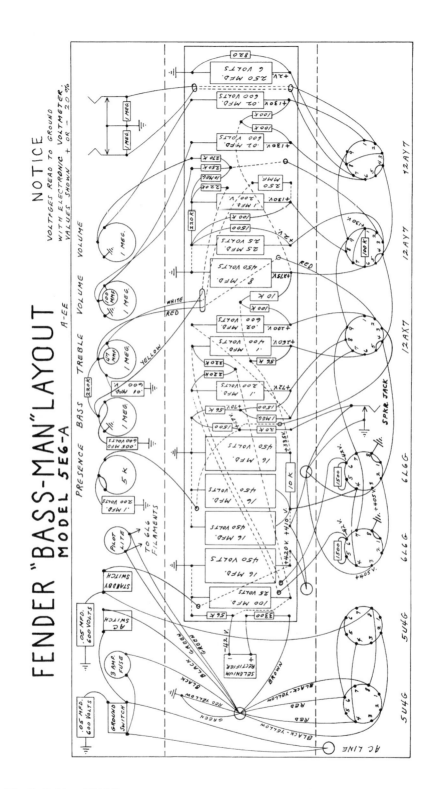

FENDER "BASS-MAN" LAYOUT
MODEL 5E6-A

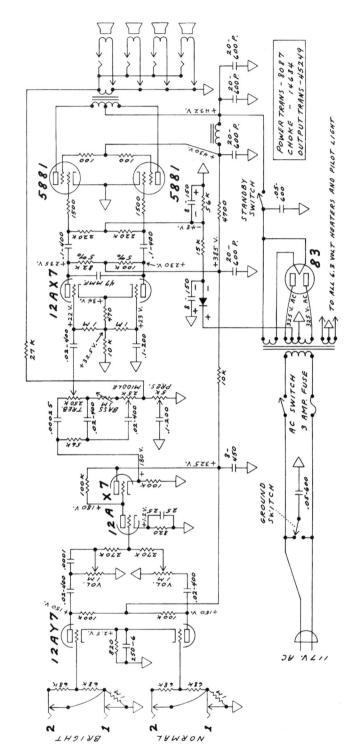

FENDER "BASSMAN" SCHEMATIC
MODEL 5F6

NOTICE

VOLTAGES READ TO GROUND
WITH ELECTRONIC VOLTMETER
VALUES SHOWN + OR − 20%

Kendricks

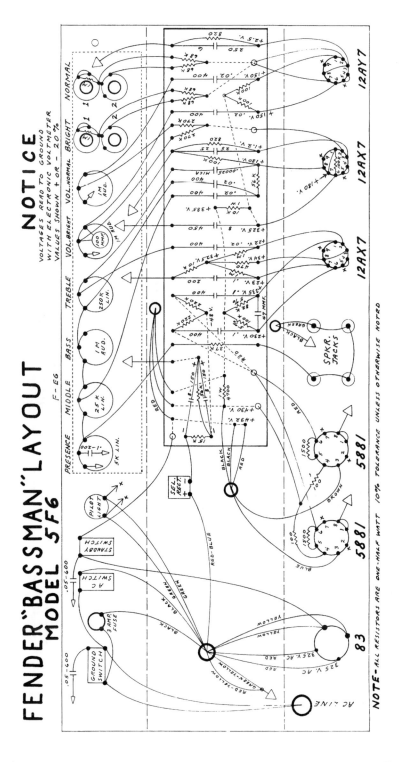

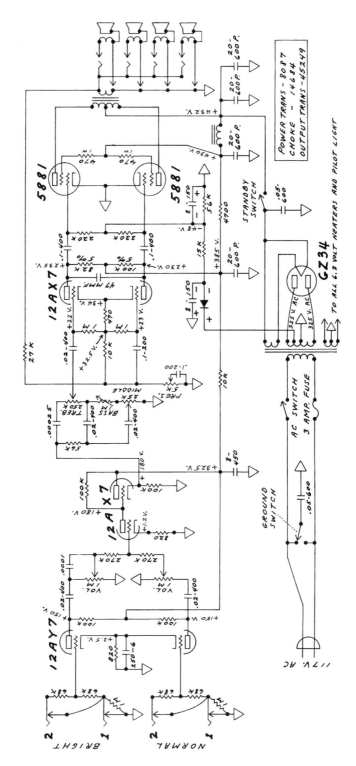

FENDER "BASSMAN" SCHEMATIC
MODEL 5F6-A
I-EG

NOTICE

VOLTAGES READ TO GROUND
WITH ELECTRONIC VOLTMETER
VALUES SHOWN + OR − 20%

POWER TRANS − 8087
CHOKE − 14684
OUTPUT TRANS −45249

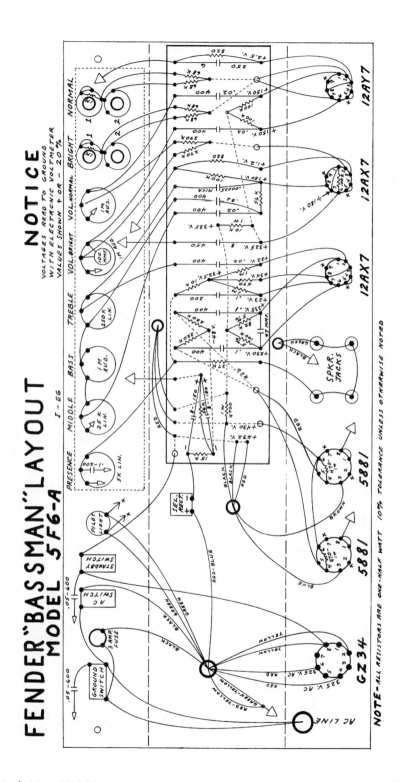

Kendricks

THE DELUXE REVERB

In June of 1963, Fender designed a brand new product: the Deluxe Reverb amp. It had vibrato, reverb, two channels and one 12" 8 ohm speaker. With an output stage running at 60 volts over the design maximum rating for the 6V6 tubes it used, the amp put out about 20 watts into a Fender special design speaker.

ABOUT THE CIRCUIT

Preamp circuitry was basically identical to all other blackface Fender amps that had two output tubes, except for a few differences. Among these differences:

1. There were no bright switches. One channel was normal and the other channel (vibrato channel) had a 47 pf cap across the volume pot to make it just a little bit brighter than the normal channel.

2. There were no adjustable middle controls. Instead, a fixed value resistor (6.8K) was installed where the middle control pot would have normally been, in the tone section of the circuit. This is the equivalent of a mid control set at about halfway up.

3. On some of the first models, a .033 mfd tone cap was used in the midrange section, making slightly clearer bass and slightly stronger upper mids. This was changed back to the familiar .047 mfd tone cap that was used on virtually all other Fenders of the day.

4. Lower plate voltages were used on the preamp tubes. This would provide less gain than other Fenders; however, it would sound browner and fatter with a preamp section that would distort more easily.

BLACKFACE vs. SILVERFACE

Only minor changes were made to the Deluxe Reverb when CBS took over Fender. Among them:

1. In 1970, the rectifier tube was changed to a 5U4GB rectifier. Although this is a very rugged and dependable tube, it was sluggish in comparison to the lower internal resistance of the earlier GZ34. To accommodate this new tube, the power transformer high voltage secondary was beefed up a little to allow for the additional losses.

2. The phase inverter voltages were increased slightly on the plates. This gave more headroom in the inverter stage—a welcome improvement.

3. The phase inverter input impedance was changed from 1 meg ohm to 330K. This was a big mistake because it loaded down the signal too much. Actually what we are talking about here is the two resistors that go to the grids (pin 2, pin 7) of the phase inverter tube.

4. The coupling cap going to the input of the phase inverter was changed from .001 mfd to .01 mfd. This was a great idea because it resulted in a richer tone. I actually prefer a .02 mfd cap in this position.

5. A parasitic suppression cap was placed from the grids of the power tubes to ground (yuck!!)! This was probably necessary in most of the silverfaced amps, because they screwed up the lead-dress which made the amps unstable. These 1200 pf capacitors kill tone! They go directly from the power tube grids (pin 5) to ground. Higher order harmonics are bled off by these caps.

AMP TIPS FOR DELUXE REVERBS

1. Never use a solid-state rectifier as a tube rectifier substitute in a Deluxe Reverb. Your amp will work for a while but tube life will be measured in minutes. However the solid-state rectifier will work if the output tubes are changed to a 6L6 style tube.

2. Biasing is critical in a Deluxe Reverb, because if the tubes are biased cold, the plate voltage will increase beyond the limits of a 6V6. 30 mA per tube is what I recommend. After biasing, I check the plate voltage and, if it is over 425 volts, I bias the output tubes for more current, until the plate voltage is no more than 425 volts. (The plate voltage decreases as the tubes draw more current because of the internal resistance of the power supply.)

3. It is okay to change output tubes to a 6L6 or 5881 style tube, but do not attempt to convert to EL34s without installing an auxiliary filament transformer. EL34s will draw too much filament

current and your power transformer will soon be history. I add a 2 amp 6.3 volt transformer by mounting it to the cap pan. I disconnect the preamp tube heaters from the main power supply and hook them to the auxiliary transformer. With the preamp heaters disconnected from the main power supply, the output tubes can easily draw an additional 1.8 amps of current. Be sure your auxiliary transformer has a center tap and ground it to the chassis or make an artificial ground by taking two 100 ohm resistors and connect them from each leg of the secondary to ground. This will eliminate hum problems.

4. Use caution if you own a model that used a 5U4GB and you want to change to a GZ34. The plate voltages may be too high.

5. Certain blackface Deluxe Reverbs had inadequate filtering on the main high voltage supply. On certain Deluxe Reverbs and Deluxes (model AB763) only one 16 mfd capacitor was on the main high voltage supply. An extra 16 mfd 450 volt capacitor should be installed in parallel with the one that goes from the hot side of the standby switch to ground. Observe correct polarity (negative goes to ground, positive goes to the circuit).

6. If you own a silverface and you would like to remove the 1200 pf cap that is going from the power tube grids to ground (pin 5), try clipping them off and see what happens. About 50% of the time, this can be done without having to change the lead dress in the preamp stage. If you clip them off and have instability problems, find a blackface as a model and route the wires inside exactly like the blackface. Also check to be sure all of the grounds are good.

GLOSSARY
K-*noun*-Abbreviation for one thousand.
VIBRATO-*noun*-The effect of pitch varying slightly higher and slightly lower than the fundamental signal.

DELUXE/REVERB

FENDER DELUXE/REVERB AMP The Deluxe/Reverb with built-in Reverberation and Vibrato assures outstanding amplification qualities and performance characteristics. The circuit incorporates the latest control and audio features to make it the finest amplifier of its type in its price range. The Deluxe/ Reverb embodies the following features: Two Channels; Normal and Vibrato, Front Panel contains four Inputs, two Volume Controls, two Treble Controls, two Bass Controls, Reverb Control, Speed and Intensity Controls and a Jeweled Pilot Light. Fifteen tube performance. 1-12" Heavy Duty Speaker. **SIZE:** Height 17½", Depth 9½", Width 24½".

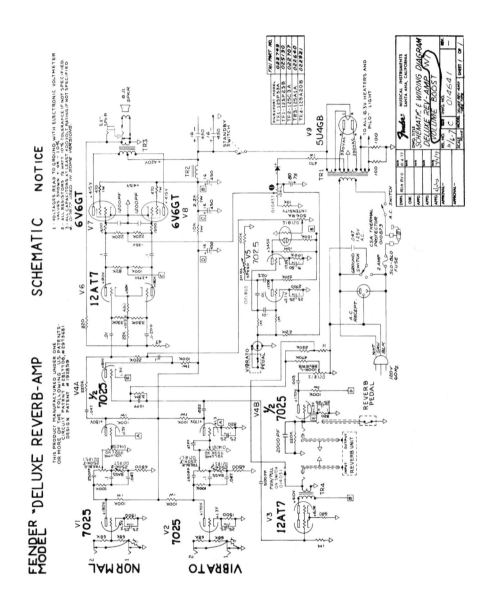

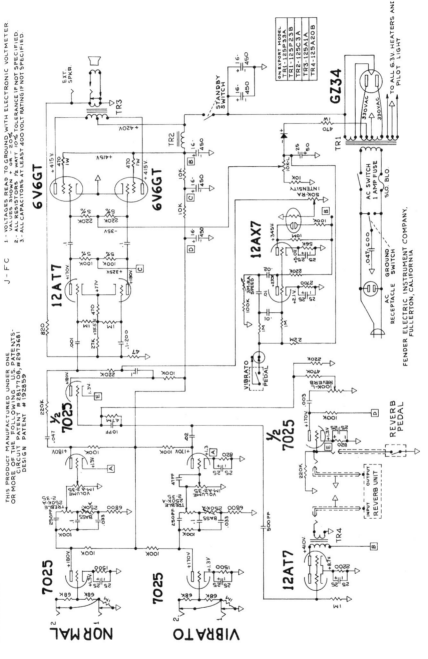

FENDER "DELUXE REVERB-AMP AA763" SCHEMATIC   NOTICE

Kendricks

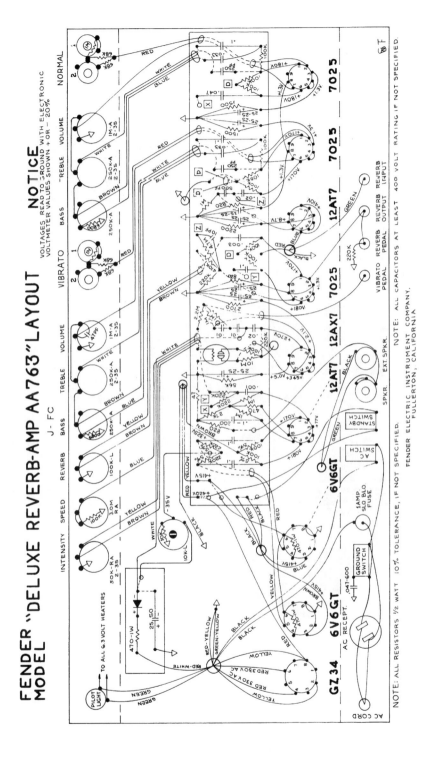

FENDER "DELUXE REVERB-AMP AA763" LAYOUT
MODEL

J - FC

NOTICE

VOLTAGES READ TO GROUND WITH ELECTRONIC
VOLTMETER VALUES SHOWN + OR − 20%

NOTE: ALL RESISTORS ½ WATT 10% TOLERANCE, IF NOT SPECIFIED.
NOTE: ALL CAPACITORS AT LEAST 400 VOLT RATING IF NOT SPECIFIED.

FENDER ELECTRIC INSTRUMENT COMPANY,
FULLERTON, CALIFORNIA.

The Deluxe Reverb   71

Kendricks

THE SUPER REVERB

In the late spring of 1964 in a small town called Groves, Texas, appearing at the City of Groves Recreation Hall was a local band called "The Misfits." I had heard this band before and I knew that the band was mediocre and not very happening. As I approached the hall I couldn't help being impressed with the music that I heard. Could it be that a substitute band was playing in their place? As I entered the place and approached the bandstand I noticed that this was indeed "The Misfits;" however, two of the players had gotten new Fender Super Reverb amplifiers. This was the first time I ever saw or heard the Fender Super Reverb amp, and was I ever knocked out.

Of course I wanted one when I heard it, but being a non-gigging 6th grader, I lacked the financial wherewithal to buy one. After all, they were selling for approximately $300 new at this time, depending on which dealer you bought from!

Of the many amps that hometown local gigging musicians bring into my shop now, I probably see more Super Reverbs than any other. My guess is that they are still the amp of choice for the working musician on a budget.

With four 10" speakers, they move a whalloping 312 inches of air. (88 more inches than a Twin Reverb or a Pro). Set up correctly, they have just the right amount of power for club gigging and rehearsal. With built-in reverb and vibrato and speakers included, they seem to simplify life for the working musician.

When Fender changed the 3X10 Bandmaster and the 4X10 Bassman to piggy-back 2X12 amps in the early 60s, the Concert amp became Fender's only 4X10 amp. At that time, the Super amp was sold with two 10" speakers. With the introduction of the Vibroverb which was already a 2X10 amp, Fender decided to add reverb to the Super and add two extra 10" speakers. This was the birth of the all new Super Reverb amp. It was advertised as a 4X10 Bassman with reverb and vibrato;

apparently Fender was getting a lot of requests, even then, to bring back the 4X10 Bassman sound. Unfortunately, Fender advertised that their new Super Reverb amp brought back the tonal characteristics of the old-style Bassman but they did very little to duplicate the sound. Not only was the circuit entirely different, but the speakers did not sound as good as the P10R Jensens used on the Bassman. The baffleboard was thicker and non-floating, which of course, sounds different.

All blackfaced Super Reverbs were nearly identical with the only difference being in a resistor value in the vibrato circuit which really didn't make much difference. Blackface models included the AA763 and the AB763 in that order.

Later 60s silverfaced Super Reverbs never really sounded all that great but could be modified to sound like their blackfaced counterparts. Almost all silverfaced Super Reverbs left much to be desired tonally because:

1. The output tube bias control was changed to a bias balance control, thus making proper biasing impossible without modifying the circuit or changing it back to blackface specs.

2. Some of them had a combination cathode-bias and fixed-bias output stage. This kind of circuit sounds absolutely horrible and is the circuit that gave silverface amps their bad reputation.

3. All of them had smaller value plate load resistors on the phase inverter stage. This caused a decrease in gain, dynamic response, punch, and sustain.

4. All of them had small value caps from the grids of the power tubes to ground which grounded out high end harmonics and made the amp sound colder than it already did.

5. Most of them used the 5U4 rectifier tube instead of the better sounding and more efficient 5AR4 used in the blackface models.

There is much than can be done to make any Super Reverb sound great. Getting the right speakers, tubes and other components would certainly make radical improvements in the tonal characteristics; but there are many mods to fatten and thicken tone, improve break-up, increase dynamic response, and improve note definition. Look for the answers to these questions in the chapter, "Ten Easy Mods For Your Super Reverb."

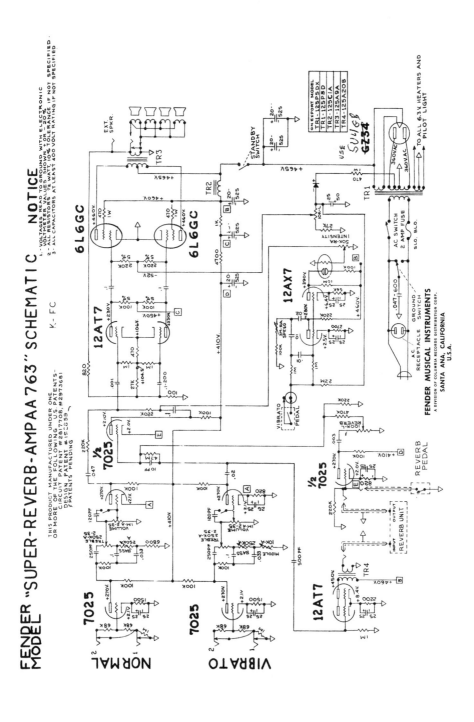

FENDER "SUPER-REVERB-AMP AA763" SCHEMATIC
MODEL

NOTICE

1. VOLTAGES READ TO GROUND WITH ELECTRONIC VOLTMETER. VALUES SHOWN + OR - 20%.
2. ALL RESISTOR VALUES ½ WATT, 10% TOLERANCE IF NOT SPECIFIED.
3. ALL CAPACITORS AT LEAST 400 VOLT RATING IF NOT SPECIFIED

THIS PRODUCT MANUFACTURED UNDER ONE OR MORE OF THE FOLLOWING PATENTS-CIRCUIT PATENT #2818708,
DESIGN PATENT #182359
PATENTS PENDING

FENDER MUSICAL INSTRUMENTS
A DIVISION OF COLUMBIA RECORDS DISTRIBUTION CORP.
SANTA ANA, CALIFORNIA
U.S.A.

ON EXPORT MODEL	
TR1-125P5DX	
TR1-125P5D	
TR2-125C1A	
TR3-125A9A	
TR4-125A20B	

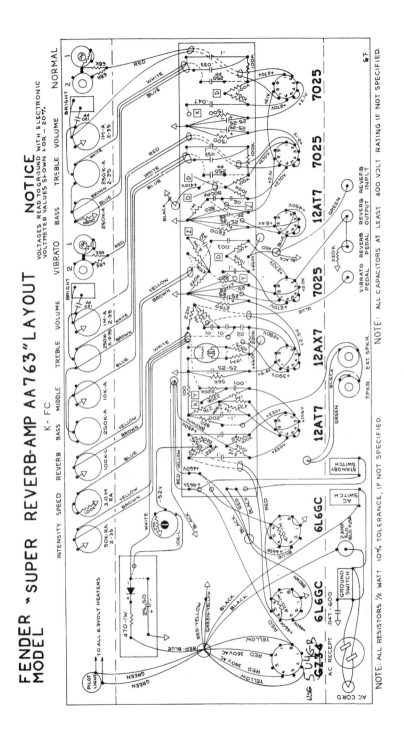

FENDER "SUPER" REVERB-AMP AA763" LAYOUT
MODEL

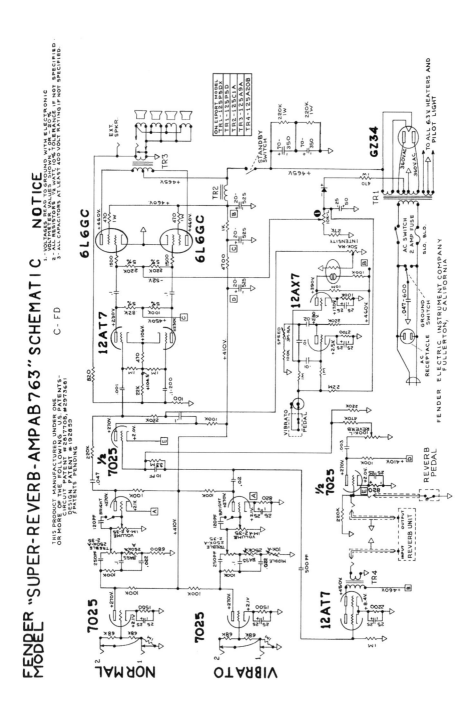

FENDER "SUPER-REVERB-AMP AB763" SCHEMATIC NOTICE

C-FD

THIS PRODUCT MANUFACTURED UNDER ONE
OR MORE OF THE FOLLOWING PATENTS—
CIRCUIT PATENT #2817708, #2973681
DESIGN PATENT #192859
PATENTS PENDING

Kendricks

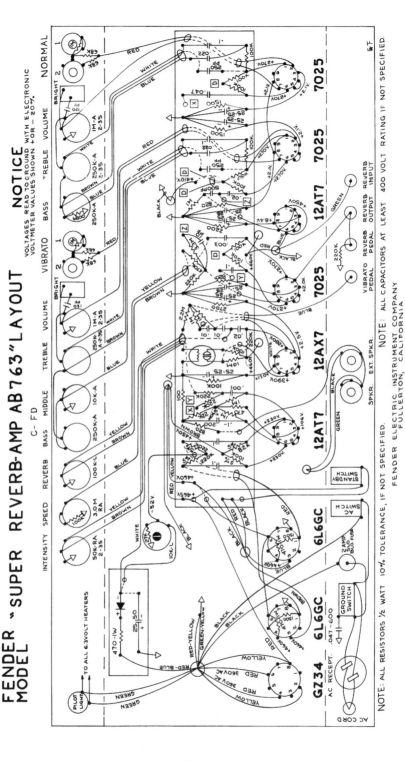

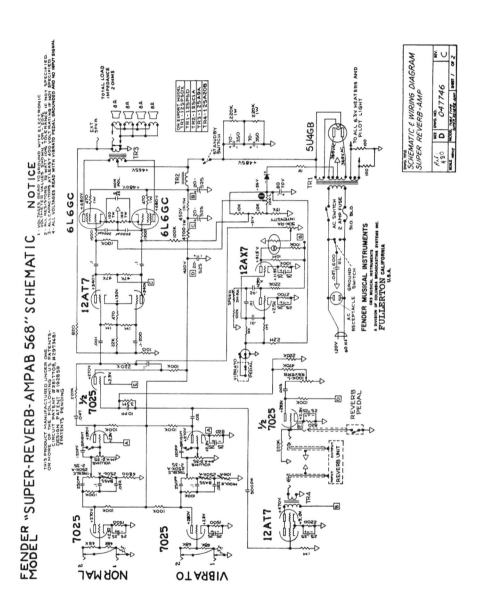

FENDER "SUPER-REVERB-AMP" AB 568" SCHEMATIC
MODEL

Kendricks

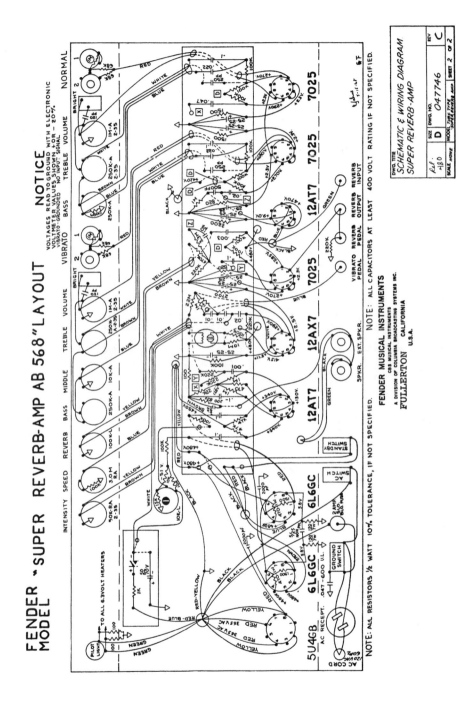

FENDER "SUPER-REVERB-AMP" SCHEMATIC
MODEL AA1069

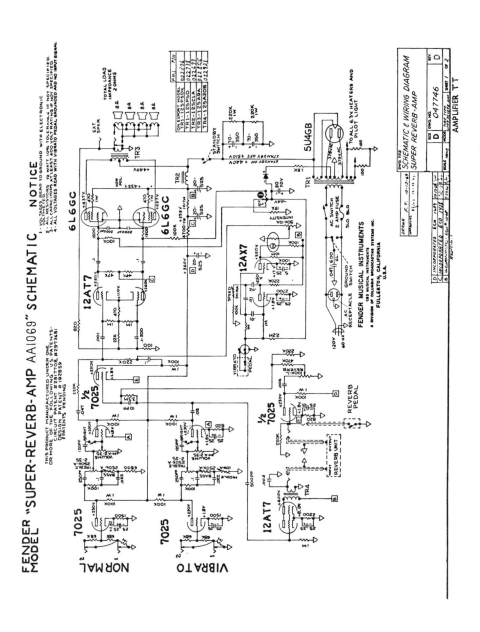

Kendricks

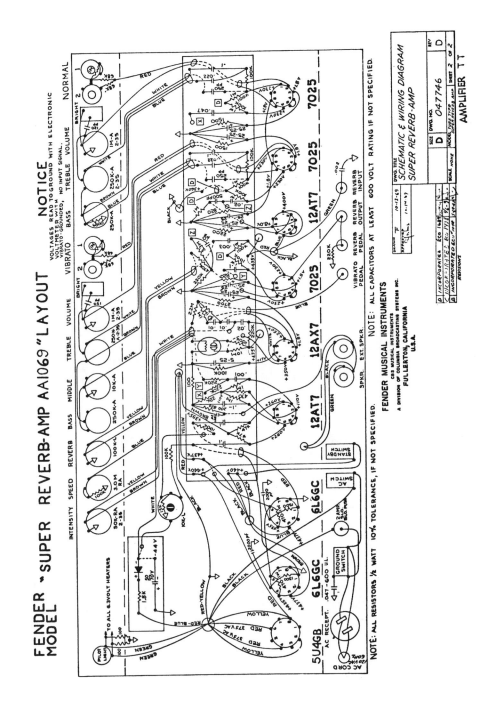

FENDER "SUPER REVERB-AMP" AA1069 "LAYOUT"
MODEL

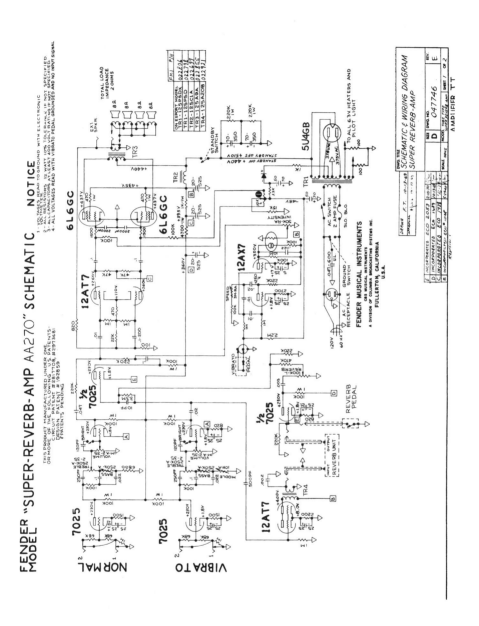

FENDER "SUPER-REVERB-AMP" AA270" SCHEMATIC
MODEL

NOTICE

THIS PRODUCT MANUFACTURED UNDER ONE
OR MORE OF THE FOLLOWING U.S. PATENTS:
CIRCUIT PATENT #2817708, #2973681
DESIGN PATENT #192859
& PATENTS PENDING

1 - VOLTAGES READ TO GROUND WITH ELECTRONIC
2 - ALL RESISTORS 1/2 WATT 10% TOLERANCE IF NOT SPECIFIED
3 - ALL CAPACITORS VALUE IN MFD VALUE IF NOT SPECIFIED
4 - ALL VOLTAGES READ WITH VIBRATO PEDAL GROUNDED AND NO INPUT SIGNAL

84   Kendricks

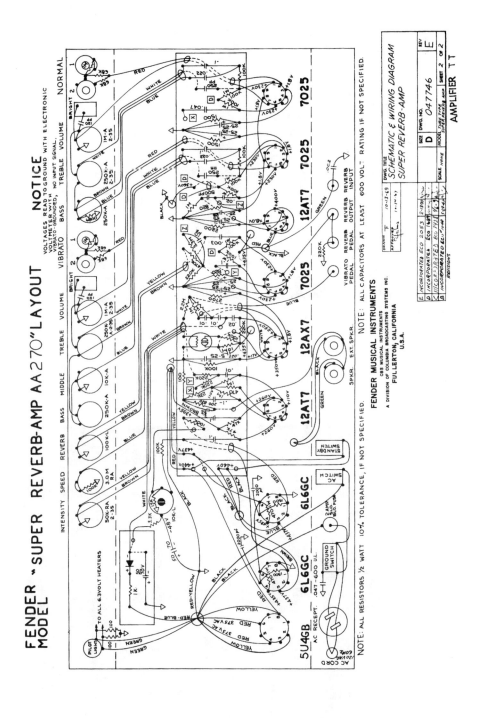

Kendricks

THE VIBROVERB

There has been a lot of talk lately about the Fender Vibroverb amps. Which model has the best tone? Which reverb circuit sounds the best? Which one has the best vibrato? Does anyone have a schematic? A layout? I personally like the 6G16 best of all; however, there is something to be said for the other models.

The 6G16 has two 10" speakers while the AA763 and the AB763 each have a 15" speaker. The 6G16 uses a vibrato circuit that modulates the power tube bias, while the other two models simply ground out the signal (immediately before the phase inverter) to achieve vibrato. Grounding out the signal was apparently Leo's favorite circuit because that type of circuit was used on all later blackface Fenders with vibrato, except the Princeton Reverb and Vibro Champ.

Unique to the 6G16 is the reverb coupling circuit which, to my knowledge, was not used in any other Fender amps. The AB763 and the AA763 use the same familiar coupling used in all blackface Fender amps. All three amps use a slightly different tone circuit, the 6G16 using the tapped treble control like many blond and brown Tolex amps of its vintage.

Also unique to the 6G16 is its 12AX7 style (7025) phase inverter tube as opposed to the 12AT7 on the other two models. This tube gives more gain generally speaking; however, since voltages on the preamp and power tube plates are lower in the 6G16, the tubes have slightly less gain before the phase inverter. In other words, one compensated for the other. One must consider that lower plate voltages give a browner sound (less high end). Also lower voltages give quicker break up, a tone I personally prefer.

For everyone out there that has been calling my shop begging for schematics of these three amps, here are the schematics and the layouts. These schematics and layouts were given to me by my good friend, tube guru Ken Fischer of Trainwreck Circuits.

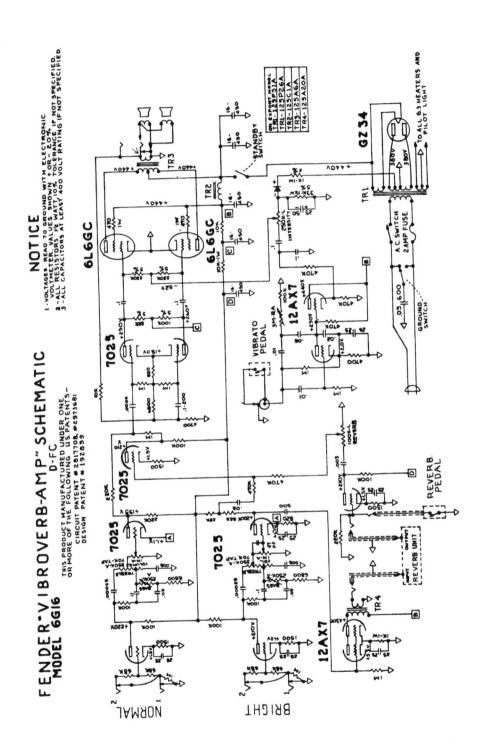

FENDER "VIBROVERB-AMP" SCHEMATIC
MODEL 6G16
D-FC

THIS PRODUCT MANUFACTURED UNDER ONE
OR MORE OF THE FOLLOWING U.S. PATENTS—
CIRCUIT PATENT # 2817708, #2973681
DESIGN PATENT # 192859

NOTICE

1 - VOLTAGES READ TO GROUND WITH ELECTRONIC
VOLTMETER. VALUES SHOWN ± 20%.
2 - ALL RESISTORS ½ WATT ± 10% TOLERANCE IF NOT SPECIFIED.
3 - ALL CAPACITORS AT LEAST 400 VOLT RATING IF NOT SPECIFIED.

ON EXPORT MODEL	
TR1-125P51A	
TR1-125P26A	
TR2-125C1A	
TR3-125A6A	
TR4-125A2OA	

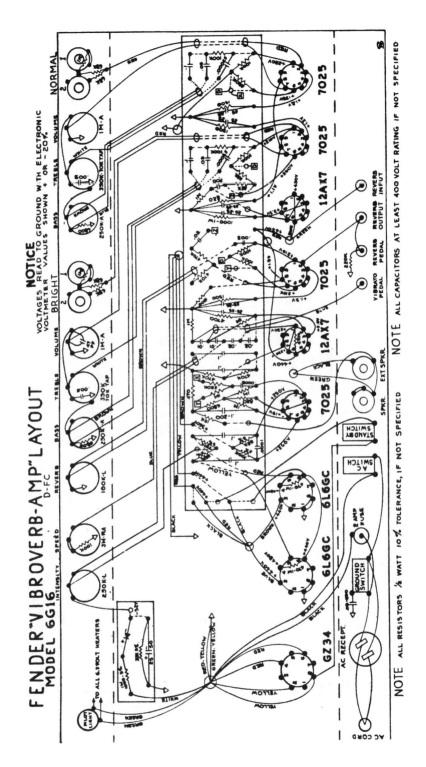

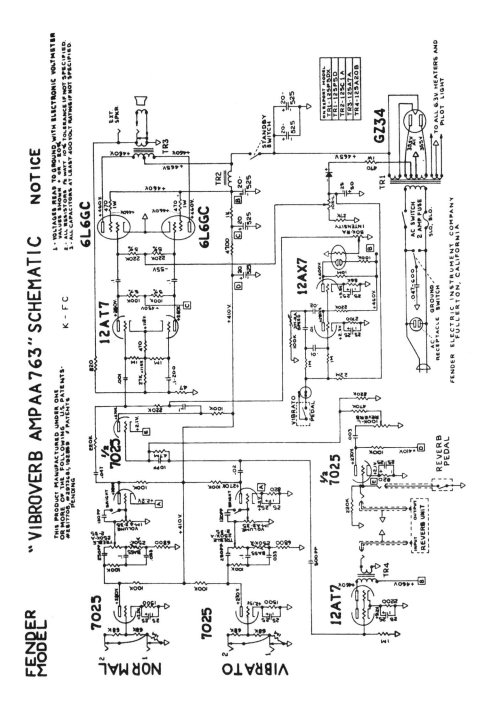

FENDER MODEL "VIBROVERB AMP AA763" SCHEMATIC NOTICE

K – FC

THIS PRODUCT MANUFACTURED UNDER ONE OR MORE OF THE FOLLOWING U.S. PATENTS. #2817708, #2973681, #2892843 / PATENTS PENDING

1 – VOLTAGES READ TO GROUND WITH ELECTRONIC VOLTMETER. VALUES SHOWN ± 20% OR LESS.
2 – ALL RESISTORS ½ WATT, 10% TOLERANCE IF NOT SPECIFIED.
3 – ALL CAPACITORS AT LEAST 400 VOLT RATING IF NOT SPECIFIED.

FENDER ELECTRIC INSTRUMENT COMPANY
FULLERTON, CALIFORNIA

Kendricks

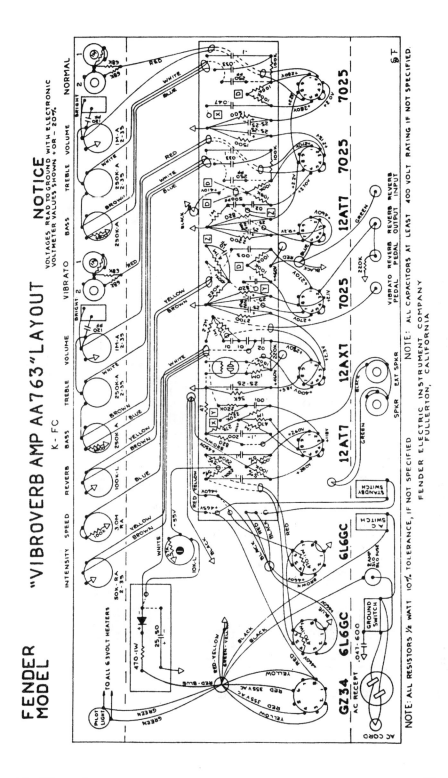

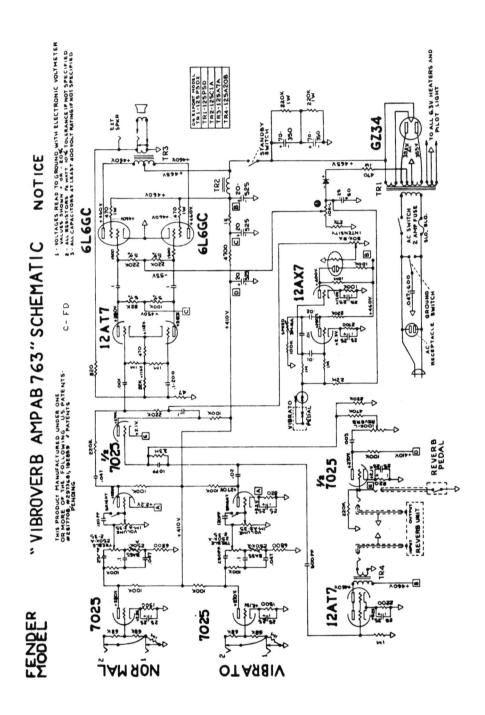

"VIBROVERB AMP AB763" SCHEMATIC NOTICE

C - FD

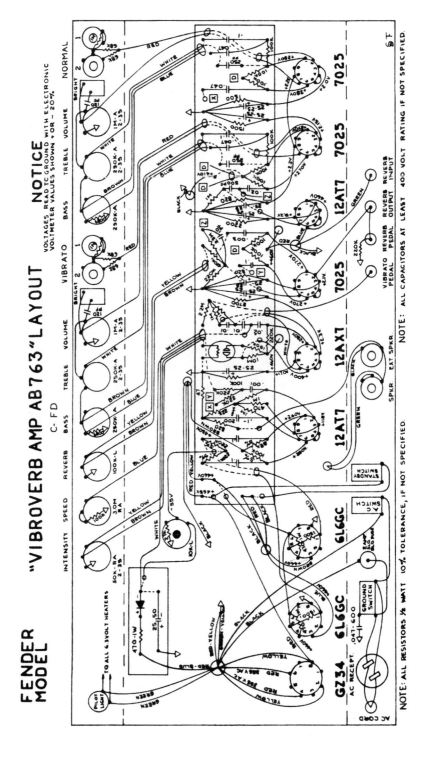

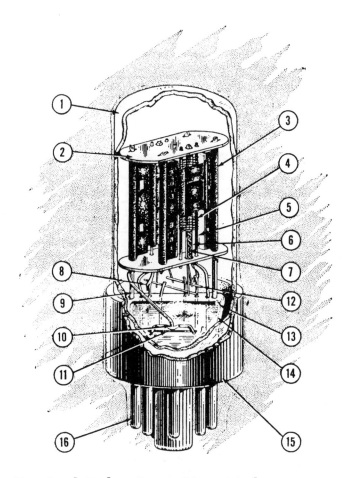

Typical Tube-Part Materials in RCA Electron Tube

1. *ENVELOPE*—Lime glass

2. *SPACER*—Mica sprayed with magnesium oxide

3. *PLATE*—Carbonized nickel or nickel-plated steel

4. *GRID WIRES*—Manganese-nickel or molybdenum

5. *GRID SIDE-RODS*—Chrome copper, nickel, or nickel-plated iron

6. *CATHODE*—Nickel coated with barium-calcium-strontium carbonates

7. *HEATER*—Tungsten or tungsten-molybdenum alloy with insulating coating of alundum

8. *CATHODE TAB*—Nickel

9. *MOUNT SUPPORT*—Nickel or nickel-plated iron

10. *GETTER SUPPORT AND LOOP*—Nickel or nickel-plated iron

11. *GETTER*—Barium-magnesium alloys

12. *HEATER CONNECTOR*—Nickel or nickel-plated iron

13. *STEM LEAD-IN WIRES*—Nickel, dumet, copper

14. *PRESSED STEM*—Lead glass

15. *BASE*—Bakelite

16. *BASE PINS*—Nickel-plated brass

Kendricks

A TUBE IS A TUBE, RIGHT?

Consider for a moment that every vacuum tube in your amplifier is a mixing bowl of electrical, geometrical, physical, and chemical properties, all acting simultaneously. Not only that, but the individual properties are affecting each other. Geometric and physical aspects would include the space between the electrodes in the tube, the specific size and shape of the electrodes, number of electrodes, size and spacing of components, as well as envelope shape and amount of vacuum. Chemical aspects include inert gases present, cathode coating chemicals, metal alloys used, including precious metal content. Electrical aspects would include the internal cathode to plate resistance, inter-electrode capacitances, cutoff grid bias, saturation grid bias, plate current, amplification factor and transconductance. Though electrical properties are dependent on the geometrics, design, and chemicals present in the tube, all physical properties (including chemical) and electrical properties affect the sound of the tube itself. It is obvious that these properties differ from one tube type to another, but what is not so obvious is that they also differ from manufacturer to manufacturer.

Also affecting the sound of a vacuum tube are the operating voltages which may differ according to the circuit they are in. This explains why two amps with the same type of tubes but different circuits will sound totally different.

Certain tube types, because of their geometric, chemical, and electrical characteristics tend to sound a certain way. This is also true of certain brands. Let's look at some specific tube types.

The 6550 power tube, because of its tighter vacuum, extra large plate size, and the fact that it can be operated at 660 volts (on the plate) gives a very clean sound and tons of low end with plenty of power. Because of this, it is a perfect tube for bass guitar, keyboards, steel guitar, or extra clean guitar. The tube is inherently clean with little sustain. This tube can be put into an amp that normally would use a 6L6GC with only a minor bias adjustment and changing the screen resistors to 1000 ohm 5 watt. It's best to use an American-made General Electric. The 6650A is better and the 6550WA is even better but much more expensive. The "A" designation means a later and modified version. The "W" designation means military grade which of course is best.

Another interesting tube is the EL84 power tube, also known as the 6BQ5. When this tube was originally designed, efficiency (power out divided by power consumed) was the primary consideration. In order to make the tube very efficient, some linearity was sacrificed. The tube cannot be operated at high voltages (340 volts is the max in class "A"), but can take plenty of current. It uses a small amount of grid bias; therefore, it is as efficient cathode-biased as it is fixed-bias. Because the linearity was sacrificed, the tube has much more harmonic distortion than other tubes. It will easily break into second and third order harmonics when pushed. Dick Denny used this tube in his first amp design in 1957, the Vox AC15. In 1959 he used this tube in the Vox AC30, although the first AC30s were not marketed until 1960. Another interesting feature of this tube is the fact that it offers gain as well as power. Most all power tubes only offer power, but the EL84 offers both; therefore, it takes little signal voltage to drive it. The best brand of EL84 today is the SovTek. It is a replication of the Mullard EL84 which of course is no longer available. Vox reissue amps come standard with the SovTek EL84. Many Gibson amps used the 6BQ5 which is the American name for the EL84.

Perhaps the sweetest sounding guitar amp tube is the 6V6. It too was designed for efficiency but compared to the EL84, it can take much higher voltages but less current. Originally designed for use in car radios, the idea was to have a tube that could play for a few hours without running down the battery. With its smaller envelope, the tube breaks into overdrive very quickly. It has a crisp sweet sound and is therefore perfect for guitar. The best sounding 6V6s are the Tung-Sol brand. Other excellent choices would include R.C.A. and SovTek.

Perhaps the most popular tube for guitar amps is the 6L6GC. Generally speaking, this tube is round sounding with good response. The Phillips ECG has loads of low end, but has a harsh top end with no middle. It is however a powerful tube that is reliable. The finest quality 6L6GC style tube being manufactured today is the SovTek 5881. It is a mil spec 6L6GWB that is smooth with mellow top end and ample lows. Never use a Chinese 6L6GC because it will not hold up, it is inefficient, and it sounds horrible. If you can find a matched set, the American made R.C.A. is probably the best sounding 6L6GC tube ever made. Since it has been years since this tube was manufactured, they are nearly impossible to find.

Another popular tube from Europe is the EL34. Different brands sound noticeably different with the Seimens EL34 being the best sounding brand currently in production. It has tight lows with sparkling highs and round mids. The Seimens is not very rugged, and must be sorted through to find good ones. A good friend of mine, who also builds high end guitar amps, takes a rubber hammer and bangs on the Seimens tube while it is operating to induce a short if the tube is flimsy. About half of them short out and he then takes the remainder and matches them for use in his amps. The best sounding EL34s of all time were probably the Mullard and the Brimar brands. The original Marshall amplifiers were designed for use with these brands.

When more than one output tube is used in an amp, it is important to use a matched set. Multiple output tubes always work as a team, just like the two front wheels on your car work together to steer your car. Just as a bad front end alignment will destroy your tires, unmatched tubes will destroy each other. Always use matched sets of output tubes for best efficiency, smoothest tone, reliability and longevity.

As far as preamp tubes, the Czechoslovakian-made "Tesla" tube is about the best sounding 12AX7 in production today. Again, you must sort through them and find some that are not noisy or microphonic, but the tone is definitely there. Chinese 12AX7s are low in microphonics, but have no tone whatsoever. The best sounding preamp tubes of all time were the Mullards, Telefunkens, and Brimars. Good luck finding some of these today. SovTek is about to come out with low microphonic preamp tubes with a fat tone. They have sent me several prototypes to test and critique. When this tube is finally out on the market, I predict that it will dominate the preamp tube market much the same as they have already done with the EL84 and the 5881.

Tubes are a lot like strings—they sound good when you use good ones and they don't last forever. Don't expect cheap ones to sound like quality ones. Select them for tone because that is why you have a tube amp in the first place. Tubes will always be available in spite of what you may have heard. Almost every country in the world uses tubes in their military equipment so you can expect good quality tubes to be available for at least the rest of our lifetimes.

GLOSSARY

CUTOFF-*noun*-A condition in which no current flows through a vacuum tube. This is achieved by having the grid potential so negative (with respect to the cathode) that current "cuts off".

MICROPHONIC-*adjective*-The tendency for a vacuum tube to pick up sound like a microphone.

SATURATION-*noun*-A condition in which maximum current is reached and no more current can possibly flow.

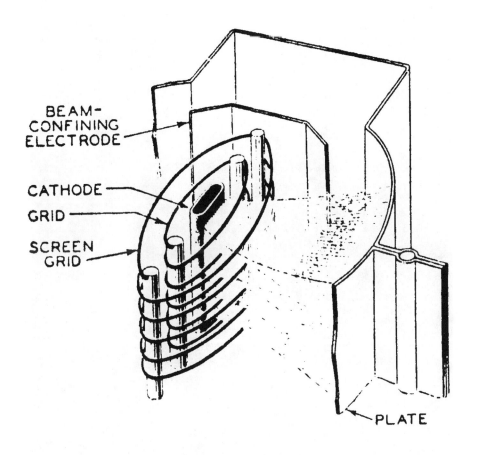

BEAM-
CONFINING
ELECTRODE

CATHODE

GRID

SCREEN
GRID

PLATE

Kendricks

THE SIMPLE TRUTH ABOUT BIASING YOUR AMP

Almost every day, someone calls and wants to know how to correctly bias their amp. In this chapter, I will explain what bias is, why it is important, the different types of bias designs, and how to bias your amp. In general, my purpose is to de-mystify what bias is all about.

WHAT IS BIAS?

To understand bias, we must first understand what is actually happening in a vacuum tube. Let's keep it simple and look at a triode. Triodes have three components (cathode, grid, and plate), hence the name triode. Generally speaking, current comes in the vacuum tube at the cathode and leaves the tube out of the plate. In actual applications, the plate is attached to the positive side of the power supply and the cathode is attached to the negative side of the power supply. Since opposites attract, the negative electrons move from the cathode to the plate and out of the tube back through the power supply and around again. The third component is the control grid, and this grid will control **how much** current will pass through the tube. How does it do this? It is physically located in between the cathode and the plate and it is shaped physically like a grid. By varying its electrical charge relationship with the cathode it can control how much current leaves the cathode for the plate. If the grid is very negative, it will stop the flow of current (cutoff), because just as opposites attract, likes repel. The negative charge on the grid simply repels the negative electrons on the cathode and they do not leave the cathode to go for the plate. If the grid is just a little negative, it will let a small amount of current pass; if it is not very negative, it will allow a large current to flow. If you varied the grid voltage charge to get the most current that could flow, varied it to get the current to stop, then averaged these two voltages to find the middle, that average would be the correct bias voltage for a class "A" triode operation. Bias then is the voltage relationship between the grid and the cathode of a vacuum tube. Bias voltage determines the quiescent (no signal) operating level of a tube.

Once the correct bias is determined and set, a guitar pickup could be connected to that grid and as the string caused varying voltages from the pickup to be applied to the grid, then varying amounts of current would pass through the tube out of the plate. What allows for amplification is the fact that a very small change in grid voltage makes a very large change in plate current.

This is exactly what happens in your guitar amp. Most guitar amps use a 12AX7 preamp tube, which is a triode. The pickup of your guitar is connected to a 1 meg ohm resistor (to complete a circuit with the pickup) with one end of the resistor to ground and the other end to the grid of a 12AX7. But how does the tube get the proper bias relationship?

We know that the grid must be negative in relationship to the cathode and we certainly don't want any D.C. voltage on our pickups. If the cathode is slightly positive with respect to the grid, the tube "sees" that as if the grid were slightly negative with respect to the cathode. Therefore a small resistor is placed in series with the cathode. As current flows through the cathode circuit, a small positive charge develops on the cathode. The grid is now negative with respect to the cathode.

All modern guitar amps use this type of biasing on the preamp tubes. It is sometimes called "cathode-bias" because of the resistor on the cathode. Many times it is called "self-bias" because if too much current tries to flow, then the positive voltage on the cathode will automatically increase thus making the grid more negative with respect to the cathode; this will have the effect of stopping some of the current flow. Conversely, if not much current flows, the positive voltage developed on the cathode will be less and the tube will "see" this as the grid being less negative and more current will flow. So as you can see, this set-up is completely self-adjusting. The preamp tube will reach a point of equilibrium.

WHY BIASING IS IMPORTANT

If you think of a sound wave as an alternating current, then you can visualize a sound wave that is going up and down (like a sine wave). Actually a guitar signal is much more complex than a simple sine wave, but for the sake of keeping this simple, think of a sine wave. In order to have a symmetrical wave, it is important for the top portion of the wave to be identical to the bottom portion of the wave. The hills must have the same characteristics as the valleys.

A vacuum tube has its limitations with regards to what it will and will not do; for instance, if the grid becomes less and less negative, there comes a point where the plate current will not go any higher. At this point making the grid even less negative will have **no effect** on the plate current (saturation). Conversely, if the grid goes more and more negative (reducing plate current), the tube can draw less and less plate current to the point of no current (cutoff). At cutoff, making the grid more negative will have **no effect** on the plate current. You can't have plate current go less than zero current.

In a preamp tube circuit, it is important to have the bias of the tubes set to where the tube is idling (no signal) in the mid-point between cutoff and saturation (class "A"). A tube will perform the most linearly in this way, without risking the severe clipping that may occur if the signal voltage is so great that it drives the tube into cutoff or saturation.

Biasing a tube affects tone greatly. As the bias level is adjusted to make the tube idle at more current, it becomes much easier for the signal voltage to drive the tube into saturation. Conversely, if the bias is adjusted to make the tube idle at less current, it becomes easier for the signal voltage to drive the tube into cutoff.

If the tube is biased where plate current is very high and a strong signal is applied, the plate watts may exceed the plate watt dissipation rating, thus causing the plates to glow red. When this occurs, tube life may be shortened to minutes!

If the tube is biased where plate current is very low, then the signal voltage may not be strong enough to get a fat tone. When this occurs, the tone is cold with not very much punch or power. Tubes that are biased cold (over-biased) can quickly reach cutoff which creates non-musical, buzzy distortion.

DIFFERENT TYPES OF BIASING DESIGNS

Cathode-biasing, a.k.a. self-biasing, is always used on preamp tubes. This never needs adjustment. Sometimes cathode-biasing is used on power tubes. Examples of amps that use cathode-biased power tubes are: all Fender tweed amps made before 1955, all late 50s Fender Deluxes, all tweed Princetons, all Champs, Vox AC30, most early Gibsons, Rickenbackers, Danelectros, Trainwreck Liverpool and the Trainwreck Rocket. You can tell if an amp has cathode-biased power tubes because it will have a resistor going from the cathode to ground. The cathode is pin 8 of the tube socket in 6L6 and 6V6 circuits. Cathode-biased power tubes have a singing quality with lots of sustain. Cathode-biased amps are generally not as loud as fixed-biased amps. Although cathode-biasing is self-adjusting in preamp tubes, that is not always the case with power tubes. Power tubes draw considerable current and sometimes aren't compatible with certain amps. More on this later.

Another biasing design used in guitar amps is the "grid leak" bias. Grid leak bias is a type of biasing that has been obsolete for years. It was only used on preamp tubes and usually only on the first gain stage. Examples of amps that used grid leak bias are: 5C3 tweed Deluxe Fender, Fender Champion 600 and 800, 5C4 Fender Super, and the 5C5 Fender Pro amp.

The most popular design, since the late 50s, for biasing output tubes is the fixed-bias design. This design is never used on preamp tubes. In a fixed-bias design, the cathode is grounded and there is a separate negative voltage power supply that is connected to the grid of the power tube. Sometimes there is an adjustment potentiometer on the negative power supply so that the bias voltage is adjustable. The reason this is called fixed-bias is because, once the negative voltage supply is adjusted, there will always be a fixed amount of negative voltage connected directly to the control grid. There are some amps that are fixed-bias, but with no adjustment potentiometer. In these amps, the bias can still be adjusted by changing the value of one or more resistors in the negative power supply that is used for the bias voltage. Most early blackface Fender amps have adjustable fixed-bias design. Later silverface Fenders have an adjustment potentiometer; however, the adjustment only adjusts the balance between output tubes and does not offer any real adjustment balance between output tubes and does not offer any real adjustment for biasing an amp. All Fender Twins, from 1956 to the present, all brown, black, and silverface Deluxes, all Mesa Boogie amps, all Marshall amps, all Kendrick combo amps 40 watts or higher, Fender Bandmasters and Pro amps since 1956, Bassmans since 1954, Jim Kelly amps, and Trainwreck Express amps—all of these and many others use fixed-bias design for the output tubes.

So now that we have talked about what bias is, why it is important, and the different types of bias designs, I will show you four excellent methods to correctly bias your fixed-biased amps and two excellent methods to correctly bias your cathode-biased amps.

To refresh your memory, we defined bias as being the voltage relationship between the grid and the cathode of a vacuum tube. Bias voltage determines the quiescent (no signal) operating level of a tube. We said that the grid must be negative in relationship to the cathode; if the cathode is slightly positive with respect to the grid, the tube "sees" that as if the grid were slightly negative with respect to the cathode. We said that in order to have a symmetrical wave, it is important for the top portion of the wave be identical to the bottom portion of the wave. "Saturation" and "cutoff" were explained as well as "cathode-biasing" and "fixed-biasing". A distinction between "adjustable fixed-bias" and "non-adjustable fixed-bias" was made.

FOUR WAYS TO CORRECTLY BIAS YOUR FIXED-BIAS AMP

TRANSFORMER SHUNT METHOD-This method was made famous by the designer of Trainwreck Amplifiers, Ken Fischer. This method has the benefits of being extremely accurate and very quick to perform. Here's how it works. Since the tube bias alters how much current the tube will pass, and since all of this current leaves the power tube directly into the output transformer, then one could simply shunt the output transformer with a milliammeter and measure the current directly. This is a lot easier than it sounds. Your negative lead on the milliammeter goes to the plate of the output tube (pin 3 on 6L6, EL34, 6V6, 7581, 6550, EL37, KT66 and pin 7 for EL84) and the positive lead goes to the center-tap of the transformer (or the transformer finish winding if single-ended amp design—i.e., Fender Champ, all amps with only one power tube.) This is almost always a red wire on

American amps. You may ask why doesn't the current split between the transformer and the meter, since they are in parallel? It's because the internal resistance of the milliammeter is only a fraction of an ohm, while the internal resistance of the transformer is several thousand times more. The current takes the path of least resistance and goes through the meter.

Now that you can measure the current flowing through the transformer, you must determine how much is going through the tube. If it's a two output tube amp or if it's a single-ended amp, then the reading on the meter is what's going through the tube. However, if the amp has four output tubes, the reading must be divided in half. On four output tube amps, two tubes feed each end of the transformer. Since you are only shunting one side, then your reading would be for two tubes and therefore must be divided in half to get an approximation of what one tube is drawing.

Now that you know how much current is flowing through the tubes, you must find the negative voltage supply that feeds negative voltage to the grids. We are going to adjust that voltage so that the output tubes are idling at the correct current. In blackface Fenders, there will be an adjustment pot that can be accessed with a small screwdriver. Marshalls also have an adjustment pot. Some amps, such as Mesa Boogies and tweed Fenders, do not have adjustment pots. In this case one must find the voltage divider resistors in the negative voltage grid supply. The circuit will have a wire going from the **power** transformer to the cathode of a solid-state rectifier and then will flow through two resistors in series. If the first of these resistors is decreased in resistance, the negative grid voltage will increase thus making the tube current **decrease** and if the second of these resistors is decreased, the negative grid voltage will go down, thus making the current go up. Decide which resistor must decrease and temporarily connect a large value pot, say 250K or 500K, across that resistor. Start with the pot at its highest resistance setting. While monitoring the current, adjust the pot until the appropriate current is reached. Turn the amp off and disconnect that pot. Measure the pot with an ohmmeter, then find a resistor of that value and solder it across where the pot was connected. You might want to re-check the tube current, but it should be the same with the resistor as it was with the pot. How can you find the appropriate value resistor if it is not a standard value? If I need 18.5K, for instance, I will simply get some 18k or 19K resistors and measure them with a meter until I find one that measures exactly 18.5K ohms.

How do you know how much idling current the output tubes want to see? Actually there is no one correct setting. There are only limits of not less than and not more than. I would say not less than 10 mA and not more than 50 mA in most cases. Certain tubes (6550, EL34) may like to see up to 75 mA. But generally speaking most 6L6 style amps sound best around 35 mA. Any setting that gives you the tone you like within those parameters is correct. Higher current settings will be louder, thicker and more easily overdriven. Lower current settings will be cleaner and somewhat thinner.

The transformer shunt method will work in almost any amp except the 5E series Fender tweed amps (these had the screen and the center tap tied together with no screen resistor, therefore shunting the transformer made the power tube into a triode.) Also silverface Fenders have an adjustment pot that looks like a blackface; however, it is not wired as an adjustment for bias, but as a balance for the output tubes. In an amp such as this, I recommend rewiring it like a blackface using the same parts and just moving a few connections around. This will make it adjustable.

CATHODE RESISTOR METHOD-This method is used on some amps already, but any fixed-biased amp can be modified for its use. Find two 1 ohm ½ watt resistors. These must be measured and matched to be **exactly** 1 ohm. Find the cathode pin on the output tube socket (pin 8 on 6L6, 6V6, etc. and pin 3 on EL84, 7189, 6BQ5) . It will have a straight wire going from the cathode to ground. Disconnect this wire and connect a 1 ohm resistor from cathode to ground. Do this on each output tube. Connect your **digital** voltmeter across one of these resistors. When you turn your amp on, the reading in millivolts will convert directly into milliamps. This will let you know how much current the one tube is passing. Now you would simply adjust the bias voltage as described in the "Transformer Shunt Method" above until the proper current is achieved. You will need a fairly accurate digital meter for this method. In this method, you can play the amp while the meter is connected. This is an advantage because you can listen for how tube current affects tone. You can not play your amp with the meter connected in the "Transformer Shunt Method" above.

Meter in "Series" With Plate Method-With this method, you will unsolder the wire that goes to the plate of one power tube and hook that wire to the positive lead of a milliammeter. The negative lead of the milliammeter goes to the plate lead on the tube socket. While monitoring current, adjust bias voltage until desired current is achieved.

Bias by Ear Method-If you think about it, the real reason for biasing an amp is tone. You can adjust the bias negative voltage supply, then listen for the desired tone. **You must be careful not to exceed the plate-watts dissipation factor.** (Translation: don't have so much current flowing through the tubes that the plates glow cherry red.) This is especially easy in most blackface amps, because the adjustment pot can be accessed without taking the amp apart. It looks like a jack on the chassis about 2 inches to the right of the power transformer, looking into the back of the amp. A small flat-blade screwdriver works nicely. Turn the adjustment one way, the amp is louder. Turn it the other way, the amp is softer. Find the sweetest spot without glowing the tube plates cherry red and you've got it!

TWO WAYS TO CORRECTLY BIAS YOUR CATHODE-BIAS AMP

Cathode-biased amps do not have a negative voltage grid supply, but instead rely on a cathode resistor to cause the cathode to be positive in relationship to the grid. Here are two correct ways to set bias with a cathode-biased amp.

Tube Substitution Method-Monitoring the current by any of the first three ways described in the fixed-bias section of this article above, try different matched pairs of output tubes until you find a set that idles at the appropriate current **for that particular amp**. You will need several matched pairs to find the set the amp likes the best. Of course, you could also do this by ear.

Cathode Resistor Substitution Method-Using any method described above to monitor current, try different value cathode resistors until the appropriate current is achieved. If the plate current is too low, a smaller value cathode resistor is needed. Conversely, if the plate current is too high, a larger value cathode resistor is needed.

Be sure and use the correct or higher wattage rating on the cathode resistor. Whatever the stock wattage is will be correct. For instance if you had a cathode-biased tweed amp that had a 250 ohm cathode resistor at 5 watts, you might try a 200 ohm at 5 watts or even a 330 ohm at 5 watts, depending on which way you are going with the current.

The one problem with this approach is that to get the correct value cathode resistor, you may have to put two or three resistors together to get an exact resistance **with the appropriate wattage rating.** Another disadvantage is that it is a trial and error approach that could be very time consuming. On the other hand, if you only have one pair of output tubes to work with, it is the only alternative for good tone. As a rule, cathode-biased amps like more current than fixed-biased amps. 50 mA to 70 mA is not uncommon, especially in a single ended amp.

WHAT TO DO

Make sure you understand these various techniques before attempting their usage. If you do not understand, don't attempt any amplifier adjustment or repair unless done with the help of a competent technician.

GLOSSARY

OHMMETER-*noun*-Meter for measuring resistance. These are almost always on a multimeter.

POTENTIOMETER-*noun*-Variable resistor that is actually a voltage divider used for volume controls, tone controls, etc.

Kendricks

UNWINDING THE TRANSFORMER PUZZLE

Transformers in vintage amplifiers can really be a problem. Many of us have purchased a vintage amp only to find out later that the transformers were replaced with non-original transformers by a previous owner. Also many vintage amps have transformers that were either wound without enough wattage capacity to handle the amp at full clip (the manufacturers probably never dreamed anyone would ever play the amp wide open) or, at best, the transformers were wound with no margin of safety. Often the core materials used were very cheap and somewhat inefficient which made them run at high temperatures because of core loss. To that, add the fact that all were wound on porous paper which can absorb moisture from humidity in the air which could later result in arcing or higher capacitive leakage. Some were actually grossly under-designed. For instance the tweed Deluxe which has a 20 to 22 watt output at full clip and the output transformer is a 15 watt design! I have replaced no less than fifty output transformers in the tweed Deluxe amps in the past year!

To compound the problem, many companies bought surplus transformers to build their amps. For instance, the first Marshall amps (JTM 45) had "off the shelf" surplus stock transformers. Marshall bought them from a mail order company called "Radio Spares." The brand used was HyGrade, mostly sold for use in P.A. amplifiers. Many companies bought surplus because custom transformers are very expensive, and buying surplus at close-out prices reduced costs dramatically. Also custom winding transformers in quantities could represent a huge capital investment; whereas, off-the-shelf items could be bought ten or twenty pieces at a time, when needed, thus reducing capital expense. Of course when supplies dwindled, the company simply bought from some other surplus distributor. This explains why Vox and Marshalls used so many different brands of transformers for their amps. In fact, a Vox AC30 could have had one of six different brands of transformers in it and yet still be original! Tweed Fenders generally used Triad brand transformers, but changed to Schumacher transformers in the early 60s. Before that time, Schumacher was building car battery chargers.

When a transformer needs replacing in a vintage amp, there are limited options for repair, since chances are nil that the transformer is in current production from the original manufacturer.

1. HAVE THE TRANSFORMER BLUEPRINTED AND REWOUND. This is very expensive. Don't take it to a transformer company, because unless their engineers are vintage amp buffs that will pay attention to **every** detail (paper thickness, insulation material, winds per layer, laminate thickness, core material, interleaving, primary incremental inductance, etc.), their rewind will sound nothing like the original. Most transformer engineers think they know so much about transformers that they will substitute this and that thinking it will be better, not understanding that the low efficiency core material, paper bobbin, etc., are all essential to the tone of a vintage guitar amp.

2. REPLACE WITH A SIMILAR TRANSFORMER. The tone will never be quite the same, but if your finances are a restriction, this may be a cheap way to get a fairly decent sound out of an otherwise broken amp. For instance, if you have a tweed Deluxe with a blown output transformer, you could substitute almost any transformer that would normally be used with a pair of 6V6 output tubes and an 8 ohm speaker (i.e., black, silver or brown Princeton; black, silver or brown Deluxe.) Similarly a Super Reverb transformer would work in a 4X10 Bassman.

3. FIND A USED ONE that is exactly the same. Although this is usually an impossible task, there are companies that "part out" vintage amps and sell the transformers. (Bremer Music is a company that does this.) Do not accept a used transformer that has rust on the core laminates. Each laminate is coated to keep it insulated from the laminates on either side of it. When the laminates rust, this causes an electrical connection between adjacent laminates. Revarnishing will not help unless the laminates are completely removed, cleaned, revarnished and

rebuilt. Electrical connection between adjacent laminates causes eddy currents, which means that instead of the output of the transformer showing up entirely on the secondary of the transformer, some of the output is induced between certain shorted laminates. The current simply goes round and round the shorted laminates. This will zap the efficiency of any transformer, and the transformer will run hot. If it is a power transformer, the voltages will be off. If it is an output transformer, the power will be down. A transformer with rusty laminates has one foot in the grave and the other on a banana peel.

4. BUY A REPLACEMENT, if someone is still making the part. Some vintage amp restoration shops will blueprint and wind several of a particular type if they know there is a demand for that part. Since 50 to 100 transformers are wound at a time, the cost will be much less due to manufacturing savings of producing quantities. For instance, a particular one-of-a-kind custom wound transformer that my company produces might sell for somewhere around $175, but if that same transformer is one we get a lot of calls for, we will make 50 or 100 at a time, thus reducing the cost to about $75.

TRANSFORMER PREVENTIVE MAINTENANCE

Often the leads for a vintage transformer will have cloth insulation. After years of humidity absorption, the cloth will literally rot and crack. Unsoldering each lead one at a time and placing shrink tubing over the entire lead is recommended to better insulate leads whose insulation has become brittle, cracked and rotted. Of course, laminate rust could also be a problem. If you already have a rust problem, do not attempt to remove any of the rust—sanding, brushing or buffing will only worsen the problem. Try spraying a little Rustoleum flat black paint on the already rusted laminates. This will not cure the problem, but will help keep it from getting worse. A small amount of surface rust may not be bad enough to cause adjacent electrical connection of laminates, in which case the paint trick will salvage a transformer that would have gone bad had it not been painted.

GLOSSARY

ARCING-*verb*-When electricity jumps across open space from one point to another, those two points are said to be "arcing."

Amplifier courtesy of Dan Courtenay, Chelsea 2nd Hand Guitars, New York, NY

Kendricks

IMPORTANT FACTS ABOUT JENSEN SPEAKERS

So you bought a vintage amplifier that has Jensen speakers and you can't help but wonder, "Are these the right speakers for this amp?" Or maybe you might ask yourself, "Are these speakers any good? If not, what would be better for my amp?" Sure the amplifier gives the guitar a voice, but the speakers are what gives the amp a voice! Think about it. The sound you hear is the result of vibrations in the air but what vibrates the air? I rest my case!

Jensen speakers came in many different varieties. They ranged in size from 4" to 18". The quality of speaker was denoted by an alpha suffix after the speaker size (in inches) that started with "J," "K," and "L" for the top of the line "Professional Series." (Actually only a very few speakers were made with these suffixes and they were 18"and 15" speakers).

The second group of suffixes was for the "Concert Series" speakers. The alpha suffix from the top to the bottom was "N," "P," "Q," and "R" in that order. These speakers came in 8," 10," 12," and 15" sizes. "Concert Series" speakers were the most common and best sounding for use with guitar amps. Almost without exception, every Jensen found in any guitar amp will be from this series.

The third and least desirable were the "Standard Series" which began with the "S," "T," "U," "V," "W," and "X." With "U" through "X," only 8" sizes and smaller were available. "Standard Series" speakers are not very efficient and do not sound very good for guitar.

Prefixes determined what type of magnet was used. Generally the "P" prefix was Alnico V magnet, the "C" prefix was Ceramic magnet, and the "F" was a Field-Coil magnet. I said generally because when Jensen quit making speakers with Alnico V, they started using the "P" prefix for Ceramic magnet speakers. Also there are some Jensens that used the "EM" prefix.

For example a "P12N" would be an Alnico V magnet speaker that was 12" and the top of the line in the "Concert Series." Incidentally, this was the Jensen used in the 1958, 1959, and 1960 Fender Twin amps. On the other hand, a "P10R" would indicate an Alnico V magnet, 10" speaker that was the bottom of the line in the "Concert Series." This was the speaker of the 4X10 Fender Bassman.

The difference with all of these speakers would be in the voice coil size, weight of magnet, cones, and ultimately gap energy. Gap energy is measured in millions of Ergs. What is an Erg?

To give you a good definition, an Erg is the unit of work in the CGS (centimeter, gram, second) system. It is equal to the amount of work produced when one Dyne acts through a distance of one centimeter. What's a Dyne? A Dyne is the force required to accelerate one gram mass at the rate of one centimeter per second. Consider a Dyne as force and if that force acts through a distance of one centimeter, then work is produced. The Erg is how much work that is produced. You might think of a Dyne as potential work and the Erg as actual work. The speakers with the higher gap energy (see chart) are better speakers and can also handle more power.

To correctly date a Jensen speaker, look for the number on the speaker frame that starts with 220. This 220 was Jensen's manufacturing code number. The next digit after the 220 will tell you the year of manufacture. For example an 8 would indicate 1958. The problem with that is that you will have to guess if it is from the 50s or 60s. The amp that it is in and the condition of the speaker should tip you off as to which decade is indicated. The next two digits after the date digit will be the week of the year it was manufactured. For instance a number of 220401 would have been made either the first week of 1954 or the first week of 1964. If a speaker dates before the amp by a few weeks or even up to a couple of months, it is most probably original, but not always.

Amp companies were not very consistent about which speakers they used in what amp. For instance the tweed Deluxe could have a

P12Q or a P12R in it and yet be original. Usually the better speakers were used in the most powerful amps. For instance you would never see a P12R in a tweed Twin; the Twin used the top of the line P12N. The 4X10 Concert amp almost always used the P10Q. Fender, Ampeg, Rickenbacker, Danelectro, Gibson, and Hammond were some of the companies that used Jensen speakers.

Just because a Jensen speaker is not blown does not necessarily mean it is any good. I found this out the hard way when I spent eight months duplicating the P10R so that I would have a speaker to use in the Kendrick 2410 amps that I build. What I found was that almost all of the old Jensen speakers have dropped voice coils. This is because the original Jensens were assembled with animal glue which deteriorates over the years. I had to buy twelve P10Rs to get four that did not have dropped voice coils. (I needed these speakers to use for testing frequency response.) A speaker with a dropped voice coil will not put out much sound! Also the speaker could have been reconed in which case it may not sound right.

The original Jensens had the polarity on the speaker marked backwards by today's standards. If it has been reconed, the chances are that the polarity is reversed from original. This is why it is so important to manually check the polarity of a Jensen speaker with a battery. This is even more important on a multiple speaker amp. Let's say that you buy a 4X10 Bassman that has had two of the speakers reconed. When the speakers were re-installed, the previous owner probably didn't know that the recones had reverse polarity from the originals. He hooked them up thinking the marked polarities were correct and now you have two speakers that are phase cancelling the other two and the amp sounds pretty bad.

But how do you check with a battery? Connect a battery to the speaker leads and watch the cone. It should either move forward or backward. If it moves backward, reverse the leads. It will now move forward. When it moves forward after you connect a battery to the leads, the positive lead from the battery is the positive lead of the speaker. Of course the negative lead of the battery will be the negative lead of the speaker. If you have a hard time telling if the speaker is moving in or out, you probably have a dropped voice coil and should replace or recone the speaker. In a multiple speaker amp, you want all of the speakers to go forward at the same time, lest one speaker would phase cancel the other. Do not leave a battery hooked to the speaker very long as D.C. could cause the voice coil to overheat.

Jensen speakers are very easy to blow because the voice coil former is made of paper which does not conduct heat. Overheat the voice coil and your Jensen is history. If you are intending to play your vintage amp, yet would like to preserve the investment that the amp represents, I highly recommend that you replace the speakers and save the original Jensen to re-install at selling time. Obviously the amp will be worth considerably more at resale time if it has the original Jensen speakers. However if you blow the Jensen speakers in the meantime (and you will blow them if the amp is played a lot at high volumes) you will depreciate the value of the amp by much more than the cost of the replacement speakers. If you take my advice, at resale time you will end up with extra speakers for future use as an added bonus.

COMPARISON CHART FOR JENSEN LOUD SPEAKERS

ALNICO 5 PM MODELS

4"	5"	6"	8"	10"	12"	15"	18"	*GAP ENERGY	DESIG-NATION	SERIES
							PMJ-18	28.1	J	professional
						PMM-15		19.5	K	professional
								13.6	L	professional
								9.5	M	concert
					P12-N	P15-N		6.6	N	concert
					P12-P	P15-P		4.6	P	concert
			P8-Q	P10-Q	P12-Q	P15-Q		3.2	Q	concert
			P8-R	P10-R	P12-R			2.2	R	concert
			P8-S	P10-S	P12-S			1.5	S	standard
		P6-T	P8-T	P10-T	P12-T			1.1	T	standard
			P8-U					.74	U	standard
	P5-V	P6-V	P8-V					.51	V	standard
								.36	W	standard
P4-X	P5-X	P6-X						.25	X	standard

R series = 1" voice coil
Q series = 1¼" voice coil
P and N series = 1½" voice coil

*GAP ENERGY IN MILLIONS OF ERGS

HOW TO MAKE YOUR AMP SOUND RIGHT

So you got that vintage amp you wanted so badly, but it just doesn't sound like the one you heard over at your friend's house. Wouldn't you like it to sound like the best sounding amp of its model and vintage? In most cases you can make your vintage amp sound perfect by simply replacing all defective components with equivalent sounding components and cleaning up the connections so that the circuit is completely sound (pun intended).

Before working on any amp, I always drain any stored electricity, thus preventing accidental electrical shock. To do this, simply use a jumper wire with one end connected to the chassis, and the other end connected to a plate of any preamp tube. The plates of a 12AX7, 12AT7, or 12AU7 will be pin 1 or pin 6. In a 6SN7, 6SL7, or 6SC7 the plates are pin 2 and 5. In a 7199, the plates are pin 1 and pin 2. Turn the amp off and unplug the power cord. After connecting any plate to ground and, with the standby switch in the play mode, wait about a minute and most of the electricity will be drained. To drain the rest, connect the jumper wire from the chassis to the plate of any power tube. On a 6L6, 6V6, EL34, 7025, or 6550, this will be pin 3. On a 6BQ5 or EL84 it is pin 7. Wait a few seconds. Now there is no more electricity stored in the amp. No chance of getting shocked. If you don't know which pin is which, read on, and we will show you know how to count it later.

The first thing to check is the filter capacitors. These capacitors filter out 120 cycle ripple current that is produced when 60 cycle 120 volt wall outlet power is converted to D.C. power. They will only last about 10 years and will last even less if the amp is not used much. (This explains why the cleanest amps cosmetically usually sound the worst tonally.) Sometimes the amp will produce sound but will not sound good. You will experience low power with a 120 cycle hum (low B flat). Also your amp may sound like a ring modulator is in the circuit because a new sound is produced that is the difference between the frequency you are playing and the 120 cycle signal that is not being filtered correctly. In other words, you will hear an out of tune note on top of every note you play.

Another tell-tale sign is that the ends of these caps will have a bubble or a rupture. Sometimes the cap will be shorted in which case the amp will not play at all because it will be blowing fuses.

The best way to find these caps, for the novice, is to locate the rectifier circuit. If the amp has a rectifier tube (unless modified, almost all vintage amps do) the first of these filter caps would start from pin 8 of the rectifier tube socket, assuming that the amp uses a standard rectifier tube. Standard rectifier tubes include 5Y3, 5AR4, 5U4, 5R4, GZ32, and GZ34. This tube is always located by the power transformer. Capacitor values are typically 8 to 40 microfarads at 450 to 600 volts. Generally there are three to five of these caps in an amp. They start at the rectifier tube and are separated by power resistors. Sometimes pin 8 of the rectifier socket goes to a standby switch with a small value cap on the rectifier side of the switch and the filter caps start on the other side of the switch. In most Fender amps, there is a pan on the chassis with the filter caps underneath the pan. Some vintage amps have a multi-cap which is actually three or four caps in one. These look like a metal cylinder on the chassis that resembles a tube in size.

Of utmost importance is getting the polarity correct. This means that the caps only go in **one** way. There is a plus or positive lead and a minus or negative lead on a filter cap. One side of the cap goes to power and the other side goes to ground. Before removing the bad caps, notice how they are in the circuit. Unless the cap is used to filter negative bias supply voltage, the plus will go to power and the minus will go to ground. On a multi-cap, one terminal will be minus (ground) and will be internally connected to all minus leads of each cap while the plus terminal will each be individual. Again the best way for the novice is to notice which way they go **before removing any caps.** Maybe a drawing would be useful, so you do not have to remember anything.

In finding replacements, you may experience difficulty in finding the correct values. For instance, what if the circuit had an 8 uf cap at 450 volts and you cannot get one; what to do? The rule is you can go the same or more on the voltage. Example: many tweed amps used 16 uf 450 volt filter caps. I typically replace them with 15 uf 500 volt caps with no change in tone. A 20 uf 450 would work just fine, but if the microfarad rating is much too small, the amp may hum. If the voltage rating is too small, the cap may short out, thus blowing a fuse and ruining the new cap. **Never** use a lower voltage rating than the original, and get exact or as close as you can on the microfarad (uf) rating.

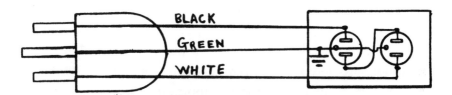

TWO SINGLE AC OUTLETS ARE WIRED IN SERIES TO MAKE THE CURRENT LIMITER, A DOUBLE OUTLET WILL NOT WORK BECAUSE IT IS PREWIRED IN PARALLEL.

Once you have soldered the new caps in, you must charge them slowly for best results. If you have a variac, you can bring them up slowly using the variac, but if you are a novice, you probably don't have a variac. Here is what you can do that will work great. Make a homemade current limiter. Get an incandescent light bulb or ordinary 100 watt lamp and hook it in series with an extension cord. The lamp will not glow unless something is plugged into the extension cord, because the lamp is in series with the extension cord and not in parallel. Now plug your amp into the extension cord. The bulb will glow somewhat and then dim as the caps charge up and the tubes heat up. If the amp has a standby switch, place it in the play position. The lamp will get somewhat brighter as the power tubes heat up and begin drawing current, but it should not glow at its full 100 watt brightness. If the light bulb glows brightly and stays bright, be aware that there is a short in the amp. Assuming there is no short, plug in to regular power. You are now ready to play with the new caps properly charged.

Another common problem with low power is bad bypass caps. These are small electrolytic caps that bypass A.C. signal to ground, thus preventing degenerative feedback. If these caps are bad, the amplifier stage with the cap will suffer from low gain because there will be degenerative feedback in that stage. Replacing them improves gain and dynamic response. These capacitors are always located across a cathode resistor. In other words, the cathode resistor of the tube goes from the cathode pin of the tube socket to ground; the bypass cap is connected with the plus side to the cathode pin and the minus side to ground. Therefore the bypass cap is actually across the cathode resistor electronically with the minus side at ground. The cathodes of a 12AX7, 12AY7, 12AT7, 12AU7 are pin 3 and pin 8 on the socket. On a 6SC7, the cathode is pin 6. On a 6SL7 or 6SN7 the cathodes are pins 3 and 6. Typical values are 2 uf to 330 uf at 6 to 35 volts. Here again, polarity is important. The positive or plus lead always goes to the cathode side while the negative or minus lead always goes to the ground side. If these caps are ten years or older consider them bad and change them. Correct value on microfarad rating is essential to maintain the original tone of the amp; however you may go more on the voltage rating without affecting the tone of the amp. For instance, if the cap you are replacing is a 25 uf at 25 volts, a 25 uf at 50 volts would not alter the tone.

How do you know how the pins are numbered if they are not marked? Looking at the socket from the underside of the chassis where the leads connect to the socket terminals, notice there is an indentation on the inner circle of an eight pin socket (called a key) or there is a large space on a nine pin socket where a tenth pin could go but is not there. From this space or indentation, the first pin going clockwise (remember you are looking from the bottom of the socket) is pin number 1. Continuing clockwise is pin 2, etc.

In some vintage amps, the power tubes are cathode-biased in which case the electrolytic bypass cap across the cathode resistor must be replaced with a new one. This improves low end, power and dynamic response. On a 6V6 or 6L6 the cathode will be pin 8 on the tube socket. On a 7591 the cathode is pin 5 on the socket. On a 6BQ5 or

EL84 the cathode is pin 3. You will know if the amp is cathode-biased because, if it is, there will be a resistor going from the cathode to ground. If it is not cathode-biased, the cathode will be grounded directly with no cathode resistor. If it is a cathode-biased amp, there will also be a cap going from the cathode to ground. Polarity will be such that the plus or positive lead will always go to the cathode. Here again, the correct value in microfarads (uf) is essential but the voltage can be the same as or more than the part you are replacing, in order to keep the original tone. Notice where the cap is physically located in the chassis. It will always be **away** physically from the cathode resistor. Cathode resistors produce lots of heat and will ruin the cap if the cap is too close to the resistor, so make sure and locate it in the same place as the original, which will probably be quite a distance from the cathode resistor. Some amps use one of the cap sections of a multi-cap to bypass the power tube cathode resistor.

All bypass caps use relatively low voltage and therefore do not require slow charging. Simply replace them, and your amp is ready to turn on and play.

The next thing to check will be the resistors. I use a solder tool with an insulated handle but you could use any small tool that is insulated (i.e. chopstick, small screwdriver, ice-pick, etc.) Visually inspect each resistor and push or pull at it a little bit with your instrument. Notice if it seems intact, physically. Resistors can become brittle, internally burnt or crystallized from years of use. These resistors must be replaced with exact values (both in watts and ohms) and exact type (carbon or wirewound.) Also there are times when the lead of the resistor will become severed from the body of the resistor, in which case the lead appears to be unsevered, since the sever is extremely small and the lead looks like it is physically where it is supposed to be. This will reveal itself when you give a gentle push to the body of the resistor and you notice the lead doesn't move with the body. Replace these resistors with exact values and type.

You also want to look for solder terminal connections that look bad. A cold solder joint usually looks dull or you may see the lead turning inside the connection when the lead is pushed. A simple re-soldering will fix that cold joint. Physical locations of bare leads are also important to notice. Are any leads in a location where they could make intermittent contact with another component? You can probably bend a lead with needle-nose pliers to move its location to where it will not make intermittent contact with other components.

Shake out all loose clippings or solder drippings, or blow debris out with compressed air. Visually inspect each component to make sure you haven't forgotten anything. Now you are ready to try it out.

It's a good idea to check for shorts before plugging it in. So take out your extension cord with the lamp in series and plug the amp in and turn it on. Let it warm up. If the lamp shines at full brightness, there is a short which must be found before using the amp. If the lamp shines a little, you are ready to plug the amp into regular 120 volt A.C. power.

Where to look if it's shorted? Look for a scrap of wire or solder dripping contacting two or more surfaces; check to see if everything was replaced correctly; take out the tubes one at a time to see if the light goes off on the current limiter.

Once you are satisfied that there are no shorts, plug it into regular 120 volt A.C. and play.

You are on your way to a great sounding amp, but you are not quite finished yet. There are a few procedures left to perform.

The contacts inside a tube socket sometimes get corroded much like the terminals on your car battery sometimes get corroded. If good contact is not made, there may still be a capacitive coupling, however the amp will not sound right. Sometimes the contact area becomes "sprung" and does not fit tightly on the tube pins. This can be corrected by first removing the tube and spraying tuner cleaner on the pins. Now re-insert the tube and work it in and out so that the cleaner dissolves any corrosion present on the inside of the tube socket connectors. You may want to remove the tube, re-spray the pins, and re-insert the tube again, just to make sure you have dissolved all of the corrosion. Do this to every tube socket in the amp.

Now that your sockets are clean, you will want to retension them for perfect contact. You will need a small tool for this. I use a dental instrument; however, a solder tool, straightened paper clip, or safety pin will also work. Looking inside the socket, notice the clips that actually contact the tube pins and bend them so that they will contact the tube pins tighter. Carefully retension each contact in all sockets.

Occasionally, you may find a socket that is so sprung it will not retension properly. If so, replace this socket. A drawing of how the bad socket is wired before it is removed will be helpful in wiring it correctly.

Potentiometer is a fancy word for a volume or a tone control. In vintage amps, the controls can sometimes be scratchy or intermittent. A little tuner cleaner can remedy this problem. Spray a small amount of tuner cleaner into the pot and rotate the control swiftly back and forth several times. You don't need very much cleaner. Repeat this procedure with every pot. If the pot is still scratchy or intermittent, you may need to replace it with another pot of identical value.

I always check the primary of the audio transformer when checking out an amp that doesn't sound right. Putting an ohmmeter between the center-tap (usually red wire) and one end of the primary, and comparing that reading to the reading you get from center-tap to the other end of the primary will usually tell if your transformer is bad, particularly if there is a huge discrepancy between the two readings. Ideally, the two readings should be almost the same; however, due to variances in turns diameter they may differ by as much as 5% and sometimes as much as 10%. The two ends of the primary go to the plates of the power tubes and are usually brown and blue. (Refer to the second paragraph of this chapter to see what the pin number is for the plates in your particular power tubes.)

To check the secondary of the output transformer, simply measure the D.C. resistance with an ohmmeter. It should be very low (½ ohm is typical). If it shows no reading or is high, consider the transformer bad. I have never seen an output transformer with a bad secondary. If a transformer goes south, it is almost always the primary that goes.

How do you check your tubes? I do not recommend a tube tester, because tube testers test the tube at much lower voltages than amps use and therefore a tube may test good on a tester, and yet not work well in a guitar amp. Also, tube testers cannot test for microphonics, noise, or actual sound. I test preamp tubes for microphonics by turning the amp on and setting its volume as high as it will go, with tone controls all the way up. Don't plug anything into the inputs. Now tap the preamp tube lightly with your index finger-nail. If the tube begins to resonate (high frequency like fine crystal-ware), the tube is microphonic and should be replaced. It is normal to get some sound from tapping a good preamp tube, but it's the resonance that you don't want.

How do you check for preamp tube noise? If your amp is noisy and you suspect a noisy preamp tube, one way to check is to turn the amp on, with volume and tone controls all the way up, nothing plugged into the inputs, and begin removing tubes, one at a time. Start at the lowest level (the side opposite the power tubes). Remove the first preamp tube. If there is still noise, remove the next tube. Still noise, remove the next tube. When the noise stops, you can suspect the last tube removed to be the noisy one. Replace only that tube with a good fresh tube. If the noise problem goes away, it was the tube; if the noise problem persists after replacing it with a known good tube, the noise is probably coming from noisy plate load resistors in that tube's circuit. (Plate load resistors are the resistors connected to the plates and usually range from 47K to 220K with 100K being most common. Check the second paragraph of this chapter for the plate pin numbers of your particular preamp tube). Replacing these resistors usually makes the problem go away.

How do you check the power tubes? If the power tubes are shorted, the amp will blow fuses and may burn out the hum balance circuit.

Remove the power tubes and put in a new fuse of the appropriate value. (Never use a fuse that is too big because you could burn up your power transformer resulting in mega-damage). Now turn on the amp. If the fuse does not blow, I would suspect either a shorted power tube or a bias problem was causing the fuse to blow initially. If it still blows with no power tubes in the socket, your problem is most likely a direct short, a bad rectifier (tube or solid-state), a shorted filter cap, or a bad power transformer. If the fuse didn't blow with the power tubes out of the socket and you replaced them with known good power tubes, and then the fuse blew, you have a bias problem.

How do you check for bias? There are two styles of biasing arrangements. Your particular amp only uses one style. One style is fixed-bias; the other style is cathode-bias. Fixed-bias almost always has the cathode of the power tube connected directly to ground (chassis) or to a resistor of 10 ohms or less in series to ground; cathode-bias style amps always have the cathodes of the power tubes connected to a big resistor (50 ohms or higher and usually rated in many watts) in series to ground. Which pin is the cathode? Pin 8 in a 6V6, 5881, 6L6, 7027, 6550, KT66, 6CA7, or EL34; pin 3 in a 6BQ5, EL84, or 7189; pin 5 in a 7591. Once you have determined if your amp is cathode-bias or fixed-bias, here is how you set it.

Cathode-bias is self-adjusting so all you have to do is check the resistor value of the cathode resistor to see if it is within its rating. If its value has drifted, simply replace it with the correct value (in ohms and watts) and you are ready to go. It is also important to know that there is also a bypass capacitor in parallel with the cathode resistor that may be shorted. Replacing this cap with the correct value in microfarads and volts will fix your problem. The cap is a polarized electrolytic and therefore should be placed with the positive side to the cathode and the negative side to ground. It is best to keep this cap physically away from the cathode resistor because the extreme heat of the cathode resistor will cause the cap to fail.

If your amp is fixed-bias, there will be a fixed amount of negative voltage on the grids of the power tubes. Grid pin numbers are: pin 5 on 6V6, 6L6, 5881, 7027, KT66, 6CA7, EL34; pin 6 on 7591; pin 2 for 7189, 6BQ5, EL34. This fixed voltage will range from minus 20 to minus 60 volts depending on the amp. To check negative voltage, put your meter in the 60 volt range with the positive lead on the meter to ground (chassis) and the negative lead to the grid. This is done with the amp on and the power tubes out of the amp. If there is no reading and you are certain that you have a fixed-bias amp, then you have a problem with the negative voltage bias supply.

What does output tube biasing do? It adjusts the operating level of your output tubes—just like adjusting the idle on your car. Bias voltage on the grid affects how much current can flow from the plates of the tubes. The more negative bias voltage on the grids, the less current flows from the plates; and conversely, the less negative voltage on the grids, the more current flows from the plates. This explains why so many people call tubes "valves." There is no exact negative voltage to bias your amp. You want enough voltage to keep the tube's output current within its operating parameters but not so much that you get crossover notch distortion. Usually anywhere from 10 to 40 milliamps of current per tube will be appropriate for most output tubes. Actually any setting that gives you the tone you want is correct. When more current is going through the tubes, the sound is beefier, with more midrange and more gain. With less current the tone not only has somewhat less gain, but is also thinner and cleaner.

The best way to set bias in a fixed-bias amp is to measure the current flowing through the output tubes (power tubes). An easy way to do this is by placing a current meter (100 milliamp range) in parallel with half of the output transformer primary. Actually the negative lead from your meter will go to the plate of one power tube (this is the start of the transformer winding) and the positive lead will go to the center tap of the output transformer (usually red wire). Since the resistance across the meter is considerably less than the transformer, the current goes through the meter without your having to unsolder anything. This must be done with the amp on and a load on the speakers and no input signal. This will give you a measurement of current in that power tube. You may move the negative meter lead from the plate of one power tube to the plate of the other power tube (with the positive meter lead still connected to the output transformer center tap), and measure the current of that tube. This will tell you how closely the two tubes are matched by how closely the current matches. If the current does not match, it may be that the output transformer is not uniform, the bias feed resistors are not matched (usually 220K), or the output tubes are not matched. Reversing the power tubes in opposite sockets will tell if it is the tubes or the circuits that are not matched. If the tubes are within 5 milliamps, they are matched closely enough. Since the amp must be on when this procedure is performed and you are dealing with the highest voltages present in the amp, this procedure is not recommended for the novice. If the current is too high, you must increase the bias voltage supplied to the grids; if the current is too low, you must decrease the bias voltage supplied to the grids. Some of the better amps have a bias trim pot to make this adjustment (most blackface Fenders and all Marshalls). However, if there is no bias pot, resistors may be added to the bias supply circuit either in series or parallel to increase or decrease the bias voltage, thus changing the idling current in the tubes.

There is nothing quite like a vintage guitar amp that has been tweaked to absolute perfection. I believe that a player's ability is linked directly to the sound of his amp. When your tone is inspiring you, how can you help being affected by this inspiration?

GLOSSARY

CAPACITIVE COUPLING-*noun*-A type of coupling between two adjacent stages that uses capacitance. Usually this is done with a capacitor; however, adjacent components/wires could have enough capacitance to couple A.C. signal.

ELECTROLYTICS-*noun*-Another name for a capacitor whose dielectric is an electrolyte. These are very small for the amount of capacitance and are therefore used in the power supply.

MICROFARAD-*noun*-One millionth of a farad (.000001 farad)

RECTIFIER CIRCUIT-*noun*-The circuit by which alternating current is changed to direct current. This always involves either a rectifier tube or a diode semiconductor.

RING MODULATOR-*noun*-An electronic device that generates the sum and difference of two or more frequencies and in doing so creates non-harmonically related sounds.

UF-*noun*-Abbreviation for microfarads.

VARIAC-*noun*-A device used to vary the A.C. line voltage. Made with a variable transformer and usually the ranges are 0 to 130 volts A.C.s

Kendricks

EASY TRICKS TO JUICE YOUR VINTAGE AMP

Ask three guru tube amp designers: What are some easy, user-friendly tricks that musicians could do to juice their vintage amplifiers? Here are the answers from Ken Fischer of Trainwreck Circuits, Jeff Bober of Precision Audio Tailoring and, of course, myself of Kendrick Amplifiers Inc.

KEN FISCHER, *Trainwreck Circuits*

1. Sweeten mids and improve gain on any blackface Fender and most silverface Fenders that have a vibrato feature by disconnecting the right terminal (looking at the back of the control with the chassis out of the case) on the intensity control. This disables the vibrato function; therefore, this is only recommended for players who don't use vibrato.

2. Re-adjust the midrange tonality of most black or silverface Fender amps that don't have a midrange control by changing the resistor that is soldered to the bass pot. Most of these Fenders have a 6800 ohm resistor. It can be changed anywhere from a straight wire (no midrange) to a 25K ohm resistor (maximum midrange). You might even try a 25K pot and then adjust it by ear. When you get the amount of mids you like, measure the pot with an ohmmeter (pot must be disconnected from the circuit for measuring) and solder in a resistor of the same value as the pot.

3. Add presence to a black or silverface Fender that doesn't have a presence control. In these amps, the circuit is like an amp with the presence control on zero. To add presence, locate the 47 ohm or 100 ohm resistor that is connected to the feedback resistor and put a 1 mfd

at 50 volts or better across the resistor. The 47 or 100 ohm resistor is connected from the feedback resistor to ground. (The feedback resistor is the 820 ohm resistor that attaches to the hot speaker jack terminal.) It is best to use a non-polarized cap, but an electrolytic will work if you observe correct polarity (negative side to ground). This mod is like having a presence control set all the way up.

4. Increase volume and rawness on a black or silverface Fender by changing the feedback resistor (usually an 820 ohm that is connected to the speaker jack) to a 1500 ohm. This reduces the amount of negative feedback, thus increasing gain and rawness.

5. Make your metal face Marshall sound like a plexi by removing the 500 picofarad capacitor that goes across the 470K ohm resistor (in the preamp section) and putting a .68 microfarad capacitor at 25 volts across the second gain stage cathode resistor (this is the 820 ohm resistor connected to pin 3 of the second preamp tube). If you use an electrolytic, positive goes to the tube side and negative goes to ground. This capacitor could also be put on a 4X10 Bassman (5F6 or 5F6A). The Bassman has no 500 picofarad cap to remove, so you would simply add the capacitor (.68 mfd) across the second gain stage cathode resistor (still pin 3 and still 820 ohms).

JEFF BOBER, *Precision Audio Tailoring*

1. If you play a Fender amp containing reverb and you don't use the reverb function, you can turn it into a gain boost/overdrive function that can be switched in and out with your reverb footswitch. Simply unplug the reverb send and return plugs coming from the reverb tank. Purchase two R.C.A. (phono) plugs and a 470K ohm ½ watt resistor. Connect the center pins of the R.C.A. plugs together using the ends of the 470K ohm resistor and leaving enough lead length so that the plugs will span the send/return jacks. (Be sure the resistor leads do not short to ground by touching the edges of the R.C.A. jack!) With this assembly plugged in, turn on the reverb footswitch and adjust the amount of drive with your reverb control.

2. This hook-up will let you have continuous footpedal control of the

overdrive mix in the trick described above. Simply plug the output jack of any volume pedal into the reverb footswitch jack. You'll need a male R.C.A. to female ¼" phone plug adaptor or compatible cable. With the pedal all the way back, you'll have no effect (off). With the pedal all the way up, you'll be at whatever the reverb control on the front panel is set for.

GERALD WEBER, *Kendrick Amplifiers Inc.*

1. Thicken tone in most two channel amps (Fender, Marshall, Ampeg) by bridging the channels. Simply plug your guitar in the number 1 input of one channel, then run another guitar cord from the number 2 input of the channel the guitar is plugged into, to the number 1 input of the other channel. Now adjust volume and tone controls of both channels. This will strengthen the signal that the power tubes get from the preamp. (Not recommended on Vox AC30 top boost or Fender blackface with reverb because of phase cancellation.)

2. Use your 6G15 Fender Reverb as a pre-gain stage. This is a little trick I noticed from building the Kendrick Reverb which uses the identical circuit of the 6G15. On the underside of the chassis is a footswitch jack (¼" phone jack). Solder a 1 megohm ½ watt resistor across this jack. Plug your guitar into the footswitch jack and unplug the cable from the reverb pan that goes to the R.C.A. jack near the footswitch jack. The mix control is now a gain control and the tone control is functional. Of course the output jack will still have to go to an amplifier. The reverb function will not work in this mode, but it is an interesting trick to boost gain. To use as a reverb, simply plug the R.C.A. reverb pan plug back into the chassis and plug the guitar into the normal chassis guitar input. (You can leave the 1 megohm resister soldered in place.)

3. Increase gain and distortion in any two channel black or silver-face Fender by removing one of the two preamp tubes. The first preamp tube is for the normal channel and the second preamp tube is for the vibrato channel. Decide which channel you want to use, then remove the other preamp tube. Since the tubes share the same

cathode resistor, removing one of the tubes causes the bias on the other tube to drop which increases gain and distortion. Also the voltages are slightly increased when one of the tubes is removed. If you don't like this one, it is an easy mod to reverse (simply plug the tube back in).

4. Increase speaker clipping by disconnecting one of the speakers in a Super Reverb or 4X10 Concert. It doesn't change the impedance that much (only ⅔ of an ohm), and many players like the sound of speakers being driven hard. Don't try this in a 4X10 Bassman because the speakers will not be able to take the wattage.

GLOSSARY

FEEDBACK RESISTOR-*noun*-The resistor in a circuit that is used to feed a signal back to a previous stage.

Kendricks

TEN EASY MODS FOR YOUR SUPER REVERB

Being in the vintage amp building and restoration business myself, I would never recommend drilling a hole or cutting the chassis or cabinet in any way. All of the following mods are simple and can be done by anyone who knows which end of a soldering iron to hold. All of these mods can be easily reversed if you don't like the result. You might want to try them one at a time and see if you like it before trying a second one. The ones you don't like, simply put back and then move on to the next one. As always when working on an amp, be sure to drain all stored electricity by unplugging the amp from the wall, put the standby switch in the "play" position, and put a jumper wire from pin 1 of any preamp tube to ground. Having said all of this, here are ten easy mods.

1. INCREASE POWER AND HARMONICS by disconnecting the negative feedback circuit. On the inside of the chassis, locate the wire that goes from the speaker jack to the circuit board. Unsolder it from the speaker jack, being careful to leave the other wires soldered to the jack, and insulate the end so that it will not accidentally brush up against some other component. Leave everything else in place in case you want to put it back in the future. The wire is easy to find because the only other wires connected to the speaker jack are the wires going to the transformer. Many amps, including all Voxes, do not have a negative feedback circuit anyway. You most certainly will notice the increase in gain and richer harmonics.

2. INCREASE GAIN AND DYNAMIC RESPONSE by removing the 12AT7 phase inverter tube and replacing it with a 12AX7. The phase inverter tube is the small preamp tube closest to the larger power tubes. A 12AX7 has a higher amplification factor than the 12AT7, but the pin configurations are identical. Fender originally used the 12AT7

because they were going for clean and didn't think anyone would want distortion.

3. ENRICH TONE AND THICKEN YOUR SOUND by increasing the size of the coupling capacitor feeding the phase inverter. This is really simpler than it sounds. Find pin 2 on the phase inverter tube socket and follow it back to the circuit board. You will see that it is connected to either a .01 or a .001 mfd capacitor, depending on the vintage. Replace this capacitor with a .02 mfd 400 volt capacitor and listen to the difference. It lets more low end and mids through the amp.

4. IMPROVE AND OPEN UP DYNAMIC RESPONSE by separating the cathodes in the preamp tubes. With the chassis opened, locate the two preamp tubes that are furthest away from the power tubes. There is a wire connecting pin 8 of one tube to pin 8 of the other tube. Also connected is a single 820 ohm resistor going from one pin 8 to ground. This resistor has a 25 mfd 25 volt capacitor across its leads with the negative lead of the capacitor going to the ground side of the resistor. Remove the wire connecting the two pin 8 leads together and change the 820 ohm resistor to a 1500 ohm. At this point, one pin 8 should have nothing on it and the other pin 8 will be going to a 1500 ohm resistor that has a 25 mfd 25 volt cap across it. The positive side of the cap is towards pin 8 and the negative side of the cap will be connected to ground (and of course the other end of the 1500 ohm resistor.) Now take the pin 8 that has nothing on it and solder a 1500 ohm resistor and the positive end of a 25 mfd 25 volt cap to it. Twist the other end of the resistor to the negative end of the 25 mfd cap and solder the both of them to ground. Both channels will now sound better. If you want to increase gain for a more Marshally type of sound, you can decrease the value of the resistor to 820 ohms but the 1500 will sound more Fendery. The one going to the preamp tube at the end of the chassis is for the normal channel, the one going to the second preamp tube from the end of the chassis is for the vibrato channel. Maybe have one channel one way and the other different. You are probably wondering if this is a misprint—didn't you just remove an 820 ohm and why are we now saying the 1500 ohm will sound more Fendery when the 820 ohm was stock? It's because when the two cathodes are tied together, more current passes through the resistor creating a larger voltage drop. Now that we have separated the

cathodes, there is half as much current flowing through each one.

5. IMPROVE LOW END by increasing the value of the first gain stage bypass caps. With the chassis opened locate the preamp tube socket furthest from the transformers. This tube is for the normal channel and the one next to it (second preamp tube) is for the vibrato channel. Decide which channel you want this mod on and select the appropriate tube. Now, looking at that tube socket, find pin 3. Follow the wire going from pin 3 to the circuit board. It will go to a 1500 ohm resistor with a 25 mfd 25 volt cap across it. Notice that the positive side of the cap is towards the tube and the negative side is connected both to the resistor and ground. Change this cap to a 250 mfd 6 volt capacitor. Take care to install it with the positive side towards the tube and the negative side connected to ground. All set—you just improved low end!

6. IMPROVE FIDELITY by eliminating series resistance on the input circuit. Decide on which channel you want improved fidelity. This mod can be done on either or both channels. Locate the input jacks of that channel. With the chassis opened, notice the two 68K resistors (blue, grey, orange) attached to the input jacks. Unsolder the wire that is soldered to both of these resistors, and move it to the "hot" lead of the number 1 jack of that channel. The "hot" lead is the one that makes contact with the tip of your guitar cord plug when it is inserted in the jack. You now have zero resistance. The number 2 jack will not work after this mod is performed, but who uses the number 2 input anyway unless you are playing accordion? I suggest that you leave the two 68K resistors in place just in case you want to put it back to stock later.

7. IMPROVE FIDELITY AND GAIN OF ONE CHANNEL by eliminating series resistance on the phase inverter input circuit. With the chassis opened, locate the phase inverter input coupling capacitor that was changed to a .02 mfd 400 volt in mod #3 above. Notice that one end of this cap goes to pin 2 of the phase inverter tube and the other end goes to two 220K resistors (red, red, yellow). Each of those 220K resistors has a single wire soldered to it. One of these wires is the output of the normal channel, and the other is the output of the vibrato channel. With this mod, we are going to move the wire that goes from the vibrato channel to the other side of the 220K resistor. Unsolder that wire and solder it directly to the .02 cap, thus bypassing one of the 220K resistors. Now take the other wire and unsolder it and insulate it to keep it from accidentally touching something. The normal channel will no longer work, but the vibrato channel will sound much better. Of course you could do this to the normal channel and have the vibrato channel disconnected, but most people just use the vibrato channel anyway. The normal channel could be hooked up to the other side of the phase inverter to make both channels work, yet still eliminate series resistance, but making it work right would depend on whether the negative feedback loop is connected and, if so, it would probably involve changing the negative feedback resistor value and the feedback load resistor value, and that is beyond the scope of this chapter.

8. Increase Volume and Punch by converting to a solid-state rectifier. With the amp opened up and the rectifier tube removed, locate the rectifier socket. It is the one that either a 5U4 or a 5AR4 tube goes into. Find four 1N4007 diodes. Solder two in series and then solder the other two in series. Be sure to observe correct polarity (cathode to anode) on each set. You should now have two pairs of diodes. Take the cathode end of each set and twist them together. Now solder them to pin 8 of the rectifier tube socket. Take the anode end of one set and solder it to pin 4. Take the anode end of the other set and solder it to pin 6. When you finish, you should have an anode on pin 6, an anode on pin 4, and both cathodes on pin 8. The cathode is the end with a band on it and the anode is the other side. You just added 10 extra watts of power!

9. Improve Fidelity by disconnecting the vibrato control. If you rarely use vibrato, you can dramatically increase fidelity, if you are willing to give up your vibrato function. With the amp opened, locate the intensity control. There are three terminals on the pot. One terminal is soldered directly to ground, the terminal in the center is soldered to a brown wire (usually) and the terminal on the end (opposite the one that is grounded) is soldered to a yellow wire. Disconnect the wire going to this terminal.

10. Improve Tone and Add Sweetness by replacing the speakers. The stock speakers in a Super Reverb are not that great. If you think about it, the speakers are what's between your amp and your ears. Take the old tired original speakers out and replace with Kendrick Blackframe 10" speakers. No kidding, I am not just saying that because my company makes the Kendrick speakers. The best sounding Super Reverbs I have ever heard use Kendrick speakers. Kendrick 10" Blackframe speakers in a blackface Super Reverb are found as house amps in many major recording studios. You have already heard them on many hit records and didn't even know you were listening to them. Save the original speakers. If you ever want to sell the amp, you can take the good ones out and put the originals back in.

GLOSSARY

ANODE-*noun*-The part of a tube or semiconductor diode that the electrical current flow exit. Also called the plate on vacuum tubes, the anode is always more positively charged than the cathode.

DIODE-*noun*-an electronic device that is the equivalent of a check valve. Electrons can go one way only. The diode can be a vacuum tube or semiconductor format.

See The Super Reverb chapter for schematics pages 76-85.

Kendricks

TEN EASY MODS
FOR YOUR
PRO REVERB

These mods refer to all blackface Pro's and most silverface Pro's. All of the following mods are simple and can be done by anyone that knows which end of a soldering iron to hold. All of these mods can easily be reversed if you don't like the result. You might want to try them one at a time and see if you like it and then move on to the next one. As always when working on an amp, be sure to drain all stored electricity by unplugging the amp from the wall, put the standby switch in the "play" mode, and put a jumper wire from pin 1 of any preamp tube to ground. Having said all of this, here are ten easy mods.

1. ADD HARMONIC RICHNESS AND IMPROVE GAIN by changing to a different value feedback resistor. This is really a lot easier than it sounds. Open the chassis and locate the speaker jack. It will be connected to wires going to the output transformer, and there will be a wire going to the component board. The wire that goes to the board is connected to the feedback resistor. It will be an 820 ohm (grey, red, brown). Change it to a 1500 ohm (brown, green, red). Since increasing the value of this resistor decreases the amount of negative feedback, you will increase volume and increase harmonics.

2. THICKEN TONE by increasing the coupling capacitor value on the phase inverter input. Find pin 2 on the phase inverter tube (the phase inverter is the preamp tube next to the power tubes.) Follow the wire on pin 2 back to the board and you will see it connected to a resistor and a capacitor. The cap will probably be a .01 or a .001 mfd cap. Replace this with a .02 mfd 400 volt capacitor. The .02 lets more mids and low end through the amp, thus thickening your tone. No

more thin tone for you!

3. ADD PUNCH AND DEPTH by changing the output transformer. Pro Reverbs had a smaller output transformer that really left a lot to be desired. Find a used blackface Bassman 4 ohm transformer and replace the Pro's cheesy transformer with the Bassman transformer. It's simple to do; the color codes on the wires are the same. When removing the Pro transformer, simply cut the leads out, leaving a sixteenth of an inch of colored insulation on the connections when taking out the original transformer. This way, when you put the new transformer in, you can see where the leads go and more importantly what colors go where. There are only five wires, and two of those go to the speaker jack. The Bassman has much more core material and consequently a richer punchier sound. Save the old transformer in case you ever want to sell the amp.

4. IMPROVE GAIN by removing the 12AX7 from the normal channel. If you are like most people, you never use the normal channel. The tube for the normal channel shares a cathode resistor on its second gain stage with the preamp tube for the reverb channel. Removing the normal channel preamp tube will automatically re-bias the reverb channel tube for better gain. The normal channel preamp tube is the small preamp tube all the way on the right of the chassis (when looking at the amp from the back while it is still in the cabinet.) Simply remove the tube from its socket and listen to the difference.

5. INCREASE GAIN AND DYNAMIC RESPONSE by removing the 12AT7 phase inverter tube and replacing it with a 12AX7. Once again, the phase inverter tube is the preamp tube next to the output tubes. You can take the 12AX7 that you just removed from mod #4 above and put it in the phase inverter socket. Since the 12AX7 has more gain, it will improve the dynamic response of the amp. This is perfectly safe for the amp, in fact all tweed amps and all Marshalls are done this way.

6. IMPROVE FIDELITY AND GAIN OF ONE CHANNEL by eliminating series resistance on the phase inverter input circuit. Since you are not going to be using the normal channel anyway, you may want to eliminate the series resistance that was an undesirable by-product of this particular two channel amp design. Locate the phase inverter coupling cap that was changed in mod #2 above. The end pointing away from the tube has two 220K resistors attached to it. The other end of each resistor has a wire going to it. One wire going to one resistor is the output of the reverb channel and one wire going to the other resistor is the output of the normal channel. Remove both resistors. Of the two wires that went to the two resistors, notice which one goes to the normal channel and which one goes to the reverb channel. This will be obvious because the physical layout of the wire. You will see one of the wires going to the side of the component board where the normal channel is physically located, and the other wire will go to the part of the component board where the reverb channel is located. Take the one wire that goes to the reverb channel and solder it to the coupling cap where the resistors were before you removed them. Leave the other wire where it was, but make sure it is not connected to anything. (Both of those 220K resistors should be out of the amp, the reverb channel wire should be connected to the phase inverter coupling cap, and the normal channel wire is soldered to an eyelet but not connected to anything.) This mod will bump up the gain and fidelity considerably, because all of the signal goes through the circuit instead of having some of the signal leak out backwards through the normal channel circuit.

7. IMPROVE FIDELITY by disconnecting the vibrato circuit. The way the vibrato circuit works, signal is leaked to ground at all times, even if you aren't using the vibrato. If you do not use the vibrato function, you may eliminate this loss by disconnecting the wire that goes to the intensity control. With the chassis out of the cabinet and the back of the amp facing you, and looking at the back of the intensity control, it is the wire on the right lead of the intensity control that you want to disconnect (usually brown colored insulation.) Tape the end up so it won't short against anything, but leave it in the amp in case you ever want to put it back.

8. IMPROVE LOW END by increasing the value of the first gain stage bypass cap. With the chassis opened, locate the preamp tube socket furthest away from the transformers. This tube is for the normal channel and the tube next to it (second preamp tube) is for the vibrato channel. Looking at that second preamp tube socket (the one for the vibrato channel), find pin 3. Follow the wire going from pin 3 to the component board. It will go to a 1500 ohm (brown, green, red) re-

sistor with a 25 mfd cap across the resistor. Notice that the positive side of the cap is towards the tube and the negative side faces the front of the amp. Change this capacitor to a 250 mfd 6 volt cap observing the correct polarity. Now you've just improved the low end.

9. IMPROVE TONE, INCREASE VOLUME AND TIGHTEN LOW END by changing the output tubes to matched R.C.A. 6L6GCs. These are the R.C.A. 6L6GCs that have a short glass envelope and the top of the tube is hemispherical. You won't find any matched pairs of these at the local music store, but it was the tube that originally came with the amp. I think (and many people agree) that this is the best sounding 6L6-style tube ever made. If you can find a matched pair, you will be amazed at the tone. It is a little louder with really strong and tight low end yet clear highs with an interesting midrange. Every time I retube an amp with these, the customer is truly amazed.

10. DRAMATICALLY IMPROVE TONE AND ADD DEPTH, FULLNESS, AND SWEETNESS by replacing the speakers. If you think about it, the speakers are what make the actual sound. Take the old tired original speakers out and replace them with KENDRICK BLACKFRAME 12" speakers. These speakers are a sonic up-grade of the original speakers. Your amp will sound like a 4X12 cabinet because of the thickness of tone and punch. Save the original speakers. If you ever want to sell the amp, pop them back in.

See the Schematics chapter for schematics pages 332-335.

Kendricks

JUICE UP THAT 6G15 FENDER REVERB

Here are fifteen easy tricks I thought you might like to juice up your 6G15 Fender Reverb unit. Reverb units of this type are a delicate interaction among physical, electronic, and mechanical properties. I have found that the least little change among these properties will offer amazing differences in actual sound.

1. IMPROVE TONAL QUALITY OF VACUUM TUBES.

A. Try changing the 12AT7 to a 12AX7. The 12AX7 is stronger gain and will drive the reverb springs harder with less signal loss.

B. Try getting an R.C.A. brand 6K6GT to replace the power tube. Try several different tubes and listen to the quality of the reverb signal to find the best sounding one. If you can't find a 6K6 style tube, a 6V6 just so happens to be the higher watt version of the 6K6. The pin configuration is identical (the 6V6 can dissipate 14 watts of heat and the 6K6 can dissipate 8.5 watts.) Some people prefer the 6V6s so you might want to try a couple of them too. When testing this tube for tonal quality, I suggest that you listen for the actual reverb slap-back quality.

C. Try different 12AX7s in the 12AX7 socket. Not only different brands, but even individual tubes within a brand sound different. When testing this tube, you may want to listen for how this tube affects the dry signal quality and gain characteristics.

2. IMPROVE REVERB TANK PERFORMANCE AND TONE.

A. Remove reverb tank and inspect both transducers. (These are located inside the tank itself. They look like small transformers and are connected to the signal springs.) If the coil bobbin is loose on either transducer your tank will have too much mechanical loss of reverb signal. Try a small bamboo shim to tighten that bobbin up.

B. Try a toothpick tip-size dab of epoxy glue where the springs clip on to the transducers. Also there will be a brass rivet in the exact center of the spring, put a dab there. This eliminates mechanical loss of signal at the junction of the spring and the transducer.

C. Notice the way the tank is actually mounted to the front board. Are the springs tight? Does it even have springs? I have seen a lot of units with homemade rubber band mounts. Today I saw one with no mounts of any kind. The tank was just sitting in there. All of this affects tone. Using small screws to mount the tank sounds different than rubber band mounts which is different than tight springs and still different yet than loose springs. I personally prefer the tight spring sound or the screw-the-tank-down-on-the-front-board sound. The loose spring sound is too jingley, and the rubber bands seem to dampen the tone slightly. If you try screwing the tank down, you will have to remove the sponge that is glued to the front mounting board. This sponge is usually used to dampen the springs when the reverb locking bar is engaged; however, on a screw down style mounting, the sponge would interfere with the spring action inside the tank.

3. IMPROVE SOUND OF ELECTRONICS.

A. Replace filter caps if they have not been replaced recently. These are located inside a 4X6 cap pan that is held on the exterior of the chassis with four sheet metal screws. Replace with 450 volt or higher electrolytic capacitors (40 microfarad or a little bit more; I use 47 microfarad). As always, when changing filter caps, you must bring the unit up slowly on a variac or use a current limiter. Make sure you check polarity of the caps and install the new ones with correct polarity.

B. Replace the three electrolytics on the circuit board with new fresh ones of the same value. If these have never been replaced, 30 years is too long. Also be sure to check polarity and observe correct polarity when installing the new parts.

C. Install a 220K resistor across both leads of the chassis footswitch jack. This is actually in parallel with the reverb return circuit. The resistor actually lowers the grid return impedance resulting in richer tone. If it didn't, I would tell you to put a resistor here anyway, because if the cable going to the reverb tank was accidentally unplugged on an unmodified unit, the 12AX7 would go into runaway. (Not good for tube life!)

4. DO SOME MODS.

A. Try replacing the 250 picofarad ceramic disc cap that connects the mix control to the tone control with a silver mica cap of the same or larger value.

B. Try bridging either one or both of the .1 microfarad caps (located on the right side of the circuit board and connected to pin 8 and pin 1 of the 12AX7 socket) with a larger value cap. The larger value cap (possibly .68 microfarad at 400 volt) should simply go in parallel with the .1 cap that is already there. The cap attached to pin 1 couples signal for the reverb sound and the cap attached to pin 8 couples the unprocessed "dry" signal. Try one cap and listen. Try the other and listen. Your personal taste is the key.

C. Do the Ken Fischer "Let's go surfing" mod and replace the 100K resistor (that is connected to pin 6 on the 12AT7 socket) with a 220K ½ watt resistor. This may make the dwell pot noisy but it might sound more like the beach.

5. IMPROVE CONSISTENT PERFORMANCE WITH ROUTINE MAINTENANCE.

A. Check shielded cable going from the tank to the chassis. Replace cables if necessary. Also check connectors on chassis to ensure a good solid connection is being made with the R.C.A. jack and R.C.A. plugs.

B. Clean and retension tube sockets. It's best to drain off voltage first by unplugging the unit and running a jumper from pin 1 or pin 6 of any preamp tube to ground and wait awhile for it to drain (20 seconds approximately). Clean the sockets first by spraying tuner cleaner inside the socket and working the tube in and out. Retension with a dental pick or a safety pin. The idea is to be certain that every pin of every tube is making good contact with the socket connector.

C. Tighten all pots and jacks to assure good grounds.

GLOSSARY
TRANSDUCERS-*noun*-An electrical device that is used to convert electrical energy to mechanical energy.

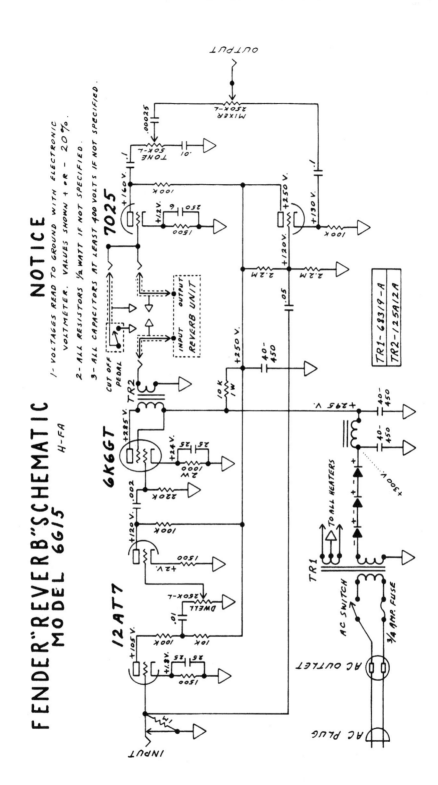

FENDER "REVERB" SCHEMATIC
MODEL 6G15 H-FA

NOTICE

1- VOLTAGES READ TO GROUND WITH ELECTRONIC
VOLTMETER. VALUES SHOWN + OR - 20%.

2- ALL RESISTORS ½ WATT IF NOT SPECIFIED.

3- ALL CAPACITORS AT LEAST 400 VOLTS IF NOT SPECIFIED.

TR1- 6319-A
TR2- 125A12A

FENDER "REVERB" LAYOUT
MODEL 6G15   H-FA

NOTICE

VOLTAGES READ TO GROUND WITH ELECTRONIC
VOLTMETER. VALUES SHOWN + OR - 20%

NOTE - ALL RESISTORS ½ WATT, 10% TOLERANCE IF NOT SPECIFIED.   NOTE - ALL CAPACITORS AT LEAST 400 VOLTS IF NOT SPECIFIED.

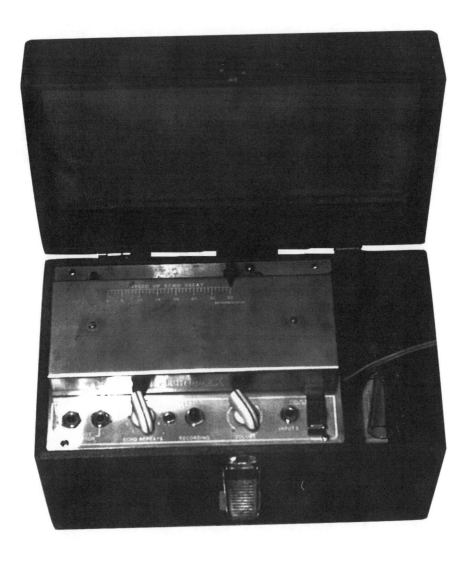

Kendricks

RESURRECTING THAT TUBE ECHOPLEX

As a tube Echoplex owner, I am always knocked out when I hear its lush, fat echo. That was not always the case; when I first acquired my Echoplex it sounded horrible. It was only after a little bit of service that the natural beauty began to come out of hiding. I'll bet that many of you own Echoplexes that sound bad but could sound great with only a minimum investment in parts and time.

Almost every Echoplex needs a good cleaning. Start with the tape heads. (You'll have to remove the tape cartridge and the top cover.) Clean both the "Record" and "Play" head with tape head cleaner and a tape head swab. I like to use the tape-head swab that is designed especially for cleaning heads, because it gently scrapes the tape head build-up off of the head. If you don't want to spend any money, an ordinary cotton swab and rubbing alcohol will get the job done. The pinch roller and capstan are next. Don't use tape-head cleaner on the rubber pinch roller. Instead try glycerin. Tape-head cleaner can be used on the capstan. Now that the heads are clean, it would probably be a good idea to clean them again! They are probably way overdue for a cleaning in which case it couldn't hurt to clean them twice.

Next, get a tape-head demagnetizer (the hand-held type are best) and do a thorough demagnetization of both the record and play-back erase head. The demagnetizer will have instructions with it on how to use it.

With the chassis out of the case, being careful not to bend the cooling fan, blow the inside chassis out with compressed air. The chassis and face panel can be cleaned with ordinary rubbing alcohol.

Notice the belt. If it looks the least bit dry-rotted, bring it to an auto parts shop and ask for an "O" ring of the same size. This will probably cost less than $1.00. In fact, since they are so inexpensive, go ahead and buy two just so you'll have a spare if you need it.

Next you'll need some new tubes. A pair of American-made 6EU7s and a 6C4 oscillator tube is all you need to get this hound dog woofing.

The only other thing left to do is to get a new tape cartridge. Dunlop sells exact replacement cartridges. I would suggest buying two or three cartridges so you will always have a few spares. If you are on a budget, you might try winding your own cartridge by cutting the tape and splicing in a new tape on the feed-in side of the cartridge. Run the tape until the splice comes back out. Now all you have to do is splice the new ends together and you are ready to enjoy the classic sound of the tube Echoplex.

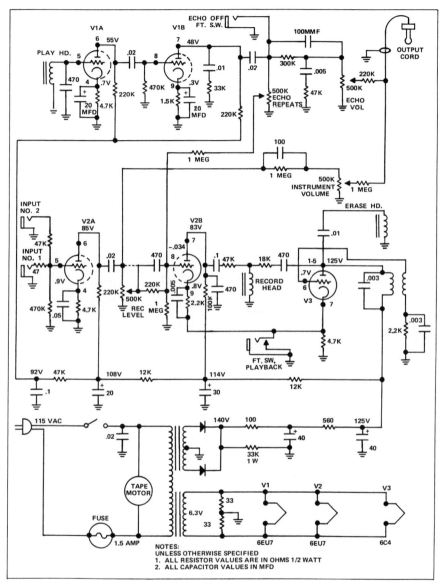

ECHOPLEX EP-1 MODEL NO. 5000 SCHEMATIC DIAGRAM

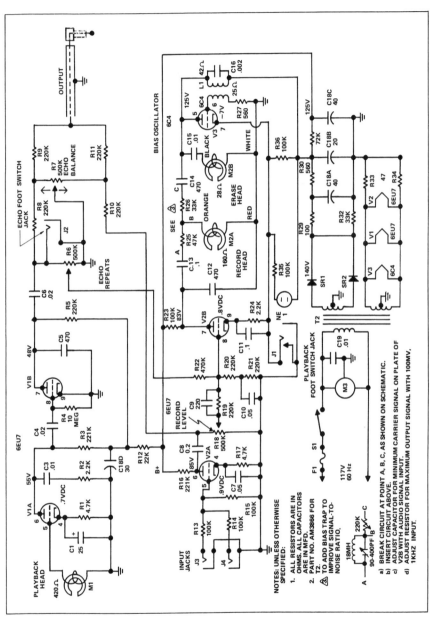

ECHOPLEX EP-2 SCHEMATIC DIAGRAM - SERIAL NO. 1549 TO 2749

NOTES: UNLESS OTHERWISE SPECIFIED:

1. ALL RESISTORS ARE IN OHMS. ALL CAPACITORS ARE IN MFD.
2. TO ADD BIAS TRAP TO IMPROVE SIGNAL-TO-NOISE RATIO.

⚠ PART NO. AM3866 FOR T2.

a) BREAK CIRCUIT AT POINT A, B, C, AS SHOWN ON SCHEMATIC.
b) INSERT CIRCUIT ABOVE.
c) ADJUST CAPACITOR FOR MINIMUM CARRIER SIGNAL ON PLATE OF V2B WITH AUDIO SIGNAL INPUT.
d) ADJUST RESISTOR FOR MAXIMUM OUTPUT SIGNAL WITH 100MV, 1KHZ INPUT.

Kendricks

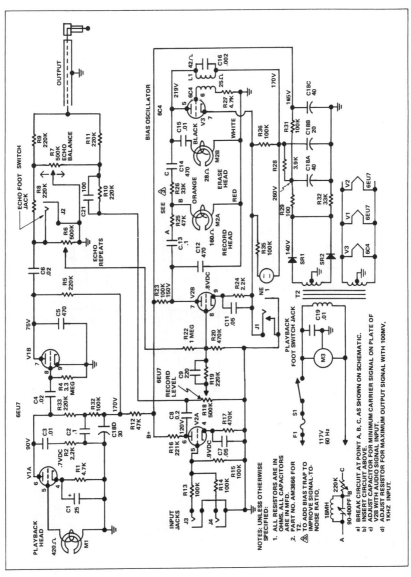

ECHOPLEX EP-2 SCHEMATIC DIAGRAM - SERIAL NO. 2750 TO 5499

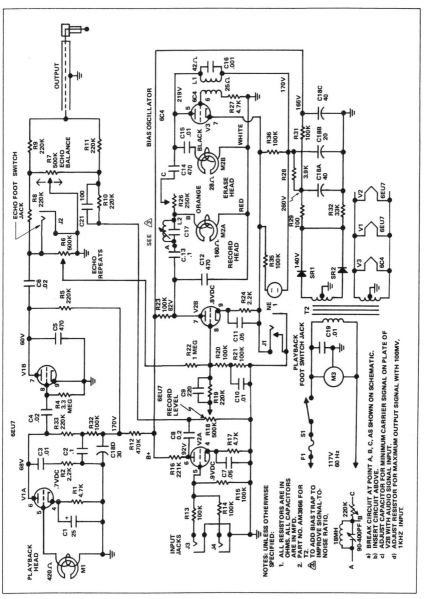

ECHOPLEX EP-2 SCHEMATIC DIAGRAM – SERIAL NO. 5500 TO 5938

Kendricks

ECHOPLEX EP-2 SCHEMATIC DIAGRAM - SERIAL NO. 5939 TO 9067

NOTES: UNLESS OTHERWISE SPECIFIED:

1. ALL RESISTORS ARE IN OHMS. ALL CAPACITORS ARE IN MFD.
2. PART NO. AM3866 FOR T2.

⚠ TO ADD BIAS TRAP TO IMPROVE SIGNAL-TO-NOISE RATIO,

a) BREAK CIRCUIT AT POINT A, B, C, AS SHOWN ON SCHEMATIC.
b) INSERT CIRCUIT ABOVE.
c) ADJUST CAPACITOR FOR MINIMUM CARRIER SIGNAL ON PLATE OF V2B WITH AUDIO SIGNAL INPUT.
d) ADJUST RESISTOR FOR MAXIMUM OUTPUT SIGNAL WITH 100MV, 1KHZ INPUT.

Kendricks

SILVER TO BLACKFACE CONVERSION FOR TWIN REVERB

Conversion from silverface Twin to blackface Twin can be accomplished in four simple steps. These are:

I. Rewire bias supply and add two 220K ohm resistors.

II. Replace five resistors and one cap in the phase inverter.

III. Remove four small capacitors.

IV. Replace two resistors in the power supply.

Do not attempt this modification unless you are certain that you know what you are doing. Always unplug the amplifier and drain the power capacitors to avoid electric shock. Having said all of this, let's begin by removing the chassis from the cabinet and setting it on a workbench with the front facing away from us and the wiring facing us.

I. Rewire bias supply and add two 220K ohm resistors.

Look at figure #1 and locate these parts in the chassis.

A. Remove both 68K resistors (blue, gray, orange). Sometimes these are 100K ohm (brown, black, yellow); at any rate, take them out.

B. Add two 220K ohm resistors (½ watt 5% or better). One goes between point "F" and "G", and one goes between point "E" and "G".

C. Move the resistor and cap lead on point "A" to point "B".

D. Move resistor on point "C" to "D" and move the wire on point "D" to "C".

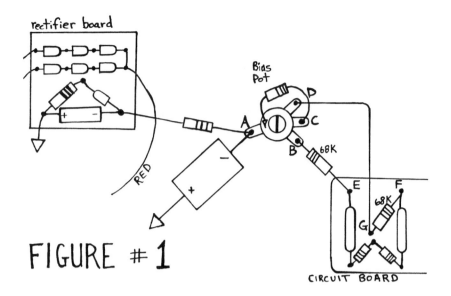

FIGURE # 1

Look at figure #2. This is how your chassis should be wired upon completion of step I.

II. Replace five resistors and one cap in the phase inverter. Look at Figure #3 and locate these parts in the chassis.

A. Replace 47K resistor (yellow, violet, orange) going from point "H" to "I" with a 100K ohm resistor (½ watt 5 % or better).

B. Replace 47K ohm resistor going from point "H" to "J" with and 82K ohm resistor (½ watt 5% or better).

C. Replace the 330K ohm resistor (orange, orange, yellow) going from point "K" to "O" with a 1 meg ohm ½ watt resistor.

D. Replace the 330K ohm resistor going from point "M" to "O" with a 1 meg ohm ½ watt resistor.

E. Replace the 270K ohm resistor (red, violet, brown) going from point "O" to "L" with a 470 ohm ½ watt resistor. Fender used various different values in this position. If there is a 680 ohm or something other than a 270 ohm, simply change it to the 470 ohm and that is correct.

F. Replace the capacitor going from point "M" to "N" with a .001 microfarad 400 volt ceramic capacitor. Sometimes the

Kendricks

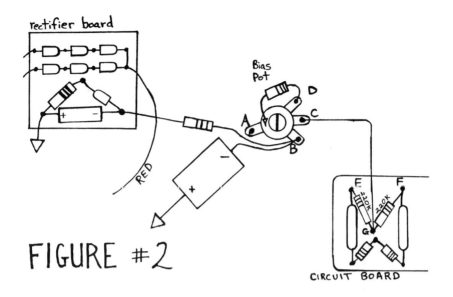

FIGURE #2

correct value will already be installed but most used a .01 mfd. If a .001 is already in the unit, leave it there.

Look at figure #4. This is how your chassis should be wired upon completion of step II.

III. Remove four small capacitors.

A. Look at pin 1 on each of the four power tubes. Two of the four will have a 2000 picofarad capacitor going from pin 1 to ground. They are usually grounded on pin 8. Cut both of these capacitors out and discard.

B. Look at the reverb pedal jack on the back panel. On the inside of the chassis you will see a 220K ohm resistor (red, red, yellow) and a .002 capacitor going from the reverb pedal jack to ground. Without disturbing the resistor, cut the capacitor out and discard it.

C. Look at the phase inverter section of the board that you re-wired earlier. A couple of components to the right of this, you will see an opto-coupler (neon bulb and light dependent resistor covered in black shrink tubing). The lead of the opto-coupler that is to your bottom left will have a 10 meg ohm resistor (brown, black, blue) with a .002 capacitor across it. Without

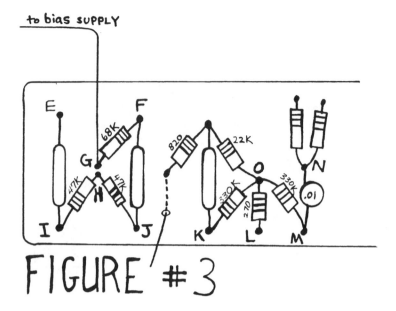

to bias supply

FIGURE #3

disturbing the resistor, cut the capacitor out and discard.

IV. Replace two resistors in the power supply. Turn the chassis over (wiring facing down) and locate the 4X6 pan that is screwed to the chassis. Unscrew the four Phillips screws holding it on and locate the 2.2K ohm resistor (red, red, red) and the 10K ohm resistor (brown, black, orange) on the circuit board underneath the pan.

A. Replace the 2.2K with a 1K ohm 1 watt resistor.

B. Replace the 10K with a 4.7K ohm 1 watt resistor.

Now would also be a good time to check the filter capacitors on that same circuit board. Look at the positive ends. If they are bubbled or ruptured at all, replace all of them using the correct values.

You are now done. However, before replacing the chassis, you must set the bias. A simple way to do this is to plug the A.C. line cord in and with the amp power switch on and the standby switch in the standby mode, put a voltmeter between point "G" on figure #4 and ground. Adjust the bias pot until the meter reads minus 44 volts to minus 50 volts. If you cannot adjust the bias to get in bias range, then the 15K ohm resistor that is soldered from the bias pot to ground (point "D" on figure #2) may have to be replaced with a 22K ohm

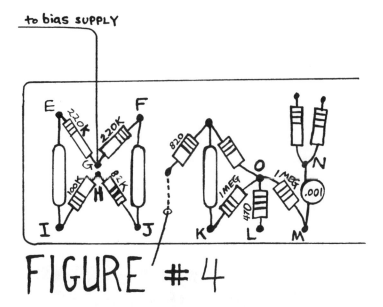

FIGURE # 4

resistor. Only rarely is this necessary. There are other ways to bias an amp, but they are beyond the scope of this chapter. Refer to "The Simple Truth About Biasing Your Amp."

Replace the chassis and listen to your "new" amp.

GLOSSARY
OPTO-COUPLER-*noun*-A device in which light is used to alter resistance.

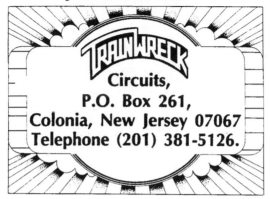

Circuits,
P.O. Box 261,
Colonia, New Jersey 07067
Telephone (201) 381-5126.

Trainwreck would like to thank the following individuals who participated in the realization of this article:

Phil Lipman
Pam Lipman
Adam Apostolos
Sue Melkisethian
Steve Melkisethian

EXECUTIVE EDITOR: ESTA FISCHER

WARNING!

WARNING: The following amplifier modifications are intended for use by qualified personnel only. Guitar amplifiers contain <u>LETHAL</u> voltages. Even unplugged filter capacitors can store enough voltage to do permanent harm or be lethal.

DISCLAIMER: Trainwreck cannot warranty the suitability of any modifications. The use of any of these modifications is done entirely at your own risk, and Trainwreck will assume no liability for any damages caused by such modifications.

TRAINWRECK IS NOT RESPONSIBLE for any misprints, typo errors or printing mistakes which may cause damage to people or equipment.

CAUTION: Unplug your amp before using any AC fuses. This will eliminate the possibility of an AC shock.

CAUTION: Certain amplifiers may have an HT (HIGH VOLTAGE) fuse. Even when unplugged, these fuse holders may contain high voltages. Use caution when changing the HT fuse. <u>NEVER</u> touch the metal end of the HT fuse with your bare fingers!

CAUTION: Tubes in amplifiers tend to get hot during operation. When changing tubes be sure to give tubes a proper cool-down period. To remove tubes grab tube gently. Rocking the tube in a circular motion, gently pull it out. Be careful not to crush the tube, which is made of glass and may cut your fingers.

WARNING: Never operate a tube amplifier without a suitable load; that is, a **19** speaker or dummy load.

THE TRAINWRECK PAGES

After years of repairing, modifying, and building amplifiers, Trainwreck has often been asked to explain the basic operation of guitar amps. The following section is intended to help those who are not experienced techs, but who are interested in how an amplifier works. The example we have used is either a fifty or one hundred watt Marshall tube amp with a Master Volume.

In this section, we will try to shed some light on the following topics: AC, DC, voltage, current, power, and wattage. These subjects can be very confusing, and we will attempt to explain them as clearly as possible.

VOLTAGE is electrical pressure. You can think of it as the speed at which electricity flows. Using a car as an analogy, you can picture that a car going ten MPH is low voltage, and a car going one hundred twenty MPH is high voltage.

CURRENT is the quantity of electrons flowing past a certain point. This can be seen as analogous to the size of a car. A Volkswagen Beetle can be seen as a low current vehicle, whereas an eighteen wheel truck would be a high current vehicle.

WATTAGE OR POWER is the combination of the voltage and the current. The formula for calculating wattage electricity is to multiply the voltage number by the current number. That gives you total power. For example, the Volkswagen Beetle going fifty MPH hitting another vehicle would impart a certain amount of power. The eighteen wheel truck travelling at the same fifty MPH would impart far more power were it to hit another vehicle.

AC VERSUS DC: Electrical voltages have what is called a polarity. The most obvious example of polarity is the positive and negative terminals which we see on batteries. The battery represents a DC voltage source, and all the electrons in it flow from negative to positive terminals in one direction. In AC, or alternating current, the terminals, which are positive and negative, alternate polarity. This reversal of polarity occurs sixty times per second in the standard household electrical system. This is what is called a "sixty cycle current".

In audio, this principle applies to a concept called frequency. For instance, when you pluck the 'A' string on your guitar, the string vibrates back and forth one hundred ten times per second. The magnetic field of the pickup is disturbed one hundred ten times per second. An alternating voltage of one hundred ten alternations per second occurs from your pickup.

The 'A' string also vibrates the air 110 times per second (that's how you hear the sound of the guitar acoustically). The air vibrates and alternately compresses and rarifies as the string vibrates. It vibrates your ear drum and you hear the tone!

Now we have established that the guitar develops a signal. The strings vibration disrupts a magnetic field generating a voltage out of your pickup, which is fed into the amp. The amps job is to make the speaker vibrate via an AC signal to reproduce this sound at the desired level.

20

THE TRAINWRECK PAGES

The power supply section of the amp is the first section we will deal with. There are several different relevant voltages which are part of its operation. One voltage, called a "filament" or "heater" voltage, is the voltage that makes the orange glow inside the tube. This filament in turn heats up an element called a "cathode" which is simply a metal cylinder coated with a substance which gives off electrons.

Other parts of the tube require positive voltages to attract the electrons. These voltages are much higher. The power transformer in your guitar amp converts the 120 volts (or 220-240 in Europe) voltage to the VARIOUS voltages needed in the amp. For example, 6.3 volts are needed to light the filaments in the tubes. The plate element in the tubes need several hundred volts for proper operation.

A transformer has a primary winding and several secondary windings. The ratios of the windings determine the amount of voltage produced. The signal coming through on the secondary windings is an AC voltage; aside from the filaments, every other required voltage in the amplifier is a DC voltage. Another circuit is called a "rectifier" circuit. It is either a tube or a solid state device which allows the electricity to flow only in one direction. It also stops the electricity from flowing in the reverse direction, and therefore converts the alternating current to a current that is going in one direction.

However, this voltage will be fluctuating sixty times per second, and to smooth out the fluctuation, a device called an "electrolytic" capacitor, also referred to as a "power filter" or "filter cap." is used. This device is similar to a battery in that it stores electricity, so that during the valleys between the pulses, the stored electricity keeps the current flowing in a smooth, orderly fashion. A SIGN OF A BAD POWER FILTER, WHEN IT DOES NOT ALLOW THE ELECTRICITY TO FLOW IN A SMOOTH, SOLID FASHION, IS A LOUD HUM.

THE PREAMP: The signal from your guitar is applied to an element called the "grid" of the preamp tube. The cathode of this tube is give off electrons and the plate of this tube, which is connected to a high voltage source, is attracting the electrons at a very high rate. The grid, which sits almost exactly between the cathode and the plate, acts as a valve or a control. The cathode in the tube is giving off electrons; the plate is attracting them at a high rate. In between you have the control grid, to which the AC signal is applied. This is sort of an electronic gate, which can be opened and closed by the amount of voltage on it. An analogy for this would be the faucet in your sink. If you turn the faucet on full, and try to stop the flow by putting your finger over the end of the faucet, you will find it impossible. But, with a little gentle pressure on the on-off valve, you can easily control the flow of the faucet. This is how a tube amplifies. A very small voltage differential applied to the grid controls a very large voltage differential on the plate of the tube.

This is what is known as a "gain stage". The gain stage can multiply the signal being applied to it many times over.

21

THE TRAINWRECK PAGES

In this Marshall amp, after the initial gain, or preamp stage, there is inserted a control known as a "preamp volume" or "gain volume". There is another important circuit which we have to understand if we are to comprehend the workings of guitar amplifiers. It is called a "voltage divider".

Essentially, what is happening inside this "volume", "gain", or "preamp" control is that there is a carbon strip which has a resistance. Signal voltage is applied at one end of the strip, from the preamp stage, and the other end of the strip is connected to a point of zero voltage.

Because this strip has a property called "resistance" (or, an opposition to the flow of electricity, which slows the electrons down, therefore reducing the voltage over its entire length) we can install a third element in this control.

This is the element that you use as you turn the shaft of the control. This element slides along the carbon granular path and allows you to select any voltage you want, anywhere between the full voltage or no voltage at all. As the slider goes down the carbon path towards ground, the less voltage you get. By selecting a point on the carbon path, you can choose the voltage, and hence the gain and volume of the sound.

In a Marshall amp, we continue on to two more gain stages. These continue to build voltage up, to the point where we can institute OVERDRIVE. Before we discuss overdrive (or distortion) it is essential that we describe the fourth stage of the Marshall amp. The fourth stage is the tube set-up and operation called the cathode follower, which basically is used to convert the high impedance signal coming from the previous three gain stages to a low impedance signal to drive the tone control circuitry. A cathode follower has no gain at all.

The next circuitry we run into on this Marshall are tone-shaping circuits. Basically, the tone shaping is an arrangement of various values of capacitors and resistors that select certain ranges of frequencies and sends them off to a voltage divider; the bass, treble, and mid-range controls. These controls work on the same principle as the volume or gain control previously discussed except that they work on the volume of only certain frequencies. Therefore, when you turn the control, you affect the volume of a certain frequency and effect the overall tonal balance of the amplifier.

22

THE TRAINWRECK PAGES

After these three tone controls is yet another voltage divider called the master volume. This selects the amount of voltage fed into the power section of the amp and thus effects the overall power generated by the amplifier. This control also affects the amount of distortion in combination with the gain or first voltage divider by the following principle: if you turn up the first voltage divider and therefore increase the amplification factor, by feeding more voltage into the later gain stages, the later gain stages will eventually reach a point called "clipping". Clipping occurs when the voltage signal being presented to that particular tube stage exceeds the tubes ability to amplify it. What happens at this point is that the tube amplifies as much as it can and then abruptly stops, chopping off part of the signal. This distorts the signal and causes the tube to generate many harmonics. By increasing the preamp volume and reducing the master volume, we have a tendency to make the later stages of the preamp clip more and more severely, thereby generating more and more distortion.
This distortion is distinct from output stage clipping, which is a type of distortion induced when the output stage delivers all the power it can and is pushed beyond its limits; it will also clip with a different sonic <u>character</u>.

From the master volume, the signal gets feed into a circuit known as the "phase inverter" or "phase splitter". Essentially, the function of this stage in the amp is to produce a mirror image voltage of opposite polarity, plus to provide drive voltage to the output tubes. This is necessary for the operation of the output stage, which is in a configuration known as "push-pull". One half of the output stage receives a negative signal and one half receives a positive signal, so that the signal is being effectively pushed and pulled through the output stage at the same time. The analogy to this would be two people behind your car pushing, and two people in front of your car pulling with ropes. It is a more effective set up than having just two people pulling, or just two people pushing. This push-pull operation gets traded back and forth between the output tubes to develop the output power. In order for one set of tubes to push, and the other to pull, they have to receive the signal in the right direction, which is the job of the phase invertor.

The last device is the output transformer, which has essentially two functions: one is to block DC voltage from being applied to the loudspeakers. Speakers do not work on DC voltages, and since such DC voltage applied to the voice coils would have very negative effects, the output transformer BLOCKS DC and will not allow it to flow into the speaker. Also, it converts the relatively high voltage/high impedance operation of the tubes to a lower voltage/lower impedance signal which matches the impedance of the speaker. Therefore, it is a matching device, as well, to the speakers.

There is one other circuit, called the negative feedback loop, which comes from the secondary, or speaker side fo the output transformer. It feeds a portion of the signal back into the amplifier in REVERSE polarity. The feedback loop goes from the output transformer stage and is fed back into the phase invertor stage. This helps the amp reduce distortion, for its clean sound.

There is one other control in the Marshall amp called the Presence control. This control increases the gain of the higher frequencies, generating a brighter sound and more 'sizzle' in the distortion. Turning up the Presence knob actually defeats the effect of the aforementioned negative feedback loop in the higher frequencies!

23

CLASS A AMPLIFIERS

There has been a lot of confusion among guitarists and technicians about what constitutes a Class A output stage in a guitar amplifier. Many people assume that all amplifiers with cathode bias output stages are Class A, and all amps with fixed output stages are Class AB-1. Either type of bias circuit does not, in fact, automatically mean that the amp in question has either Class A or Class AB-1 operation. The definition of Class A operation is that the output tube conducts signal for 360 degrees (or the full signal swing). This automatically means that any single-ended amp (that is, any amp with just one output tube such as the Fender Champ) must operate in Class A, or they would clip even on the clean signals.

Class AB-1 operation is when the signal flows for at least 180 degrees of signal swing, but less than 360 degrees of signal swing. This is commonly used in "push-pull" circuitry, because the phase inverter supplies only 180 degrees of signal swing to each side of the output stage. The two sides of the output stage combine their 180 degree signal swings to make the full 360 degree signal swing. A Class AB-1 amp can be converted to a Class A amplifier by adjusting the bias so that the tube will conduct during the full 360 degree signal swing.

However, this is often impractical, as lowering the bias voltage without lowering the plate voltage will cause the tube to exceed its current handling ratings in some amplifiers. It may also cause the output transformer to saturate on DC current, which will block it from producing the AC signal current, and it may exceed the current-supplying capability of the power supply, resulting in overheating (burnt transformers) and other components.

Push-pull Class A amps, such as the Vox-AC-30 may be easily biased into Class AB-1 operation. Basically, the only modification necessary to accomplish this is to increase the value of the bias resistor to achieve Class AB-1 operation. A common misconception is that Class A operation is always notoriously inefficient, but amplifiers, such as the Vox AC-30 and the Trainwreck Liverpool 30 are relatively efficient, and lose only a few watts compared to Class AB-1 operation.

This inaccurate reputation stems from a particular type of Class A operation used by audiophiles, the "CLASS A TRIODE". The power output tubes used in amplifiers are a five-element tube called a "pentode". However, the screen grids in these tubes are hooked directly to the plate and operated as a three-element tube, or "triode"; this class of operation dramatically increases the screen current, requiring that the voltages be substantially reduced, hence the inefficiency. These audiophile amps are actually fixed bias amplifiers, rather than cathode-biased.

Most Class A guitar amplifiers are cathode-biased. The way in which we arrive at the correct bias voltage for a fixed-bias Class A amp is to raise the bias voltage to the exact point of tube cutoff, and then divide that voltage in half. This way, the tube will reach clipping and zero bias with exactly the same voltages, just in the opposite directions of opposite polarities. If the tube is operated on an AC filament line, then one half the filament voltage must be added to the bias voltage to compensate for the swing of the filament voltage.

24

THE ADVANTAGES AND DISADVATAGES OF CLASS A OPERATION

In a typical "push-pull" amp, one of the characteristics most guitarists want to avoid is the type of distortion known as "crossover-notch" distortion. This distortion has a harsh, non-musical quality to it, and tends to appear when a tube amp is overbiased . the amp sound is characteristically very weak, but also very "broken up".

The advantage of Class A operation is that it minimizes the crossover-notch distortion under severe overdrive conditions. Therfore, a smoother, more musical distortion sound is produced. However, many heavy metal players prefer the sound of a fixed-bias CLASS AB-1 amplifier, such as a Marshall, for its aggressive, crunchy tone. Blues and fusion players, and players who prefer a less aggressive sound often prefer a cathode-bias, Class A amplifier. A fixed-bias Class A amplifier has a sound which falls about halfway in between these sounds. Mesa Boogie uses fixed-bias Class A in their Simulclass amps, for example.

AMPLIFIER BIASING

WARNING: The Trainwreck method of biasing an amplifier requires that you work with a "live" amp at the points which contain the most LETHAL voltages!!! If you are not thoroughly familiar with the safety precautions for working with live amps at high voltages, Trainwreck recommends having a trained technician do the biasing work on your amplifier.

1. There are two systems most commonly used to bias the output stage of a guitar amp. One system is called "cathode bias". In this system, a resistor is connected in series from the cathode to ground. This type of biasing system adjusts itself automatically by the current draw of the output tubes. It requires no adjustment.

2. The other common method of biasing an amp is called "fixed bias" In this method a negative voltage is applied to the control grid of the output tube to adjust the tube to its optimum operating range. This adjustment might be seen as comparable to the setting of the level of idle in a car. If you set the idle level too slow, the car will hesitate, acceleration might be too sluggish, and the car could possibly stall out. If you adjust the idle too high, the engine will be racing, and may overheat or damage the transmission.

The same holds true for the output stage of a guitar amplifier. An underbiased amp can destroy both output tubes and output transformers. Underbiased amps characteristically sound muddy and tend to hum abnormally. An overbiased amp will not play clean under most circumstances. Its clean channel will sound fuzzy and thin, and its distortion sound will be weak and thin. Certain overbiased amps have a tendency for ARCING (just like an arc welding rig!) across the output sockets!

HOW TO ADJUST THE BIAS ON A FIXED-BIAS AMP

There is an incorrect, yet commonly recommended method for biasing amps being circulated by many sources, including the manufacturers of tubes and amplifiers. This method instructs the repairman to connect the amp to a 'dummy load', attach it to an oscilloscope and put a signal into the amp with a signal generator. Then the instructions are to bring the amp to full power, raise the bias voltage until a crossover notch appears, and lower the bias voltage back until the crossover notch just disappears. *25*

THE TRAINWRECK PAGES

The problems with this method of adjusting the bias are plentiful! Number one, this method is extremely inaccurate, and if you repeated this operation three or four times and measured the bias voltage, each time you would have a different bias voltage! The point at which the crossover notch disappears is a very subjective concept, and bound to be a highly unreliable method for gauging an adjustment such as this one. The second major flaw with this method is that it leaves the tubes OVERBIASED, and in a few months when the tubes age, the crossover notch will reappear, and in this overbiased condition the amp will sound weak.

WARNING!!! TRAINWRECK DOES NOT RECOMMEND THE ABOVE METHOD FOR BIASING AN AMP! IT IS INTERESTING TO NOTE THAT NO HIGH-END AUDIOPHILE AMPLIFIER USING VACUUM TUBES RECOMMENDS THIS METHOD OF BIASING! INSTEAD, THEY UTILIZE THE SAME BIASING TECHNIQUE FAVORED BY TRAINWRECK CIRCUITS!

There is another system for biasing an amp using fixed bias, called THE VOLTAGE MEASUREMENT SYSTEM. This method requires measuring the bias voltage at the tube (usually Pin 5 on most common output tubes used today), and adjusting it to a specified voltage. This method does have an advantage over the CROSSOVER NOTCH DISTORTION METHOD, but is still not the most accurate method of biasing an amp.

Trainwreck's preferred biasing system is called the MEASURED CURRENT BIASING SYSTEM. This method actually measures the current flow through the output tubes and is thus an extremely accurate measurement as compared to either the Crossover Notch Distortion or Voltage Measurement System.

This method also makes it very easy to repeat exactly the same setting from one set of tubes to another, and allows for a very consistent sound when changing tubes. This method also allows you to adjust the tubes within the safe operating range to achieve the desired tone. For instance, with an amp with a very high bias, the sound may tend to be crunchy, but thinner.

With the bias lower and the current increased, the same amp might have a beefier tone and more gain. The tradeoff is that you may have to sacrifice a certain amount of crunch. By using the CURRENT METHOD you are able to fine tune the amp to your particular sound, and have it remain consistent from one set of tubes to another (especially when using "matched" sets of tubes).

TWO METHODS FOR MEASURING CURRENT IN THE OUTPUT STAGE

WARNING!!! Amplifier must be on for all tests detailed below, and must be connected to a speaker or a dummy load with no signal being applied to the input to measure the current.

1.) One method involves unsoldering the center tap of the output transformer and putting a current meter in series with the tap to the voltage source. This measures the current of all of your output tubes simultaneously. Using this method, you can determine the amount of current for each individual output tube by taking the total amount of current and dividing it by the number of output tubes. Therefore, if you have two output tubes, the single tube current is equal to half the total output tube current. If you have six output tubes, the single tube current would be one-sixth the total output tube current.

26

Kendricks

THE TRAINWRECK PAGES

Using this method on a typical amplifier (such as a Fender, Mesa, Marshall, etc....) the safe operational range per tube is generally from 10-40 milliamperes (a milliampere is one thousandth of an ampere) per tube. For example, using a 100 watt Marshall with four power tubes as an example, four times ten is forty, and the minimum current you would adjust for would be forty milliamperes. Four times forty is one hundred sixty, and one hundred sixty milliamperes would be the maximum current. WITHIN THOSE PARAMETERS, ANY CURRENT THAT YOU FIND PRODUCES THE TONE YOU DESIRE IS THE "CORRECT" SETTING!

Conventional amplifier designs using fixed bias generally run 10-40 milliamperes per tube. Unsoldering the center tap and putting a meter in series can be extremely inconvenient on some amps. Trainwreck uses another system for measuring current, which does not require any wires to be disconnected in the amplifier.

Instead, the positive lead of the current meter will connect to the point of the center tap of the output transformer, and the negative lead of the current meter should be connected to the plate pin of one of the output tubes. The plate pin is often Pin 3 in many tubes. Examples of tubes which would commonly utilize Pin 3: 6L6, KT66, KT 77, KT88, 5881, 6550, 6V6, EL34, 6CA7. Some tubes, such as the EL84 (AC-30!), 7591, 7027A, 7868, have the plate appear on a different pin.

However, as we are measuring only ½ of the primary, we will only be measuring the current for half the "push-pull" output. This method is accurate primarily because of the very low resistance of the meter which effectively shunts the winding of the output transformer, and allows the total current to flow through the meter. Please bear in mind, however, that you are only measuring one half the output stage current. For example, if you want to set a four output tube amp to 30 milliamperes per tube, first mulitply four tubes times 30 milliamperes to equal 120 milliamperes total. Now, since this method only measures one half of the total current, you would adjust the bias until the meter reads 60 milliamperes (one half of the 120 milliamperes total).

Some amplifiers are equipped with a variable bias adjustment which may be turned with a screw driver to obtain the proper operating range. Some amps have fixed resistors, and values of resistors must be substituted until the proper bias current is observed.

CAUTION: This system of biasing amps will not work for every make! For instance, Music Man, Hiwatt 200 and 400 have different systems fo biasing. The Ampeg SVT has a built-in biasing system where you measure a voltage on the front panel through access terminals, and it measures a voltage which is dependent on current.

CBS Fender amps often have a different biasing system. In the late '60s CBS used a biasing system which adjusted the balance of bias between the two output tubes. These amps are easy to detect, as the bias voltage on each half of the output tubes is not necessarily equal.

27

THE TRAINWRECK PAGES

In other words, the voltage on Pin 5 on one half of the output, and Pin 5 on the other half of the output may actually be different. Any Fender amp which has a bias adjustment on the back panel is an amp of this variety. The way the bias is adjusted on these particular amps is to turn the control until you observe the minimum amount of hum in the speakers. This is a poor system, as the bias tends to drift and change as the amp warms up. We recommend that these amps be converted to the earlier Fender system which allows you to adjust the current. This modification combined with the use of balanced output tubes will generally cancel out any problematic hum.

CAUTION: DO NOT ATTEMPT TO ADJUST FENDER AMPS WITH A BALANCE TYPE BIAS SYSTEM BY THE CURRENT METHOD!!!!!

BIASING THE TRAINWRECK AMPLIFIER

The Trainwreck Circuits Liverpool 30 amp employs a cathode-biasing system which requires no adjustment. Four EL-84 (VOX STYLE) output tubes are used to power the output section. The Trainwreck Express amp is unique in that it is capable of using either two 6V6 (typical of Fender Princetons, Deluxes, etc.) or EL-34 (generally associated with Marshall amps) output tubes. They can be switched without adjusting the amp. Because of this feature, a Trainwreck Express amp should not be biased by current. Instead, it is recommended that biasing be done by the Voltage Method.

The correct bias voltage for a Trainwreck Express amp in operating position using a digital multimeter is -30 volts on Pin 5 of the output tube, which may be adjusted by using the variable adjuster inside the chassis . Normally, this adjustment will never have to be made. A special process at Trainwreck manufacturing headquarters insures that there will be little need for bias adjustment for many years!

CBS FENDER AMPLIFIERS: On January 5, 1965 CBS became the official owners of the Fender Musical Instruments group, (formerly known as the "FENDER ELECTRIC INSTRUMENT CO."). Although in 1965 they did not start changing circuit designs, eventually they started changing circuits in all of their amplifiers. These legendary changes were not for the better. There was an eight month period of trying to combine cathode and fixed-bias technologies in one product! These units were a dismal failure, and among the worst sounding of the CBS Fender amplifiers. Unfortunately, CBS never returned to their production of pre-CBS circuitry, however the amps made just after CBS took over are easily converted back to the coveted pre-CBS Fender specifications.

Obtain a copy of AA763 or AB763 schematic for your Deluxe, Tremolux, Super, Twin, Showman, Bandmaster, etc. Following the schematic, it is possible to remove the dreaded CBS circuitry to match the pre-CBS schematic. If modified correctly, your amp should have that pre-CBS Fender sound.

28

THE TRAINWRECK PAGES

It is also important to note that CBS routed wires differently in the amplifier and started having a problem with a phenomena called "parasitic oscillation". The aural manifestation of this problem was a sound not unlike the buzz of an insect which would appear on top of the clean note produced by the guitar and amplifier. To eliminate this problem, Fender added a .002 capacitor across the output tubes to shunt this oscillation to ground. Unfortunately, most amplifiers which were produced with the .002 capacitors across the tube circuit require them to be there even after the conversion back to pre-CBS specs.

The only way to eliminate this problem is to use the original wiring layout. As you would require a pre-CBS amp to copy the layout from, this operation is not particularly practical, and we don't recommend it.

Later, Fender increased the output of their amplifiers in another attempt to keep up with the times. Super Reverbs became 70 watts, Twin Reverbs and Bassmans were increased to 135 watts. These amplifiers can never be brought back to the original pre-CBS sounds due to their larger transformers.

PICKUP TESTING FOR VINTAGE GUITAR OWNERS (HOW TO TELL IF A PICKUP IS OK WITHOUT REMOVING IT FROM THE GUITAR)

Our first premise is that anyone owning or rewiring vintage speaker cabinets or pickups should own, or have access to a device known as a "multimeter". This device measures voltage, current, and resistance. Such a multimeter may be purchased at a very low cost at most electronics stores. We recommend that anyone purchasing a multimeter be sure to get one with a digital (or LCD) readout rather than the model with the swinging needle. The digital units are far easier to use.

With the popularity of vintage guitars we are finding that some unfortunate collectors have purchased guitars which function, but contain open pickups. This occurs because a break in the wire in the middle of the pickup will allow the pickup to function because of capacitance effect, but the tone is hardly vintage! A telltale sign of this syndrome is a harsh, shrill tone coming from the pickup, and the fact that the tone control does not appear to work correctly. This is a particularly common problem with older Fender Telecaster bridge pickups, and occasionally with Gibson P-90 'soapbar' pickups. It is a rare occurrence with humbuckers.

Your pickup may be very easily checked for continuity, without removing it from the guitar, through the output jack of the instrument. A ¼" phone plug should be inserted into the jack of the guitar, the multimeter is to be set on an appropriate resistance range, and one lead of the meter is connected to the hot terminal, and the other meter lead is connected to the ground terminal of the jack. The volume control is to be turned all the way up.

29

PICKUP TESTING (CONT.)

The pickup resistance can be measured, and should read slightly lower than it would outside of the guitar due to the parallel effect of the pot.
Examples of typical readings for various pickups are as follows: #1). A Fender type pickup will typically read from 4,000-10,000 OHMS maximum.

If you find that your Fender-style pickup reads over 10,000 OHMS, your pickup is probably either overwound or a non-vintage replacement. Pickups reading over 20,000 OHMS can be generally considered "open". These pickups are worthless! #2). Humbuckers generally read somewhere between 6,000-18,000 OHMS.

WHEN PERFORMING THIS TEST, BE SURE TO REMEMBER TO USE YOUR PICKUP SELECTOR TO TEST ALL OF YOUR PICKUPS INDIVIDUALLY!

Marshall SUPER BASS to SUPER LEAD Conversion

This modification applies to standard four-input fifty, hundred, and two hundred watt models. Chassis should be removed and placed upside down (with transformer and tubes facing downwards). The back panel should be facing the technician, and the control panel faces away from the technician. This will put power tubes to the left and preamp tubes to the right of the technician.

STEP ONE: Locate first preamp tube (all the way to the right hand side). Locate pin 3 on the first preamp tube. Pin 3 is connected to an 820 ohm resistor with either a 250 or 320 MFD capacitor. From Pin 3, jumping across the tube socket is a wire. Remove this jumper wire but leave the 820 ohm and 250MF capacitor connected to Pin 3. From Pin 8, run a wire to a 2.7K half watt resistor to ground. Run a .68 capacitor to ground to Pin 8. This capacitor may be a low voltage type.

STEP TWO: Locate Pin 6. Pin 6 connects to a 100K half watt resistor. There is a .022 or 22N capacitor. Remove this capacitor and replace it with a .0022 capacitor, sometimes labeled 2N2. Locate the treble potentiometer. From the right hand terminal of the treble potentiometer a wire runs to the circuit board and connects to a 250 p.f. capacitor. Replace the 250 p.f. with a 500 p.f. capacitor. The opposite end of the 500 p.f. capacitor connects to a 56K half watt resistor. The other end of that resistor connects to the .022 capacitor which runs to the bass and midrange controls. Change this 56K resistor to 33K. Locate the volume control for the first channel. Across the center and the right hand terminal (the slider and the hot terminal), install a .005 m.f.d. capacitor. Locate the third tube (the phase inverter) which is the third from the right. The plates on these tubes are PINS 1 and 6. Both Pin 1 and Pin 6 run to their individual .1 m.f.d. capacitors. Replace the .1 m.f.d. capacitors with .022 m.f.d. capacitors. This completes the normal "SUPER BASS TO SUPER LEAD" modification.

On some Super Lead amplifiers (particularly the earlier ones) there was an additional .68 m.f.d. capacitor used. Locate the second preamp tube. From Pin 3, a wire runs to an 820 ohm (sometimes this is a 1K) resistor to ground. Add from the same pin the .68 capacitor to ground. This will add slight high end and slightly more distortion. **30**

THE .68 CAPACITORS AND THE .005 CAPACITORS MAY BE OF A LOW VOLTAGE TYPE. ALL OTHER CAPS MUST HAVE A VOLTAGE RATING OF 400 VOLTS OR BETTER!

MODIFICATION FOR INCREASING OUTPUT TUBE RELIABILITY FOR MARSHALLS

PREFACE: Marshalls were originally intended to run on Mullard or Brimar brand EL-34 output tubes. Unfortunately, the output tubes being manufactured throughout the world today cannot take the the same stress as the original tubes. A very simple modification for increasing tube life without altering the tone of the amplifier is to lower the value of the bias feed resistors in the output stage.

STEP ONE: Going to Pin 5 of each (or pair of, in the case of a hundred watter) output tubes there will be a 220K resistor each side from the bias circuit. We want to reduce those 220K bias feed resistors to 100K. This will increase the longevity of your output tubes. In the case of the early fifty-watt Marshalls, which did not include "screen resistors", installing a screen resistor on each output tube will allow it to use the modern tubes without instant self-destruction! This is accomplished by removing the wire from Pin 4, connecting one end of a 1000 OHM 5 watt resistor to Pin 4 and connecting the wire that previously went to Pin 4 to the remaining wire on the resistor.

Another way to achieve roughly the same result is to solder this resistor between Pin 4 and Pin 6, and connect the wire that previously went to Pin 4 to Pin 6. The primary negative impact of using a screen resistor is a slight reduction in power, and a change of tone which may or may not be desirable. However, when using the modern EL-34 tube, this modification becomes almost a necessity, as the average tube life can be as short as five minutes! If you do not wish to do this modification to your Marshall and you cannot find original Mullard or Brimar tubes, you may use the American Phillips brand 6CA7, which is a large bottle type EL-34. These are available from many sources including MESA/BOOGIE, Groove Tubes, TNT, etc. This tube does not require the installation of the screen resistor, as it can competently handle the screen current "as is".

BIAS INFO SUPPLIED WITH MARSHALL MATCHED TUBE SETS

Prior to packaging, Marshall EL34M replacement tubes are subjected to a series of specially designed inhouse test and selection procedures.

These not only select the tubes to a band of parameters that have been shown to produce the optimum in terms of performance reliability and creating the genuine Marshall sound, but also subject the tubes to an abnormal check, in real world amplifier conditions, recreating the harsh tube situations found in a guitar amplifier.

Unless your amplifier has been reworked or serviced since it left the Marshall factory then these tubes are a direct replacement without the need for rebiasing. If it has, or you are unsure, the bias should be checked, and if necessary adjusted, by a competent audio electronics engineer to the following figures.

50w JCM 800 MODELS – 39 VOLTS

50w PRE JCM 800 – 32 VOLTS

100w ALL AGE MODELS – 42 VOLTS

When fitting these tubes to pre JCM 800 50 watt models, it should be checked that the amplifier is fitted with screen grid resistors, if not, these should be fitted – 1Kohm 5 watt being the required value. If not, premature failure can arise.

When fitted to other makes of amplifier, the bias should be set to the manufacturers specifications.

Genuine Marshall spares No: O/PV

31

MASTER VOLUME Mods For MARSHALLS: Four Types

Types 1,2, and 3 master volume go after the phase inverter section. This type of modification is to be done to four-input Marshall amplifiers which are to remain four-input Marshalls and uses the extra gain stage of the phase inverter to achieve adequate distortion. The type 4 Master Volume is used directly after the preamp and before the phase inverter. That is the type of Master Volume used when adding a gain stage. It is the type of Master Volume which is "stock" in two-input Master Volume Marshalls straight from the factory.

Type 1 uses a double one meg audio taper potentiometer and is the type used in certain old Marshall combos and certain other Marshall amps as a factory Master Volume. However, this type of Master Volume has the unfortunate side effect of limiting the quality of the amplifiers original fully 'cranked' sound. If it is important to maintain the option of producing the original sound of the Marshall on '10', this mod will not achieve your goals.

Types 2 and 3 both allow the amp to return to its original 'fully cranked' sound with the volume set to '10'. One circuit (which is a Trainwreck exclusive) uses a double 100K linear taper potentiometer and Type 3 uses a single 1 Meg audio taper pot and is the simplest style of Master Volume to install in a Marshall. However, all three Master Volume circuits have distinctly different sounds when using the Master Volume, and the user should be aware of the sound he or she is shooting for in selecting a particular style of Master Volume.

Type 4 Master Volume, which is used on the later Marshall amps tends to produce the more modern 'heavy metal', harDCore sound. With the addition of an outboard overdrive unit, channel-jumping on four input Marshalls or the actual installation of an additional preamp stage will tend to produce the most distortion.
SEE DIAGRAMS FOR TYPES ONE, TWO, THREE, AND FOUR MASTER VOLUMES.

THE BEST TUBE AMP MADE TODAY
32

Here's a gain stage you can use with a Fender, Marshall, or almost any tube amp. The gain stage described here can be used as the input stage; the guitar goes directly into it for a boost before it goes into the amps normal circuitry. This gain stage can also be inserted between any points in the preamp of the amp you want to modify. For example, in a Marshall you would use this gain stage in either the first position as the very first preamp (the first thing the guitar signal "sees"), or you would use it in the second position AFTER the guitar amps first preamp; it would be inserted right after that point. Typically, in a Fender, this gain stage would be used all the way at the end of the preamp, after it has gone through the amplifiers entire preamp stages. In a Fender, then, the last stage you would add would be this stage.

WARNING! THIS IS A VERY COMPLICATED PROJECT. IT REQUIRES A CERTAIN LEVEL OF EXPERTISE. IT IS VERY IMPORTANT IN USING AN EXTRA GAIN STAGE TO USE PROPER LEAD DRESS, TO USE SHIELDED WIRE WHERE NECESSARY TO KEEP THE AMP FROM OSCILLATING AND TOTALLY FREAKING OUT!

If you intend to use this circuit as a first gain stage, then the guitar input would be connected to Point B on the diagram. The R-2 resistor would be a ONE MEG OHM ½ watt type. Resistor R-1 and capacitor C-1 would not be used if this gain stage is being used as the first stage in the amplifier.

If this is being used as the second stage in the amp, for instance as in a Marshall, then R-1 and C-1 WOULD be used. C-1 is optional; if you find the amp is too brilliant with C-1 in place. Removing C-1 will reduce the treble response.

R-4, the cathode resistor, can be anywhere from 820 to 10,000 ohms! The lower the resistance, the more gain the circuit will have. The higher the resistance, the less gain the circuit will have. In a factory Master Volume Marshall in this particular position they use a 10,000 ohm resistor with no bypass capacitor (in our diagram C-4 functions as a bypass capacitor). Capacitor C-4 on the diagram is optional; it increases the gain, and will also increase the gain at certain frequencies, depending on the value selected. A .1 capacitor across R-4 will increase only the very highest frequencies. A .68, which is standard Marshall value, increases the upper midrange to treble frequencies. A 25MFD, 25 Volt capacitor will increase all frequency ranges equally. Typically, when using the .68 capacitor, Marshall would use a 2.7K resistor in that position, though anything from 820 ohms to 10K ohms can be used.

The higher the value of the aforementioned resistor used, the more effect capacitor C-4 has.

R-3 is the plate resistor. This is a 100K ½ watt resistor. Some amps have a problem with oscillation. If so, you may choose to try a 250pf, a 500pf, or .001 cap across R-3. This will tend to suppress oscillation, but will also limit high frequency response. Unless this added cap is necessary, don't use it! I would recommend starting with the smaller value cap and working your way up in value. Also, on the input jack of the amp, a 250 pf from the hot terminal to ground often helps to suppress oscillation (not included on the diagram, but an extra tip you may want to try out).

We come out of the plate of the tube and go to capacitor C-3, which would be a .02 or .002, that is the OUTPUT capacitor. The .002 slightly suppress the bass frequencies. This is a very minor difference; most people can't hear it but I put it in anyway! On a Super Lead Marshall, the lead channel uses a .002 and the standard Super Bass and the 'dull' channel on a Marshall, for example, would use a .02.

We then come to resistors R-5 and R06, which are 470K ohm ½ watt resistors. If you want the full output of this circuit, you would connect the next stage to Point C on the diagram. If you connect the input of the next stage to point D, you will have half the gain of the stage: connecting to that point reduces the gain by one half. In a Marshall JCM 800 factory Master Volume, they would have connected the gain stage at Point D.

This tube has to be powered. The way we arrive at the power is to connect a 10K ohm two watt resistor to the positive terminal of any power filter in the preamp stage, and that runs to an electrolytic capacitor whose value may range from 8 MFD to 50 MFD, 450-500 Volt rating. Be careful to observe polarity! This is a polarized capacitor, as is the bypass cap! If you use a 25 MFD 25 Volt capacitor for C-4, the negative end connects to ground, and the positive end goes toward the cathode.

If you install an extra tube for this circuit it will also require 6.3 volts to power the filaments. Tie pins #4 and #5 of the new socket together at the socket and connect them with a wire to pins #4 and #5 of the closest existing 12AX7 socket. Now connect a wire from pin #9 of the new socket to pin #9 of the same closest existing socket.

A 12AX7 actually contains two separate triode tubes. You can use either one for this mod! For triode #1, pin #1 is the plate, pin #2 is the grid, and pin #3 is the cathode. For triode #2, pin #6 is the plate, pin #7 is the grid, and pin #8 is the cathode. Either use pins #1, #2, and #3 together, or pins #6, #7, and #8 together; do not intermix them!

That completes our universal gain stage! Basically, the way it is set up here, if you were using it in a Marshall the way Marshall does it, would be to connect the first stage of a four-input model lead channel into Point A, and take the output from Point D. TO MAXIMIZE THE GAIN, YOU CAN CONNECT INTO POINT B AND COME OUT OF POINT C!

M.O.V. MODIFICATION

In order to give the amp some protection from dangerous power 'spikes' that can appear in most household wiring systems, Trainwreck recommends connecting an M.O.V. across the primary of the power transformer. If the amp is to be run on 95-120 volts, we recommend a 130 volt M.O.V. If the amp is to be run in Europe, on 210-240 volts, we recommend a 250 volt M.O.V. across the primary. The 130 volt M.O.V. CANNOT be used across the 240 primary of the amp for Euro use or DAMAGE will result! The 250 volt M.O.V. cannot be used on a 120 volt U.S. amp as it will not effectively protect the amp. These devices are particularly useful for people who use amps that are played off of portable generator systems, such as found at carnivals and other outdoor "geek" shows, as these generators are very poorly regulated and can do severe damage to your amp!

34

This modification involves taking three 1-N 4007 silicon diodes, putting them in series, the banded end connects to pin three of your output tubes, and the the other end to ground. You use one on each side of a push-pull output.
So, for example, on a 100 watt Marshall, the two tubes on the left, either pin three of either one of those tubes can connect to this diode to ground.
And, on the other side, either pin three can connect to the other set of diodes to ground, as the pin threes on either side are in parallel.

We use 1-N 4007 silicon power diodes which are effective in supressing spikes at certain frequencies. These will not necessarily prevent spiking on all amps! There is a fast recovery, or high speed diode which will suppress higher frequency arcing, however these diodes have a very distict disadvantage, as they alter the tone of the amp! They make the amp sound muddy as they bleed off high frequencies from the output transformer! Trainwreck does not use these kinds of diodes because of their effect on the sound.

While the Trainwreck method does not eliminate spiking in every amp, it does not effect the sound at all. Every other method which will totally eliminate spiking will have a negative effect on the sound of your amp.

Another point to remember, concerning spiking, is that underbiased amps tend to generate more high voltage spiking than properly biased amps.

50 WATT MARSHALL BIAS MOD

Many early '70s Marshalls came from the factory with the bias connected to the cold side of the Standby switch. That is, a terminal on the Standby switch which does not have voltage until the switch is moved to the On position. What this means to you, is when you turn on the amp to warm-up, no bias voltage appears on the output tubes! When the amp is put into the On position, the bias voltage takes several seconds to build. In the meantime, the tubes draw an extreme amount of current, which can cause damage to the tubes, or 'pop' the HT or High Voltage fuse in your amp!

To determine if you have one of these amps, you can put the amp "ON", leave the Standby switch in the standby position, and check pin 5 of a power tube for bias voltage, which generally runs in the 30 volt range. If no bias voltage appears on pin 5 of the power tubes (also known as "output tubes"), you have an amp that requires this modification.

To accomplish this mod, first determine which terminals are the hot terminals on the Standby switch. Take a voltmeter, put it on an AC voltage range capable of measuring AC voltages over 300 volts. Connect one lead of the AC voltmeter to the chassis. Then probe terminals on the Standby switch with the other lead until you find one that reads AC voltage. Locate the wire coming off the terminal terminal on the Standby switch that runs to the bias diode, and move it to one of the two terminals (it does not matter which one of these two) that has AC voltage on it.
WARNING! SHUT OFF THE AMP BEFORE SOLDERING THIS WIRE!! AFTER YOU FIND THE PLACE THAT HAS THE VOLTAGE, UNPLUG THE AMP!! ALSO, MAKE SURE THE FILTERS ARE DISCHARGED BEFORE YOU MOVE THE WIRE FROM THE 'COLD' TERMINAL AND SOLDER IT TO EITHER ONE OF THE 'HOT' TERMINALS!

35

Fuses on the Marshall: the "HT" fuse connects to the output transformer, the output tubes, and some electrolytic capacitors. The vast majority of times when you blow an HT fuse in a Marshall is because of shorted output tubes. If your HT fuse blows, and you replace it, and it blows again, substitute output tubes! The second biggest cause of HT fuse blowing is a tube socket that has carbonized from high voltage arcing and has shorted out.

After eliminating these two possibilities, then one would check for others, such as a bad filter cap, which is probably the next most common cause. Then, of course, check the output transformer itself, the power diodes, etc.

When looking at a standard Marshall, either a four-input model or a factory M-V with three preamp tubes, from the back (with the chassis in the normal upright position) the first tube on the left (actually, a 12AX7 contains <u>two</u> tubes in one glass envelope!) contains your gain stages. If you experience a lot of noise or microphonics in the amp, the tube on the FAR LEFT when viewing the amp from the back is the culprit.

The next tube (the middle one of the three) is a gain stage plus a cathode follower stage. The cathode follower stage is a circuit used to turn high impedance signals into low impedance signals to drive the tone circuitry. So, the middle tube is also a gain stage and affects the tone controls.

The third tube is the phase inverter, which splits the signal into equal but opposite signals to drive the push-pull output stage.

For troubleshooting purposes, one spare tube can be substituted one position at a time until the problem is eliminated. If the problem is not solved by this subsitution technique, take the amp to a service technician!

Make sure that the old style output selector is always CLEAN and TIGHT! Gaffer tape is NOT the recommended method of accomplishing this! A loose output selector or a bad speaker output cable can cause damage to output tubes and output transformers.

It is not recommended to use a Marshall with a conventional 'power soak', as the transformer was not designed to be used in this manner! POWER SOAKS CAN CAUSE DAMAGE TO THE OUTPUT TUBES AND THE OUTPUT TRANSFORMER! There does not seem to be any problems caused by the 'speaker emulators' on the market, such as the Groove Tube or Harry Kolbe "Silent Speaker" units, but time will tell!

NEVER operate a tube amp without a suitable dummy load or speaker connected, or DAMAGE will occur!

Trainwreck does not recommend the use of a Variac to boost the voltage going into a Marshall, since it can drastically shorten the life of many components.

On certain early metal face Marshalls you may hear a "buzz" along with the normal Marshall "hiss", especially as you turn up the volume. Many of these amps had a ground loop problem. The ground from the diodes in the power supply section were connected to the front panel of the amp forming a ground loop, which causes the "buzz". On those amps, removing the ground from the front of the amplifier and reconnecting it to the back side of the chassis will eliminate this annoying buzz.

36

37

Lead dress (HOW wires are routed) in Marshalls is critical for reducing noise.
On old four-input Marshalls, the filament leads, typically red and black, should
be routed away from the tube socket and against the chassis.
The green grid leads, which are the leads that run to pins two and seven on the
first two preamp tubes, should be raised in the air away from all the other leads.
Also, the leads on the controls, with the amp controls facing forward and the amp
upside down, looking in, should be brushed toward the top of the chassis and
towards the right side. There is a purple lead going to the "Presence" control,
which comes from the feedback loop of the amp, and that should be moved as much
to the LEFT as possible.
On certain old Marshalls, they connect some of the grounds through the controls by
soldering directly to the backs of the controls. The controls complete a
mechanical ground connection to the chassis which can sometimes corrode. If you
have a Marshall that has a "buzzy" or humming sound you can try jumping an alligator
clip to the front of the chassis and connect it to the wire soldered across
the backs of all the controls. If the hum or noise is eliminated, a wire may be
soldered directly from that wire to the chassis, to ensure a positive connection.

On many old Marshalls, the pilot light burns out, and some collectors do not
wish to alter the appearance by removing the original lens bezel. The bulb
in question is a 6.3 volt incandescent job, and a Trainwreck trick is to cut
off the back of the pilot light (an EXACTO brand razor saw for plastics works
great, says Steve) inside the amp CAREFULLY! Obtain a 6.3 volt "grain of wheat"
bulb, solder it to the original leads, put it inside, and reconnect the back
(Steve uses Jet Super Fast Dry crazy glue). The pilot assembly even looks stock
from the outside and will continue to function as Marshall intended!

TUBE TIPS

Trainwreck often gets asked the difference between a 12AX7, a 7025, and an
ECC-83. In days bygone, a 7025 was a premium version of a 12AX7. That is, a
12AX7 selected for its low noise.
An ECC-83 is just the Euro designation for a 12AX7.
In modern times, manufacturers label the same tubes 12AX7, ECC-83, or 7025
depending on the preference of the distributor! Though these 'types' are
completely interchangeable, it should be noted that different brands of tubes
can produce different tones, just as different brands of guitar strings or
speakers have their characteristic tones. Anyone who is truly interested in
experimenting may buy several different brands and types of these tubes and
give them a trial! Also, you can mix and match; you can use a 12AX7 in one
position, an ECC-83 in the next position, and a 7025 in another position.
You don't have to use the same brand in every position, nor do you have to use
designation. Try different types and LISTEN; use the ones you like the sound of.
It should also be noted that the 12AX7, 7025, and ECC-83 are all good substitutes
for the 12AY7 found in some older Fender amps, including the 4X10" tweed
Bassman. They are directly interchangeable. We would not recommend that if you
run across some 12AY7s you try them in your Marshall; they are lower in gain
and 'flatter' sounding than the 12AX7 types.
The 12AT7 used to drive the reverb tanks on Fenders, and in the phase inverter
of certain amps, have the same pin configuration as 12AX7 types and, in a pinch,
you may substitute a 12AX7 and a 12AT7. However, the 12AT7 has a greater
current handling capacity than a 12AX7, and 12AT7s should generally be used *37*
where specified!

THE TRAINWRECK PAGES

FENDER TROUBLE SHOOTING GUIDE FOR TWO CHANNEL REVERB AMPS WITH SIX PREAMP TUBES

Looking at the back of the amp with the upper back panel removed, the first tube on the right (7025 or 12AX7) is the tube for the first, or "Normal" channel. If this "Normal" channel is not working properly, or making noises, this tube would be the one to suspect. The second 7025 is the tube (first preamp stage tube and tone driver tube; they do both functions) for the "Vibrato" channel. If you get microphonics or excessive noise in the second, or "Vibrato" channel, this would be the one to suspect. The third tube from the right is a 12AT7; it sits next to the right hand side of a small transformer (the reverb transformer) and acts as a reverb drive tube. This third tube supplies the signal to drive the reverb tank, through the reverb drive transformer. If the reverb is not working, but you can rock the amp with reverb control up and hear the springs 'crashing' I would suspect this 12AT7 first! If changing this 12AT7 does not cause the reverb to work, then I would suspect an "open" driver or a break in a wire in the reverb tank. Also, make sure that the reverb tank is plugged in the proper polarity; it will only work in one direction.
The fourth tube in the preamp (7025/12AX7) is the reverb recovery tube, and a third gain mixer stage for the Vibrato channel. If the reverb is not functioning and rocking the amp does not cause a reverb 'crash' with the reverb control up, this 7025 is the one to suspect. If replacing this tube does not cause the reverb to function, an 'open' reverb tank is a likely culprit.
The fifth tube from the right (12AX7) is the tremelo oscillator tube. If your tremelo does not work, this is the tube to suspect. Note that in Fender amps, the tremelo works by closing a circuit with the footswitch. If the footswitch is not plugged into the amp, or not functioning properly to CLOSE the circuit, the tremelo will not work.
The sixth and final tube (12AT7) is the phase inverter tube. This 12AT7 drives the output tubes (provides the inverted signal for the output tubes). On the pre-CBS Fender circuitry, a 12AX7 may be used in this position for a different sound with no harm. On the later models, a 12AT7 should be used.
The next tubes over to the left are the power tubes. These are the tubes that do the amplifying and supply power to the speakers. It is very important in this position to have a fresh, preferably MATCHED set of tubes to get the maximum efficiency out of your amplifier.
If your amp has an odd number of output tubes, such as three, the one all the way over to the left is the RECTIFIER tube, typically a 5Y3GT, a 5AR4/GZ34 or 5U4GB. The function of this tube is to convert AC into DC. These tubes will either work or they won't! Occasionally, one will have an intermitent short, which will cause the fuse to blow.

MORE FENDER TROUBLE SHOOTING TIPS

On the pre-CBS Fender blackface series amplifiers, they used half watt carbon resistors in the preamp. With age, these tend to get very noisy. As the amp sits idling you will hear an assortment of snaps, crackles, pops, and other noises. The first thing to try, to correct this, is a fresh set of preamp tubes. If the noise remains, replace all 100K ohm resistors in the preamps with fresh ones of good quality. The 100K ohm resistors are the ones with the brown, black, and yellow bands around them. One half watt resistors are fine. There are eight of them altogether: three on each preamp and two in the reverb circuit (these last two resistors don't really make all that much noise).

38

WARNING! BEFORE ATTEMPTING ANY REPAIRS, MAKE SURE THAT ALL CAPACITORS IN THE
AMP ARE DISCHARGED! DO NOT ATTEMPT ANY REPAIRS IN THIS SECTION UNLESS THE AMP
IS UNPLUGGED FROM THE AC LINE!

With age, controls will become noisy. Tube sockets can become loose, or corroded.
Obtain a good, commercial quality control or contact cleaner spray from a
reputable electronics supply house. Be sure to obtain a brand that states on the
container that it is "safe for plastics"; some control cleaners contain a solvent
that may actually dissolve parts inside your amp!
The way to clean controls is to squirt a <u>SMALL</u> amount of cleaner into the
control and rapidly rotate the shaft back and forth along the entire length
of travel.
Repeat this process for every control. This may also be used on open type
switches, such as the mid-range and treble switches used on the Ampeg amps or
the "Bright" switches used on Fender amps.

Tube socket contacts can spread over time, not making proper contact with the
pins of the tubes. Using a strong pin or other object, <u>slightly</u> bend the contacts
inward, closing the gap slightly on the contacts in the sockets. You can also
clean socket contacts with the same control cleaner spray described above. This
will do much to reduce amplifier noise and increase reliability.

NOTE: DO NOT SOAK THE SOCKETS WITH CONTACT CLEANER! USE NO MORE THAN IS NEEDED
TO DO THE JOB!

If you notice that the tube sockets do not respond to re-tensioning (have little
'spring' to them) it is time to replace that whole socket. Also, note any
charring or carbon build-up on the socket; these sockets, too, must be replaced.
Sockets that are exceptionally dirty, with pitting of the metal surfaces, are
also best replaced.

It should be noted that certain controls on certain amps will make noises no
matter how much you clean them, such as the "PRESENCE" control on many
Marshall amps (also on Trainwreck amps), as these contain DC voltages. If a
typical control cannot be made silent using cleaner, it is probably worn out
and should be replaced.
The exception to this rule, if you are a collector of vintage amps, and you
want to retain your amps originality, as long as the control functions and the
noise that results does not drive you crazy, I would leave it alone.

The same control cleaner described above can be used to clean the controls and
switches in your guitar. However, I recommend HUGE amounts of paper towels
behind and around the controls and switches so that you do not get control
cleaner on the finish of your guitar, or saturate the wood!

RECTIFIER TUBES

3g

The common rectifier tubes used in guitar amps are the 5Y3, 5AR4/GZ34 or 5U4.
These tubes are directly interchangeable in most guitar amps. However, each
tube produces a slightly different tonal characteristic in the amp. The 5AR4
produces a sound closest to solid state silicon rectifiers that are most common
in amps today. This is because this rectifier has less of a characteristic known
as "sag"; that is, as the amplifier draws current, the voltage across the tube
drops (there is a voltage drop across the tube that increases with current draw).

The 5AR4/GZ34 has the least loss of voltage with current draw. The 5U4 tube has slightly more voltage loss with current draw than a 5AR4/GZ34. The 5Y3 has the most loss of voltage with current draw and therefore has the 'softest' sound. Also, if you have an amp that "eats" output tubes, it will be easiest on the amp to use a 5Y3. One can subsitute these tubes and judge for one's self which one provides the basic tone that one likes.

Many companies make a solid state replacement for these rectifier tubes. These solid state units tend to 'tighten up' the sound, make it more dynamic. However, they also tend to remove the 'singing' quality in certain amps! If you are going to substitute, make sure that the voltages will not exceed the voltage ratings of your output tubes and power filters!
For example, a Fender blackface Deluxe with a solid state rectifier in place will exceed the voltage ratings of both the tubes and the power filters and is most emphatically NOT recommended! However, the same mod will work just fine on a Super Reverb!

TIPS FOR HIWATT OWNERS

The vintage DR series amps were bullet proof! They had only one MAJOR design flaw from the factory. That was the decision to use one watt carbon screen resistors. While I'm sure Hiwatt thought that their amps were phenomenally loud, and no one would ever want to turn one up to the point of distortion, actually many people do! When a Hiwatt equipped with EL-34s reaches distortion, especially when outfitted with modern EL-34s, the screen current draw exceeds the ratings of these one watt resistors and they do burn up.
When these resistors burn, they open up, shutting off that tube, and eventually shutting down the amp. Trainwreck recommends that anyone with a Hiwatt replace all one watt screen resistors with five watt wirewound types.

Another Hiwatt mod which may be useful concerns wiring layout. Although the Hiwatt layout and wiring is among the neatest of any guitar amp ever built, they do have a problem with buzz and noise caused by ground loops.
In order to obtain the neat appearance inside the amp, one ground point was connected to another by ground wires which are hidden underneath the preamp circuit board. This can result in an amp, which, when turned to "10", is buzzy and noisy. Locating all the grounds in a Hiwatt, disconnecting the subterranean wire, and running each ground individually to the front of the chassis will make the Hiwatt much quieter and also tends to improve the tone! This is a tricky operation, as these ground wires are hidden, and should be done by a tech with some experience with this brand.

wanted: input
STEVE AT ANGELA INSTRUMENTS IS COMPILING A LIST OF RECOMMENDED AMP REPAIR PERSONS FOR PUBLICATION IN OUR NEXT CATALOG. PLEASE WRITE OR CALL IF YOU KNOW OF ANYONE THAT YOU WOULD LIKE TO SEE MENTIONED! IF YOU'VE HAD A BAD EXPERIENCE, HE'D BE INTERESTED IN HEARING ABOUT THAT AS WELL! IF YOU'VE GOT A MOD OR SERVICE TIP THAT YOU'D LIKE TO SHARE WITH OTHERS, SEND IT ALONG!

40

MASTER VOLUME "TYPE-1"

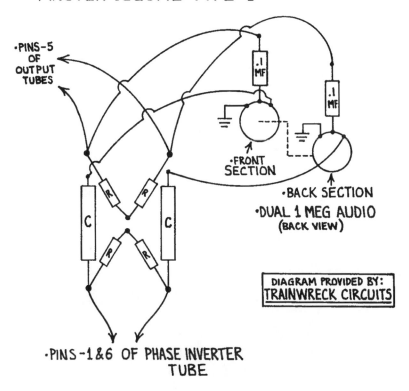

·PINS-5
OF
OUTPUT
TUBES

.1 MF

.1 MF

·FRONT
SECTION

·BACK SECTION
·DUAL 1 MEG AUDIO
(BACK VIEW)

DIAGRAM PROVIDED BY:
TRAINWRECK CIRCUITS

·PINS-1&6 OF PHASE INVERTER
TUBE

·R= RESISTER   ·C = CAPACITOR

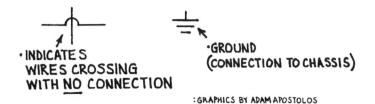

·INDICATES
WIRES CROSSING
WITH NO CONNECTION

·GROUND
(CONNECTION TO CHASSIS)

: GRAPHICS BY ADAM APOSTOLOS

41

MASTER VOLUME "TYPE-2"

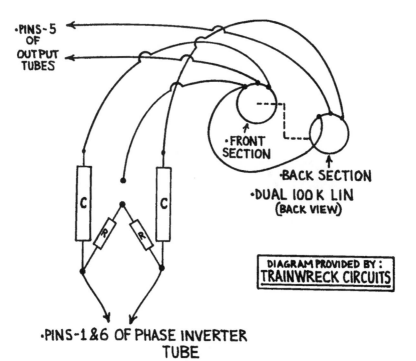

·PINS-5
OF
OUTPUT
TUBES

·FRONT
SECTION

·BACK SECTION
·DUAL 100 K LIN
(BACK VIEW)

DIAGRAM PROVIDED BY :
TRAINWRECK CIRCUITS

·PINS-1&6 OF PHASE INVERTER
TUBE

·R=RESISTOR   ·C= CAPACITOR

·INDICATES
WIRES CROSSING
WITH NO CONNECTION

:GRAPHICS BY ADAM APOSTOLOS

42

MASTER VOLUME "TYPE-3"

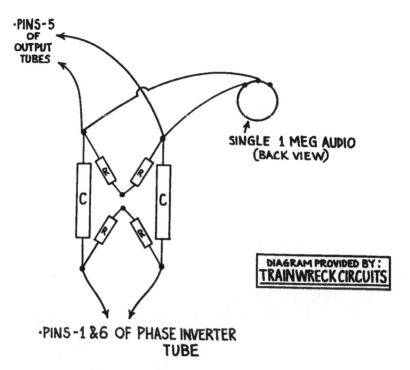

·PINS-5 OF OUTPUT TUBES

SINGLE 1 MEG AUDIO (BACK VIEW)

C   C

R   R
R   R

DIAGRAM PROVIDED BY :
TRAINWRECK CIRCUITS

·PINS-1 & 6 OF PHASE INVERTER TUBE

·R=RESISTOR   ·C=CAPACITOR

·INDICATES WIRES CROSSING WITH **NO** CONNECTION

: GRAPHICS BY ADAM APOSTOLOS

43

MASTER VOLUME "TYPE-4"

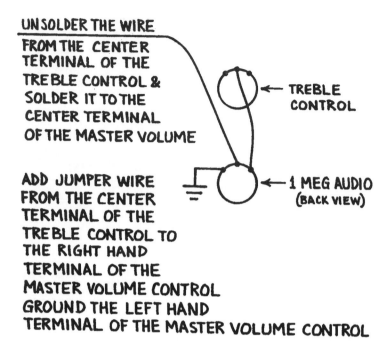

UNSOLDER THE WIRE
FROM THE CENTER
TERMINAL OF THE
TREBLE CONTROL &
SOLDER IT TO THE
CENTER TERMINAL
OF THE MASTER VOLUME

← TREBLE CONTROL

← 1 MEG AUDIO
(BACK VIEW)

ADD JUMPER WIRE
FROM THE CENTER
TERMINAL OF THE
TREBLE CONTROL TO
THE RIGHT HAND
TERMINAL OF THE
MASTER VOLUME CONTROL
GROUND THE LEFT HAND
TERMINAL OF THE MASTER VOLUME CONTROL

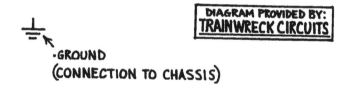

DIAGRAM PROVIDED BY:
TRAINWRECK CIRCUITS

•GROUND
(CONNECTION TO CHASSIS)

:GRAPHICS BY ADAM APOSTOLOS

44

"UNIVERSAL GAIN STAGE" 12AX7, 7025, ECC83, ½ TUBE

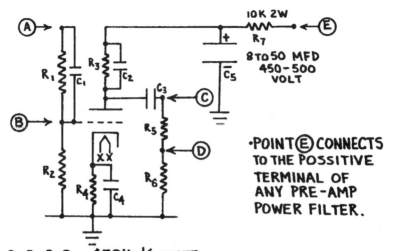

·POINT Ⓔ CONNECTS TO THE POSSITIVE TERMINAL OF ANY PRE-AMP POWER FILTER.

R_1 R_2 R_5 R_6 = 470K ½ WATT

NOTE: IF GUITAR INPUT IS APPLIED TO POINT Ⓑ USE 1 MEG ½ W FOR R_2

C_1 (OPTIONAL) 500 PF	
R_4 820 TO 10,000 OHMS (LOWER VALUES = MORE GAIN)	
C_4 (OPTIONAL) .1, .68, OR 25 MFD	
R_3 100 K ½ WATT	
C_2 (OPTIONAL) 250 PF, OR 500PF, OR .001 MFD (1000 PF)	
C_3 .002 MFD OR .02 MFD	
C_5 8 TO 50 MFD 450/500 VOLT	
R_7 10K 2 WATT	

DIAGRAM PROVIDED BY:
TRAINWRECK CIRCUITS
: GRAPHICS BY ADAM APOSTOLOS

45

"MOV MOD"

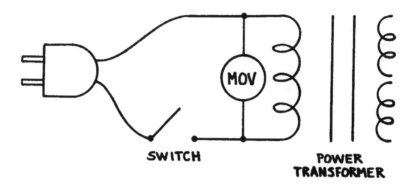

SWITCH   POWER TRANSFORMER

- 130 VOLT MOV FOR AMPS USED ON 100-120 VOLTS

- 250 VOLT MOV FOR AMPS USED ON 210-240 VOLTS

DIAGRAM PROVIDED BY:
TRAINWRECK CIRCUITS

GRAPHICS BY ADAM APOSTOLOS
46

OUTPUT TUBE &TRANSFORMER "PROTECTION MOD"

NOTE: A SHORTED TUBE CAN SHORT THE DIODES. ALWAYS TEST DIODES AFTER REPLACING A SHORTED TUBE.

·OUTPUT SOCKETS

·TUBE TYPES
6L6 , 5881 , EL-34,
6CA7, 6V6 , 6550,
KT66, KT77,KT88,
6K6

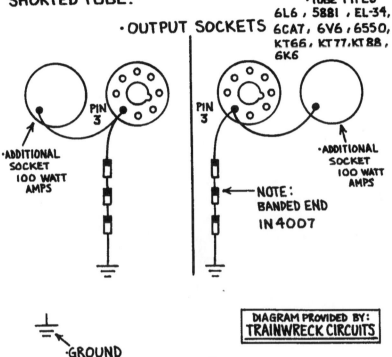

PIN 3

·ADDITIONAL SOCKET 100 WATT AMPS

·ADDITIONAL SOCKET 100 WATT AMPS

NOTE: BANDED END IN4007

DIAGRAM PROVIDED BY:
TRAINWRECK CIRCUITS

·GROUND
(CONNECTION TO CHASSIS)

: GRAPHICS BY ADAM APOSTOLOS

47

Q & A

FENDER

What other output tubes can I put in my Fender Deluxe amp? More specifically, could I use 6L6 style tubes?

With slight modifications (auxiliary 6.3 volt filament transformer, rewiring of pin 1 on the socket, and a bias adjustment), a Fender Deluxe amp could use EL34 or 6550A. With only a bias adjustment, the amp could use KT66, EL37, 6L6GC, 7581A or 5881. The 5881 would be an excellent choice because the tubes' load impedance would be a very close match for the output transformer. The Sovtek 5881 would be the best brand to use. This tube is actually a military grade 6L6GB that would probably last many years in a Deluxe. The sound would become much tighter particularly in the low end. If you could find some, the Mullard brand EL37 would also be an excellent choice.

Would changing to different output tubes in my Deluxe give me more power?

In most cases the power would be about the same or only a couple of watts more. If you want more power when changing output tubes, you might try going to a solid-state rectifier. This would up the wattage considerably. But remember, **you must never use a solid-state rectifier** in a Deluxe that uses 6V6 output tubes. I am recommending the solid-state rectifier only for use with the output tubes mentioned in the previous answer.

You said never to use a solid-state rectifier in a blackface Deluxe. I use one in my Deluxe and it sounds great.

All tube amps seem to sound their best when they sound like they are about to blow up. That may very well be the case with your amp. I didn't say it wouldn't work, I said don't do it. Both the General Electric and the R.C.A. Tube Manuals show the 6V6 style tube as having a design maximum rating of 350 volts for the plate and 315 volts for the screen. Blackface Deluxes with a tube rectifier are running about 420 volts on the plate and 415 volts on the screen. Simple arithmetic will tell you that's already about 70-100 volts over the design maximum rating. If you change to a solid-state rectifier, you will add approximately 30 more volts to both the plate and the screen. The odds are that your power tubes will blow up, and when they do, you will know why they did. This is the same story for Princeton Reverb amps. However, on tweed Deluxes, the supply voltages are much lower and a solid-state rectifier would definitely work well. In a tweed Deluxe, I prefer a 5V4 rectifier to the 5Y3 stock tube. The 5V4 gives a little more voltage than a 5Y3 but still retains the rectifier tube envelope that a solid-state rectifier loses. In amps without a standby switch, the solid-state rectifier will cause all of the tubes to wear out quickly, because it will provide the high voltage before the other tubes have a chance to warm up. This causes cathode stripping. (The alkaline earth coating on the cathodes will boil off of the cathodes if high voltage is present before the tube is warmed up.) With a tube rectifier, the rectifier tube will not supply the high voltage until it is warmed up, but by that time, the other tubes have had a chance to warm up.

I would like to change the power tubes in my Princeton Reverb to 6550s. How do I adjust the bias without a bias trim pot?
I will give you the answer but only after saying that I do not recommend changing the Princeton Reverb to 6550s without other extensive modifications. In the bias supply circuit, there is a 22K resistor going from the voltage supply to ground. This resistor must be made smaller in order to correctly bias 6550s. The easy way to adjust it would be to put a 250K ohm pot across the resistor and adjust the pot while monitoring the tube current with a milliammeter. (To monitor current on this particular amp, the positive lead of the milliammeter goes to pin 8 on the 5U4 rectifier tube and the negative lead goes to pin 3 of one of the output tubes.) When the current is

Kendricks

right (about 40 to 60 milliamps for 6550s depending on tone desired), turn off the amp and disconnect the pot from the circuit. Now measure the pot with an ohmmeter and find a resistor that matches the resistance. Solder the resistor across the 22K resistor and you are set. If you ever wanted to return the amp to stock, simply remove the resistor and you are back to stock.

A word of caution: A 6V6 tube, the stock output tube in a Princeton, draws heater current of .45 amps per tube, making the total heater current for the output tubes a total of .9 amps. A 6550 tube requires heater current of 1.8 amps per tube, so a pair would require 3.6 amps, a difference of 2.7 amps or 300% more current. **You will need an auxiliary heater filament transformer** to supply this kind of current or you will overheat your power transformer and it **will burn up!** Best to over-design, probably a 10 amp 6.3 volt transformer would be right. Also a pair of 6550s would put out about 40 to 50 watts in a Princeton and the output transformer is designed for about 20 watts. To avoid burning it up, you will need a heftier output transformer. A 40 to 50 watt Fender transformer will do nicely. Perhaps a Bassman, Pro, or Bandmaster would be a good choice. Of course the speaker will not be able to take that kind of power. Maybe you should upgrade to a 12" speaker rated at 50 watts or better **to avoid blowing up the 10" speaker that is stock.** With all the extra current on the B + circuit, it might be a good idea to double or triple the filtering on the main B + voltage to avoid annoying ghost notes and unnatural harmonics. Best to double the screen supply filtering also to keep the screen supply stable. I would recommend saving all parts so that the amp could easily be returned to stock if desired.

Recently a power tube fell out of its socket in my Princeton Reverb (a 1979 silverface) and it sounded GREAT. I replaced the prodigal tube, but at low volume the tone with one tube is better. If I purposely pulled a power tube, would there be dire consequences? Also, is there much difference in circuitry (and resulting tone) between my late 70s Princeton and a pre-CBS? Very interesting. Here's what happened when your tube fell out. Normally a Princeton Reverb amp is a Class "AB" amp. This means that the output tubes conduct plate current for less than 360 degrees of the signal cycle. In order to have a good sounding class "AB" amp, there are two output tubes and when one of the tubes is not conducting plate current, then the other tube is conducting plate current. In a class "AB" amp, the signal voltage has to be strong enough to drive each of the tubes into "cutoff" for a brief time during each cycle of the input signal. One tube is driven into "cutoff" during the first half-cycle and the the other tube is driven into "cutoff" during the next half-cycle. (See more info in the chapter titled "The Simple Truth About Biasing Your Amp.") When the amp has only one tube and when the amp is set at low volume, the signal voltage is not enough to drive the tube into "cutoff"; therefore the one tube is conducting plate current for the full 360 degrees of the signal cycle. This then would be class "A" operation. In class "A" operation, the tube conducts plate current during the entire 360 degrees of the signal cycle.

Also, with one tube, you were operating the amp single-end whereas with two tubes you would be operating push-pull. Push-pull amps sound different because a push-pull design will cancel second order harmonics (even order), and they cancel power supply hum.

Some amps could be operated with one tube without much consequence; however, the Princeton already has a very high plate voltage for 6V6 output tubes, and removing one would cause the plate voltage to go up. This is due to the fact that one tube draws half as much current as two tubes and a decrease in current will reduce the voltage drop across the power supply, thus increasing plate voltage. Also the impedance of the output transformer for one tube should be twice what it is for two tubes, so operating only one tube would have that tube wear out very fast because it would "see" itself as operating into a somewhat "shorted" circuit. If you like the way one tube sounds, and you want to play the Princeton Reverb with one tube, I recommend that you do it with a single 6L6 or 5881 tube. This tube can easily take the extra voltage, and it normally has a lower operating impedance making it a much closer impedance match than a 6V6. Also you might want to re-bias the one tube for class "A" operation and change the first gain stage preamp tube to a 12AY7 or a 12AT7 to reduce gain.

The silverface and blackface Princeton Reverb amps are almost identical, the only difference being that the silverface has a small cap across the reverb return signal that would ground out some of the highs of the reverb signal. This would make the reverb less bright. As far as the tonality differences and similarities, it would depend on the individual amp.

I own a Fender Bandmaster 6G7-A, tube chart dated "LF" and I have two questions I hope you can answer for me.
1. What is the output impedance? The number on the transformer is 022871. Is there a code on the transformer?
2. The 2X12 bottom did not have any speakers in it and I was wondering what could have come in it originally and what ohmage?

That's actually four questions! 1. The output impedance of the transformer 022871 is 4 ohms. That transformer is the same transformer that is used for a 6G6-A Bassman. This information is contrary to the output transformer that is supposed to be in the 6G7-A Bandmaster. The Bandmaster should have a 45217 which is 8 ohms. However, the schematic of this amp shows it with only one speaker, and Fender could have used a different transformer for the 2X12 design. The actual transformer number determines what impedance it is and there is no code.

2. You could have had Jensens, or perhaps Oxfords or whatever Fender had available at the time. Upon consulting the Fender catalog for your particular amp, I could see they were very vague and only referred to the speakers as "heavy duty". Almost all early Fender speakers were 8 ohms, with the only exception being the Champ at 4 ohms.

I have a Fender blackface Pro Reverb amp. The normal channel breaks up more than I would like. Can I increase the value of the 220K resistor that feeds the phase inverter or is there something you could recommend?

Do not increase the value of the 220K resistor that feeds the phase inverter; you will simply add series resistance which will hurt fidelity. Instead, try decreasing gain of the first gain stage by increasing the value of the cathode resistor that is connected to pin 3 of the first preamp tube. Stock value is 1500 ohms. Try going to a 2.7K ohm. You must keep the 25 mfd cap across the resistor just like it was on the 1500 ohm resistor. If that doesn't do the trick, try increasing the value of the cathode resistor on the second gain stage (pin 8, same tube). To do this simply snip the wire that goes to pin 8, and install a 2.7K resistor from pin 8 to ground. Put a 25 mfd 25 volt capacitor across this resistor with the negative end of the cap to ground and the positive side on pin 8. If this still doesn't do the trick, put the amp back like it was and put it up for sale. A Pro Reverb amp with obnoxious gain would probably sell really fast!

In Fender blackfaces and early silverfaces, is it possible to substitute a 5751 (industrial 12AX7) for a 7025/12AX7 in either the preamp or phase inverter sections? Would a 5751 give more gain?
The tube pin out for both the 12AX7 and the 5751 are identical. You may drop the 5751 directly into the 12AX7 socket and it is perfectly safe to do so; however, the gain characteristics of the the 5751 are lower than the 12AX7. The 5751 is the General Electric 5 star tube that was developed by using the 12AX7 as a prototype; however, it has lower ratings and higher heater current (not much higher). I have used this tube on occasion and had good luck with it. Try it and go with what your ears tell you! The amplification factor of the 12AX7 is 100 whereas the amplification factor of the 5751 is 70. Some other special type 12AX7s that you might try: 6057, 6681, 7729. All of these have an amplification factor of 100.

Some friends bought an old house belonging to a deceased TV and radio repairman. I found a Deluxe Reverb amp in the attic and some tubes. The Deluxe has broken springs in the reverb tank but worked perfectly otherwise. Can you describe where to attach these springs and also would you list some collectible R.C.A. tubes for a guitarist?
I do not recommend repairing the reverb pan. It could be done; however, it is very tricky because the wire that holds the spring must be magnetic in order for it to work. Also, if you overheat the place where it must be soldered, the plastic mounting will melt. Simply get another pan. Avoid the hassle.
Collectible tubes for a guitarist would include any tubes used in guitar amp circuits. Some examples would be 6L6GC, 5881, 7025, 12AX7, 7199, 7189, 7591, 6SJ7, 6SN7, 6SL7, 6X4, 12AT7, 12AU7,

6550, 6BQ5, 6V6, 6CA7, 6CG7, 12DW7, 12BH7, 5AR4, 5Y3, 5V4, 5U4, 12AY7, 6SC7, 7027, 7581. Of course these same tubes with a "W" or an alpha suffix "A", "B", etc. are improved versions of the tubes listed and are also desirable.

My favorite sounding Fender amps all use a GZ34 rectifier tube. How does this differ from the 5U4 used in Pro Reverbs, etc.? Could you substitute a GZ34 in an amp made to take a 5U4? Also who makes the best replacement GZ34s today?

Although both the 5U4 and the GZ34 are both high vacuum full wave rectifier tubes with virtually the same pin configuration, the 5U4 rectifier tube has different construction and geometry than a GZ34 (a.k.a., 5AR4) that results in a higher internal resistance. In a 5U4, there is only a filament and two plates; therefore, since there is no cathode, the filament acts as the cathode. This is referred to as a directly heated cathode design. In this type of design, arcing can be a big problem, so the plates must be moved a relatively long distance away from the plates to prevent arcing. Since the plates are further away, the electrons must move a longer distance in a vacuum which results in a higher resistance. The higher resistance will cause a voltage drop of up to 50 volts across the tube. Of course lower voltages will affect the rest of the amp's sound, but the higher resistance will also affect the dynamic envelope of a pick attack. The 5U4 also draws more filament current (3 amps total) than the 5AR4 (1.9 amps total).

In a 5AR4 rectifier tube there is a separate cathode that is between the filament and both plates. This is called an indirectly heated cathode design. Since the cathode provides a shielding from the filament heater to plate, the tube is less likely to arc and the cathode can be placed very close to the plates (approximately two-hundredths of an inch!) This results in a much lower internal resistance, since it is so much easier for the electrons to move such a short distance in a vacuum. The voltage drop is therefore very small and the attack envelope is much more percussive.

Generally speaking, 5U4s and 5AR4s are interchangeable but not always. Some Fender Deluxes (and other amps with 6V6 output tubes) used a 5U4 and developed about 410 to 420 volts on the plates of the output tubes. If you changed to a 5AR4 in an amp such as this, you would most definitely have a problem keeping power tubes from shorting. In amps that were originally designed with a 5AR4, installing a 5U4 could possibly cause the power transformer to overheat which would ultimately result in transformer failure. This is due to the fact that a 5U4 draws almost twice the filament heater current. The good news is that almost any amp that originally used a 5U4 will take a 5AR4 and since most people prefer the 5AR4, why not try it?

As far as availability, 5AR4s have not been manufactured in years, therefore the only ones available are new old stock. The British-made ones are preferred. Many new old stock American brands are British-made. **Buyer beware:** There are a couple of designer tube companies from California (as well as a few other companies with otherwise good reputations) that buy 5V4 or 5Y3 tubes and rebrand them GZ34/5AR4. These 5Y3 and 5V4 rectifier tubes will work in a 5AR4 circuit for a few hours and then short out. They will always short because they simply cannot deliver the current that a real 5AR4 delivers. (A 5Y3 is only good for 125 mA output, a 5V4 is good for 175 mA output and the 5AR4 is good for 250 mA output.) How do you spot a phony? The phony will have four pins instead of five; a real 5AR4 has a glass envelope about the same size as the base, whereas the phony will have a glass envelope smaller than the base. Also a real one has a fairly flat top whereas the phony has a rounded top.

The good news is that SovTek is currently working on a GZ34 prototype. They have made several prototypes, one of which is very promising. This tube will probably not be available for another year. If it actually comes out, it will be the only GZ34 in current production in the world.

I have a tweed Deluxe amp with a P12R Jensen speaker. The speaker sounds awful. I have checked around and no one has the exact original cone to recone it. I want to keep the amp original and therefore do not want to replace the speaker with a new speaker. What should I do?

You have a real dilemma. 3KSP paper recone kits from the original manufacturer are not commercially available. If you had the speaker reconed, it wouldn't sound the same as an original, and if you get a new speaker the amp is no longer original. I suggest two possibilities depending on whether you are a player or a collector. If you are a player, get a new speaker that you like the sound of, and save the old speaker in case you ever want to sell the amp. When you eventually decide to sell, change the speaker back to the original and you will have an amp to sell that is dead stock and someone else will have the problem of what to do about the speaker. If you are a collector, shop around and find a P12R that has never been reconed to replace the speaker. When buying a used speaker I strongly recommend listening to the speaker first. The used speaker you buy could sound worse than the one you are trying to replace. On old speakers, the voice coils can become unglued causing a huge drop in efficiency (almost no volume); often the paper can become mushy due to years of use (and years of humidity absorption) causing tired sound and bad response.

I recently acquired a 1950 (pot-dated 304-016) two-tone "Champion 600" to go with my small collection of amps. The "Champion 600" is almost mint, but it has a Kletron 6" speaker in it, made by Cleveland Electronics of Cleveland, Ohio. It is very old with a code on the cone of the speaker (2005-3). Did Fender ever use Kletrons?

When Fender was making amps in the late 40s and early 50s, they used whatever they could get at a good price. Buying closeout inventory or surplus parts was not uncommon. Therefore it is very likely that your Kletron speaker is original. Check the D.C. resistance of the speaker. If it measures around 3.2 ohms, my guess is that it probably came with the amp.

Can I hook my Super Reverb cabinet to my blackface Deluxe Reverb amp?

Yes and no. Do not hook the speakers up to the Deluxe without first rewiring the speakers in the Super Reverb to reflect an 8 ohm load. A stock Super Reverb cabinet is 2 ohms, and the output of a Deluxe Reverb is 8 ohms. If you hooked this up without modifying the speaker wiring to be 8 ohms, the amplifier would think it was operating into a somewhat shorted circuit. 0 ohms is a direct short, so you can see how 2 ohms would look almost like a short for an amp designed to run at 8 ohms. There are two ways that the modification can be done and each way sounds different.

1. Series parallel: This way has more branch inductance and therefore will have less high end, better low end, and an overall crunchier tone. To do this, simply wire two speakers in series, then wire the other two speakers in series. You should now have two pairs of speakers. Next wire one set in parallel with the other set. You're done. Impedance is 8 ohms.

2. Parallel series: This way has less branch inductance and therefore will have better clarity in the high end, a little less low end and an overall cleaner tone. To do this, simply wire two speakers in parallel, then wire the other two speakers in parallel. You should now have two pairs of speakers. Next wire one set in series with the other set. You're done. Impedance is 8 ohms.

I have a 8 ohm output Fender Showman amp and would like to hook it up to two 8 ohm 12" speakers. What is the best way to wire them?
There are only two ways that you can possibly wire them, in series or in parallel. If you wire them in parallel (positive to positive and negative to negative on each speaker with positive and negative being leads to the amp), you will have a 4 ohm speaker load. If you wire them in series (positive and negative tied together and then use the other positive and negative of each speaker as your leads to the amp), you will have a 16 ohm load. From an electrical standpoint either one would work. I would suggest that you try the speakers both ways and see which one sounds best to you. The 4 ohm will probably have more high end because of less inductance and consequently the 16 ohm load would probably have less high end and greater low end. Best to try them both ways and let your ears decide.

How does the external speaker jack on a Fender amp work, and what ohms should the extension speaker be? Also what will happen if the ohms are not correct?
Almost all Fender amps have the same setup for speaker output jacks. There are two jacks, one labeled "speaker" and the other labeled "ext. speaker". The "speaker" jack is a shorting jack that shorts both output leads from the output transformer when a plug is not in the jack. This is a type of safety circuit so that if you try to run the amp without a

speaker, the jack shorts the output side of the output transformer thus protecting the amp from damage. That is the reason why you must always use the "speaker" jack if you are only using one speaker output. The "ext. speaker" jack is simply a two terminal jack that is in parallel with the "speaker" jack, but it has no shorting terminal hook-up. In other words, you should only use the "ext. speaker" jack if the "speaker" jack is already being used. When you use the "ext. speaker" jack while using the "speaker" jack, the two are in parallel. To get the power divided equally between the speakers in the "speaker" jack and the "ext. speaker" jack, you should use the same impedance speaker in the "ext. speaker" as you used in the "speaker" jack. This would divide the power evenly, but if the efficiency of one speaker is much greater than the other, you may still have more sound coming out of the more efficient speaker. Using the "ext. speaker" jack will alter the actual speaker impedance that the amp "sees". Fender amps are very tolerant of mismatched output impedances as long as they are not more than 100% off.

For instance, a stock Twin has two 8 ohm speakers in parallel; this makes a 4 ohm load. If you plug in an extra cabinet with two 8 ohm speakers in parallel (also a 4 ohm load), you would now have both 4 ohm loads in parallel. The amp would then see 2 ohms (two 4 ohm loads in parallel equals 2 ohms). Another example would be a Deluxe amp with one 12" speaker (8 ohms). Plug in an additional 8 ohm speaker and the amp would now "see" 4 ohms (two 8 ohm loads in parallel equal 4 ohms).

As far as your question concerning what will happen if the ohms are not correct, let me say this. Maximum signal transfer occurs when the impedance of the speakers match the impedance of the output transformer of the amp. If you have an impedance mismatch you may lose a little power, but wait. Did you know that the actual impedances of the amp and speakers are constantly changing somewhat with frequency? It's true, because of inductive reactance, the impedances go higher on high frequency notes and lower on lower frequency notes. One thing to consider, lower impedances approach a short circuit which is not good for the output tubes in the amp. A short circuit has zero ohms. If you have a Fender amp, let's say a Deluxe, that is supposed to run at 8 ohms and you run it at 4 ohms, you have a 100% mismatch. The amp can tolerate this very well. Now take the same 8 ohm amp and plug a

2 ohm 4X10 cabinet in the extra speaker jack. Your speaker load is now 1.6 ohms (8 ohms times 2 ohms divided by 8 plus 2 ohms). The tube life would definitely be shortened, the 2 ohm speaker would get almost all the power and some of that power would be lost because of the 240% impedance mismatch (8 ohm to 4 ohm is 100% mismatch, 4 ohm to 2 ohm is 100% mismatch and 2 ohm to 1.6 ohm is 40% mismatch; a total of 240%). 1.6 ohms approaches a short circuit.

Similarly, I would never use the "ext. speaker" jack on a Super Reverb without rewiring the stock 2 ohm load (four 8 ohm speakers in parallel equals 2 ohms) to an 8 ohm load (series parallel or parallel series).

I read that the old 4X10 Bassman has a thinner baffle board than the Super Reverb. What will changing the baffleboard to thinner material on a Super Reverb do to the sound of the amp? The 4X10 Bassman does have a thinner baffleboard than a Super Reverb. The Bassman is $\frac{5}{16}$ inch whereas the Super Reverb is $\frac{1}{2}$ inch. Thinner baffleboards are easier for the speakers to vibrate and therefore should give a fuller, rounder sound, but you are limited because the baffleboard must be thick enough to support the speakers without the wood ripping apart near the mounting screws. Conversely, thicker baffleboards have a tendency to suppress certain frequencies. Most people can hear the difference.

I recently purchased a 1966 blackface Fender Bassman amp. The speaker grille cloth was badly ripped and torn so I replaced it with new grille cloth. The replacement grille cloth appears to be identical to the original; however, it is brand new and of course does not match the cloth on the amp head which is a bit dirty, faded and perhaps oxidized. I can easily replace the clothe amp head grille to match but it will not have the vintage look. Do you or your readers have any suggestions on aging the new grille cloth? Although I have never tried it, many collectors that I know, soak new grille cloth in strong coffee or black tea for a few hours to age their grille cloth. The trick is to make sure the coffee or tea is strong enough and to let the cloth soak long enough to get that "nicotine from the barroom" color. I would recommend checking it ever so often for color, and when it looks right, remove it from the soak and let it air dry before applying.

I have a blackface Fender Twin Reverb. The grille cloth has no tears or holes in it but appears loose. Is there any way to tighten up the grille cloth without have to completely remount the grille?

Yes, there is a way. In fact it is the same basic way that Fender originally tightened up the grille in the first place. Use even heat. Not a heat gun, but rather a large area of even heat such as a portable electric heater or a radiator. It's best to heat up the edges of the grille first, taking care to do each edge individually. By the time you have done that, the grille will probably be very tight; if not, try doing each edge again. Only on rare occasions would I apply heat to the middle of a grille because the lines of thread in the grille are likely to go wavy. Of course you need not remove the grille or speakers from the amp to perform this procedure. This process only works on Fender, Ampeg, and a few other amps. It will not work on Vox or any other amp that has a textile fabric type grille.

I have a tweed amp that a previous owner painted with black paint. I would like to get it recovered except I would like to keep it original. Is there anything to use to remove the paint, and how much would I devalue it if I got it recovered?

The bad news is that there is nothing that will restore the tweed to its original look. Tweed is fabric and therefore, when it was painted, the black paint soaked into the actual fibers thus making complete removal impossible. You say you want to keep it original but the amp is not original now. To my knowledge no tweed amp left the factory with a coat of black paint on it. Getting it recovered by an upholstery shop using original tweed would be a waste of time and money, because there are special ways to cut the corners and a special direction that the tweed stripes must go and other special details around the top cutout and back panels that only an amp recovering specialist would know how to do correctly. I have seen recovered amps that, although covered with the right tweed fabric and done by a professional upholstery shop, could be spotted from across a convention center as being unoriginal. Your best bet is to have the amp professionally recovered by a tweed amp recovering specialist. The amp would look original and of course would have its value enhanced. Using a car analogy, which would you pay more money for—a '56 Porsche that had been brush painted by a professional house painter or a '56 Porsche that had been repainted in the exact original color by a shop that specializes in Porsche restorations?

I have a 1974 Fender Princeton Reverb amp that I have owned since it was new. I misplaced the cover at a gig. Can I buy an original Fender amp cover for my Princeton? Also what is the RMS rating on my amp? I think it is 12 watts.

Unless you find someone with a 1974 Princeton Reverb amp that is willing to sell you his cover, you are SOL. Fender does not make them anymore; the last ones were sold out in 1985. You have a few alternatives. If you could find a cover from another Fender amp, let's say a Showman cabinet or something large, you could have a seamstress use the original Tolex and make a cover for you. Another possibility would be to use current issue Tolex and have a cover made. As far as the actual wattage of your amp, it is probably around 18 watts although the actual wattage would vary depending on what brand and type of tubes you have in it as well as how hot you have it biased. The apparent loudness is also dependent on the efficiency of the speaker.

My Fender blackface Pro Reverb amp makes a loud "thump a dee thump" when I turn it from standby to play. Any suggestions?

Fender blackface amps used an under-designed standby switch that was not rated for the B + voltage used. (Probably a 250 volt at 3 amps.) This would work OK on a 450 volt circuit because the current was only somewhere around 100 milliamps during switching. However, over a period of time, the switch will arc during switching and that causes the "thump a dee thump." Many a Fender amp has done that for years and no one bothered to change the switch. When changing the switch, try upgrading to a 600 volt switch at 2 or 3 amps.

Can any of the mods mentioned in the chapter "Ten Easy Mods For Your Super Reverb Amp" be used on other Fender amps?

Mods #1 and #6 can be done on all Fender amps. Mods #2 and #3 can be done on all Fender black and early silverface amps that have two or more output tubes. Mods #4, #7, #8 can be done on all black, early silver, and some brownface amps that have two channels. Mod

214   Kendricks

#5 can be done on all black, brown, or silverface amps with two channels. This mod could be done on other amps (with only one channel) but the tube to do it on would be the preamp tube furthest away from the transformers. Mod #8 can be done on all tweed amps but only on black, brown, and silverface amps that use 6L6 power tubes. Never put a solid-state rectifier in a black or brown Deluxe, Princeton, or Champ. It will reduce output tube life to minutes. Mod #9 can be done only on Fender amps that use an optocoupler style vibrato circuit. The optocoupler is a neon bulb that flashes against a light dependent resistor. Trying Mod #9 on a Fender amp that does not use an optocoupler will result in immediate power tube failure. Mod #10 can be used on any tweed, brown, black, or silverface amp that uses 10" or 12" speakers.

I have a Fender amp with reverb that crashes more than any other I've had. It seems that the reverb springs are too loose, so vibrations (like walking) cause them to crash into each other and the box. Is there an easy way to solve this problem?

You are right, the springs are sprung from many years of movement. The easy way to fix this problem is to replace the tank. Tanks are relatively inexpensive and a new one will clear up your problem. Since your tank is virtually unusable as it is now, you could try unhooking the two long signal conducting springs from the inside of the tank, then clip about a half inch off one end and bend a small hook on the end just shortened (so that the newly shortened spring can be re-installed). My experience has been that the spring material is very brittle and hard to shape into a new end hook without stressing the metal. Also the hair size wire that the spring attaches to (on the transducers) is extremely delicate and will break if you look at it funny. That is why you would remove the spring completely before attempting to shorten it. To reshape the hook on the end of the spring, it is best to use rounded tip needle nose pliers. If this doesn't work, get a new tank. You needed one anyway.

My blackface Pro Reverb amp used to have plenty of reverb but now it seems that the reverb is not very strong. How can I bring it back?

Often one or both transducers inside the reverb pan itself (in the black bag in the bottom of the amp) become loose. A transducer is a coil wrapped around an iron core much like a small transformer. Its job is to convert electrical energy to mechanical energy (like a speaker), or to convert mechanical energy into electrical impulses (like a microphone). When the input coil gets loose, signal is lost and the springs are not driven as hard. On the output side transducer, the coil can also become loose causing even greater loss. When the coils are loose, the energy is used to vibrate the coil instead of the springs. You might think of this as a helicopter with the blade stationary and the fuselage turning instead. The energy is being transferred to the wrong part. Often this problem can be remedied by wedging a small shim between the coil and the core (I use a small slice of a bamboo chop-stick). Also, while you are working with the pan itself, be sure to check and make sure that **both** reverb springs are in the reverb pan. Sometimes one of the two springs will break, thus making the reverb weak.

Another problem could exist in either the reverb drive tube or the reverb recovery tube. These tubes are a 12AT7 and a 12AX7 respectively. They are located on either side of the reverb drive transformer. The reverb drive transformer is the smallest transformer on the chassis and it is near the reverb input and output jacks on the back of the chassis. Change both tubes, one at a time, and do a sound test after each change. Make sure that you use tubes that are known to be good.

If you still haven't got the life back, try another pan. Sometimes the transducers are too far gone to bring back and another pan is the only solution.

When I bridge the two channels on my Deluxe Reverb amp, I get a decrease in the volume as I turn the control up to around 4. As I continue to turn the volume control, it will then begin to get louder. This occurs on both channels and when I use either volume control. This does not happen when I bridge the channels of my Bandmaster. Thanks for any help you can give.

I am assuming that your Bandmaster does not have reverb. The Deluxe, since it has reverb, has one extra gain stage in the reverb channel that the normal channel does not have. Since a stage of gain inverts phase 180% and coupling capacitors also alter phase, my guess is that when your volume is on 4, you are experiencing maximum phase cancellation. On the Bandmaster, both channels are in phase and therefore you don't have the same situation. To understand phase relationships, think of a sound wave as vibrating "up" and "down" (going "up" first and "down" second.) Now if you had an identical wave except it started its vibration as "down" first then "up" second, and you had both waves on top of each other, then they would have a tendency to cancel each other out. It is like adding minus one and plus one; you get zero.

How does the "bright" switch on Fender amps work?

On every Fender amp, the "bright" switch is simply a switch that puts a small value capacitor (100 picofarads in tweed amps, 120 picofarads in blackface amps, and 47 picofarads in most Deluxes) across the volume control, from input to output. Since higher frequencies see a small capacitor as an almost dead short, the high frequency signal bypasses the volume control altogether. The lows and mids get attenuated by the volume control, but the very highs go around the volume control through the capacitor without much attenuation. We hear this as bright. For this reason, the control is more effective as the volume control is turned down and conversely, the "bright" switch will have hardly any effect when the volume is turned up. If the volume is all the way up, it will have no effect whatsoever!

Would sealing the back of a Fender amplifier produce a "tighter" sound that is more characteristic of the British speaker cabinets of this type?

I don't think it's that simple. I do not recommend sealing a Fender combo amp, because the tubes need the ventilation to stay cool enough not to burn up! Remember the Vox AC100s and how they would typically catch on fire while being used. This was caused by too much heat without adequate ventilation. I think the power supply impedance, kind of speakers, tubes and transformers have more to do with the British sound than whether the back is closed or open. A Fender Showman and Bandmaster (blackface) for instance, are both closed back and do not sound British.

I have a tweed Champ that has a wonderful tone, but I cannot use it in a gig situation because it isn't loud enough. I have tried miking it but it doesn't sound the same and I can't hear it on stage. Do you have any suggestions?

If I were you, I would use the Champ as a preamp for good tone and then take a line level signal off the Champ and feed it into a power amp. A simple mod that would not alter the collector value of your amp could be made from a ¼" phone jack and two resistors. This could be mounted on the speaker terminals of your amp speaker and of course could be taken off at any time. To do this simple mod, find a ¼" phone jack (like a guitar cable plugs into) and you will also need a 2.2K ohm resistor, a 400 ohm resistor and a 3" piece of hook-up wire. The jack has two terminals on it. One is ground (sleeve) and one is hot (tip). Take a stripped end of the 3" hook-up wire and one lead from the 400 ohm resistor and twist them together, then solder the twisted part to the ground of the jack. Now take the free end of the 400 ohm resistor and one end of a 2.2K resistor and twist them together. Solder these to the hot lead of the jack. Now it's time to hook it up to the speaker. The free end of the 2.2K resistor goes to one speaker lead and the free end of the wire goes to the other speaker lead. Plug a guitar cable into the jack and plug the other end into either a power amp or the low gain input of a guitar amp. How do you know which speaker lead connects to the wire and which one to the resistor? Try it both ways, the one that sounds the best is correct. The one that doesn't sound the best will be out of phase with the auxiliary amp. The only way to know for sure is by listening because some amps invert signal (reverse phase) and others do not.

I have a '71 Twin Reverb with two problems:
1. While playing, a slight ringing type feedback will occur and continue even after I stop playing. To stop it I simply give the cabinet a slap.
2. The second problem occurs when certain single notes are played. When these notes are played the amp does not reproduce the note properly but rather grunts or coughs. This problem goes away if I disconnect the internal speakers and use a separate speaker cabinet. Do you have any suggestions?

In regards to problem number one, you probably have a microphonic preamp tube. Take the tube shields off of the preamp tubes and make the amp start its feedback ringing. While it is ringing, and starting with the first preamp tube, hold the tube with your hand to dampen any ringing. If dampening the first tube does not affect the ringing, go to the next tube and dampen it. Continue until you find the tube that, when dampened, stops the ringing. When the ringing stops, notice which tube you were dampening to make the ringing stop. Take this tube out and replace it. If that doesn't do the trick, you may have a ringing in the reverb circuit. Unplug the reverb tank (both R.C.A. connectors) and see if this affects the problem. My guess is that your problem is probably the second preamp tube, because this is the tube most likely to ring due to its gain characteristics.

Regarding your second problem, it sounds to me like you have either a bad socket connection or a bad output tube. To check this, with tube covers removed, the amp on with both channels volume control on 4, and starting with the first tube, rock the tube gently from side to side to see if it is making noise. If it is quiet, go to the next tube and rock it gently. Continue this process until you find which tube makes a commotion when it is rocked in its socket. When you find out which socket, turn the amp off, but leave the standby switch in the play mode (to drain off the charge in the caps) for about 30 seconds. What to do next? Clean the socket by spraying a little tuner cleaner on the tube pins, re-insert the tube and rock it in a scrubbing motion. Next, re-tension the connectors inside the socket with a small tool (safety pin, dental pick, etc.) so that you are sure that the pins will make tight contact with the inside of the socket connectors. Re-insert the tube and repeat the test to see that the problem has disappeared. If the problem seems to be with an output tube (6L6GC) and cleaning and re-tensioning the socket doesn't work to stop the problem, you might have loose internal components in the power tube. Check for this by thumping the tube with your finger while it is in the play mode. If you get commotion by thumping it, it is definitely time for a new matched quartet of output tubes.

I have a 1955 Bassman that sounds great except occasionally it seems to cut out on me while in use. This is very unpredictable and disappointing because I cannot use it on a gig, thus making the amp worthless. I have brought it to several different amp

shops that have checked and rechecked the amp, but the bottom line is that no one can fix it. What should I do?

Your amp can be repaired to play perfectly. It seems to be suffering from a phenomenon known as parasitic oscillation. Parasitic oscillation is a problem that occurs when the amp is oscillating (usually at a higher frequency than can be heard) and it feeds back more and more until the amp simply shuts down. Why does it oscillate? There are many things that contribute to this problem. Old amps usually have questionable ground connections, especially on the control panel where corrosion is a factor. Perhaps humidity has been absorbed in the cloth hookup wire making it more susceptible to leakage, or even the circuit board, when old, could become somewhat conductive. This could cause a type of coupling (capacitive coupling), where the amp feeds back positively on itself. The feedback gets stronger and stronger until it is so strong that no other signal can even pass through the amp. All of the power supply's power is being used to amplify the feedback. Since the feedback is at a frequency higher than humans can hear, all we actually notice is that the amp seems to shut down for no apparent reason. Sometimes parasitic problems don't shut down the amp, but instead show up as a buzzy sound on top of the note being played. This can be very annoying to a repairman who checks everything on the amp and everything checks perfectly except the amp sounds awful. Most of the time parasitic problems appear to be a tube problem because when you put your hand on a particular tube and rock the tube, the problem may seem to go away temporarily. You think it's the tube or the socket that is giving the problem. What's actually happening is that the capacitance of your body is altering the way the feedback is occurring. Depending on the degree of parasitic oscillation there are five things that could be done to stop it. My recommendation would be to check all grounds and perhaps install a grounding buss first. If that doesn't solve the problem, simply rewire the amp, using a new circuit board and new wire. The other four things that could be done involve parasitic oscillation suppression circuits which would probable degrade the fidelity of the amp and therefore I cannot recommend them.

I have two mid-60s Fender amps with the same problem. At zero volume on both channels, a smooth 60Hz type hum comes

out. **By turning one (and only one) channel up to about 3 or so, the hum goes away! I tried replacing the power caps, tubes and adjusting the "hum" control, but no luck. What else should I try? Why does it go away when one channel is turned up?**

Some mid-60s amps had the grounds on the filter caps in the wrong place. This is obviously the case with both of your amps. The filter cap for the screen supply is improperly grounded to the phase inverter filter. The screen supply filter should be grounded to same ground as the main power filter ground. This main filter actually consists of two 70 mfd caps in series to ground whose most positive lead feeds the output transformer. The ground wire should then run from the filters to the chassis near the B + center tap ground. Best to have the B + center tap ground and the main power filter ground along with the screen filter ground near the power transformer (the further away from the inputs the better). Also the first gain stage filter (this is the one that feeds the first two preamp tubes and the reverb recovery tube) should be grounded separately inside the chassis on the grounding buss near the normal volume control. All of the filters mentioned are physically located in the cap pan on the outside of the chassis. There are wires running underneath the circuit board in the cap pan, so you would have to unscrew the board to remove some of the connections that are underneath the board. Changing the grounds to the ones I recommend should clear up the problem, but if it doesn't, you could always simply not play the amp on zero volume.

I have a '75 Fender Vibrolux which is now schematically the same as my friend's '64 blackface Vibrolux, but his has that sweet Fendery distortion characteristic and mine just won't "give it up" so to speak. Did Fender change something about the output transformers, i.e. magnetic core material, spacing, etc., after Leo left? Also my power transformer output voltage is considerably higher than his—an attempt to increase power or inadvertently mess up a good thing? Finally, the blackface models have an 82K and 100K for the phase inverter plate resistors and the silver models use a 47K for each plate. What was the purpose of the different values in the blackface amps?

First of all there is more to a guitar amp than a schematic. The transformers are a very important part of the sound, but so are the kind of tubes, the way the tubes are biased, the speaker, and the wood of the enclosure, and the actual layout of the amp (tube spacing, lead dress, component spacing, type of capacitors, type of resistors, etc.). But to be specific and answer your questions, the transformers were different. The CBS engineers were going for a clean sound with harmonic distortion eliminated. One way to do that was to increase the voltages of the power transformer. A tube tends to distort more at lower voltages and less at higher voltages, so they had the power transformer voltages increased. This gave more headroom with a brighter high end. There is a simple mod that you could do to get the voltages down to blackface spec. Buy a 56 volt 50 watt zener diode (N.T.E. part number 5278A). This is a stud mount device and you will have to drill a couple of holes in the chassis to mount it correctly. Insert it reverse-biased in series with the B + center tap and ground. The cathode side goes to ground and the anode side gets connected to the B + center tap. Of course you must first disconnect the ground on the B + center tap connection. Make sure that the cathode side is grounded in the same place that the center tap was originally grounded. This simple mod will drop the voltages to blackface spec without your having to buy an expensive power transformer (the zener diode only costs about $10.) When this is done, you will have to re-bias the output tubes to draw more current. You will notice a remarkable difference in the tone.

In regards to the 47K plate resistors on the silver amps, this was another attempt to get rid of distortion. The 47K has less gain than the 100K and 82K setup. I always go to the higher value for better tone and dynamics.

Can anything be done to reduce the pulsating noise of Fender amp vibrato?

Yes and no. It depends on where the noise is coming from, and what type of vibrato circuit you are using. Fender used four different types of vibrato circuits. The four types of vibrato (actually three of these are tremolo and only one type is true vibrato, even though Fender did not make the distinction) are:

1. Preamp tube bias modulation. This was only used on a very few Fender amps. The black Vibrochamp and the tweed 5E9A Tremolux are really about the only two I can think of that used this circuit.

2. Output tube bias modulation. Though rarely used, this circuit was found on the brown Deluxe, blackface Princeton, tweed Vibrolux (model 5F11 and 6G11) and perhaps the most famous—the brown Vibroverb.

3. Pitch vibrato. This was used on most brown amps such as the Bandmaster, Concert, Pro, Showman, Twin, and Super. You will never find this circuit on a blackface or tweed amp. It uses two or three tubes and actually alters the pitch of the notes.

4. Optocoupler grounding of the signal. This was used on almost all blackface amps except the Princeton and the Vibrochamp. You will never find this circuit in a tweed or brown amp.

Now we must look at the source of the noise. If the noise is coming from the preamp tubes, changing to quieter preamp tubes will help dramatically. Because the vibrato circuit is actually making the gain of the amp increase and then decrease on all of the circuits mentioned except type #3 above, noise coming from preamp tubes or just gain hiss will be more noticeable with the vibrato circuit on. Circuit type #3 above will have a swirling sound if the preamp tubes are noisy.

Sometimes noise will be coming from the plate load resistors. (These are the resistors connected to pin 1 and 6 of the 12AX7 and 12AT7 tubes.) These are made from compressed carbon and can have small pockets of air inside. Electrons will sometimes arc across the small pockets and cause noise. Changing the resistor with the same value resistance, but upgrading to twice the wattage rating of the original will cure this problem. Sometimes humidity will be absorbed into the carbon, in which case the noise will be more of a popping sound. This can sometimes be remedied simply by leaving the amp on and in the play mode for three or four hours.

Pitch vibrato has a beating that is not caused by resistors, humidity or tube noise. It is caused by the oscillator clipping. Using a weaker 12AX7 in the oscillator socket (usually the third socket from end opposite side of power tubes) will help. Try a Sovtek 12AX7WA, these have slightly less gain. Voltage tweaking may also help, but I have never seen one that didn't beat a little.

GIBSON

I have recently acquired a 1961 Gibson GA-5T amp. It has a 12AX7, 5Y3, and a 6BM8 tube in it. I'm familiar with the 5Y3 and the 12AX7, but I've never heard of a 6BM8. Is it like a 6BQ5? How much output can I expect from it? Is there a better replacement available? Also it has an 8" Special Design Jensen blue label speaker in it. Could you tell me something about this speaker?

A 6BM8 is two tubes in one; a triode and a pentode. The triode has an amplification factor of 70. The pentode section can handle a maximum of 5 watts. Load impedance for the pentode section ranges from 15K to 20K. There is no substitute that you can use to replace the 6BM8. Both the 6FY8 and the 6HC8 have pin configurations identical to the 6BM8; however, the operating characteristics are radically different and they cannot be substituted for the 6BM8. Of course the 6BQ5 is nothing like the 6BM8 either. Your Jensen 8" speaker is probably the same 4 ohm speaker that was used in the Fender Champ amp.

I have recently seen two Gibson amps, the Hawk GA-25 and the Super Medalist, both of which use 7591 output tubes and 6EU7 and 12AT7 preamp tubes. Please tell me about the power rating of the 7591s and anything about the 6EU7s. Are there other tubes that can be substituted for these?

The 7591 output tube has a nice tone, maybe even sweeter than the 6L6GC style tube; however, a pair will deliver about 10 watts less power than a pair of 6L6GCs in the same circuit. Do not attempt to substitute any other tube in a 7591 socket without rewiring the socket. To my knowledge, there is no other tube (save a 7591A) that can be used in a 7591 socket. The power rating of the 7591 is a design maximum of 19 watts per tube. Gibson didn't run them at the maximum. As far as the 6EU7, there is no substitute tube that will work in a socket wired for a 6EU7. The operating characteristics, load impedance, transconductance, maximum ratings, etc. are all identical to a 12AX7; however, the internal inter-electrode capacitances for the the 12AX7 are slightly higher. A 12AX7, though technically a 12.6 volt tube, has a center-tapped filament which means that it can be wired for 6.3 volts humbucking. Almost all 12AX7s in guitar amps are wired this way. The 6EU7 can only be wired 6.3 volts (non-humbucking). Since all vintage amps had an A.C. filament supply, the 12AX7 would have less hum, provided, of course, that it was wired in the standard humbucking fashion.

The Gibson Super Medalist has two C12N Jensen speakers. How do these speakers stack up in relation to other Jensens?
The C12N was a top of the line Jensen 12" speaker. It had a 1½" voice coil and better than twice the gap energy of the C12Q, C12R, C12S, or the C12T. Rumor has it that this was Clapton's favorite speaker. This speaker was in Jensen's "Concert" line as were the "P", "Q", and "R" series speakers.

MARSHALL

I have a Marshall 4X12 cabinet with the 16 ohm speakers wired together to make 16 ohms. Is there more than one way to wire them to get 16 ohms and, if so, which way is better?
Yes, there are two ways that you can wire the four 12" speakers to get 16 ohms. Assuming we are talking about four 16 ohm speakers, you can wire them in parallel/series or series/parallel. Either way will give you the same 16 ohm impedance, but the parallel/series will have clearer and stronger high end because of lower branch inductance. Conversely the series/parallel will have browner highs with stronger lows because of greater branch inductance. To wire parallel/series, simply wire two speakers in parallel; then wire the other two speakers in parallel; then wire one pair in series with the other pair. To wire series/parallel, simply wire two speakers in series; then wire the other two in series; then wire the two pairs in parallel. There is no better way. I recommend that you

try both ways and see which sounds better with your amp/playing style. If your particular amp is too clean or in need of a browner tone, perhaps the series/parallel would be the ticket. If your particular amp and guitar are plenty brown and what you really need is some clarity and definition, then maybe the parallel/series will please your ear.

VOX

I have a well-preserved custom color blue JMI VOX AC30 Combo amp that has been painted black. I tried nail polish remover on a very inconspicuous part of the amp and the black did come off, but it almost took the blue off too. I would like to know what can be used to take off the remainder of the black so I can restore it to the original color?

There are a variety of different paint strippers/removers that could be used to remove the paint without hurting the vinyl. There are also a variety of different paints (lacquer, enamel, acrylic, epoxy, etc.) that could have been used on the vinyl! Therefore, I recommend that you bring the amp to a paint store, tell them what you need, and request that they help you with a patch test to see which product works best with the particular type of paint that is on your amp. As with your fingernail polish remover test, keep the paint remover test in an inconspicuous place.

I have a Vox Berkeley II in new condition which seems totally original. The footswitch has reverb and tremolo and a switch marked "M." Did Vox use a footswitch with a function not pertinent to a control on the amp? Is this function a gimmick? If there's a tonal change by hitting the switch, it's minimal at best, and could be my imagination.

To answer your first question: Yes, Vox did have a midrange boost function with no control on the amp. However it was on the Berkeley III and not on the Berkeley II. You must have a footswitch from the Berkeley III on your Berkeley II. Look on the footswitch connector on the chassis and see if there is a wire on pin 4. If I am correct, there will be no wire on pin 4. The Berkeley III amp has a red wire on pin

Kendricks

4 that goes to an inductor (one Henry). This inductor is part of a "T" filter that grounds out or ungrounds midrange.

I have a Vox AC30 top boost which has a louder than normal hum especially in the Brilliant channel. I find that the hum goes away when I use a ground lift adapter on the A.C. cord. Is the problem in the amp or the A.C. and is it safe to use the ground lift adapter? Also there are two caps that are labeled 561J and 100J, which appear on the schematic as 500 pf and 100 pf respectively. Are these the right values or does the 100J actually mean 10 pf? Could this be part of the problem? Any help would be appreciated.

Hum chasing is a problem that plagues almost everyone. There are dozens of things that could cause hum. If you get less hum with a lifted ground, use a ground lift adapter. Amps were made for decades without a ground to the wall. You might encounter a shock problem with other equipment such as microphones; however, you could always reverse the plug or use a ground fault interrupter if it makes you feel any better. On your caps, the 561J is probably a 560 pf. Usually, but not always, the last digit is a multiplier times ten. Therefore 561 would mean 56 times one ten which equals 560. Using this same code 100J would mean 10 times zero tens which would be 10 pf. However this is not always the case. A different manufacturer might mark a 100 pf as 100J. The 100 pf cap in an AC 30 is in the tremolo circuit, so if the tremolo is doing what it is supposed to, it's probably correct. If you want, you can always take the cap out of the amp and test it with a capacitance checker to satisfy your own curiosity. Those two caps are not part of your hum problem. A capacitor to stop hum would have a much larger value. Check to see if the hum goes away when nothing is plugged into the input. If it does, you might have the hum coming from your guitar or cord.

MISCELLANEOUS

What about triode/pentode switches? Pentode seems to have a lot more high end but the triode is really sweet.

Switching a pentode to a triode is a myth. Even if the screens are connected directly to the plates, you still have a suppressor grid which triodes do not have. The suppressor grid on a 6L6 or a 6V6 is internally connected to the cathode. On an EL34 it is not internally connected; however, if you connected it to the screen and plate to try to make a triode there would be too much secondary emission and you would probably get a runaway tube. At best you would have a tetrode. Also triodes do not have beam forming plates. I know that there are many people connecting the screens to the plates and calling that a triode; it will only work if the plate voltage is low enough to keep from drawing excessive screen current. Also the internal capacitances (especially the grid to plate capacitance) is increased, thus altering the sound. Efficiency would be decreased. If you like the way a tetrode connected pentode sounds, then by all means do it; if you like the way it sounds, then it is correct for you!

Would adding a 3 prong A.C. plug to an older amp help prevent shocks and, if so, how is it wired? Is there a line conditioner that could be used for safety's sake to prevent shocks?
Adding a 3 prong A.C. cord could stop annoying shocks if the receptacle that you are plugging it into is wired correctly. You would simply wire it exactly like the 2 prong except the extra wire would be connected to the amp chassis. This wire is almost always green. As far as a three prong connector eliminating shock hazards, it will only work if the receptacle is wired correctly. A receptacle checker can be bought at almost any electronics supply for $11.00 to $15.00. The line conditioner is designed for voltage regulation, spike protection, RF interference filter, and EM interference filter, but will not help for shock protection.

I would love to build my own amp. Does anyone have a kit available?
At the present time, I know of no one with an actual kit available; however, Dan Torres at Torres Engineering has several mod kits available for Fender, Marshall, Ampeg, Traynor, as well as many other amps. Kits are modestly priced and are available with different skill levels from beginner to advanced. Kits come with diagrams, parts, schematics, and whatever else you would need for a particular mod.

The same problem exists on three amps I own, a 1966 Pro Reverb, a 1965 Bandmaster, and a Teisco Checkmate 50. Once the amps

have been on for a while (i.e., 5 - 10 minutes) they develop massive crackling, popping, and crunching noises somewhat like a dirty pot only much, much louder. The noise is triggered by vibrations such as simply tapping the control panel, thumping the cabinet, or vibrations from playing at moderate volume levels. The volume of this noise is unrelated to volume settings; all controls including the volume can be set to zero and the noise will persist. All the tubes test O.K. Note: all amps are stored in a basement with humidity around 50 to 65%. Also all amps were fine when I purchased them with the problem only occurring 2 to 8 weeks after entering the basement. What do I do?

Get those amps out of the basement. All of those amps have paper insulated transformers that could easily absorb humidity during storage. The crackling you heard (I hope I am wrong) could very easily be arcing in the output transformers. Once a transformer arcs, it can only rarely be saved. I don't want to sound like a parent, but don't ever put a vintage amplifier in a place you wouldn't sleep. Like any other fine instrument, an amplifier is a delicate piece of equipment. I can not diagnose the amp for sure without having it available for inspection, but the cloth wire that is used in the wiring of a vintage amp can also absorb humidity and become conductive. Then it too can arc to the chassis (ground), thus making a crackling sound.

My tech replaces the 1.5K resistors that are on the power tube sockets (pin 1 to pin 5 on most Fender amps) with a 2.2K on both the 6L6 and 6V6 style amps I own. What is the purpose and what effect will this change have on the tone?

The original purpose of this resistor in the first place was to help stabilize the output stage. Certain amps (due to layout and tube spacing) are prone to parasitic oscillation instability problems. By putting a resistor on the grid of the power tube (the resistor must be located directly on the socket for this to work), positive feedback created by electromagnetic radiation is decreased. The actual value of the resistor is determined by the value needed to stabilize the amp. For instance a 100 watt Marshall uses a 5.6K whereas a Vox AC100 uses a 57K. When the resistor value increases, the high end sparkle decreases and the attack softens. Although these resistors were used originally only to stabilize the amp, technicians started noticing the difference in tone and began to develop opinions about which value sounds best. I personally like either no resistor at all or the smallest value that will keep the amp stable.

I would like to get into tube amp repair and mods. Where is a good place to start getting info? My good friend Bart Whitrock with Rockin' Robin Guitars in Houston advised me to get The Tube Amp Book II by Aspen Pittman and buy "wrecked amps" and then get my hands dirty. What would you do? I respect your candor.

Your friend's suggestion to get Mr. Pittman's book is a good idea. Find an older university near your area and obtain a non-student library card. Often in the engineering library, there will be shelves just full of tube technology material. Much of this material will be from the 30s to the 60s. After you have familiarized yourself with basic tube technology, study schematics of your favorite amps and see if you understand the signal path. Another good book, available today in most bookstores, is "Basic Electronics Volume 1", Bureau of Naval Personnel, NAVPERS 10087-C. This book covers test equipment, power supplies, tube audio circuits, and other useful information. It is written so that a beginner can understand the material very easily. You will know when it is time to start looking into amps and getting your hands dirty. Stay away from printed circuit board amps in the beginning, but use hand-wired amps to study because it is easier to see how they are wired. Develop relationships with people that you can call for help if you need it. Of course you can always call me. Good luck!

I recently acquired this amp head that I'm totally unfamiliar with. I'm not sure if the tubes in it are correct. It came with two 8417 output tubes (one blown) and two empty sockets. The 5 amp fuse and fuse cap are gone, so I figured something is wrong with the amp. The only writing on the amp is the company name : Soundtronics, Inc., 5111 W. Chicago Ave., Chicago, Illinois, S/N 0155. Two of the pots date to 1966 and one dates to 1968. Would you know where I could find a schematic for this amp? Also the prongs that hold the tube pins in place on the output tubes appear to be too small for the 8417 or the 6L6 tube. I put a EL34 in and the prongs seem to fit the base pins of it. So now I'm guessing the

8417 is not original and a smaller base tube is. I turned the amp on without any tubes and it did stay on. If I had the correct tubes in place, I believe it would work. Any suggestion?

If you turned the amp on with no tubes in it and it did stay on, the good news is that the power transformer is not shorted. An EL34, 6L6, and 8417 all use the same socket size! I am not familiar with the amp you describe and I have only one suggestion as to where to get a schematic. If the amp does not appear to have been rewired, you could always draw a schematic. This is not as difficult as it may seem if you start out by drawing the tube sockets first and then simply filling in what is connected to each pin on the socket. As far as which tubes go in the output stage, an educated guess might be appropriate. First you must determine if the four sockets that are power tube size are all power tubes, or if two of the tubes are used as output tubes and two are used in the power supply. If the original design used two 8417s, it is possible that the amp used two tube rectifiers! The fuse and fuse cap being gone might suggest that serious problems exist with the amp. Maybe the amp doesn't use any of the tubes you think it uses and someone tried the 8417 and blew it up. One or both could be regulator tubes (not likely, but possible). A 6L6, 6550, 5881, 8417, as well as many other power tubes are possibilities as power tubes in your amp. Pin outs are the same for all of these tubes. The big tip off as to which ones were originally used would be: 1. the way the socket is wired, 2. the screen resistor values, 3. the plate voltage, 4. the output transformer. 8417s could handle up to 660 volts on the plate, meaning a 6L6 would not work if the plate circuit used that high of voltage. The output transformer could be used to guess the possible wattage and thus guess which tubes would have developed that kind of wattage. A 5 amp fuse indicates some serious current which may suggest high wattage output. My suggestion is to send the amp to an experienced tech if you aren't sure of yourself; he could use intelligent guesswork to solve your problem. This is not a problem that can be easily solved by a lay person or an inexperienced tech.

What happened to Jensen, CTS, Utah, Oxford and Altec? Someone said that CTS, Utah, and Oxford became Eminence? Someone else out there would probably find this interesting also.

You are right, a lot of people ask the same question. Although there are employees in speaker manufacturing that move from one company to another, the best of my knowledge is that Jensen, CTS, Oxford, and Altec are all still in business. Jensen has converted all of its manufacturing for the car stereo market. All of these companies except Utah are listed in the Electronic Industry Telephone Directory. One thing I know for sure from having manufactured speakers myself is that the opportunity for big profits in the speaker business is in car stereos and home entertainment and not in guitar amps.

You said a reconed speaker wouldn't sound the same as the original speaker. This makes no sense whatsoever, because it seems to me that if you had a part replaced in a speaker (or anything else for that matter), then that part would be the same as new. Please correct me if I am wrong.

You are right generally speaking. If you could get the exact original parts and reconed the speaker with those parts, then the speaker would more than likely sound the same. However, the context of the conversation was concerning Jensen speakers and those exact parts are no longer available. If you bring a Jensen speaker to a recone shop and ask them to recone it, they do not have cones made by the same company as the original (nor do they have voice coils, voice coil formers, spiders, or dust caps that are original). They will have something that will make the speaker work. The cone may even be made of 3KSP paper like the original. It may even look the same. However one company's 3KSP paper is not like another company's 3KSP paper. The ingredients and recipes may be the same but the finished product is different. Consider this: my grandmother makes the world's best German chocolate cake. If she gave you her recipe and told you what brand of flour, sugar, shortening, leavening, etc., to use, do you think your cake would come out exactly like hers?

I have an early Gibson amp that has a field coil type speaker that really needs replacing. Do I get the thing reconed or is there a good replacement alternative? Also why does this speaker have five leads?

I do not recommend getting a field coil type speaker reconed. The five leads are not all for the speaker! Only two of the leads are going to the field coil itself. The field coil was used in the days before Alnico was used for a speaker magnet. The field coil is actually a big electromagnet that simply replaces the magnet portion of the speaker. Because the coil was expensive to make and because a large coil of wire has considerable inductance, all field coil speakers had the field coil wired to the power supply where the choke would normally go. Advantage was taken of the inductance and the field coil acted as the smoothing choke as well as an electromagnet. The other three leads are actually going to the output transformer. One lead is the center tap of the transformer and the other two leads are the top and bottom of the transformer winding. If the output transformer is good and you would like to change to a conventional magnet speaker, here's what to do. Remove the output transformer from the field coil speaker frame and mount it on the new speaker frame if possible. The three connections that were wired to it before stay wired exactly the same. The two output side wires of the output transformer get wired to the terminals of the new speaker. The other two leads that went to the actual field coil must be connected to a choke. To find the right choke, you must have one with the same inductance as the field coil. This value could be measured with an inductance meter if it is not printed on the speaker. Its value will probably be anywhere from 4 to 15 Henrys. It is also important to use one with the correct current rating. If you don't know the current rating guess high (150 mA?) and then correct the resistance by measuring the D.C. resistance in the field coil and then measuring the D.C. resistance in the choke. If the choke has a higher current rating, the D.C. resistance of the choke will be less than the coil. After you determine how much less, find a resistor of this value (use high wattage rating) and install this resistor in series with the choke. In other words, one of the original field coil wires is now connected to a choke, the other wire from the choke is connected to a high wattage (10 to 20 watt) resistor, whose D.C. resistance added to the D.C. resistance of the choke equals the same D.C. resistance as the field coil, and the other end of this resistor connects to the other lead of the two original field coil leads. As always, don't attempt any of this unless you are certain of what we have been talking about!

I bought a Fuzz Face distortion pedal recently in a hock shop for a very good price. It was sold as is and the price was so reasonable that I just couldn't pass it up. The problem is that it doesn't work. It looks as if it has been modified. What should I do?

I do not have enough information without looking at it to tell you what to do; however, Jeff Bober, at Precision Audio Tailoring, sells a Fuzz Face kit that is exactly like the original except it has no housing. Even the two germanium transistors, circuit board, all parts values, the layout, and the wire color codes are identical to the original. It takes an hour to assemble. Although your unit could be sent to Jeff for repair, it might be more cost-effective to order the kit (it costs $60) and build all new guts. Then, using the kit as a model, you could correct your unit and you would have an extra Fuzz Face left over. Also, you will be able to determine if there are parts missing on your unit by comparing. I own one of his Fuzz Face kits and I really like it a lot.

I've heard of people modifying early 50s Fender Deluxes to the later 50s style circuits by changing the 6SC7 preamp tubes to 12AX7s using step down sockets. What's involved in doing this and is it worth it?

Whether it's worth it is subjective opinion. The 12AX7 will give considerably more gain, having an amplification factor of 100, while the 6SC7 has an amplification factor of 70. No circuit change is necessary, but you will need a 9 pin socket and a washer with the inside hole big enough to mount the 9 pin socket. If you want to try it, here's how you do it:

6SC7		12AX7
pin 2	goes to	pin 1
pin 3	goes to	pin 2
pin 6	goes to	pins 3 and 8
pin 7	goes to	pins 4 and 5
pin 5	goes to	pin 6
pin 4	goes to	pin 7
pin 8	goes to	pin 9

Note: This will only work for the 6SC7 conversion. There is a different pin out for 6SN7s or 6SL7s. The 6SJ7 is a pentode and therefore cannot be replaced with a 12AX7 without circuit modification!!

I have an Ampeg Reverberocket with 6V6 power tubes and 6SL7 and 6SN7 preamp tubes. How can I increase the treble and bass

response? I've tried various capacitors across the volume control and nothing worked.

Small value caps across the volume control are only effective when the volume control is turned down. You are not going to improve bass with a cap across the volume. Those are used only to increase treble or upper midrange (depending on the value.) I would start off by replacing **all** electrolytic capacitors in the amp. Make sure and get the cathode bypass caps on the board as these influence bass response. Having good power supply, electrolytics insure proper voltages which are also needed for good highs and lows. Next, I would change the output tubes to R.C.A. new old stock matched 6V6s because output tubes can make or break your highs and lows. And finally, I would replace the speaker with a Kendrick Blackframe 12". This speaker has plenty of efficiency that results in stunning low end and it also has frequency response with a hump at 8K for crisp and sparkling high end. Your amp may be producing plenty of highs and lows, but if you speaker doesn't reproduce them, you won't get a chance to hear those frequencies. And one other thing, look at your output transformer and check for rust. If it is rusty around the laminates, replace it. Rusty transformers cause an electrical connection between laminates which results in eddy currents. This will zap your power and your low end response, because the energy that should be coming out of the secondary simply goes around and around the laminates instead.

In previous chapters, you referred to the Alnico V speakers. My blackface Bassman has two C12N speakers. How do those compare to the Alnico? Also, would you be a little more specific on the battery test? What type of battery do you use?

Your C12N speakers are the same as the Alnico V P12N except they have ceramic magnets instead of Alnico V magnets. Because they are ceramic, they are probably smoother with less high end harshness. Also they will be about 1 or 2 decibels less efficient. To do the battery test on speakers, I generally use a 9 volt battery, simply because the leads are on both sides and it is more convenient than having to use hook-up wire. If you connect the battery to the speaker leads, the cone of the speaker should move with some enthusiasm. If it doesn't move, or is sluggish in its movement, or it just moves so little that you are wondering if it is really moving or if it is your imagination, then it is time to replace your speaker or get it reconed.

How do you bias preamp tubes and what are your recommended plate voltages? Also what are some ways to increase output tube distortion, other than by increasing plate current?

There is no need to bias preamp tubes. All preamp tubes are class A cathode-bias and are biased with a cathode resistor. Since a preamp tube draws very little current (usually 1 mA) there is almost no variance from different brand preamp tubes placed in the same socket. You could alter the bias of a preamp tube by changing the value of the cathode resistor; however, this is almost never necessary unless you are purposely modifying the gain characteristics. There are a few amp designs that use a diode instead of a resistor, but you will never see that arrangement on a vintage amp.

I do not recommend certain plate voltages without knowing what I am trying to accomplish. Higher voltages will increase headroom and high end as well as gain. Lower voltages will sound browner with somewhat less gain and easier break-up.

To answer your last question, there are only two other ways to increase output tube distortion (other than increasing plate current). One way is to decrease plate voltage. A tube distorts easier at lower voltages. The other way is to increase grid signal. A stronger signal will drive the tube into saturation easier.

My Fenders get kind of muddy at high volume on the low "E". Would changing the output transformers help? What do you recommend?

Your problem could be many things other than your output transformer. Check the laminated core for rust. If it is rusty, you should replace it. I'm talking about the power transformer as well as the output transformer. Low plate voltages could cause muddiness. How's your rectifier tube? Old filter capacitors can cause lower voltages in the power supply thus loosing headroom on low-end performance. Worn out speakers or output tubes could also be your problem.

Is it possible to use the vibrato section of a Fender amp (without reverb) to add reverb or an extra gain stage? Also, I have a blackface Princeton with an 80 mfd capacitor connected from the filter capacitor to ground. Can you tell me what it is for?

Yes, you can add an extra gain stage or reverb to your non-reverb Fender amp! A friend of mine, Dan Torres, sells inexpensive kits complete with all the parts and detailed instructions to do the kind of mods you are seeking. In answer to your second question about the Princeton: The cap you described is definitely not stock. Apparently one section of the multi-section filter capacitor was probably not doing its job, and a service technician probably put the 80 mfd capacitor from one lead to ground, thus bridging the defective section with a good part. Although I would not repair an amp this way, many techs would. I would simply replace the entire multi-section filter cap. The other possibility is that someone was trying to beef up the main power filter by adding extra capacitance. This would improve low end and reduce rectifier sag (envelope) resulting in an overall tighter sound.

I have a very early silverface Pro Reverb amp. The amp sounds great, but the face is oxidized. I see a lot of silverfaces in this condition. What would you recommend?

Unfortunately there is no way to remove the oxidation and keep the lettering. If you really want it to be perfect, call Tom Bremer at Bremer Music and buy a new face. The face is very easy to replace!

What is "B+" voltage? What type of capacitors do I buy to replace my filter capacitors? Must I use a variac to raise voltage slowly on capacitors when changing filter capacitors?

In the early days of tube development, batteries were often used to operate tube equipment. Two or three batteries were needed. The first battery was called the "A" battery and was used to supply filament voltage. This is the part of the tube that lights up and heats the cathode. The second battery, called the "B" battery, was used to provide high voltage on the plates of the tubes. This voltage was always positive. The third battery, called the "C"battery, was used for grid bias supply and was always negative. Some devices were cathode-biased and did not need a "C" battery. When batteries were made obsolete by modern electricity, a transformer with multiple secondaries was made into a multiple power supply. The supply for the filaments was then called the "A" supply. The high voltage plate supply, since it was always a positive supply, became known as "B+"

voltage. The bias voltage supply, since it is always negative, became known as the "C-minus" voltage.

Use aluminum electrolytic capacitors for filter capacitor replacement. When filter capacitors are brand new, there is no dielectric present. Therefore, subjecting them to high voltages as found in a guitar amp circuit could puncture them electrically. The dielectric is actually formed by an electro-chemical process when the initial D.C. voltage is first placed across the capacitor. Bringing an amp up slowly on a variac (also called an autotransformer) is the best way to charge newly replaced capacitors; however, if you don't have access to a variac, a current limiter can be made with a fairly low wattage (75 watt) light bulb placed in series with the amp A.C. line cord and this is the next best thing.

I have done extensive testing and experimenting on charging capacitors and they will sound noticeably better when initially charged slowly, just like your car battery will perform better when charged slowly. I like to charge my capacitors for 12 hours in the amp and with the amp on a variac set for 40 volts, and then bring the variac up 10 volts per hour for the next 8 hours.

Variacs are usually fairly expensive; however, the best deal going is a 10 amp, zero to 130 volts with a built in ammeter for under $100 from MCM Electronics. The part number to order is #72-110. The phone number is in the back of this book in the chapter "Dealers and Sources."

You showed how to date Jensen speakers. What about other manufacturers? What are other manufacturer's codes?

The dating of speakers was standardized by the Electronics Industries Association. The first three digits are the E.I.A. source code, the next digit is the year of manufacture (you will have to guess the decade because a 6 could mean either 56 or 66), and the next two digits are what week of the year it was produced. I am printing a chart of the E.I.A. Manufacturing Code Numbers for reference.

E.I.A. SOURCES CODES NUMERICAL LIST

The Electronic Industries Association has assigned code numbers to most manufacturers of speakers. The first digits stamped on the speaker may indicate the E.I.A. Source Code. For example: 465741. The first three digits are the E.I.A. Source Code number and indicate that the speaker is an Oxford type speaker.

Code	Manufacturer	Code	Manufacturer
24	Becker	371	Best
67	Eminence	391	Altec-Lansing
101	Admiral	394	Foster Transformer
119	Automatic Mfg.	416	Heath
125	Bendix	433	Cleveland
130	Matsushita	449	Wilder
130	Panasonic	465	Oxford
132	Talk-a-Phone	466	Delco
137	C.T.S.	549	Midwest
145	Cinaudagraph	575	Heppner
145	Consolidated	589	Bogen
150	Crescent	649	Electro-Voice
169	Hitachi	706	Pioneer
185	Motorola	719	Carbonneau
188	General Electric	742	Esquire
220	Jensen/Viking	748	Russell
232	Magnavox	756	Universal
245	National	767	Quincy
252	Dukane	787	Sonatone
252	Operadio	789	McGregor
260	Philco	794	Harman Kardon
270	Quam-Nichols	795	Atlas
274	RCA	828	Midland
277	Emerson	840	Ampex
277	Radio Speaker	847	University
280	Raytheon	918	Oaktron
285	Rola	1056	Fisher
286	Ross	1056	Gefco
296	Solar	1059	Channel
308	Stromberg-Carlson	1098	Pyle
312	Sylvania	1113	Acoustic Fiber Sound
328	Utah	1149	Curtis Mathes
336	Western Electric	1191	Micro Magnet
343	Zenith		

GLOSSARY

HENRY-*noun*-A unit of measure of inductance.

MILLIAMETER-*noun*-A device used for measuring current of less than an amp. Most multimeters are also milliammeters.

PF-*noun*-Abbreviation for picofarad.

SMOOTHING CHOKE-*noun*-An inductor that is made from a single coil of wire around a metal core. This component is actually part of the power supply and it smoothes out the ripple current that occurs when A.C. is converted to D.C.

SCHEMATICS

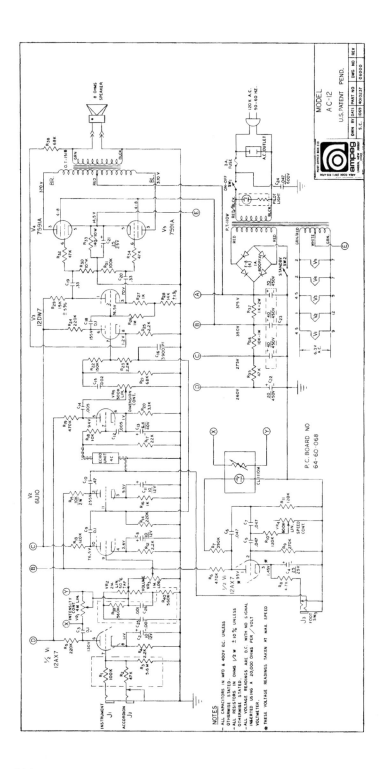

4/69   67

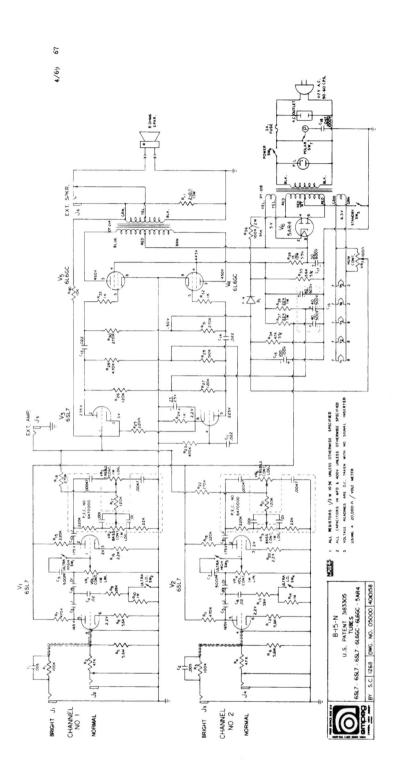

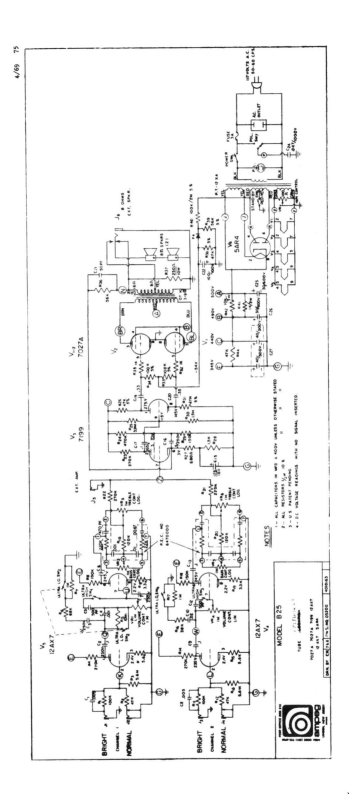

Kendricks

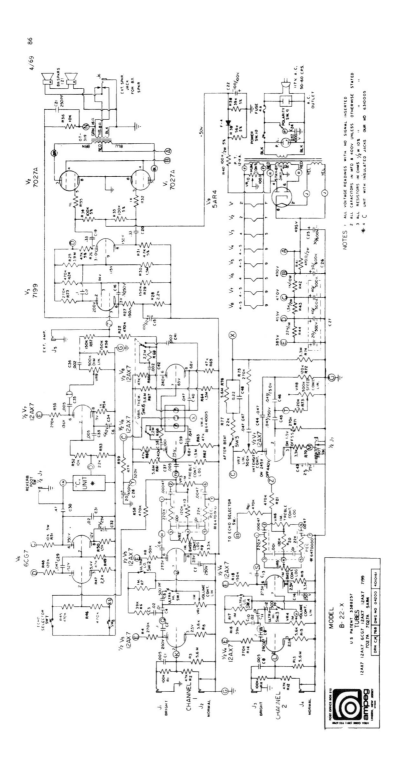

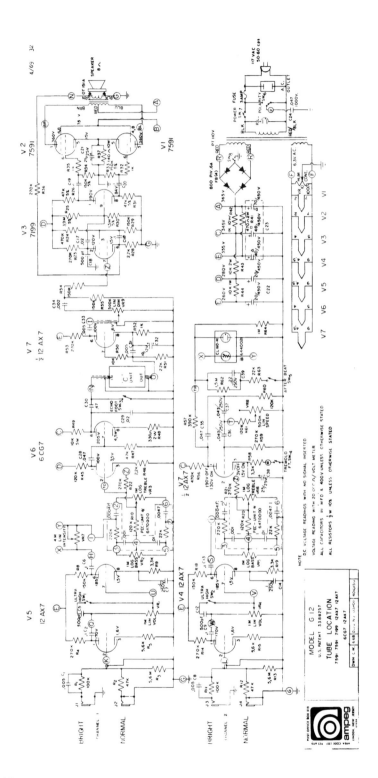

Kendricks

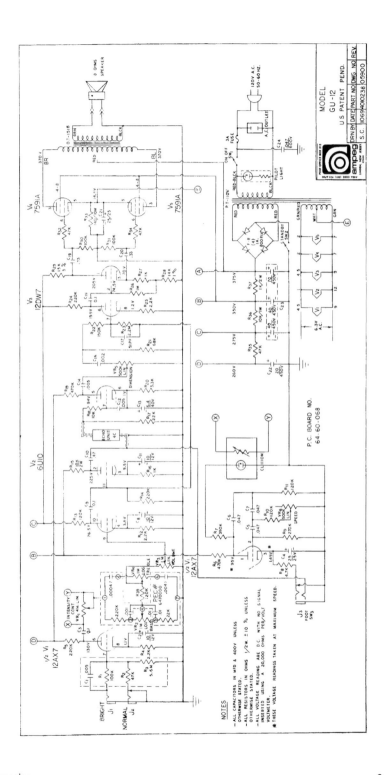

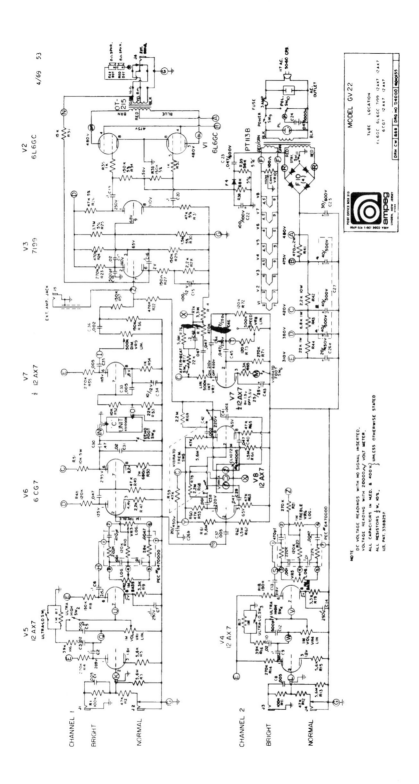

MODEL GV 22

Kendricks

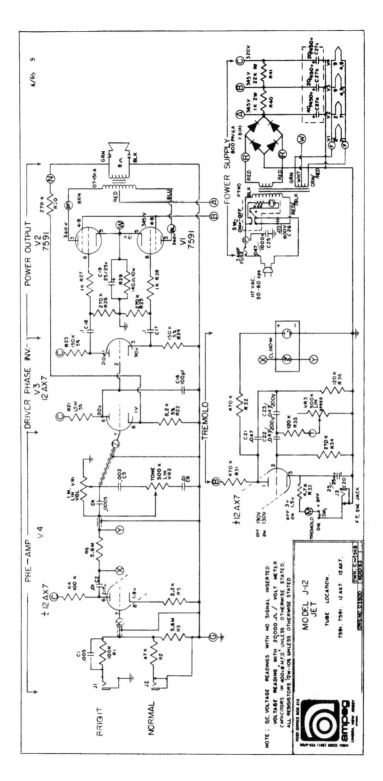

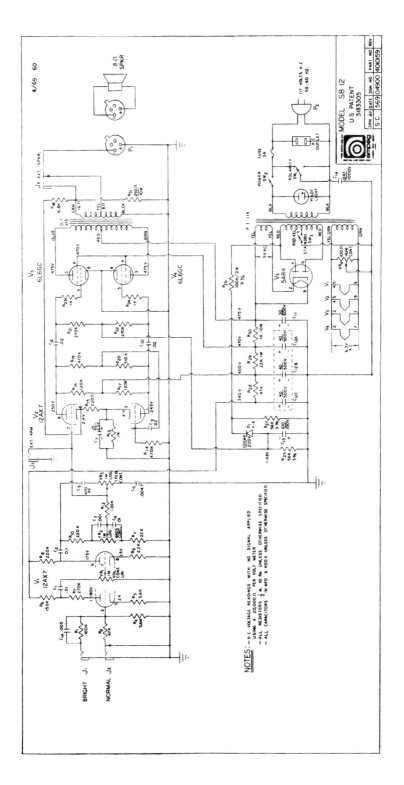

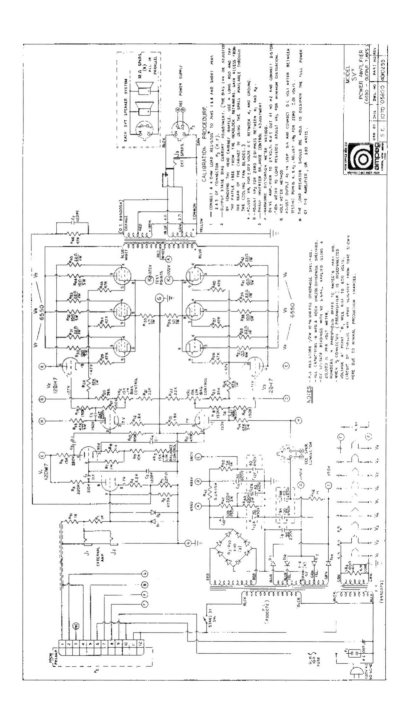

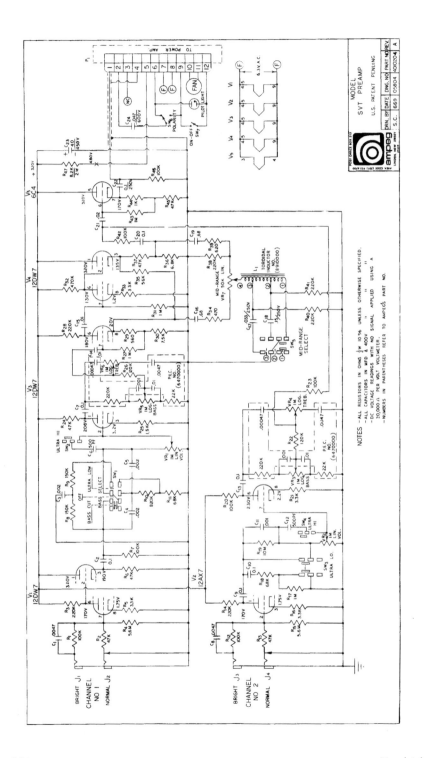

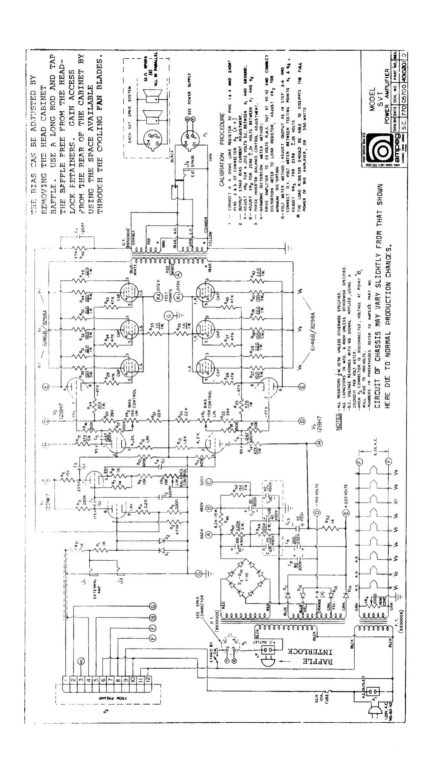

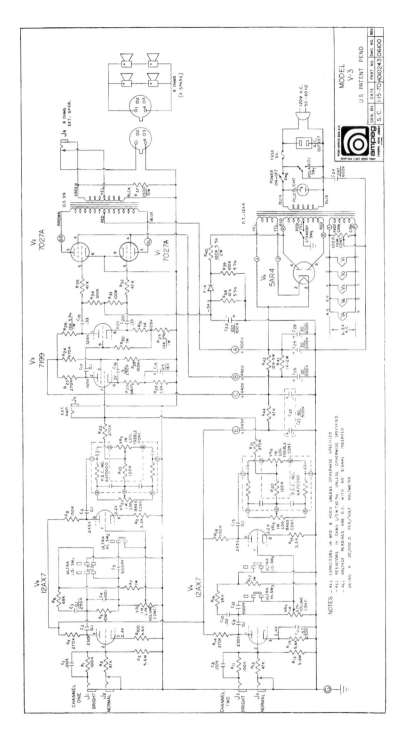

Kendricks

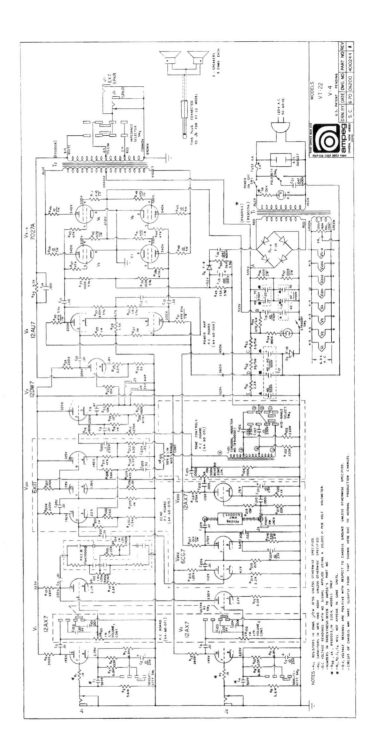

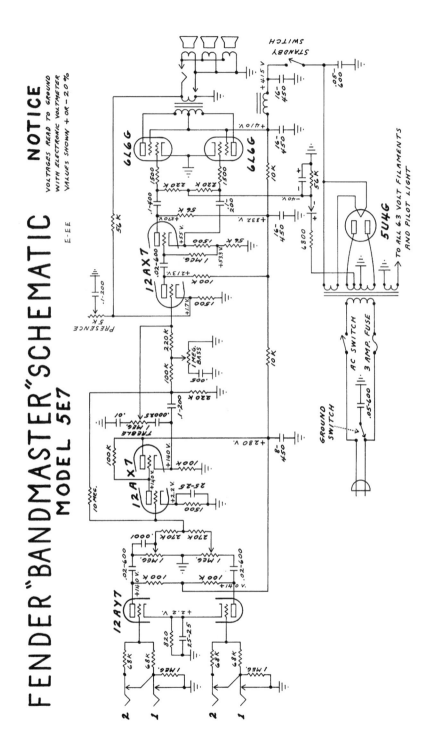

FENDER "BANDMASTER" SCHEMATIC
MODEL 5E7

E-EE

NOTICE

VOLTAGES READ TO GROUND
WITH ELECTRONIC VOLTMETER
VALUES SHOWN + OR − 20%

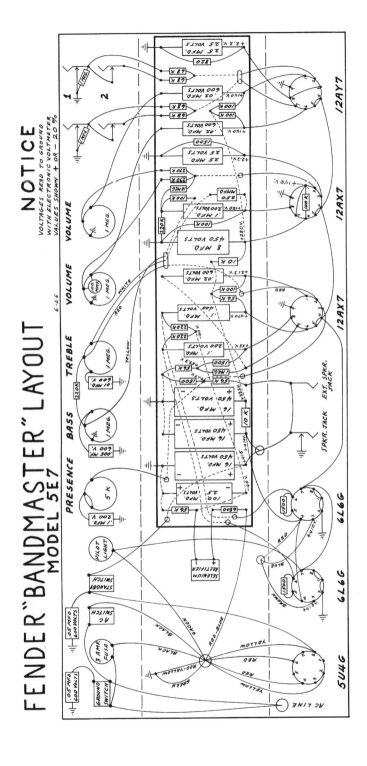

FENDER "BANDMASTER" LAYOUT
MODEL 5E7

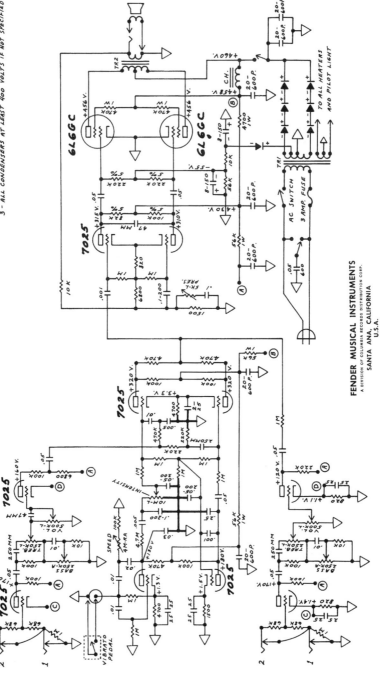

FENDER "BANDMASTER" SCHEMATIC
MODEL 6G7
A-F-J

FENDER MUSICAL INSTRUMENTS
A DIVISION OF COLUMBIA RECORDS DISTRIBUTION CORP.
SANTA ANA, CALIFORNIA
U.S.A.

NOTICE

1 - VOLTAGES READ TO GROUND WITH ELECTRONIC VOLTMETER. VALUES SHOWN + OR -

2 - ALL RESISTORS ½ WATT IF NOT SPECIFIED

3 - ALL CONDENSERS AT LEAST 400 VOLTS IF NOT SPECIFIED

FENDER "BANDMASTER" LAYOUT
MODEL 6G7
A-F-J

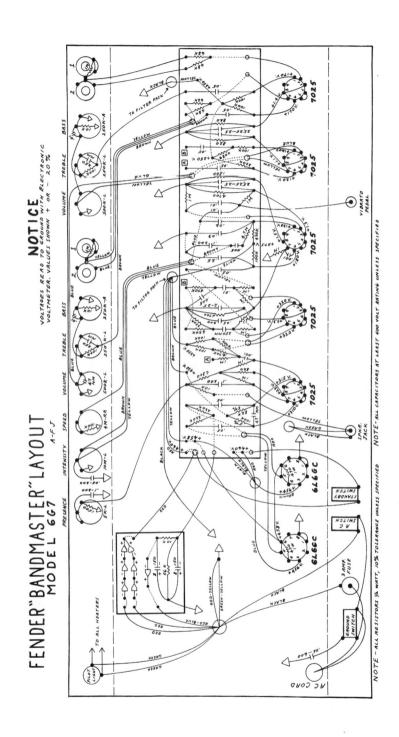

FENDER MUSICAL INSTRUMENTS
A DIVISION OF COLUMBIA RECORDS DISTRIBUTION CORP.
SANTA ANA, CALIFORNIA
U.S.A.

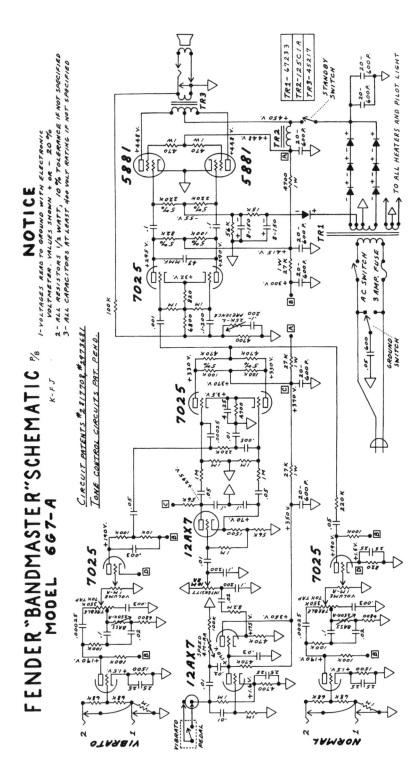

FENDER "BANDMASTER" SCHEMATIC P/B
MODEL 6G7-A
K-F-J

CIRCUIT PATENTS #2817708 #2776348L

TONE CONTROL CIRCUITS PAT. PEND.

NOTICE
1 — VOLTAGES READ TO GROUND WITH ELECTRONIC VOLTMETER. VALUES SHOWN + OR - 20%
2 — ALL RESISTORS 1/2 WATT, 10% TOLERANCE IF NOT SPECIFIED
3 — ALL CAPACITORS AT LEAST 400 VOLT RATING IF NOT SPECIFIED

TR1	67233
TR2	125C1A
TR3	45217

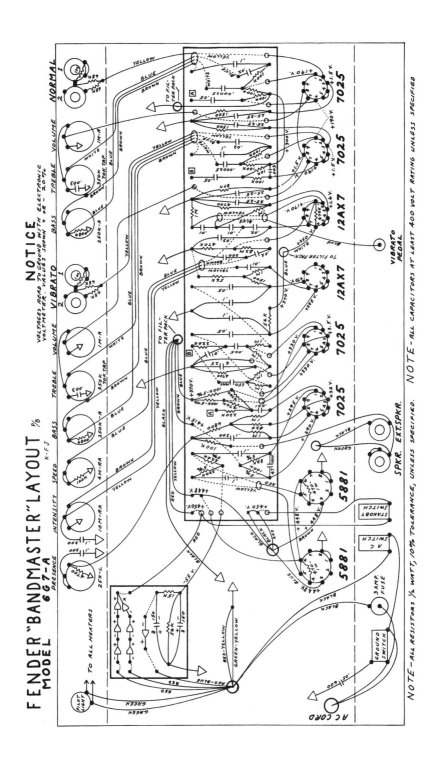

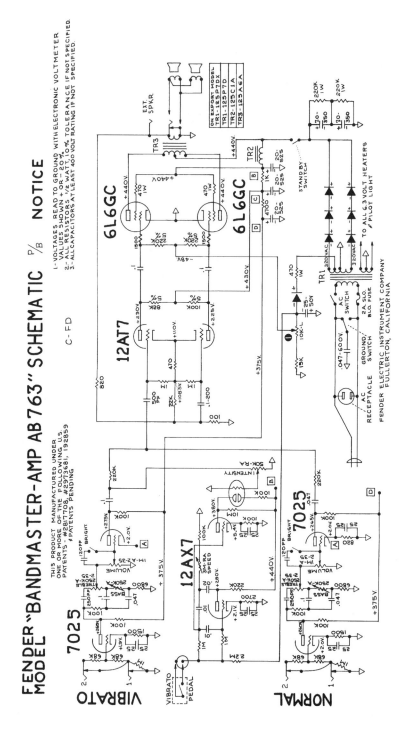

FENDER "BANDMASTER-AMP AB763" SCHEMATIC P/B NOTICE
MODEL

NOTICE

1- VOLTAGES READ TO GROUND WITH ELECTRONIC VOLTMETER
   VALUES SHOWN +OR-20%.
2- ALL RESISTORS ½ WATT, 10% TOLERANCE IF NOT SPECIFIED.
3- ALL CAPACITORS AT LEAST 400 VOLT RATING IF NOT SPECIFIED.

ON EXPORT MODEL
TR1-125P7DX
TR1-125P7D
TR2-125CIA
TR3-125A6A

C-FD

THIS PRODUCT MANUFACTURED UNDER
ONE OR MORE OF THE FOLLOWING U.S.
PATENTS- #2817708, #2971368I, 192859
#PATENTS PENDING

FENDER ELECTRIC INSTRUMENT COMPANY
FULLERTON, CALIFORNIA

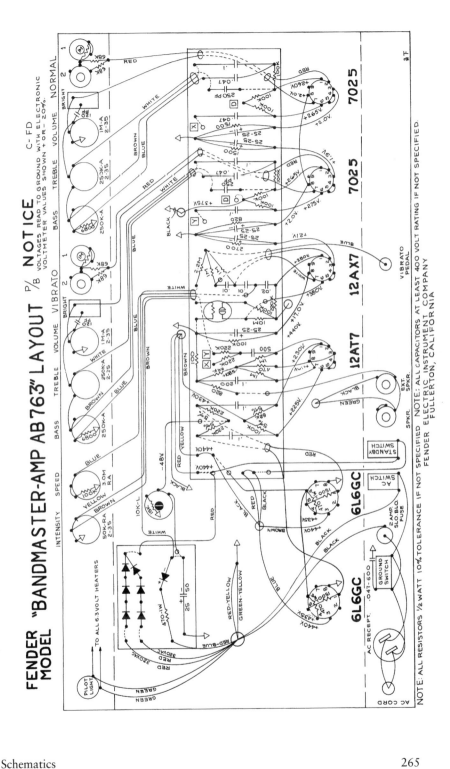

Schematics

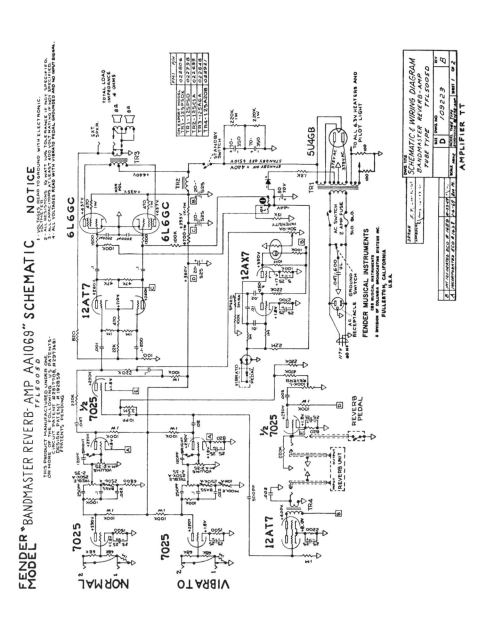

FENDER "BANDMASTER REVERB-AMP AA1069" SCHEMATIC
MODEL *TFL5005D*

Kendricks

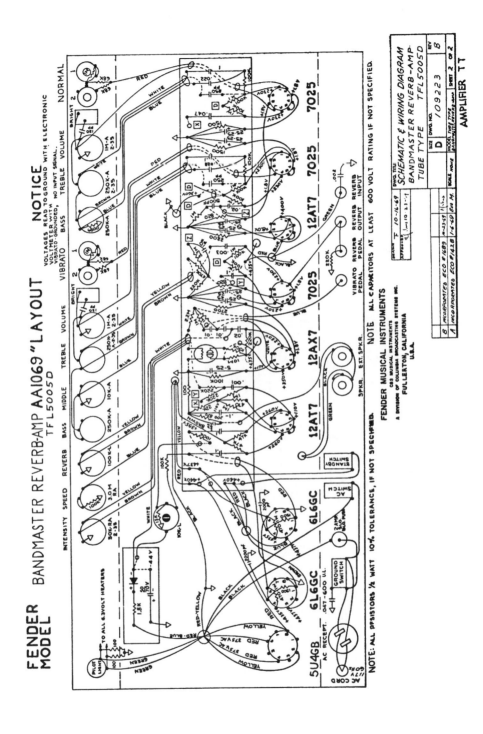

BASSMAN SCHEMATIC
5B6 ?

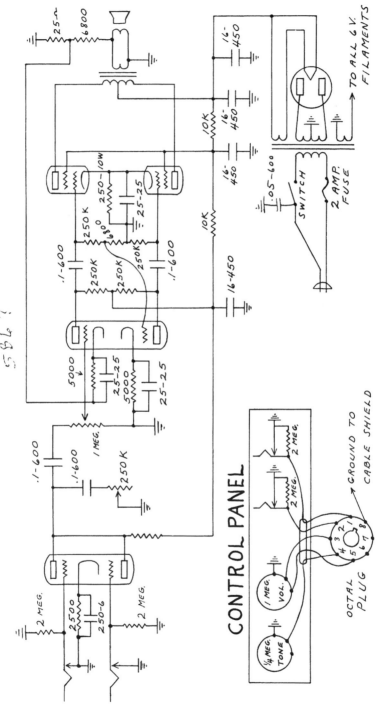

CONTROL PANEL

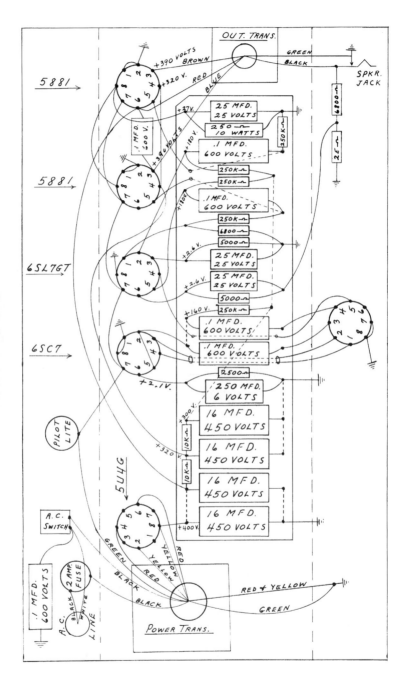

FENDER "BASSMAN" AMPLIFIER PARTS LAYOUT

FENDER "BASSMAN" SCHEMATIC

MODEL 6G6

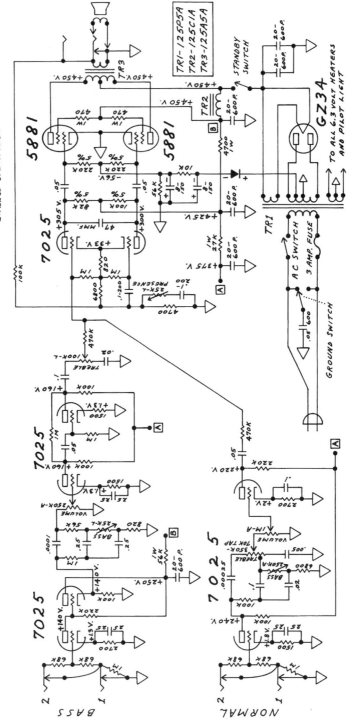

Kendricks

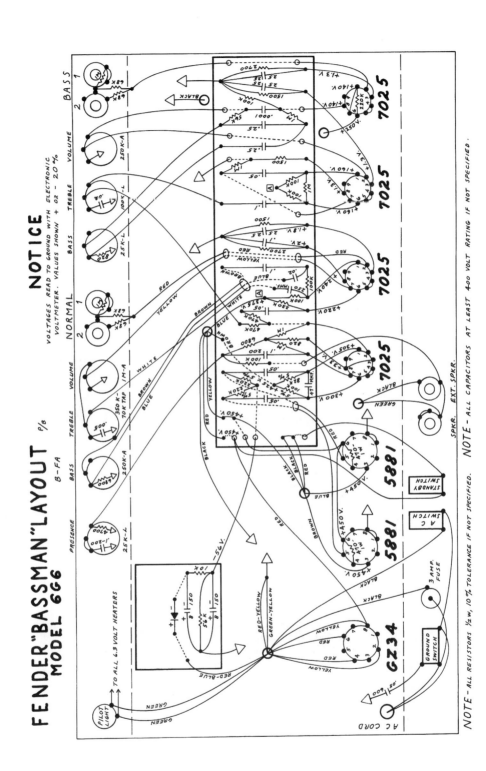

FENDER "BASSMAN" LAYOUT ⁶/₈
MODEL 6G6

B-FA

NOTICE

VOLTAGES READ TO GROUND WITH ELECTRONIC
VOLTMETER. VALUES SHOWN + OR - 20%

NOTE - ALL RESISTORS ½W, 10% TOLERANCE IF NOT SPECIFIED.   NOTE - ALL CAPACITORS AT LEAST 400 VOLT RATING IF NOT SPECIFIED.

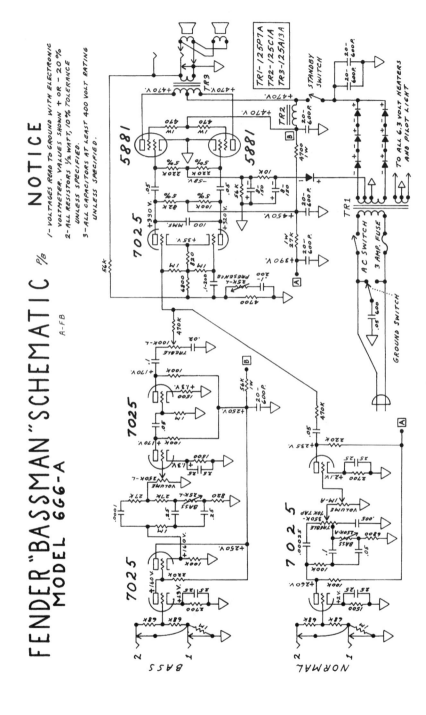

FENDER "BASSMAN" SCHEMATIC
MODEL 6G6-A

A-FB

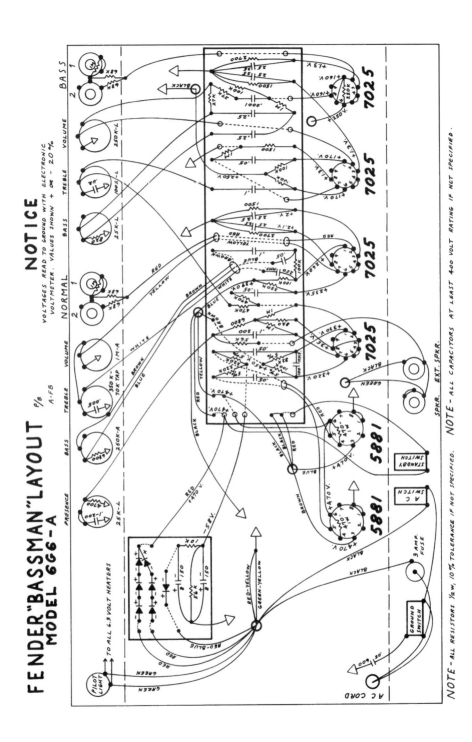

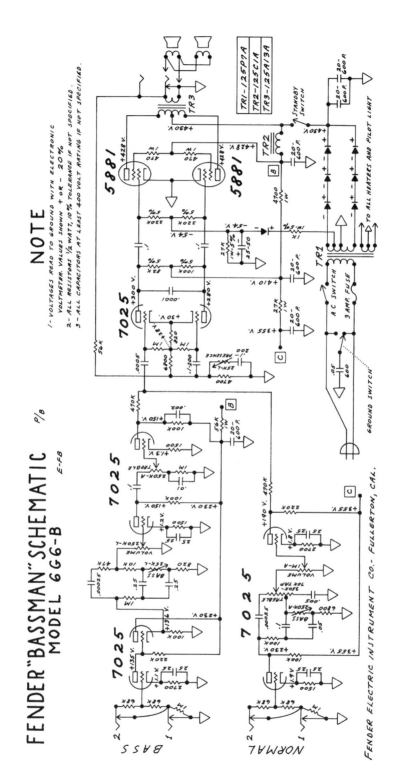

FENDER "BASSMAN" SCHEMATIC
MODEL 6G6-B

NOTE

1 - VOLTAGES READ TO GROUND WITH ELECTRONIC VOLTMETER. VALUES SHOWN + OR - 20%
2 - ALL RESISTORS 1/2 WATT, 10% TOLERANCE IF NOT SPECIFIED.
3 - ALL CAPACITORS AT LEAST 400 VOLT RATING IF NOT SPECIFIED.

FENDER ELECTRIC INSTRUMENT CO.- FULLERTON, CAL.

Kendricks

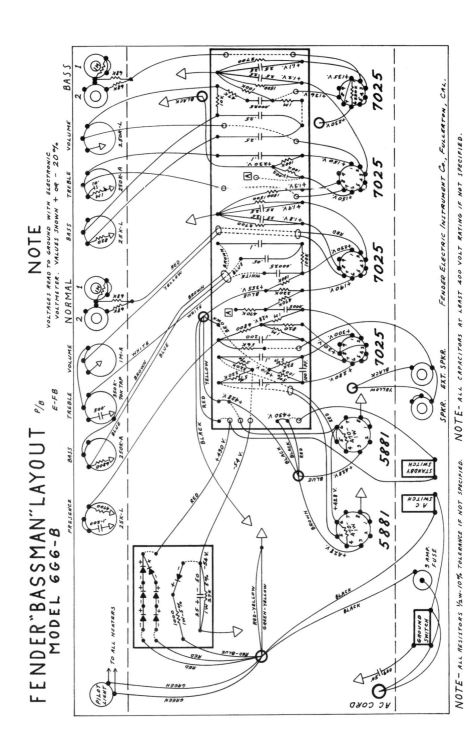

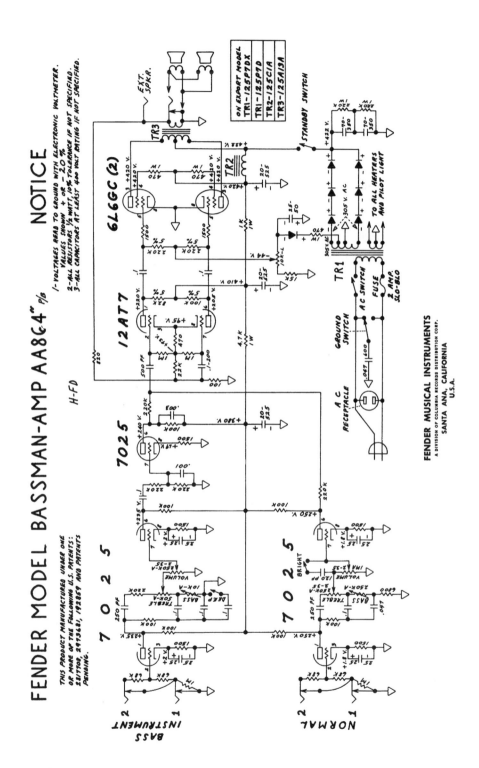

FENDER MODEL BASSMAN-AMP AA864" P/B

H-F-D

NOTICE

1—VOLTAGES READ TO GROUND WITH ELECTRONIC VOLTMETER. VALUES SHOWN +OR – 20%
2—ALL RESISTORS ½ WATT, 10% TOLERANCE IF NOT SPECIFIED.
3—ALL CAPACITORS AT LEAST 400 VOLT RATING IF NOT SPECIFIED.

THIS PRODUCT MANUFACTURED UNDER ONE OR MORE OF THE FOLLOWING U.S. PATENTS: 2617784, 2947061, 1932869 AND PATENTS PENDING.

ON EXPORT MODEL
TR1-125P7DX
TR1-125P7D
TR2-125C1A
TR3-125A13A

FENDER MUSICAL INSTRUMENTS
A DIVISION OF COLUMBIA RECORDS DISTRIBUTION CORP.
SANTA ANA, CALIFORNIA
U.S.A.

276

Kendricks

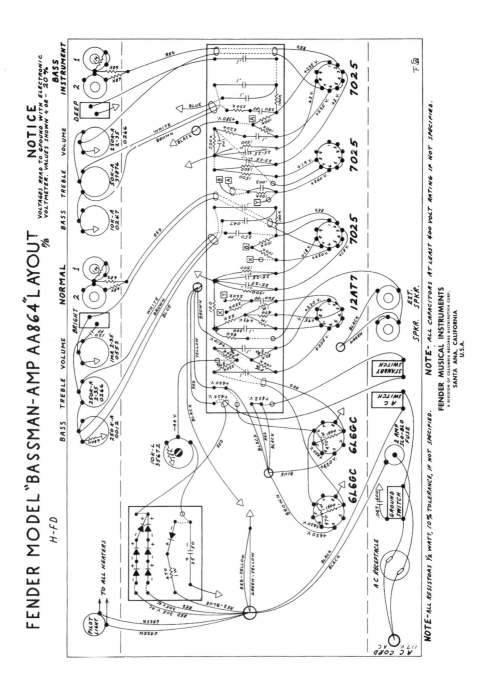

FENDER MODEL "BASSMAN-AMP AA864" LAYOUT

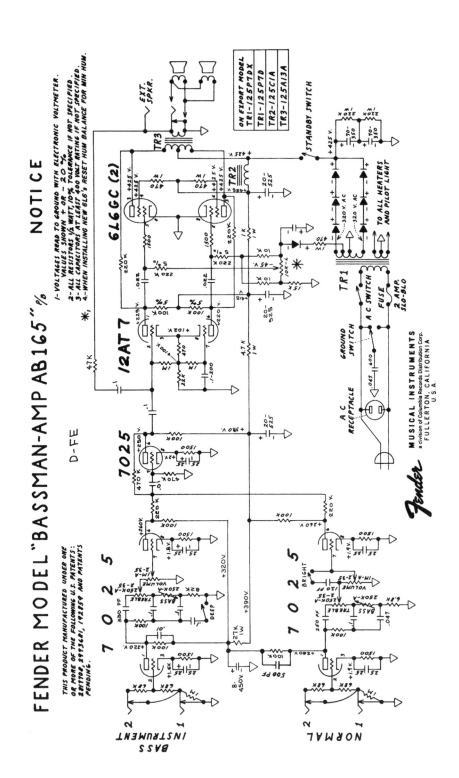

FENDER MODEL "BASSMAN-AMP AB165"

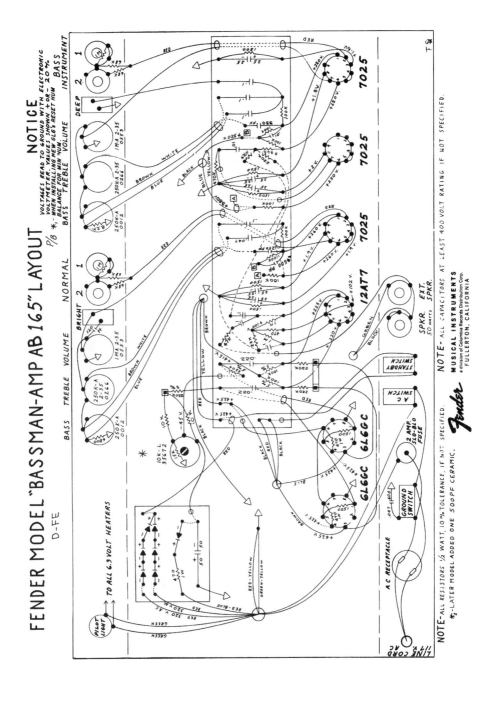

FENDER MODEL "BASSMAN-AMP AB 165" LAYOUT

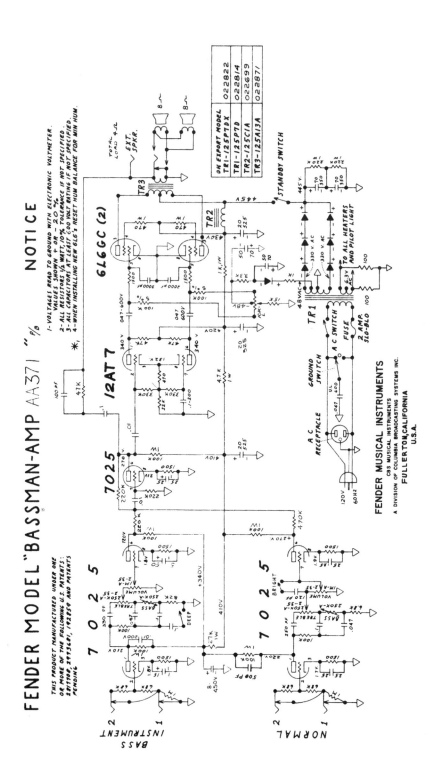

FENDER MODEL "BASSMAN-AMP" AA371 "%" NOTICE

Kendricks

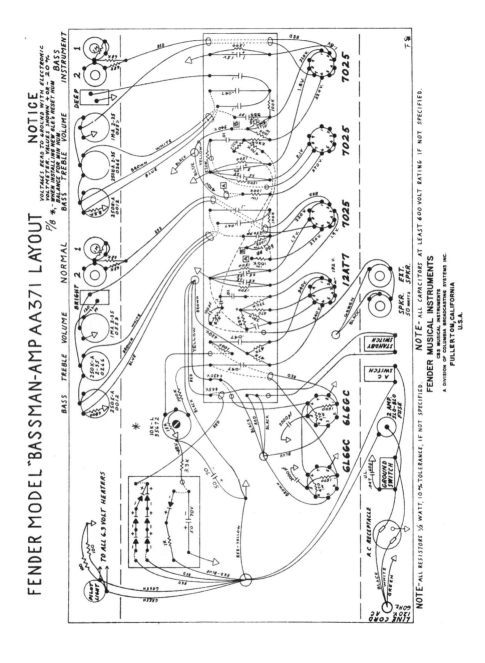

FENDER MODEL "BASSMAN-AMP AA371 LAYOUT"

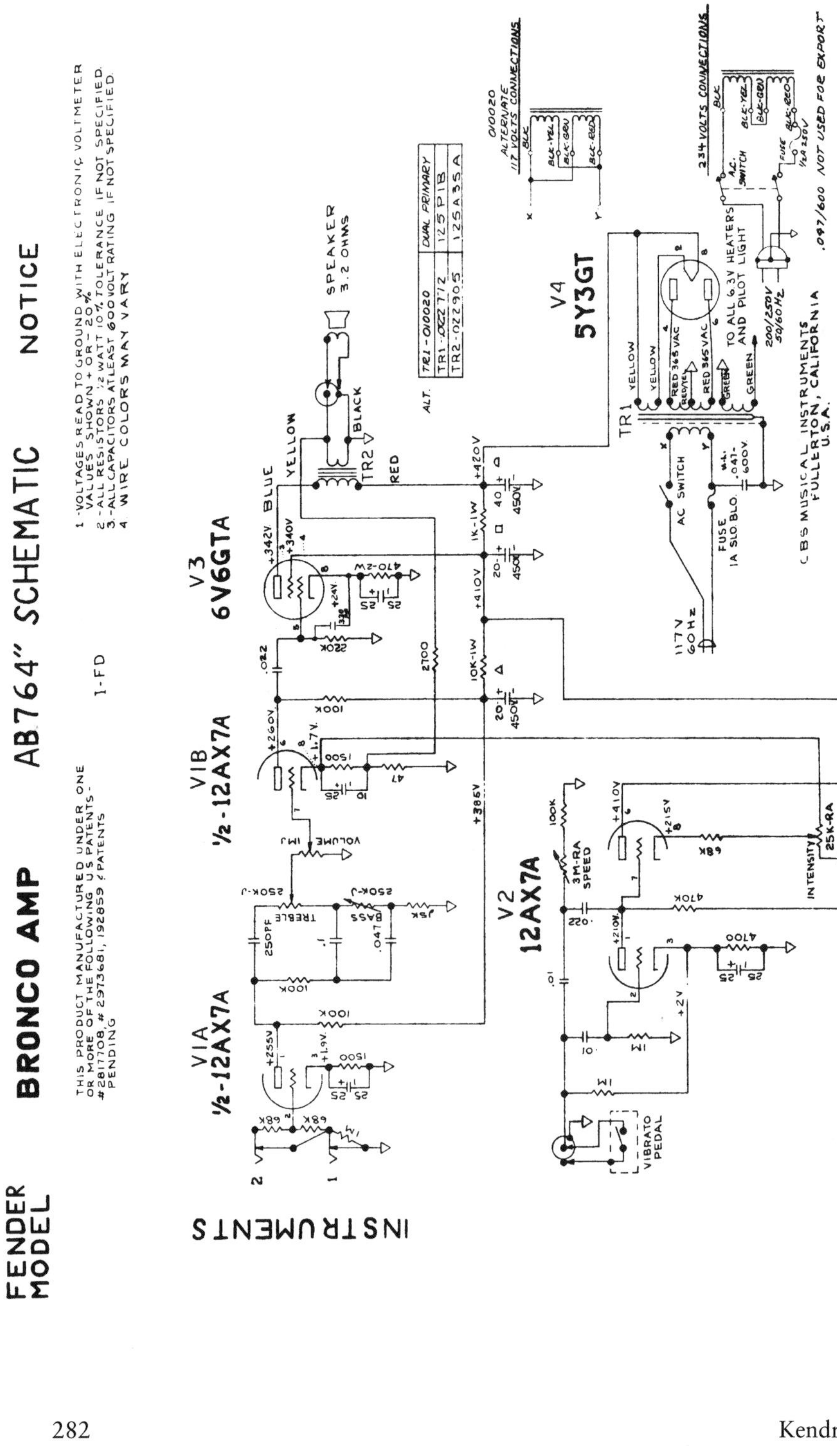

FENDER MODEL
BRONCO AMP
AB764" SCHEMATIC
NOTICE
1-FD
THIS PRODUCT MANUFACTURED UNDER ONE OR MORE OF THE FOLLOWING U.S. PATENTS - #2817708, #2973681, 192859 & PATENTS PENDING
1 - VOLTAGES READ TO GROUND WITH ELECTRONIC VOLTMETER VALUES SHOWN + OR - 20%
2 - ALL RESISTORS 1/2 WATT 10% TOLERANCE IF NOT SPECIFIED.
3 - ALL CAPACITORS AT LEAST 600 VOLT RATING IF NOT SPECIFIED.
4 WIRE COLORS MAY VARY
INSTRUMENTS
V1A ½-12AX7A
V1B ½-12AX7A
V3 6V6GTA
V2 12AX7A
V4 5Y3GT
SPEAKER 3.2 OHMS
VIBRATO PEDAL
117V 60 Hz
CBS MUSICAL INSTRUMENTS FULLERTON, CALIFORNIA U.S.A.
.097/600 NOT USED FOR EXPORT
234 VOLTS CONNECTIONS
010020 ALTERNATE 117 VOLTS CONNECTIONS

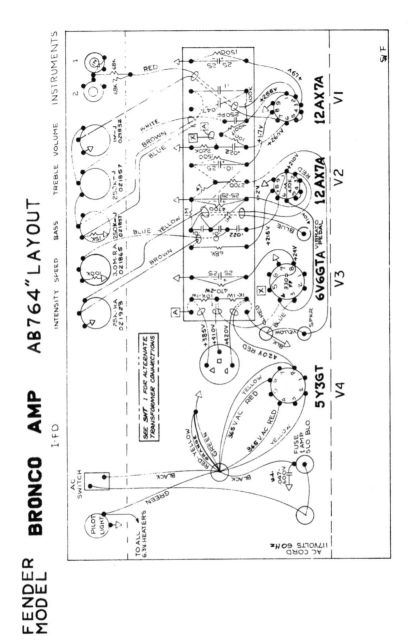

FENDER **BRONCO AMP** AB764" LAYOUT
MODEL I-FD

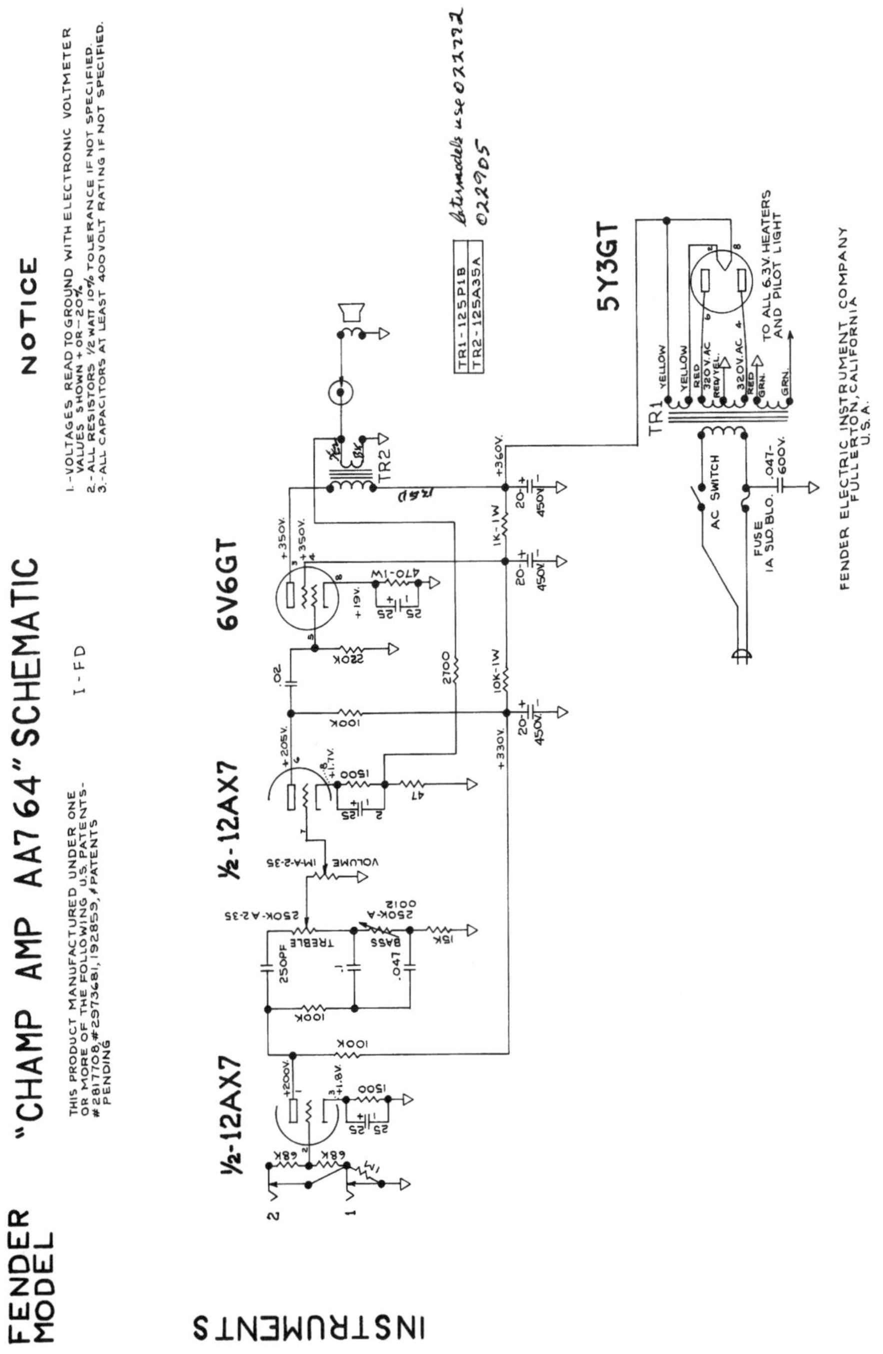

FENDER
MODEL "CHAMP AMP AA7 64" SCHEMATIC

I - F D

NOTICE

1.- VOLTAGES READ TO GROUND WITH ELECTRONIC VOLTMETER
    VALUES SHOWN + OR - 20%.
2.- ALL RESISTORS 1/2 WATT 10% TOLERANCE IF NOT SPECIFIED.
3.- ALL CAPACITORS AT LEAST 400 VOLT RATING IF NOT SPECIFIED.

THIS PRODUCT MANUFACTURED UNDER ONE
OR MORE OF THE FOLLOWING U.S. PATENTS-
#2811708, #2973681, 192853, PATENTS
PENDING

TR1-125P1B
TR2-125A35A

later models use 022772

022905

5Y3GT

6V6GT

1/2 - 12AX7

1/2 - 12AX7

TR1
    YELLOW
    YELLOW
    RED
    320V. AC
    RED
    320V. AC
    GRN.
    GRN.

TO ALL 6.3V. HEATERS
AND PILOT LIGHT

AC SWITCH

FUSE
1A SLO BLO.

.047-
600V.

FENDER ELECTRIC INSTRUMENT COMPANY
FULLERTON, CALIFORNIA
U.S.A.

INSTRUMENTS

284   Kendricks

FENDER MODEL "CHAMP-AMP AA764" LAYOUT

FENDER ELECTRIC INSTRUMENT COMPANY
FULLERTON, CALIFORNIA
U.S.A.

NOTICE

1. VOLTAGES READ TO GROUND WITH ELECTRONIC VOLTMETER
2. ALL RESISTORS 1/2 WATT 10% TOLERANCE IF NOT SPECIFIED.
3. ALL CAPACITORS AT LEAST 400 VOLT RATING IF NOT SPECIFIED.

VALUES SHOWN +OR– 20%

NOTE ALL RESISTORS 1/2 WATT 10% TOLERANCE, IF NOT SPECIFIED. NOTE ALL CAPACITORS AT LEAST 400 VOLT RATING IF NOT SPECIFIED.

12AX7   6V6GT   5Y3GT

FENDER MODEL "VIBRO-CHAMP AMP AA764" SCHEMATIC NOTICE

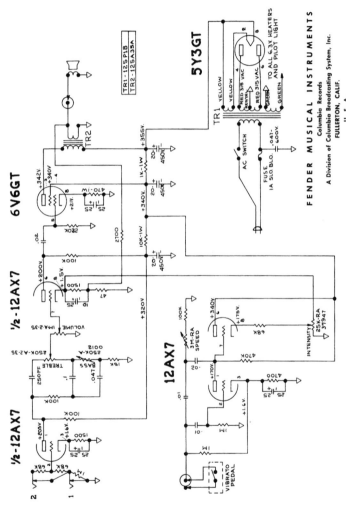

1 - FD

THIS PRODUCT IS MANUFACTURED UNDER
THE FOLLOWING U.S. PATENT: DES. 192859

1 - VOLTAGES READ TO GROUND WITH ELECTRONIC VOLTMETER.
    VALUES SHOWN + OR - 20%
2 - ALL RESISTORS ½ WATT 10% TOLERANCE IF NOT SPECIFIED.
3 - ALL CAPACITORS ATLEAST 400 VOLT RATING IF NOT SPECIFIED.

TR1 - 125P1B
TR2 - 125A35A

5Y3GT

FENDER MUSICAL INSTRUMENTS
Columbia Records
A Division of Columbia Broadcasting System, Inc.
FULLERTON, CALIF.
U. S. A.

045401

INSTRUMENTS

Kendricks

FENDER "VIBRO-CHAMP-AMP AA764" LAYOUT
MODEL

NOTICE

1- VOLTAGES READ TO GROUND WITH ELECTRONIC VOLTMETER. VALUES SHOWN +OR- 20%.
2- ALL RESISTORS ½ WATT 10% TOLERANCE IF NOT SPECIFIED.
3- ALL CAPACITORS AT LEAST 400 VOLT RATING IF NOT SPECIFIED.

FENDER MUSICAL INSTRUMENTS

Columbia Records
A Division of Columbia Broadcasting System, Inc.
FULLERTON, CALIF.
U. S. A.

NOTE- ALL RESISTORS ½ WATT 10% TOLERANCE, IF NOT SPECIFIED   NOTE- ALL CAPACITORS AT LEAST 400 VOLT RATING IF NOT SPECIFIED.

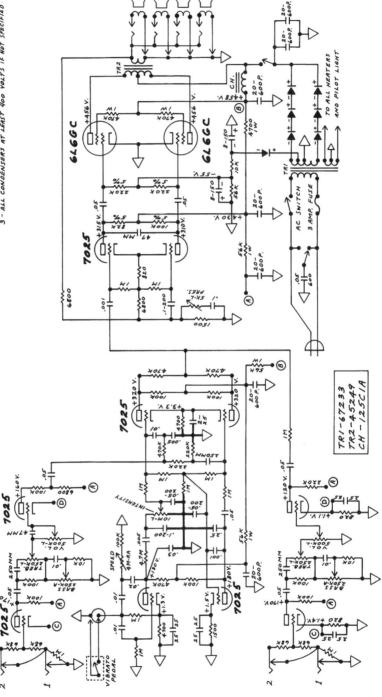

FENDER "CONCERT" SCHEMATIC
MODEL 6G12
A-FJ

NOTICE

1 - VOLTAGES READ TO GROUND WITH ELECTRONIC VOLTMETER. VALUES SHOWN + OR −

2 - ALL RESISTORS ½ WATT IF NOT SPECIFIED

3 - ALL CONDENSERS AT LEAST 400 VOLTS IF NOT SPECIFIED

TR1-67233
TR2-45249
CH-125C1A

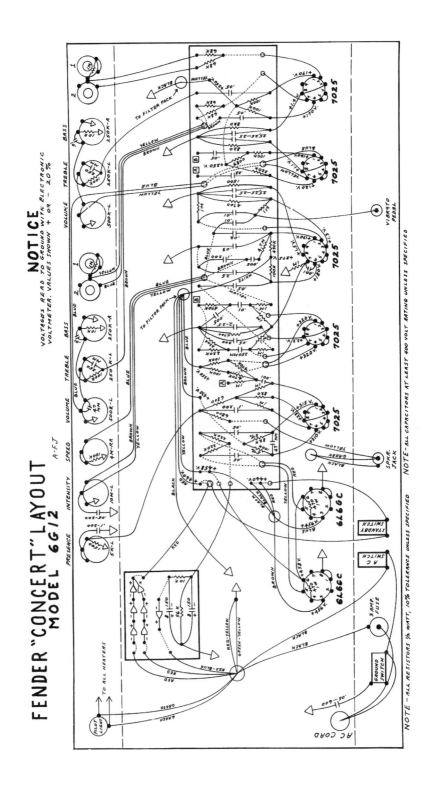

FENDER "CONCERT" LAYOUT
MODEL 6G12   A-FJ

NOTICE
VOLTAGES READ TO GROUND WITH ELECTRONIC
VOLTMETER. VALUES SHOWN + OR − 20%

NOTE − ALL RESISTORS ½ WATT, 10% TOLERANCE UNLESS SPECIFIED

NOTE − ALL CAPACITORS AT LEAST 400 VOLT RATING UNLESS SPECIFIED

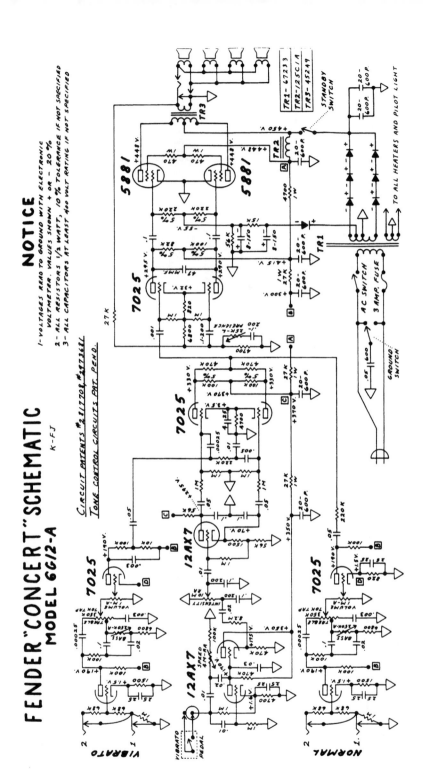

FENDER "CONCERT" SCHEMATIC
MODEL 6G12-A

K-FJ

CIRCUIT PATENTS #2817170 & #2773388L
TONE CONTROL CIRCUITS PAT. PEND.

NOTICE

1 - VOLTAGES READ TO GROUND WITH ELECTRONIC
     VOLTMETER. VALUES SHOWN + OR - 20%
2 - ALL RESISTORS 1/2 WATT, 10% TOLERANCE IF NOT SPECIFIED
3 - ALL CAPACITORS AT LEAST 400 VOLT RATING IF NOT SPECIFIED

TR1 - 67233
TR2 - 125C1A
TR3 - 45249

STANDBY SWITCH

TO ALL HEATERS AND PILOT LIGHT

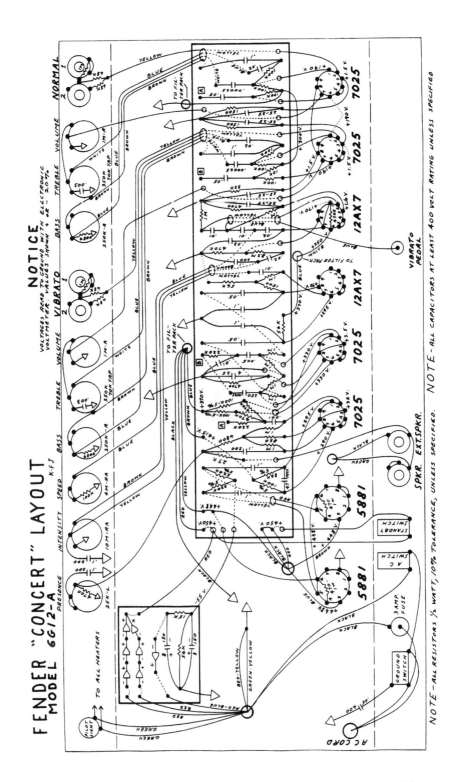

FENDER "CONCERT" LAYOUT
MODEL 6G12-A

NOTICE

VOLTAGES READ TO GROUND WITH ELECTRONIC VOLTMETER. VALUES SHOWN + OR - 20%.

NOTE - ALL RESISTORS ½ WATT, 10% TOLERANCE, UNLESS SPECIFIED.

NOTE - ALL CAPACITORS AT LEAST 400 VOLT RATING UNLESS SPECIFIED.

FENDER DELUXE"SCHEMATIC
MODEL 6G3
I-FA

NOTICE

1 - VOLTAGES READ TO GROUND WITH ELECTRONIC VOLTMETER. VALUES SHOWN + OR - 20%
2 - ALL RESISTORS ½ WATT, 10% TOLERANCE, IF NOT SPECIFIED
3 - ALL CAPACITORS AT LEAST 400 VOLT RATING, IF NOT SPECIFIED

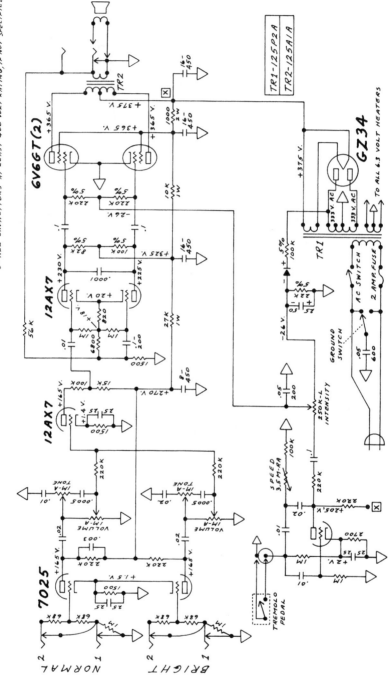

292   Kendricks

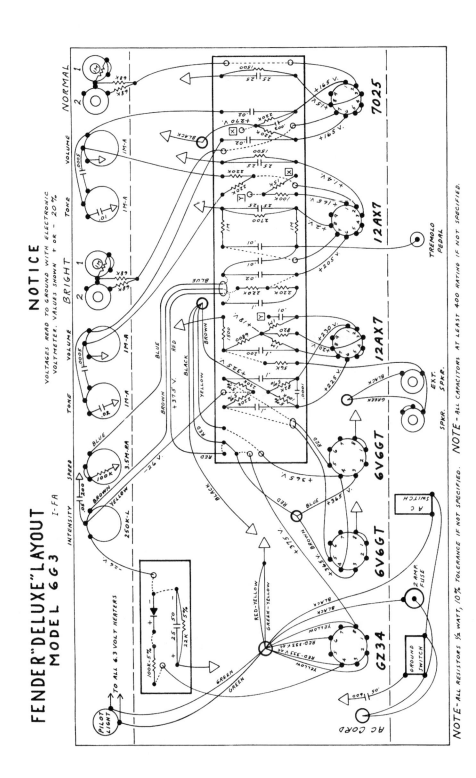

FENDER "DELUXE" LAYOUT
MODEL 6G3
I-FA

NOTICE

VOLTAGES READ TO GROUND WITH ELECTRONIC
VOLTMETER. VALUES SHOWN + OR - 20%

NOTE - ALL RESISTORS ½ WATT, 10% TOLERANCE IF NOT SPECIFIED.   NOTE - ALL CAPACITORS AT LEAST 400 RATING IF NOT SPECIFIED.

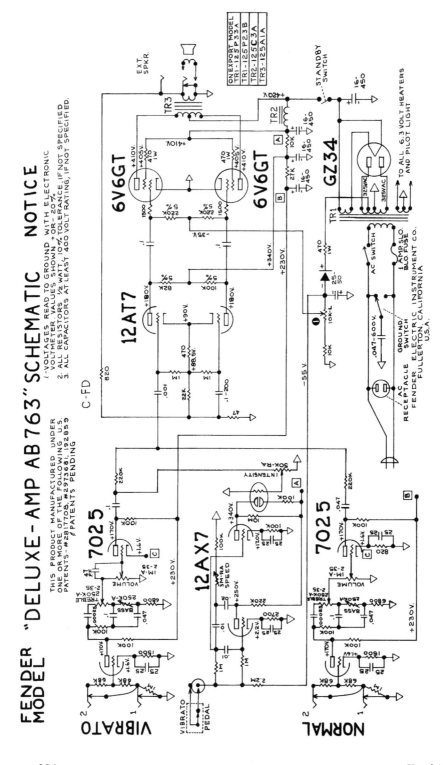

FENDER MODEL "DELUXE-AMP AB763" SCHEMATIC NOTICE

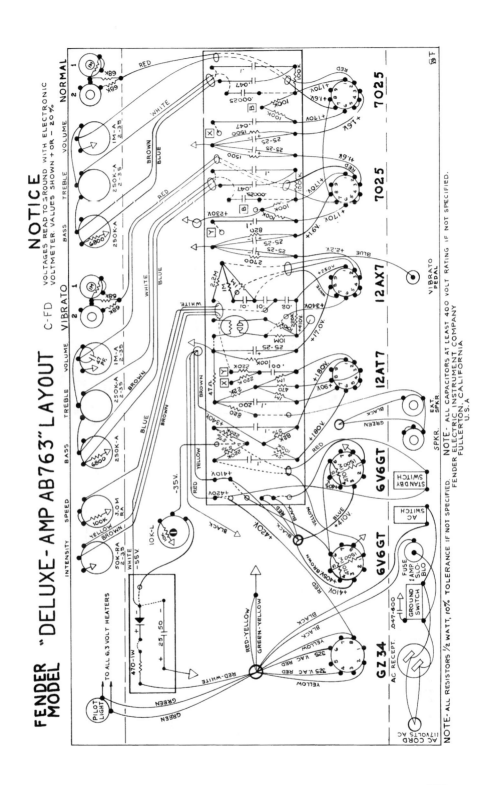

FENDER MODEL "DELUXE-AMP AB763" LAYOUT

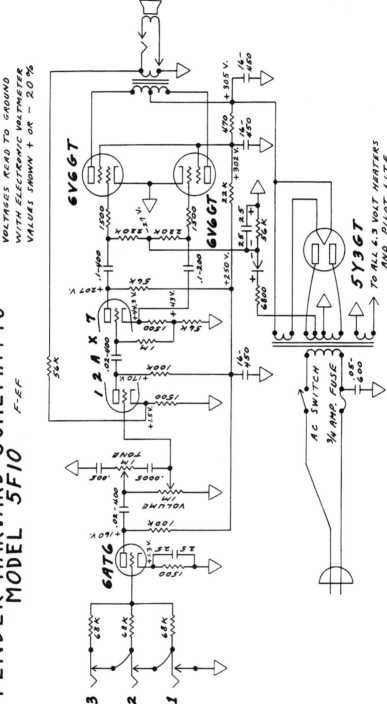

FENDER "HARVARD" SCHEMATIC
MODEL 5F10 F-EF

NOTICE

VOLTAGES READ TO GROUND
WITH ELECTRONIC VOLTMETER
VALUES SHOWN + OR − 20 %

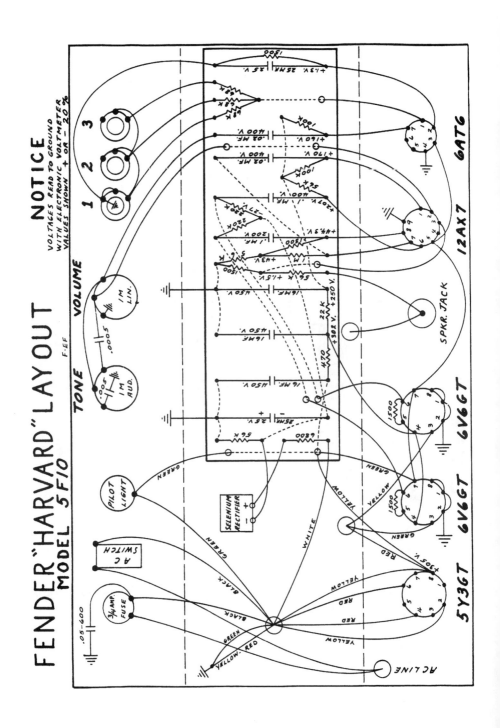

FENDER "HARVARD" LAYOUT
MODEL 5F10

NOTICE

VOLTAGES READ TO GROUND
WITH ELECTRONIC VOLTMETER
VALUES SHOWN + OR - 20%

FENDER PRINCETON AMP

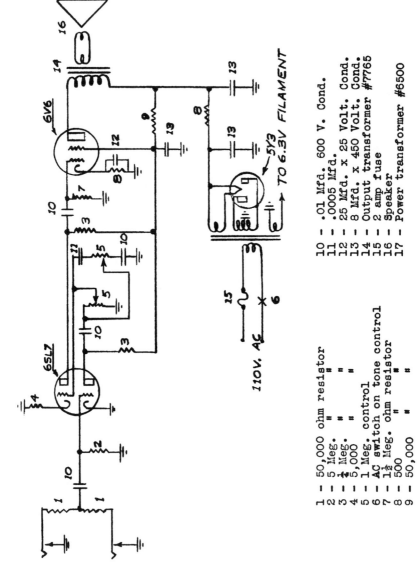

1 — 50,000 ohm resistor
2 — 5 Meg.   "   "
3 — 1 Meg.   "   "
4 — 5,000   "   "
5 — 1 Meg. control
6 — AC switch on tone control
7 — 1½ Meg. ohm resistor
8 — 500   "   "
9 — 50,000   "   "

10 — .01 Mfd. 600 V. Cond.
11 — .0005 Mfd.
12 — 25 Mfd. x 25 Volt. Cond.
13 — 8 Mfd. x 450 Volt. Cond.
14 — Output transformer #7765
15 — 2 amp fuse
16 — Speaker
17 — Power transformer #6500

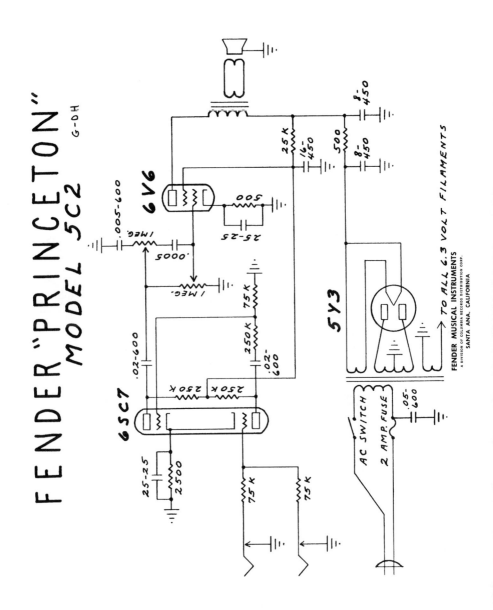

FENDER "PRINCETON"
MODEL 5C2
G-DH

6V6

.005-600

1MEG.

.0005

500

25-25

25 K

16-450

500

8-450

8-450

1 MEG.

6SC7

.02-600

250K

250K

75 K

250 K

.02-600

25-25

2500

75 K

75 K

5Y3

AC SWITCH

2 AMP. FUSE

.05-600

TO ALL 6.3 VOLT FILAMENTS

FENDER MUSICAL INSTRUMENTS
A DIVISION OF COLUMBIA RECORDS DISTRIBUTION CORP.
SANTA ANA, CALIFORNIA

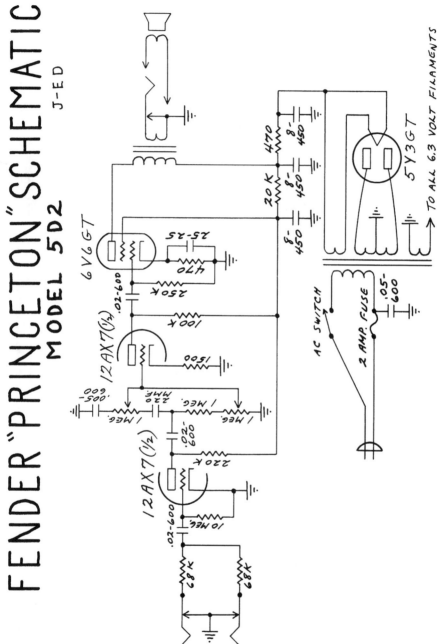

FENDER "PRINCETON" SCHEMATIC
MODEL 5D2
J-ED

Kendricks

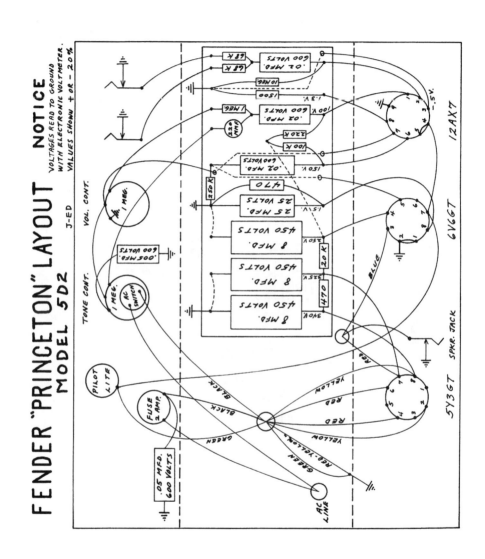

FENDER "PRINCETON" LAYOUT
MODEL 5D2

J-ED

NOTICE
VOLTAGES READ TO GROUND
WITH ELECTRONIC VOLTMETER.
VALUES SHOWN + OR − 20%

FENDER "PRINCETON" SCHEMATIC
MODEL 5E2

E-EE

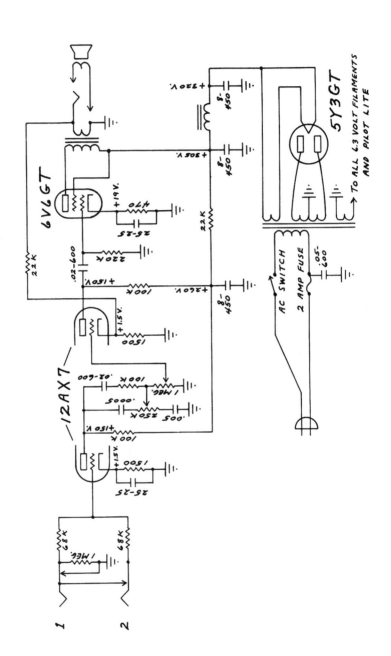

Kendricks

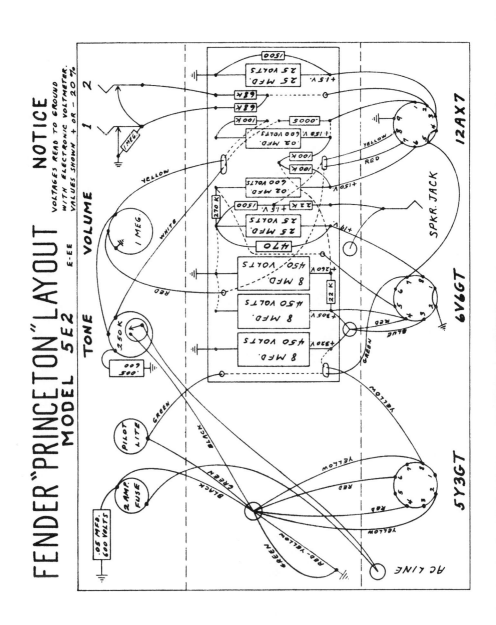

FENDER "PRINCETON" LAYOUT
MODEL 5E2

NOTICE

VOLTAGES READ TO GROUND
WITH ELECTRONIC VOLTMETER.
VALUES SHOWN + OR - 20%

E-EE

FENDER "PRINCETON" SCHEMATIC
MODEL 5F2

A-EF

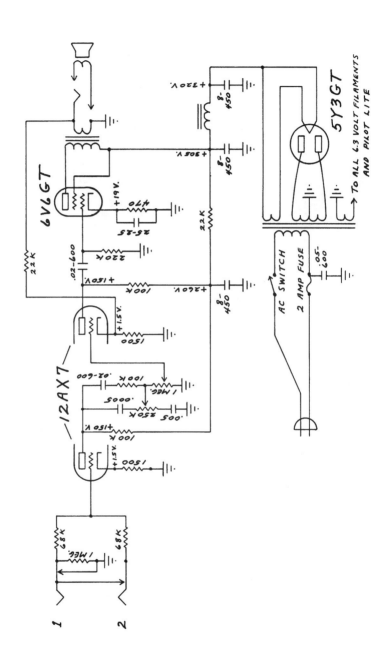

Kendricks

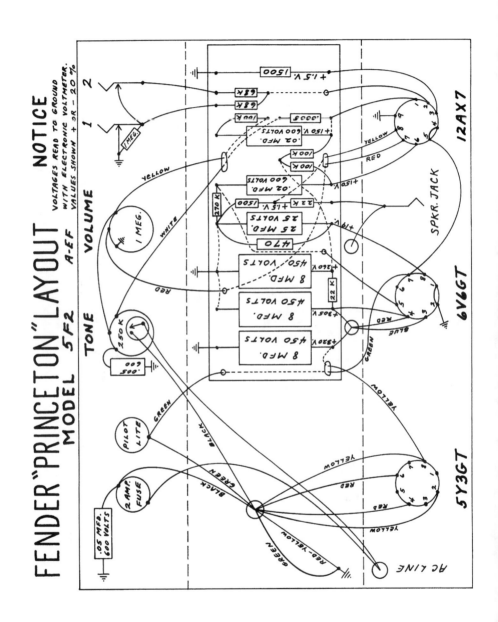

FENDER "PRINCETON" LAYOUT
MODEL 5F2   A-EF

NOTICE

VOLTAGES READ TO GROUND
WITH ELECTRONIC VOLTMETER.
VALUES SHOWN + OR - 20 %

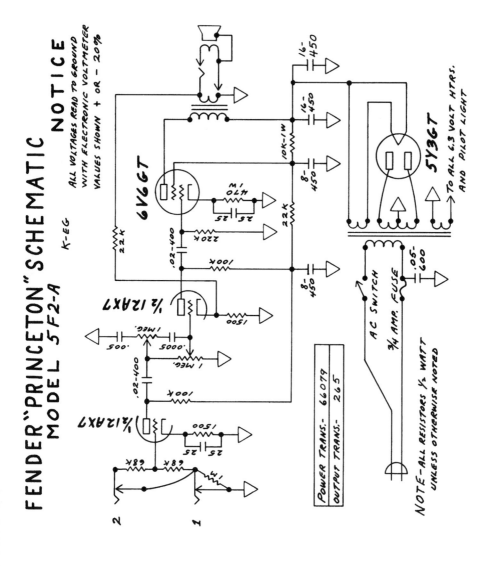

FENDER "PRINCETON" SCHEMATIC
MODEL 5F2-A

K-EG

NOTICE

ALL VOLTAGES READ TO GROUND
WITH ELECTRONIC VOLTMETER
VALUES SHOWN + OR − 20%

6V6GT

5Y3GT

→ TO ALL 6.3 VOLT HTRS.
AND PILOT LIGHT.

½ 12AX7

½ 12AX7

AC SWITCH

¾ AMP. FUSE

| POWER TRANS.- | 66079 |
| OUTPUT TRANS.- | 265 |

NOTE − ALL RESISTORS ½ WATT
UNLESS OTHERWISE NOTED

16-450
16-450
8-450
8-450
10K-1W
22K
22K
220K
100K
100K
1 MEG.
1 MEG.
.05-600
.02-400
.02-400
.5000
.500
.25
.25
.25
.25
1500
1500
470 1W
68K
68K
1M

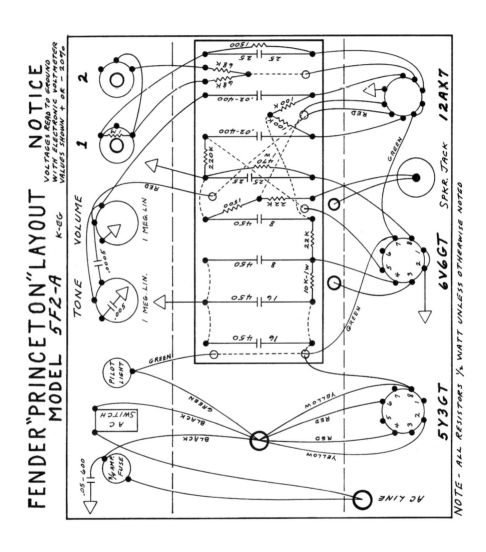

FENDER "PRINCETON" LAYOUT

MODEL 5F2-A   K-EG

NOTICE

VOLTAGES READ TO GROUND
WITH ELECTRONIC VOLTMETER
VALUES SHOWN + OR – 20%

NOTE – ALL RESISTORS ½ WATT UNLESS OTHERWISE NOTED

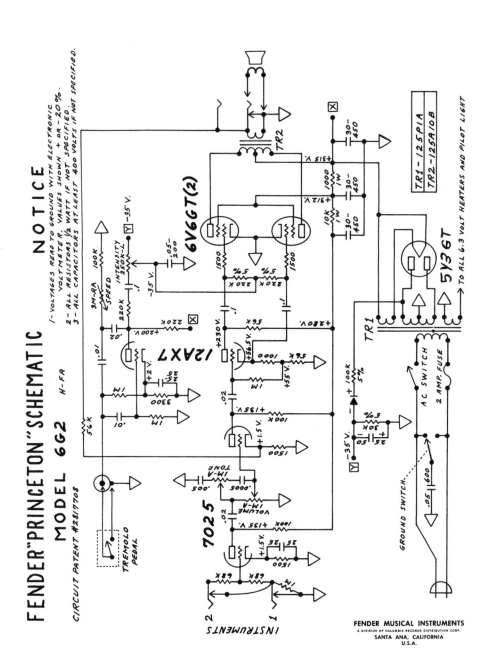

FENDER "PRINCETON" SCHEMATIC
MODEL 6G2   H-FR

NOTICE

1 - VOLTAGES READ TO GROUND WITH ELECTRONIC
VOLTMETER. VALUES SHOWN + OR -20%.
2 - ALL RESISTORS ½ WATT IF NOT SPECIFIED.
3 - ALL CAPACITORS AT LEAST 400 VOLTS IF NOT SPECIFIED.

CIRCUIT PATENT #2817708

TR1 - 125P1A
TR2 - 125A10B

FENDER MUSICAL INSTRUMENTS
A DIVISION OF COLUMBIA RECORDS DISTRIBUTION CORP.
SANTA ANA, CALIFORNIA
U.S.A.

Kendricks

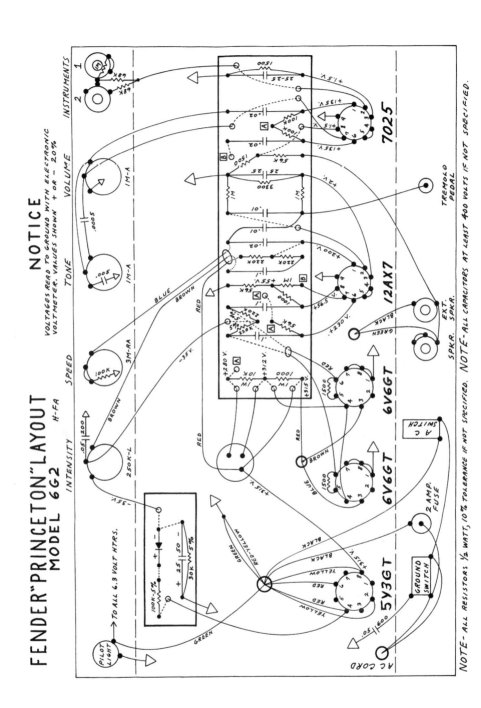

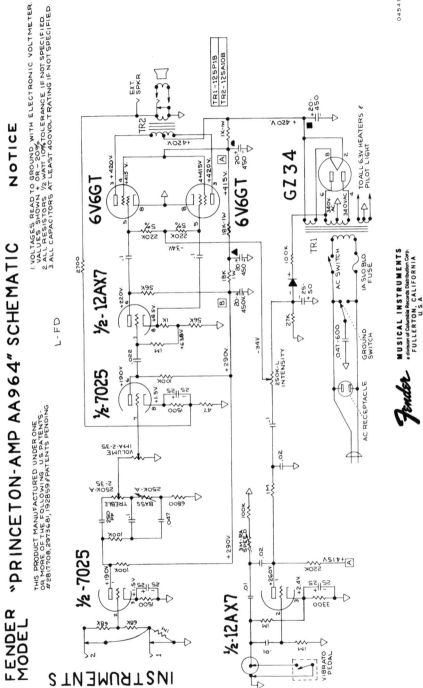

FENDER MODEL "PRINCETON-AMP AA964" SCHEMATIC

NOTICE

1. VOLTAGES READ TO GROUND WITH ELECTRONIC VOLTMETER. VALUES SHOWN + OR - 20%.
2. ALL RESISTORS 1/2 WATT 10% TOLERANCE IF NOT SPECIFIED.
3. ALL CAPACITORS AT LEAST 400 VOLT RATING IF NOT SPECIFIED.

L-FD

THIS PRODUCT MANUFACTURED UNDER ONE OR MORE OF THE FOLLOWING U.S. PATENTS - #2817708, 2973681, 192859 & PATENTS PENDING

MUSICAL INSTRUMENTS
a division of Columbia Records Distribution Corp.
FULLERTON, CALIFORNIA
U.S.A.

310

Kendricks

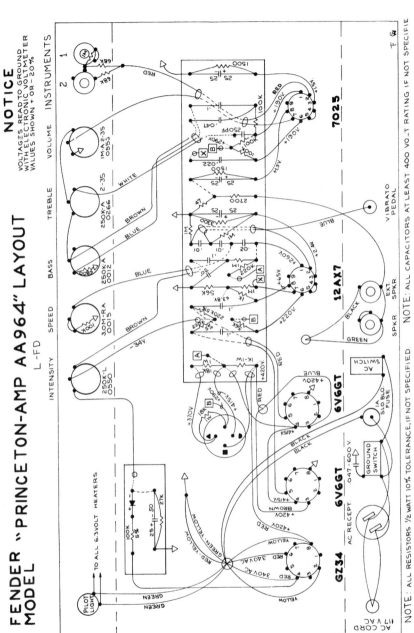

FENDER "PRINCETON-AMP AA964" LAYOUT
MODEL L-FD

NOTICE
VOLTAGES READ TO GROUND
WITH ELECTRONIC VOLTMETER
VALUES SHOWN + OR - 20%

MUSICAL INSTRUMENTS
a division of Columbia Records Distribution Corp.
FULLERTON, CALIFORNIA

NOTE: ALL RESISTORS ½ WATT 10% TOLERANCE, IF NOT SPECIFIED
NOTE: ALL CAPACITORS AT LEAST 400 V-T RATING IF NOT SPECIFIE

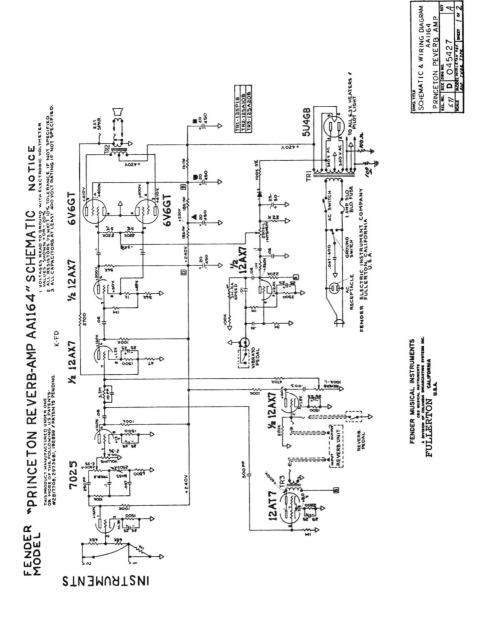

FENDER MODEL "PRINCETON REVERB-AMP AA1164" SCHEMATIC NOTICE

Kendricks

FENDER "PRINCETON REVERB-AMP AA1164" LAYOUT NOTICE
MODEL

VOLTAGES READ TO GROUND WITH ELECTRONIC
VOLTMETER VALUES SHOWN + OR – 20%

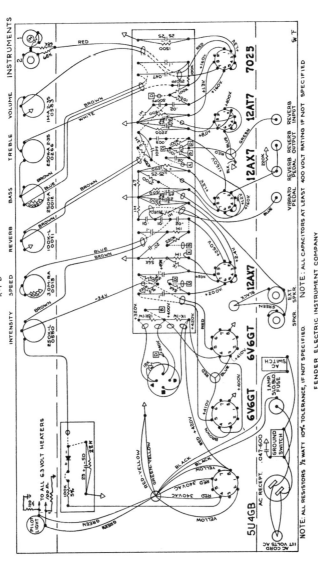

DWG TITLE				
SCHEMATIC & WIRING DIAGRAM AA1164				
PRINCETON REVERB AMP				
REL. NO.	SIZE	DWG NO.		REV
571	D	045427		A
SCALE	MODEL		SHEET 2 OF 2	

FENDER MUSICAL INSTRUMENTS
CBS MUSICAL INSTRUMENTS
A DIVISION OF COLUMBIA BROADCASTING SYSTEMS INC.
FULLERTON   CALIFORNIA
U.S.A.

NOTE: ALL RESISTORS ½ WATT 10% TOLERANCE, IF NOT SPECIFIED.

NOTE: ALL CAPACITORS AT LEAST 400 VOLT RATING IF NOT SPECIFIED

FENDER ELECTRIC INSTRUMENT COMPANY
FULLERTON, CALIFORNIA
U.S.A.

PRO-AMP

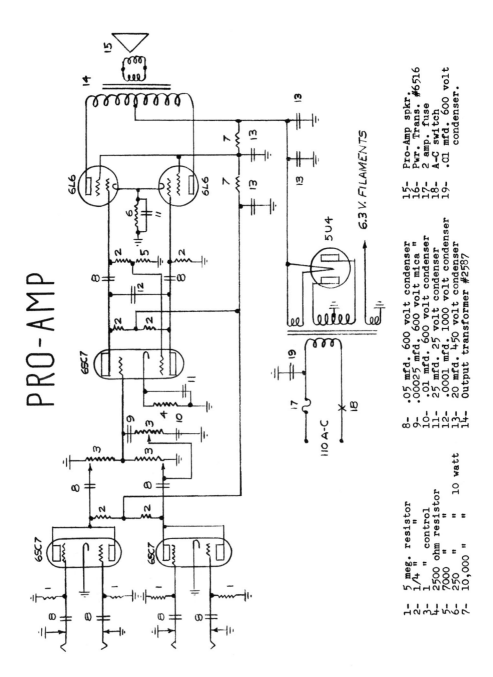

1— 5 meg. resistor
2— 1/4 "   "
3— 1 "   control
4— 2500 ohm resistor
5— 7000 "   "
6— 250 "   "
7— 10,000 "   " 10 watt

8— .05 mfd. 600 volt condenser
9— .0025 mfd. 600 volt mica "
10— .01 mfd. 600 volt condenser
11— 25 mfd. 25 volt condenser
12— .0001 mfd. 1000 volt condenser
13— 20 mfd. 450 volt condenser
14— Output transformer #2587

15— Pro-Amp spkr.
16— Pwr. Trans. #6516
17— 2 amp. fuse
18— A-C switch
19— .01 mfd. 600 volt
     condenser.

6.3 V. FILAMENTS

110 A-C

FENDER "PRO-AMP" SCHEMATIC
MODEL 5C5

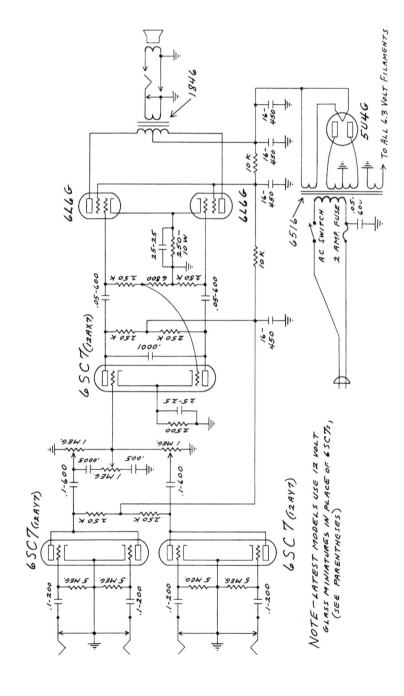

NOTE — LATEST MODELS USE 12 VOLT GLASS MINIATURES IN PLACE OF 6SC7s, (SEE PARENTHESES)

Kendricks

FENDER "PRO-AMP" LAYOUT
MODEL 5C5

NOTICE

VOLTAGES READ TO GROUND
WITH ELECTRONIC VOLTMETER.
VALUES SHOWN + OR – 20%

NOTE – EARLY MODELS HAVE ONLY ONE SPEAKER JACK.
– LATER MODELS HAVE 1 MEG. FEEDBACK RESISTOR FROM
VOICE COIL TO GRID OF 2ND 6L6G.
– LATEST MODELS USE 12 VOLT GLASS MINIATURES IN PLACE
OF 6SC7S (SAME CIRCUIT) SEE PARENTHESES AT BOTTOM

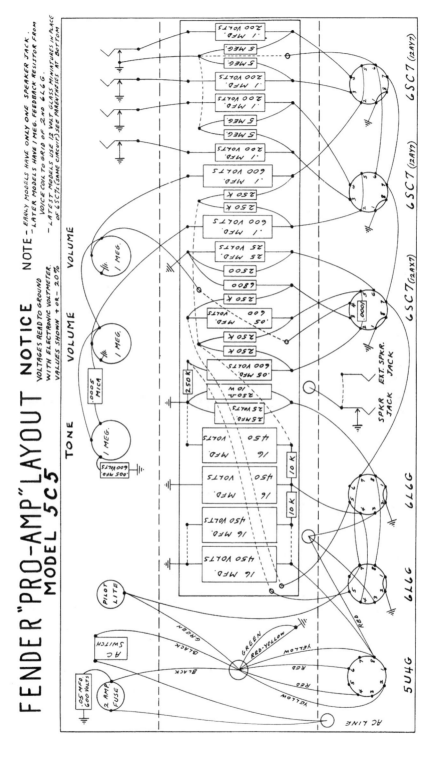

FENDER "PRO-AMP" SCHEMATIC
MODEL 5D5
1-ED

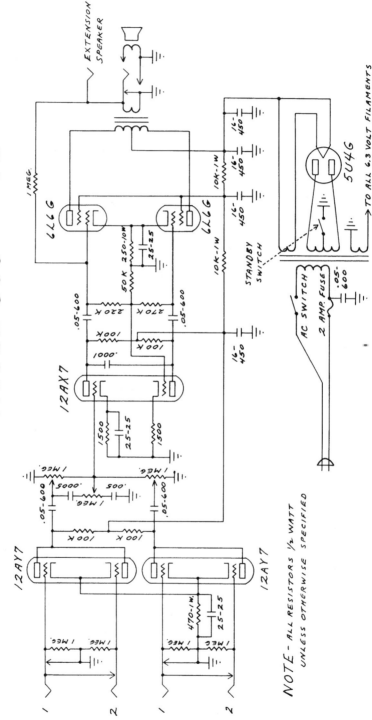

NOTE - ALL RESISTORS ½ WATT
UNLESS OTHERWISE SPECIFIED

Kendricks

FENDER "PRO-AMP" LAYOUT

MODEL 5D5

NOTICE

VOLTAGES READ TO GROUND
WITH ELECTRONIC VOLTMETER.
VALUES SHOWN + OR − 20 %

I - ED

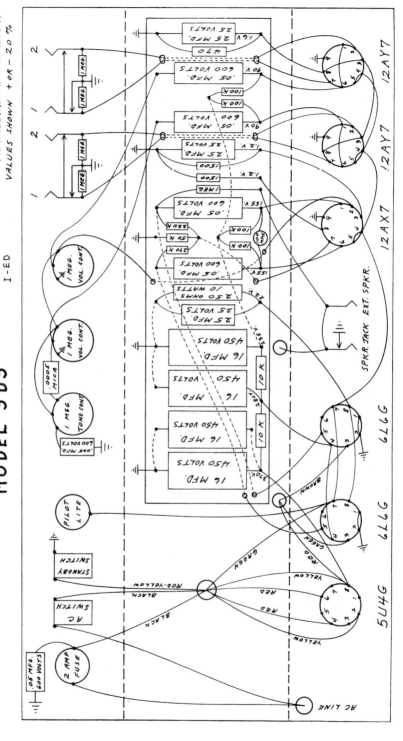

SPKR. JACK EXT. SPKR.

12AY7
12AY7
12AX7
6V6G
6V6G
5U4G

FENDER "PRO-AMP" SCHEMATIC
MODEL 5E5

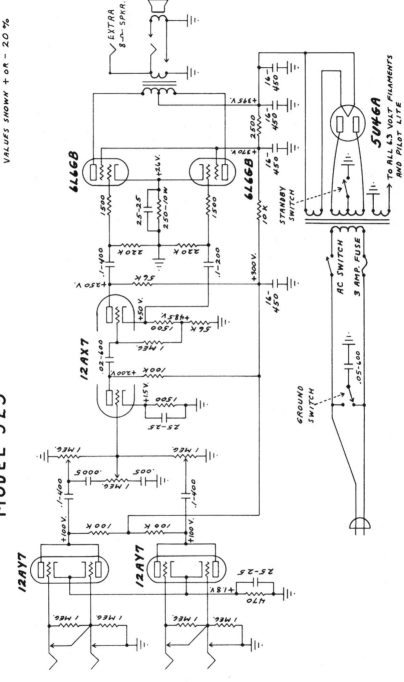

N O T I C E

VOLTAGES READ TO GROUND
WITH ELECTRONIC VOLTMETER.
VALUES SHOWN + OR − 20 %

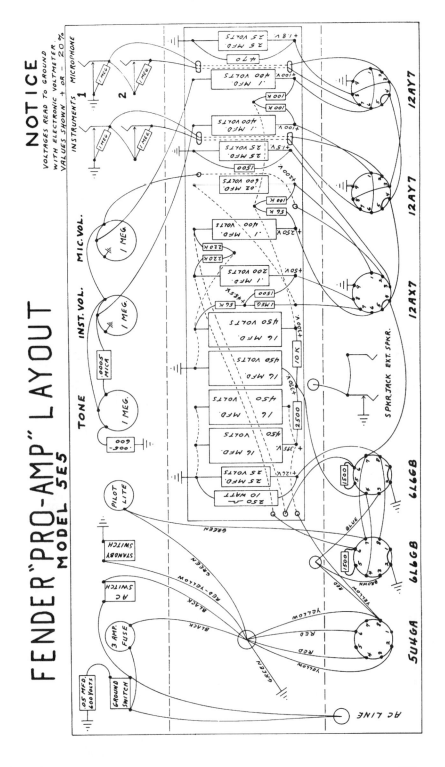

FENDER "PRO-AMP" LAYOUT
MODEL 5E5

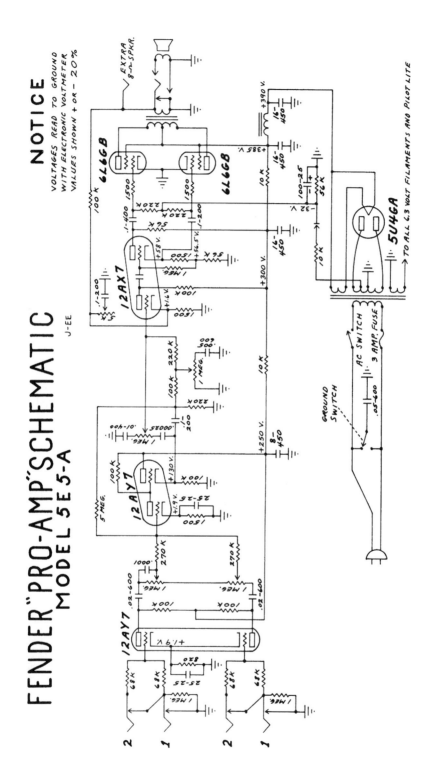

FENDER "PRO-AMP" SCHEMATIC
MODEL 5E5-A

J-EE

NOTICE

VOLTAGES READ TO GROUND
WITH ELECTRONIC VOLTMETER
VALUES SHOWN + OR - 20%

Kendricks

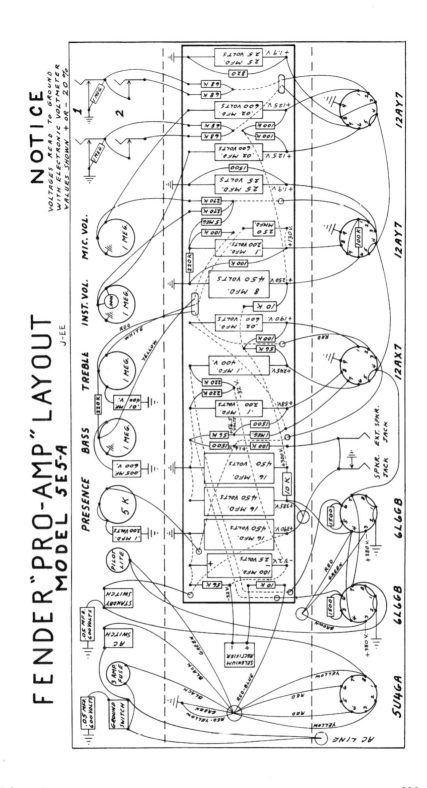

FENDER "PRO-AMP" LAYOUT
MODEL 5E5-A

FENDER "PRO-AMP" SCHEMATIC
MODEL 6G5

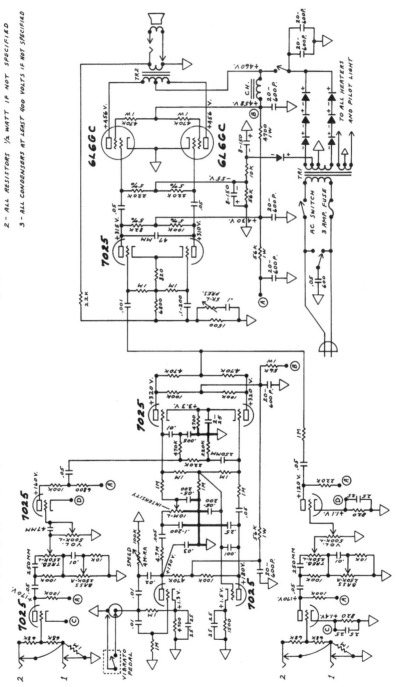

NOTICE

1 – VOLTAGES READ TO GROUND WITH ELECTRONIC
VOLTMETER. VALUES SHOWN + OR –

2 – ALL RESISTORS ½ WATT IF NOT SPECIFIED

3 – ALL CONDENSERS AT LEAST 400 VOLTS IF NOT SPECIFIED

A-FJ

Kendricks

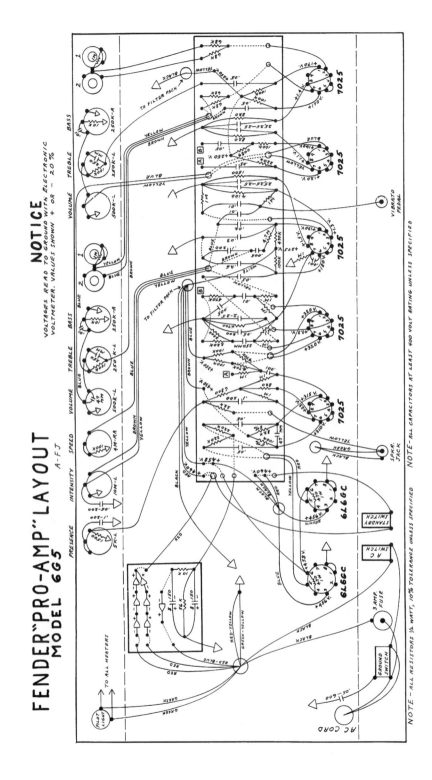

FENDER "PRO-AMP" LAYOUT
MODEL 6G5
A-FJ

NOTICE

VOLTAGES READ TO GROUND WITH ELECTRONIC
VOLTMETER. VALUES SHOWN + OR − 20%

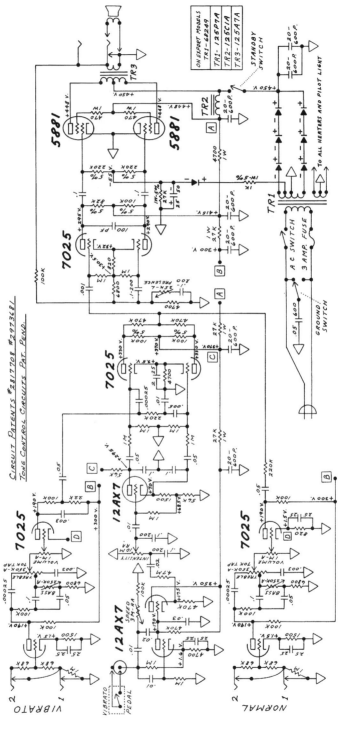

FENDER "PRO-AMP" SCHEMATIC
MODEL 6G5-A   K-FJ

NOTICE

1 – VOLTAGES READ TO GROUND WITH ELECTRONIC
      VOLTMETER. VALUES SHOWN + OR – 20%
2 – ALL RESISTORS ½ WATT, 10% TOLERANCE IF NOT SPECIFIED.
3 – ALL CAPACITORS AT LEAST 400 VOLT RATING IF NOT SPECIFIED.

CIRCUIT PATENTS #2817708 #2973681
TONE CONTROL CIRCUITS PAT. PEND.

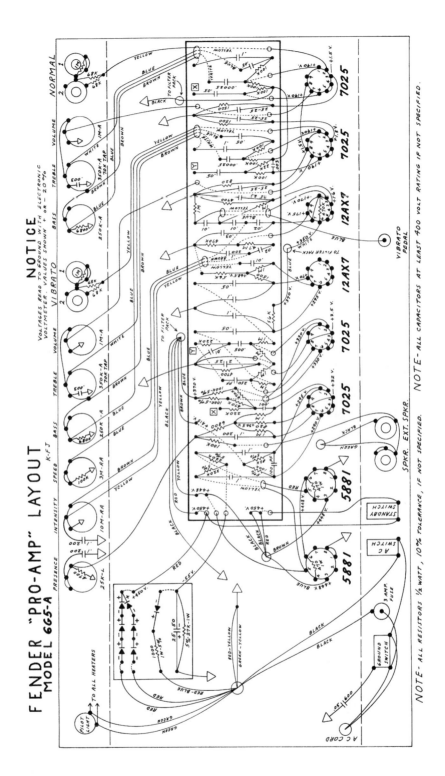

FENDER "PRO-AMP" LAYOUT
MODEL 6G5-A

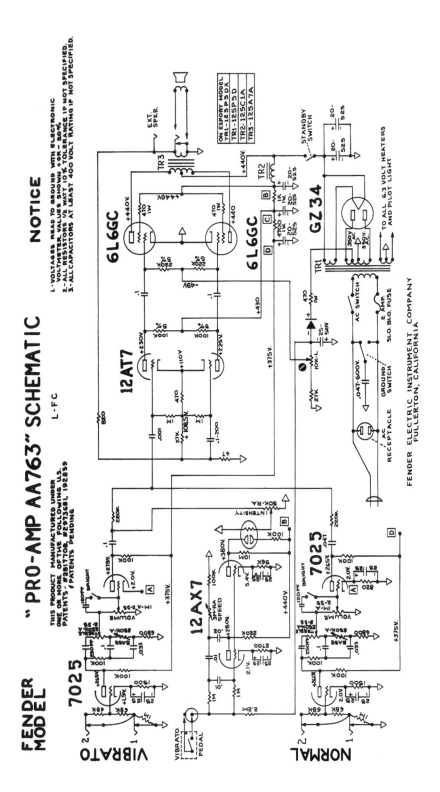

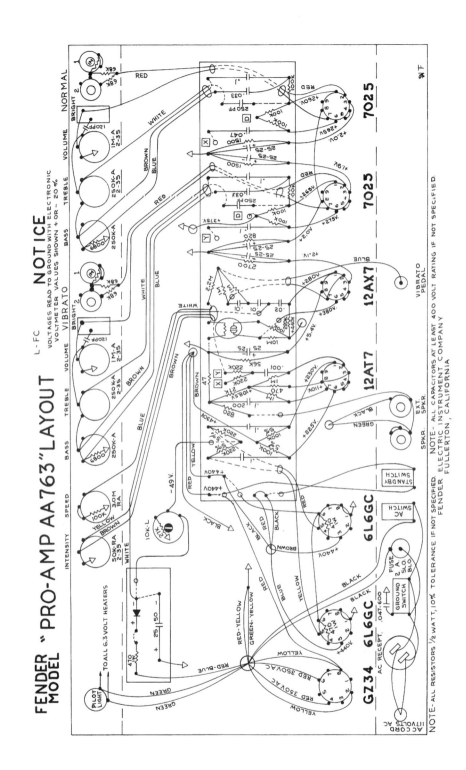

FENDER "PRO-AMP AA763"LAYOUT MODEL

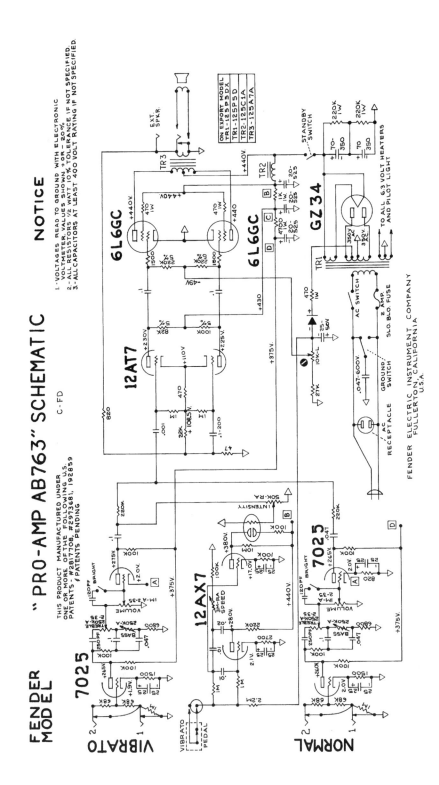

FENDER MODEL "PRO-AMP AB763" SCHEMATIC

C-FD

THIS PRODUCT MANUFACTURED UNDER ONE OR MORE OF THE FOLLOWING U.S. PATENTS - #2817708, #2973681, 192859 & PATENTS PENDING

NOTICE

1.- VOLTAGES READ TO GROUND WITH ELECTRONIC VOLTMETER. VALUES SHOWN +OR- 20%
2.- ALL RESISTORS 1/2 WATT 10% TOLERANCE IF NOT SPECIFIED.
3.- ALL CAPACITORS AT LEAST 400 VOLT RATING IF NOT SPECIFIED.

ON EXPORT MODEL	
TR1-125P5DX	TR1-125P5D
TR2-125C1A	
TR3-125A7A	

FENDER ELECTRIC INSTRUMENT COMPANY
FULLERTON, CALIFORNIA
U.S.A.

FENDER "PRO-AMP AB763" LAYOUT
MODEL

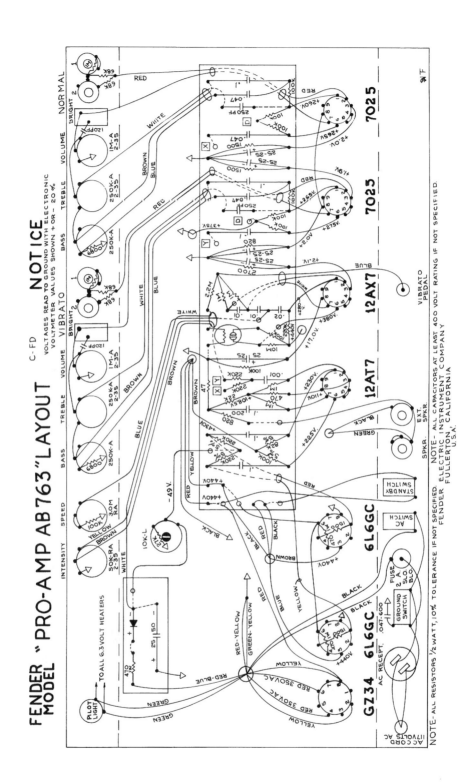

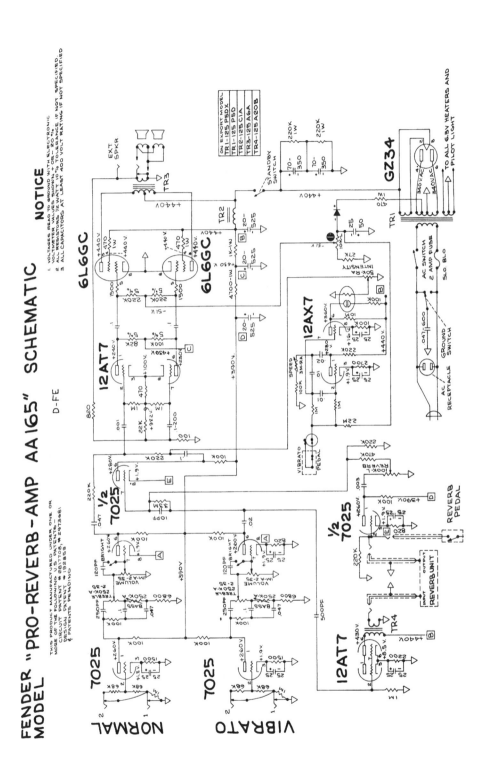

FENDER "PRO-REVERB-AMP AA165" SCHEMATIC MODEL

D-FE

Kendricks

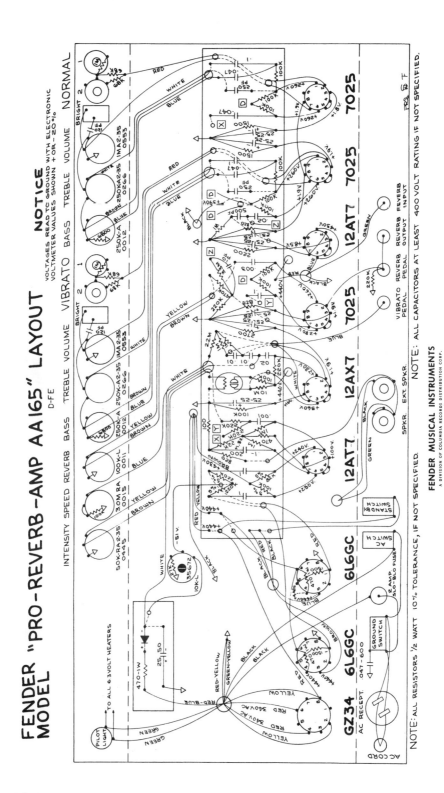

FENDER "PRO-REVERB-AMP AA165" LAYOUT
MODEL D-FE

FENDER "PRO REVERB-AMP AA1069" SCHEMATIC

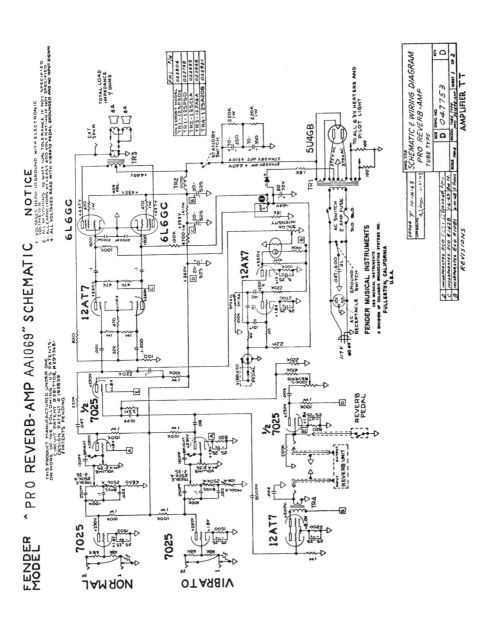

Kendricks

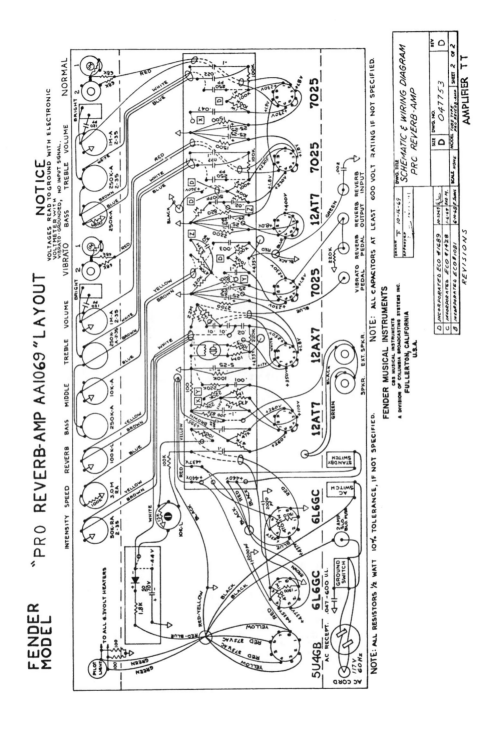

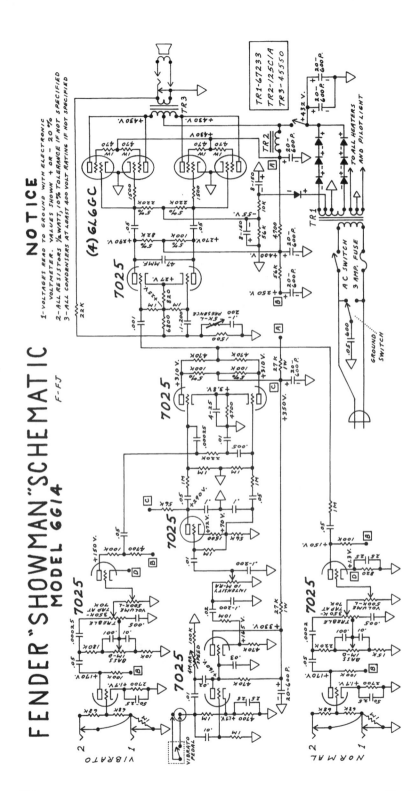

FENDER "SHOWMAN" SCHEMATIC
MODEL 6G14
F-FJ

NOTICE

1 - VOLTAGES READ TO GROUND WITH ELECTRONIC VOLTMETER. VALUES SHOWN + OR - 20%

2 - ALL RESISTORS ½ WATT, 10% TOLERANCE IF NOT SPECIFIED

3 - ALL CONDENSERS AT LEAST 400 VOLT RATING IF NOT SPECIFIED

TR1-67233
TR2-125C1A
TR3-45550

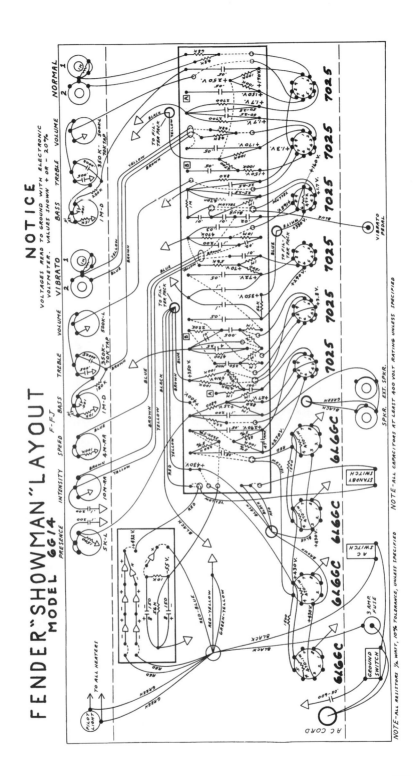

FENDER "SHOWMAN" LAYOUT
MODEL 6G14

Kendricks

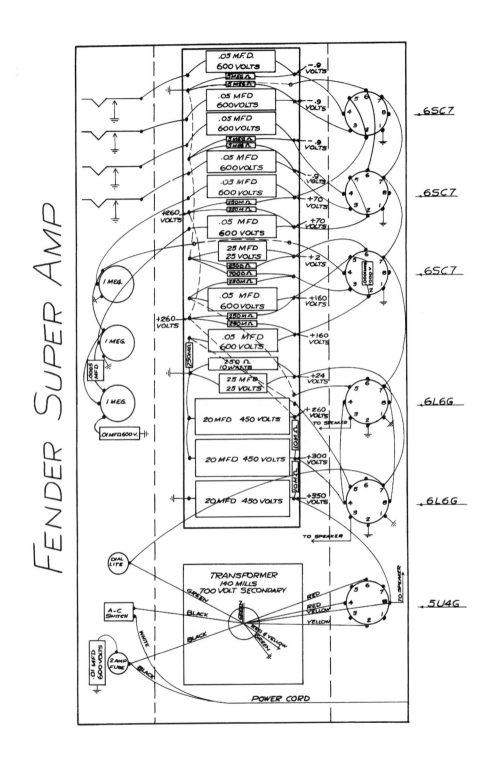

FENDER "SUPER-AMP" SCHEMATIC
MODEL 5C4

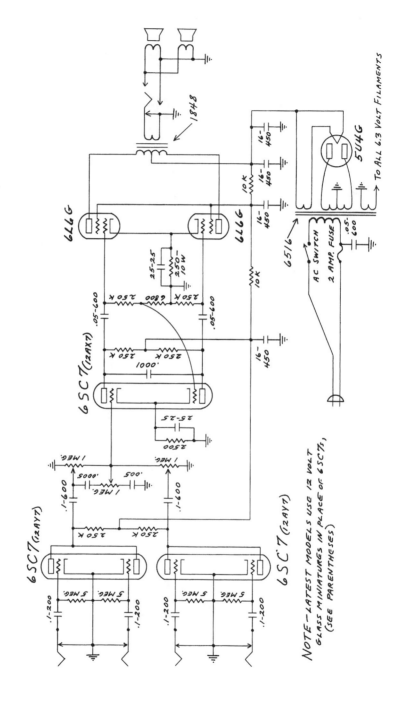

Kendricks

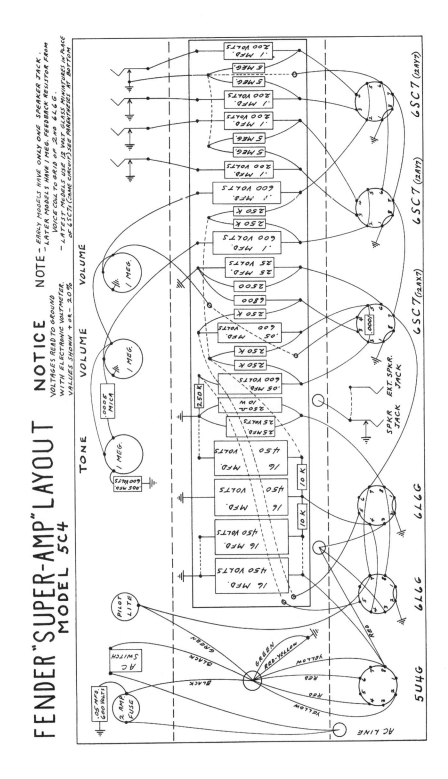

FENDER "SUPER-AMP" LAYOUT
MODEL 5C4

NOTICE

VOLTAGES READ TO GROUND
WITH ELECTRONIC VOLTMETER.
VALUES SHOWN + OR - 20%

NOTE – EARLY MODELS HAVE ONLY ONE SPEAKER JACK.
– LATER MODELS HAVE 1 MEG. FEEDBACK RESISTOR FROM
VOICE COIL TO GRID OF 2ND 6L6G.
– LATEST MODELS USE 12 VOLT GLASS MINIATURES IN PLACE
OF 6SC7s (SAME CIRCUIT) SEE PARENTHESES AT BOTTOM

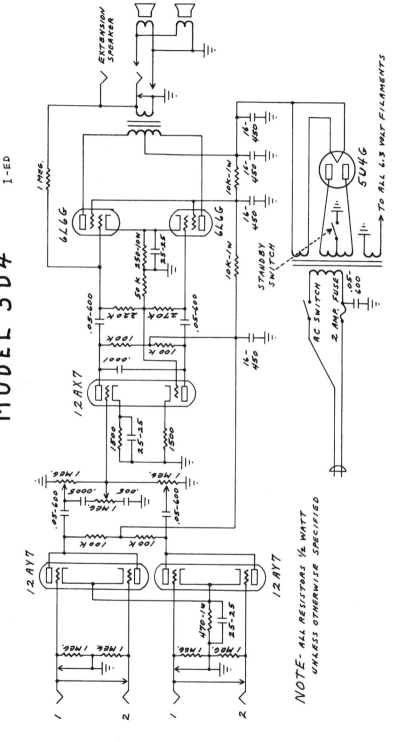

FENDER "SUPER-AMP" SCHEMATIC

MODEL 5D4

I-ED

Kendricks

FENDER "SUPER-AMP" NOTICE
MODEL 5D4 I-ED

VOLTAGES READ TO GROUND
WITH ELECTRONIC VOLTMETER.
VALUES SHOWN + OR - 20 %

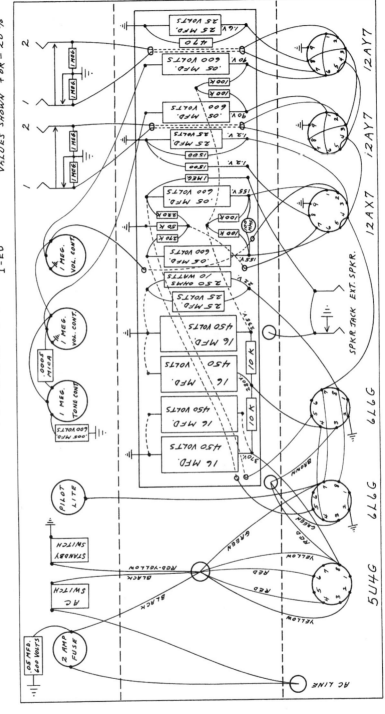

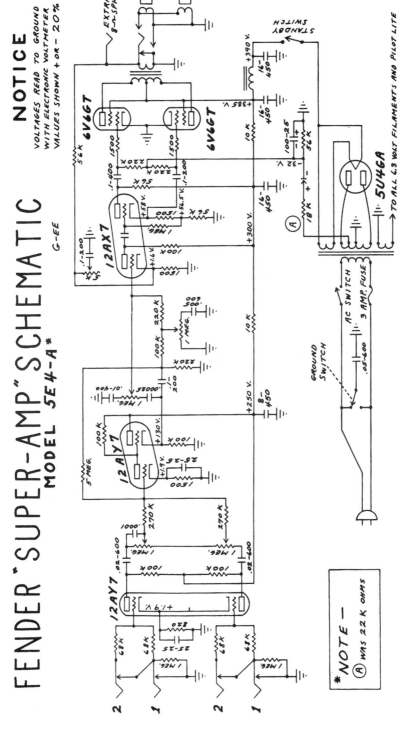

FENDER "SUPER-AMP" SCHEMATIC
MODEL 5E4-A*

G-EE

NOTICE

VOLTAGES READ TO GROUND
WITH ELECTRONIC VOLTMETER.
VALUES SHOWN + OR - 20%

*NOTE —
Ⓐ WAS 22 K OHMS

Kendricks

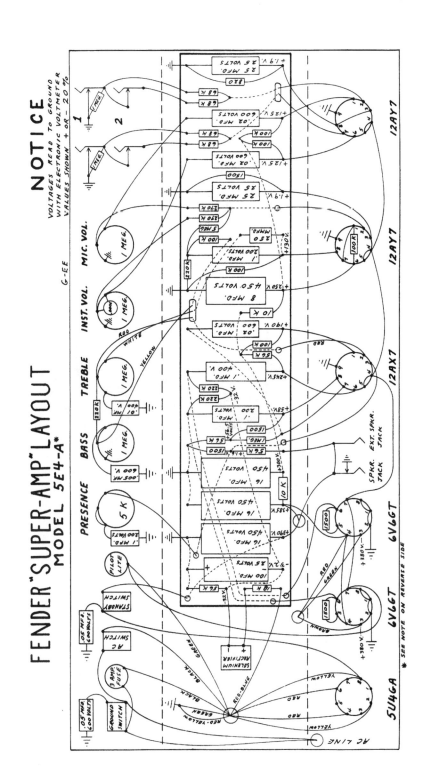

FENDER "SUPER-AMP" LAYOUT
MODEL 5E4-A*

NOTICE

VOLTAGES READ TO GROUND
WITH ELECTRONIC VOLTMETER
VALUES SHOWN + OR − 20%

G-EE

* SEE NOTE ON REVERSE SIDE

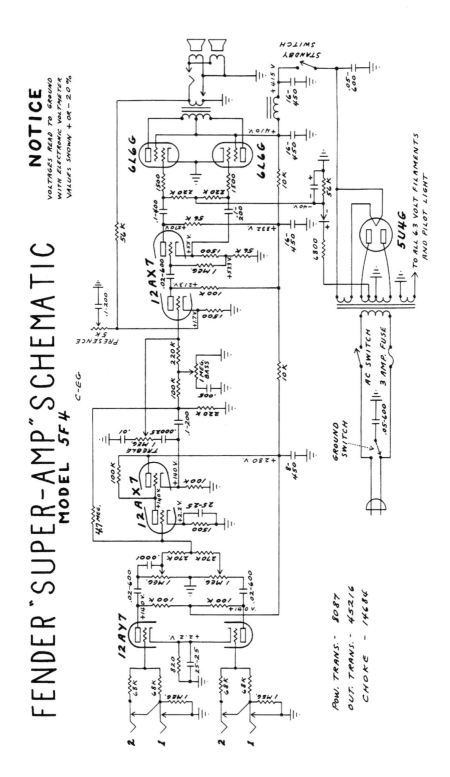

FENDER "SUPER-AMP" SCHEMATIC
MODEL 5F4

NOTICE
VOLTAGES READ TO GROUND
WITH ELECTRONIC VOLTMETER
VALUES SHOWN + OR − 20%

POW. TRANS.- 8087
OUT. TRANS.- 45216
CHOKE - 14684

Kendricks

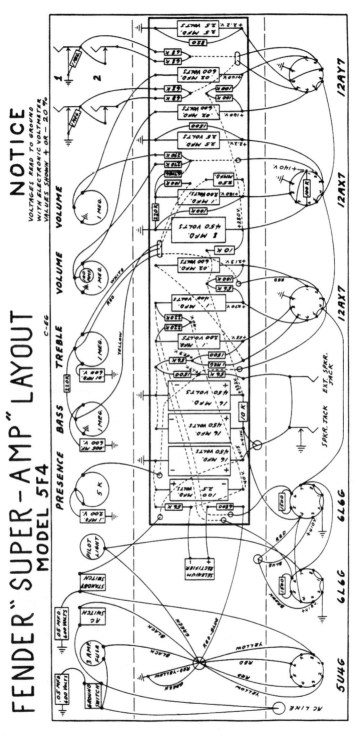

FENDER "SUPER-AMP" LAYOUT
MODEL 5F4

FENDER "SUPER-AMP" SCHEMATIC
MODEL 6G4
A-FJ

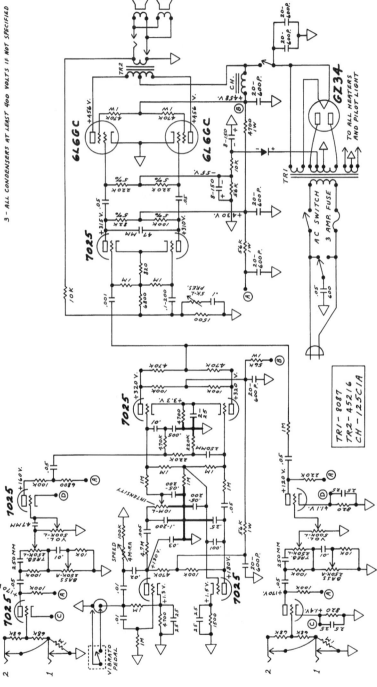

NOTICE

1 - VOLTAGES READ TO GROUND WITH ELECTRONIC VOLTMETER. VALUES SHOWN + OR -

2 - ALL RESISTORS ½ WATT IF NOT SPECIFIED

3 - ALL CONDENSERS AT LEAST 400 VOLTS IF NOT SPECIFIED

TR1 - 8087
TR2 - 45216
CH - 125C1A

Kendricks

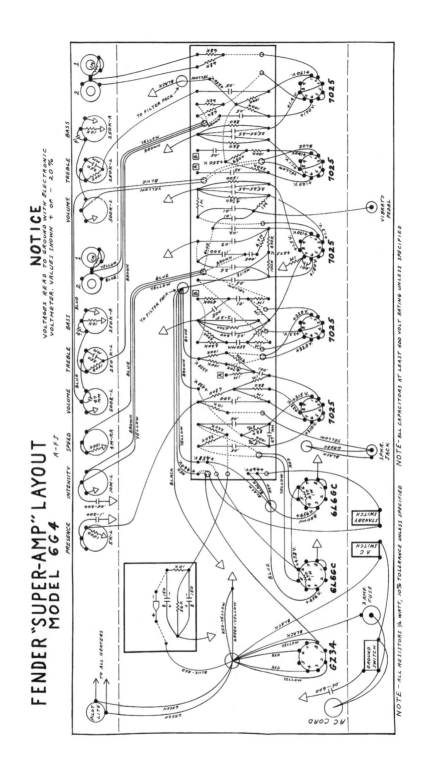

FENDER "SUPER-AMP" LAYOUT
MODEL 6G4

A-FJ

NOTICE

VOLTAGES READ TO GROUND WITH ELECTRONIC
VOLTMETER. VALUES SHOWN + OR - 20%

NOTE - ALL RESISTORS ¼ WATT, 10% TOLERANCE UNLESS SPECIFIED

NOTE - ALL CAPACITORS AT LEAST 400 VOLT RATING UNLESS SPECIFIED

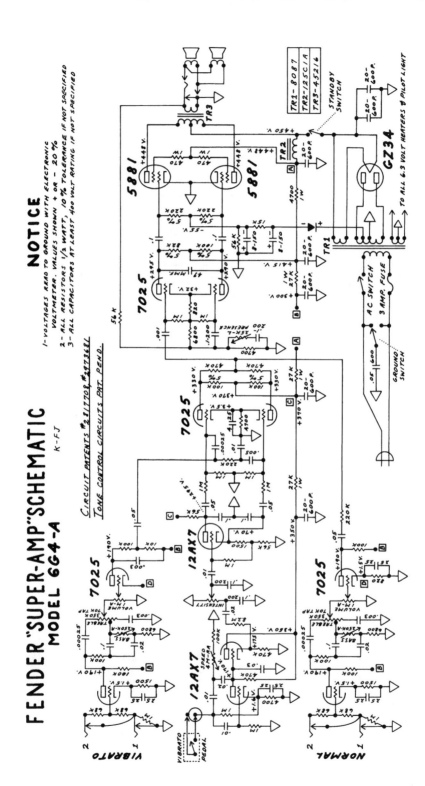

FENDER "SUPER-AMP" SCHEMATIC
MODEL 6G4-A

K-FJ

CIRCUIT PATENTS #2,517,708, #2,973,386L
TONE CONTROL CIRCUITS PAT. PEND.

NOTICE

1 – VOLTAGES READ TO GROUND WITH ELECTRONIC
VOLTMETER. VALUES SHOWN + OR – 20 %
2 – ALL RESISTORS 1/2 WATT, 10 % TOLERANCE IF NOT SPECIFIED
3 – ALL CAPACITORS AT LEAST 400 VOLT RATING IF NOT SPECIFIED

Kendricks

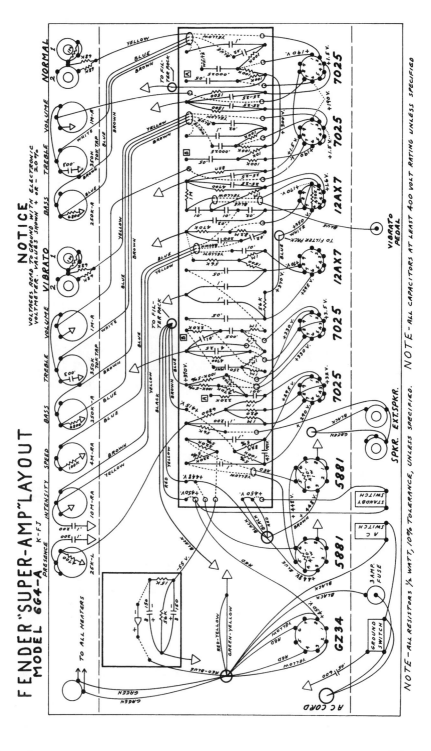

FENDER "SUPER-AMP" LAYOUT
MODEL 6G4-A   K·F·J

FENDER "TREMOLUX" SCHEMATIC
MODEL 5E9-A

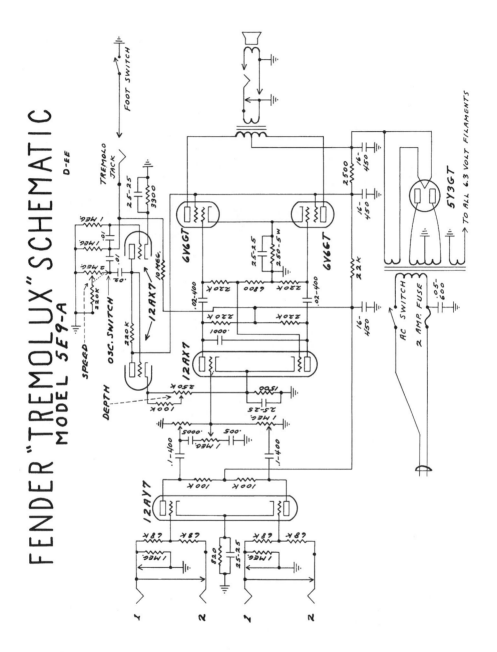

Kendricks

FENDER "TREMOLUX" LAYOUT
MODEL 5E9-A
D-EE

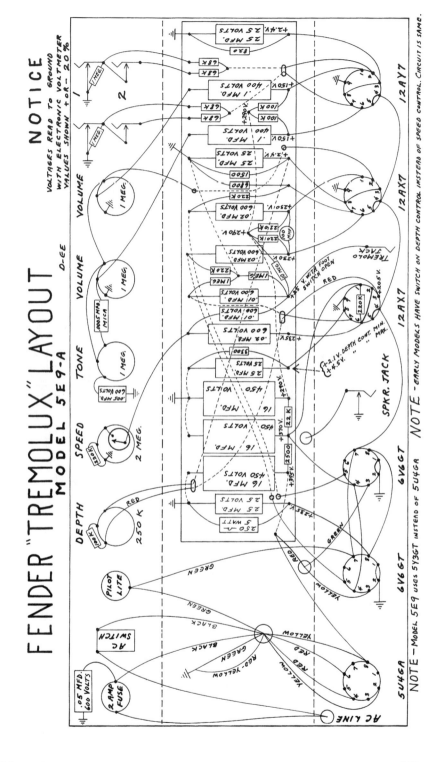

NOTICE

VOLTAGES READ TO GROUND
WITH ELECTRONIC VOLTMETER
VALUES SHOWN + OR - 20%

NOTE - EARLY MODELS HAVE SWITCH ON DEPTH CONTROL INSTEAD OF SPEED CONTROL. CIRCUIT IS SAME.

NOTE - MODEL 5E9 USES 5Y3GT INSTEAD OF 5U4GA

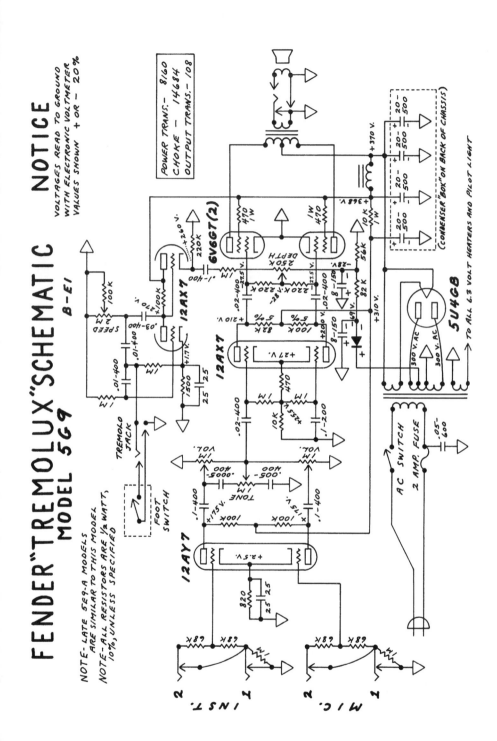

FENDER "TREMOLUX" SCHEMATIC
MODEL 5G9
B-E1

NOTE- LATE 5E9-A MODELS ARE SIMILAR TO THIS MODEL
NOTE- ALL RESISTORS ARE ½ WATT, 10%, UNLESS SPECIFIED

NOTICE
VOLTAGES READ TO GROUND WITH ELECTRONIC VOLTMETER
VALUES SHOWN + OR - 20%

POWER TRANS.- 8160
CHOKE - 14684
OUTPUT TRANS.- 108

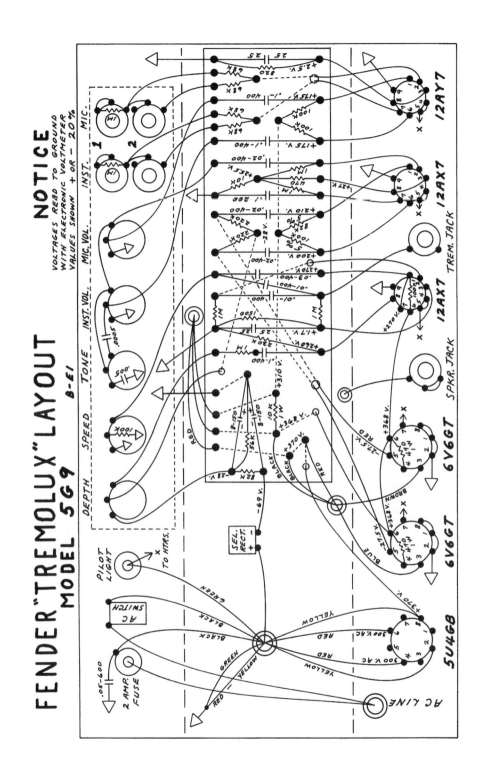

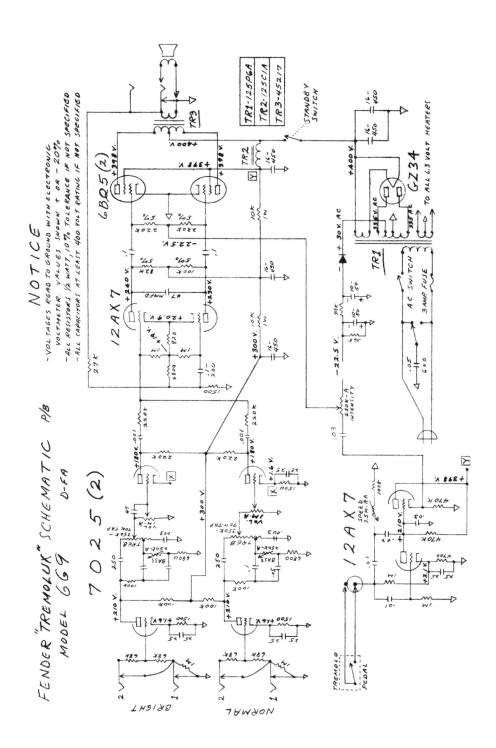

FENDER "TREMOLUX" SCHEMATIC P/B

MODEL 6G9   D-FA

Kendricks

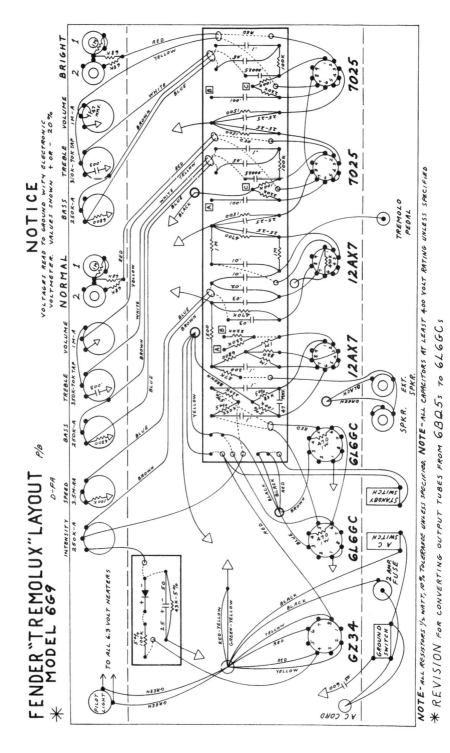

FENDER "TREMOLUX" LAYOUT
MODEL 6G9

NOTICE
VOLTAGES READ TO GROUND WITH ELECTRONIC VOLTMETER. VALUES SHOWN + OR − 20%

NOTE − ALL RESISTORS ½ WATT, 10% TOLERANCE UNLESS SPECIFIED. NOTE − ALL CAPACITORS AT LEAST 400 VOLT RATING UNLESS SPECIFIED.

✱ REVISION FOR CONVERTING OUTPUT TUBES FROM 6BQ5s TO 6L6GCs

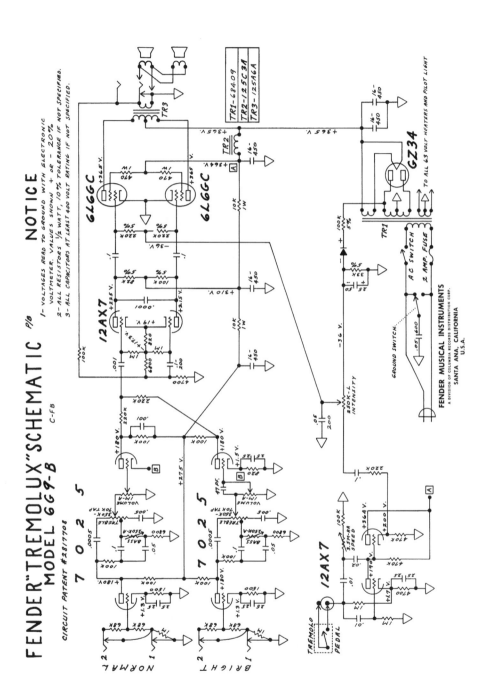

FENDER "TREMOLUX" SCHEMATIC P/8
MODEL 6G9-B
C-FB

CIRCUIT PATENT #2817704

NOTICE

1- VOLTAGES READ TO GROUND WITH ELECTRONIC VOLTMETER. VALUES SHOWN + OR - 20%.
2- ALL RESISTORS 1/2 WATT, 10% TOLERANCE IF NOT SPECIFIED.
3- ALL CAPACITORS AT LEAST 400 VOLT RATING IF NOT SPECIFIED.

| TR1-684-09 |
| TR2-125C3A |
| TR3-125A6A |

FENDER MUSICAL INSTRUMENTS
A DIVISION OF COLUMBIA RECORDS DISTRIBUTION CORP.
SANTA ANA, CALIFORNIA
U.S.A.

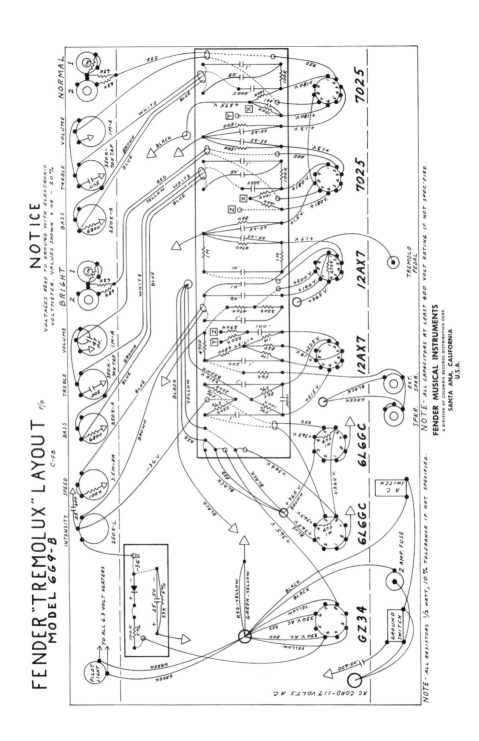

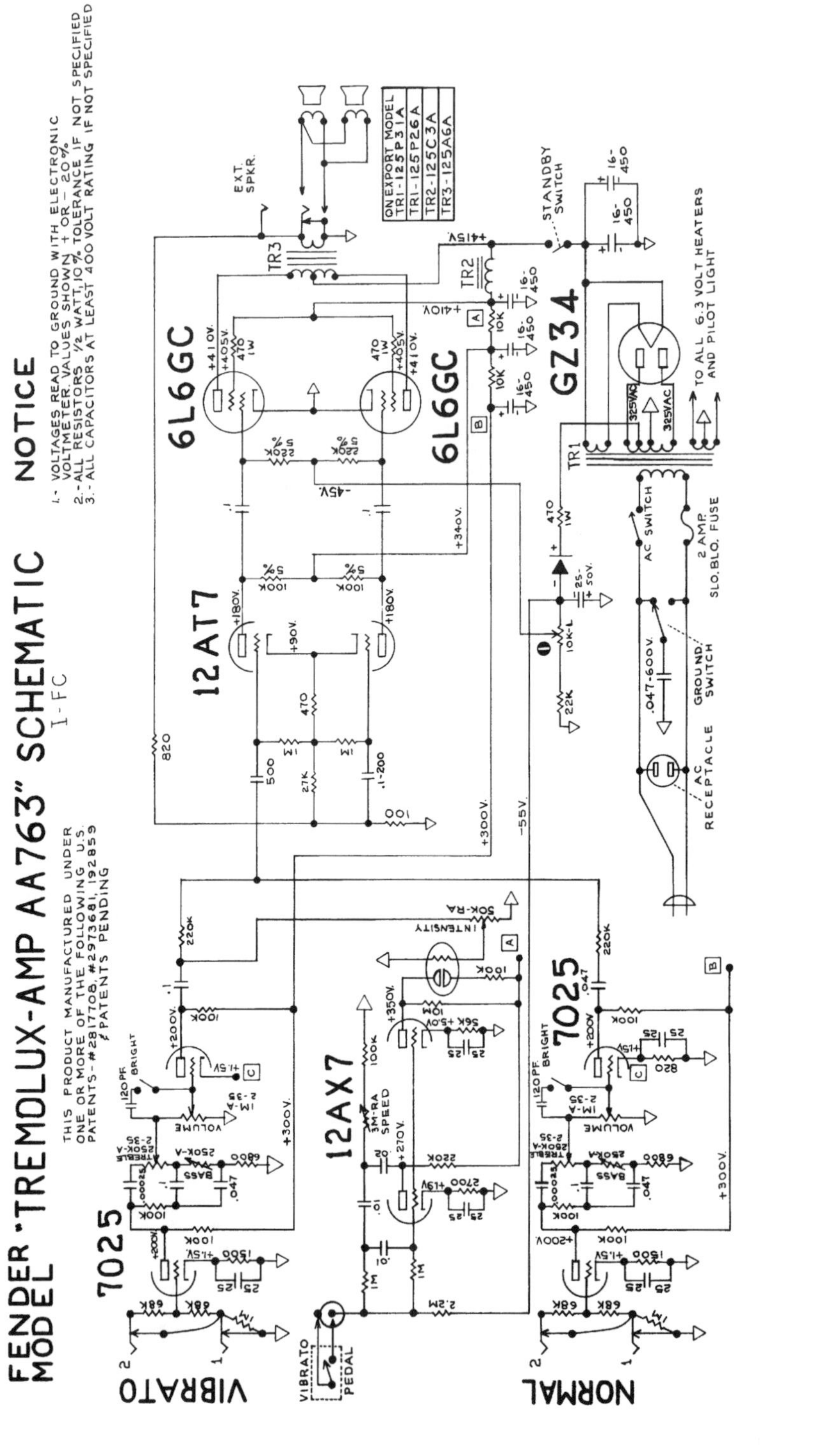

FENDER MODEL "TREMOLUX-AMP AA763" SCHEMATIC
I-FC
NOTICE
1.- VOLTAGES READ TO GROUND WITH ELECTRONIC VOLTMETER. VALUES SHOWN + OR - 20%
2.- ALL RESISTORS 1/2 WATT, 10% TOLERANCE IF NOT SPECIFIED
3.- ALL CAPACITORS AT LEAST 400 VOLT RATING IF NOT SPECIFIED
THIS PRODUCT MANUFACTURED UNDER ONE OR MORE OF THE FOLLOWING U.S. PATENTS - #2817708, #2973681, 192859
PATENTS PENDING
VIBRATO
NORMAL
VIBRATO PEDAL
7025
12AX7
12AT7
6L6GC
GZ34
7025
ON EXPORT MODEL
TR1-125P31A
TR1-125P26A
TR2-125C3A
TR3-125A6A
EXT. SPKR.
TR1
TR2
TR3
STANDBY SWITCH
TO ALL 6.3 VOLT HEATERS AND PILOT LIGHT
AC SWITCH
2 AMP. SLO.BLO. FUSE
GROUND SWITCH
AC RECEPTACLE
INTENSITY
SPEED
BRIGHT
VOLUME
TREBLE
BASS

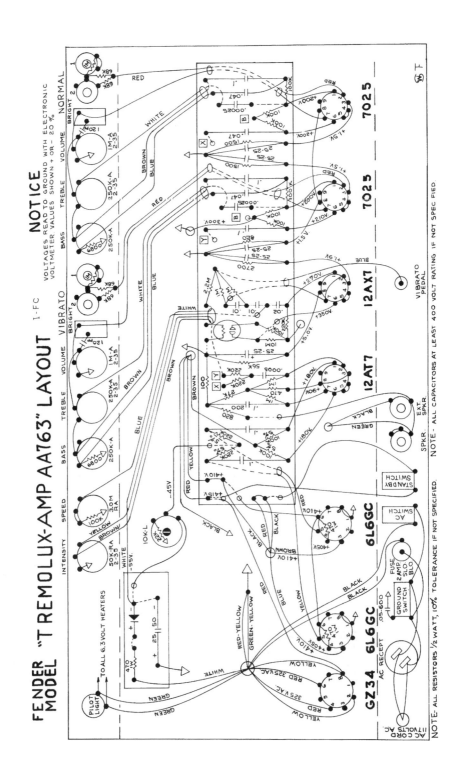

FENDER "TREMOLUX-AMP AA763" LAYOUT 1-FC
MODEL

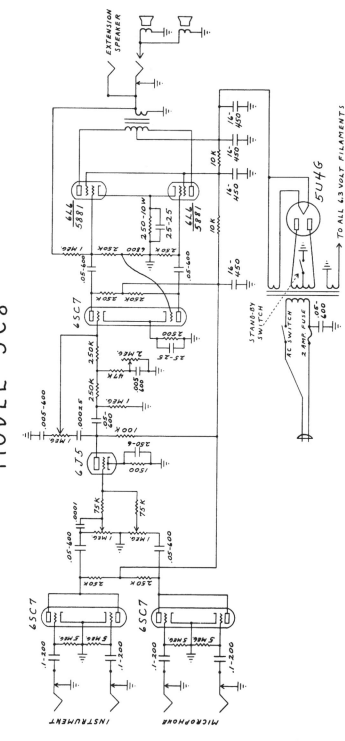

FENDER "TWIN-AMP" SCHEMATIC
MODEL 5C8

Kendricks

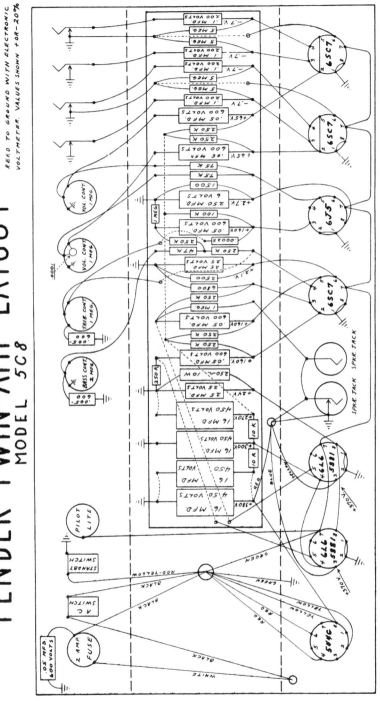

FENDER "TWIN-AMP" LAYOUT

MODEL 5C8

NOTICE

ALL VOLTAGES

READ TO GROUND WITH ELECTRONIC

VOLTMETER. VALUES SHOWN + OR - 20%

FENDER MUSICAL INSTRUMENTS

A DIVISION OF COLUMBIA RECORDS DISTRIBUTION CORP.

SANTA ANA, CALIFORNIA

U.S.A.

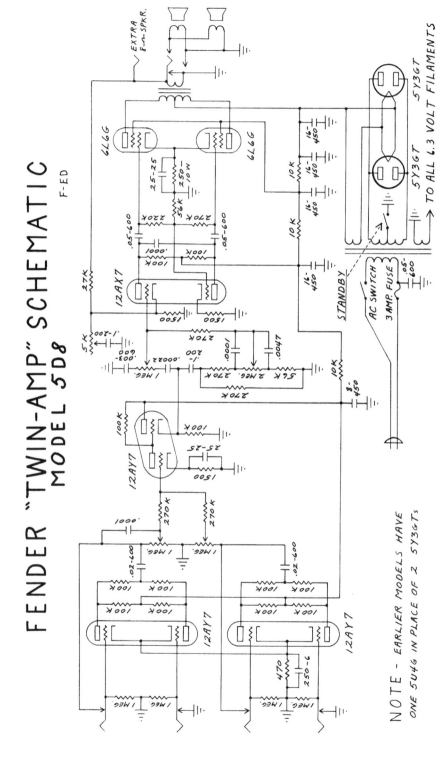

FENDER "TWIN-AMP" SCHEMATIC
MODEL 5D8

F-ED

NOTE - EARLIER MODELS HAVE
ONE 5U4G IN PLACE OF 2 5Y3GTs

364

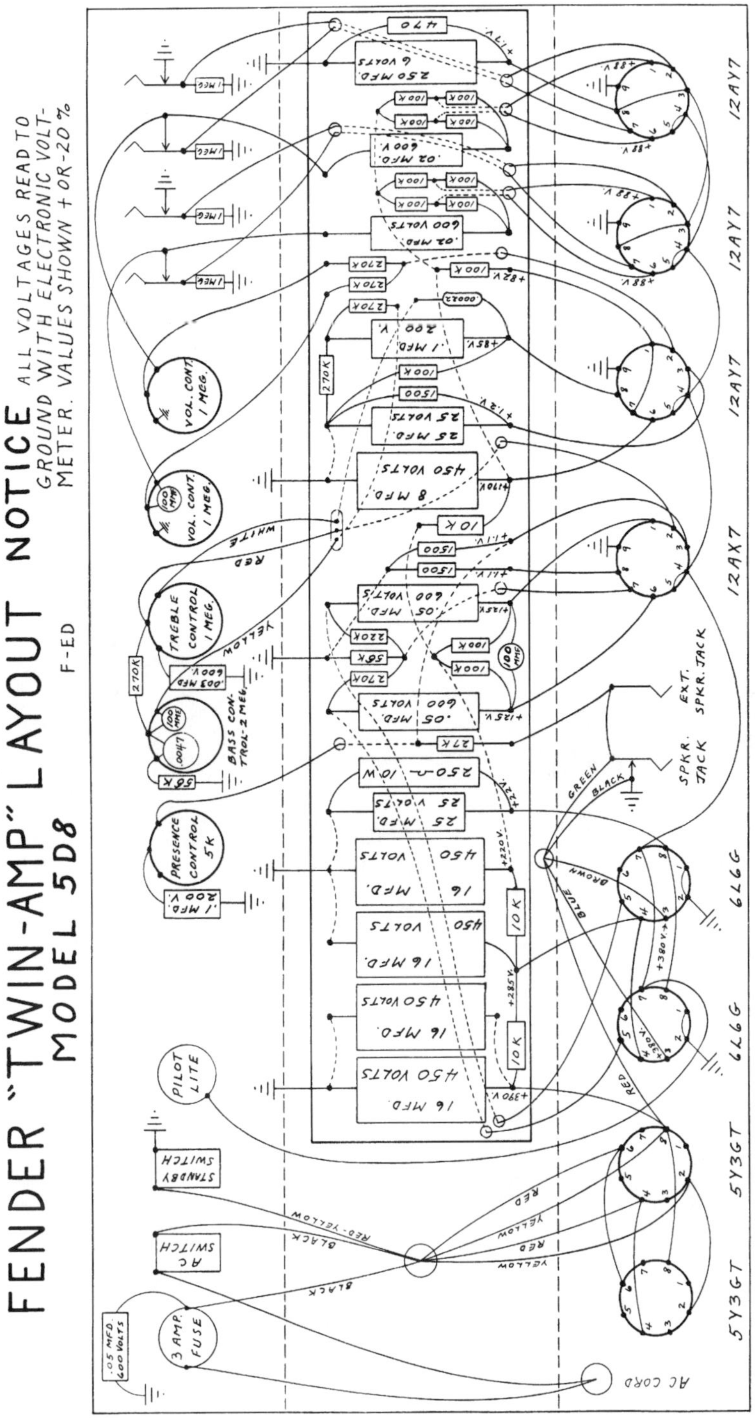

FENDER "TWIN-AMP" LAYOUT

NOTICE ALL VOLTAGES READ TO GROUND WITH ELECTRONIC VOLT-METER. VALUES SHOWN + OR −20%

MODEL 5D8

F-ED

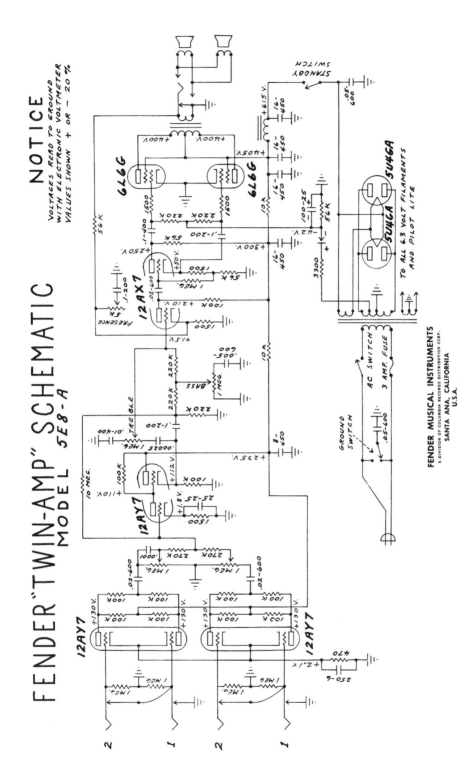

FENDER "TWIN-AMP" SCHEMATIC
MODEL 5E8-A

NOTICE

VOLTAGES READ TO GROUND
WITH ELECTRONIC VOLTMETER
VALUES SHOWN + OR - 20%

FENDER MUSICAL INSTRUMENTS
A DIVISION OF COLUMBIA RECORDS DISTRIBUTION CORP.
SANTA ANA, CALIFORNIA
U.S.A.

Kendricks

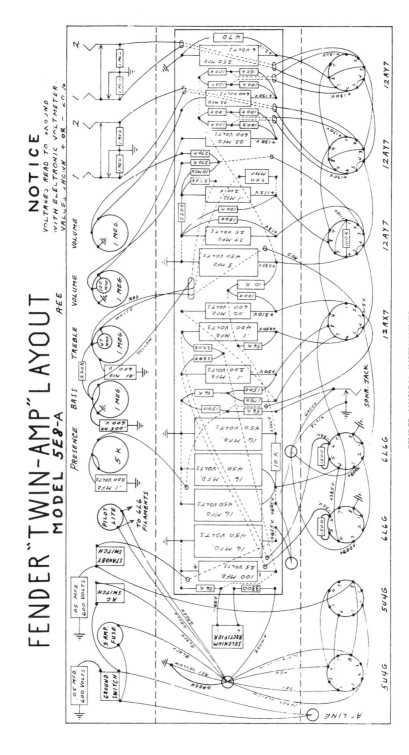

FENDER "TWIN-AMP" LAYOUT

MODEL 5E8-A

FENDER MUSICAL INSTRUMENTS

A DIVISION OF COLUMBIA RECORDS DISTRIBUTION CORP.

SANTA ANA, CALIFORNIA

U.S.A.

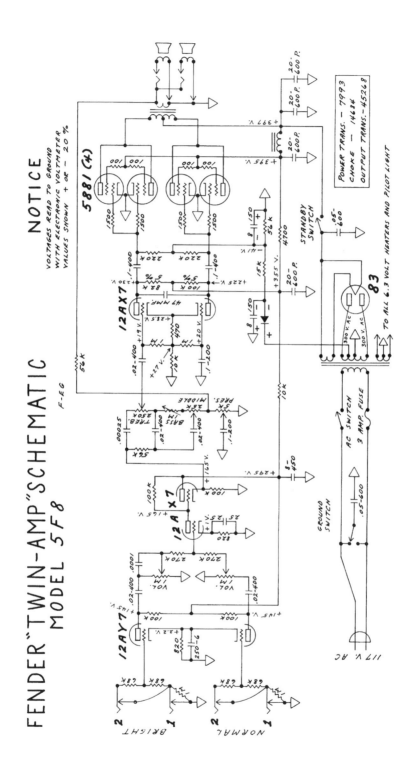

FENDER "TWIN-AMP" SCHEMATIC
MODEL 5F8
F-EG

NOTICE

VOLTAGES READ TO GROUND
WITH ELECTRONIC VOLTMETER
VALUES SHOWN + OR - 20 %

5881 (4)

12AX7

12A X7

12AY7

BRIGHT   NORMAL

POWER TRANS. - 7993
CHOKE - 14634
OUTPUT TRANS. - 45268

TO ALL 6.3 VOLT HEATERS AND PILOT LIGHT

83

300 V. AC

300 V. AC

STANDBY SWITCH

GROUND SWITCH

AC SWITCH
3 AMP. FUSE

117 V. AC

Kendricks

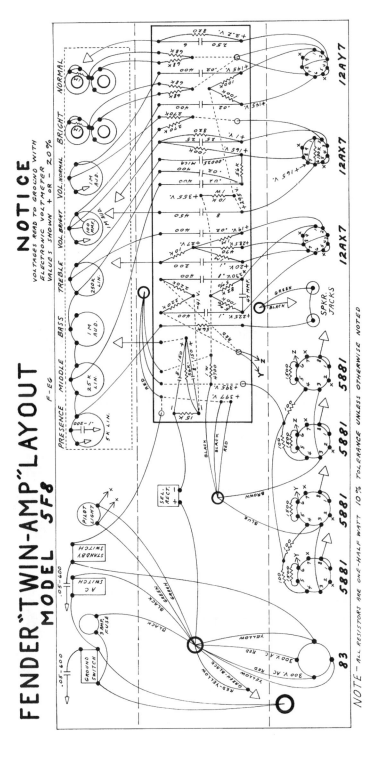

FENDER "TWIN-AMP" LAYOUT
MODEL SF8

F-EG

NOTICE

VOLTAGES READ TO GROUND WITH
ELECTRONIC VOLTMETER WITH
VALUES SHOWN + OR – 20%

NOTE – ALL RESISTORS ARE ONE-HALF WATT   10% TOLERANCE UNLESS OTHERWISE NOTED

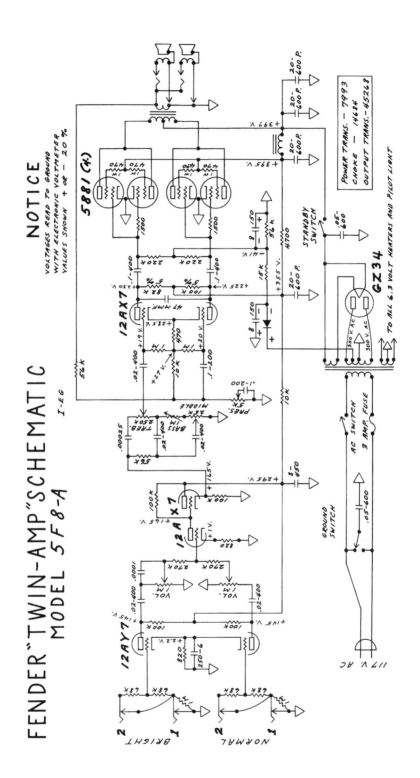

FENDER "TWIN-AMP" SCHEMATIC
MODEL 5F8-A
I-EG

NOTICE
VOLTAGES READ TO GROUND
WITH ELECTRONIC VOLTMETER
VALUES SHOWN + OR − 20%

POWER TRANS. − 7993
CHOKE − 14634
OUTPUT TRANS. − 45268

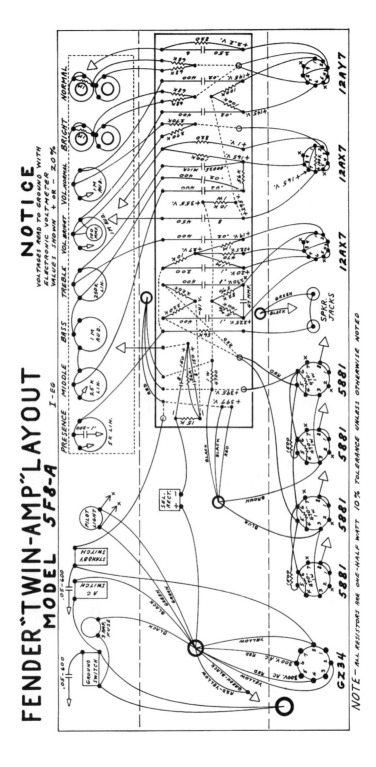

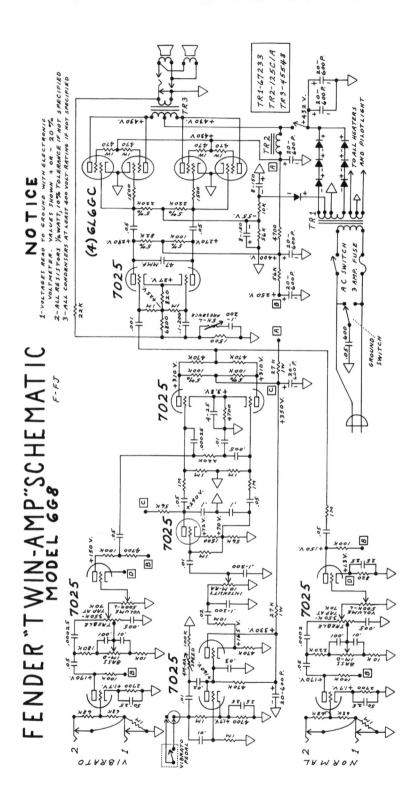

FENDER "TWIN-AMP" SCHEMATIC
MODEL 6G8
F-FJ

Kendricks

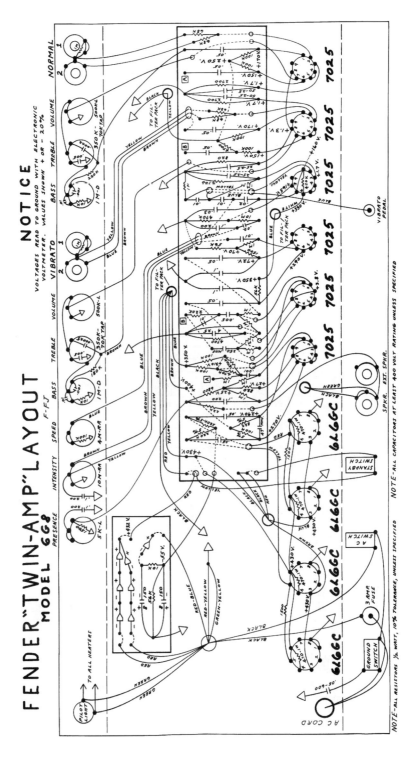

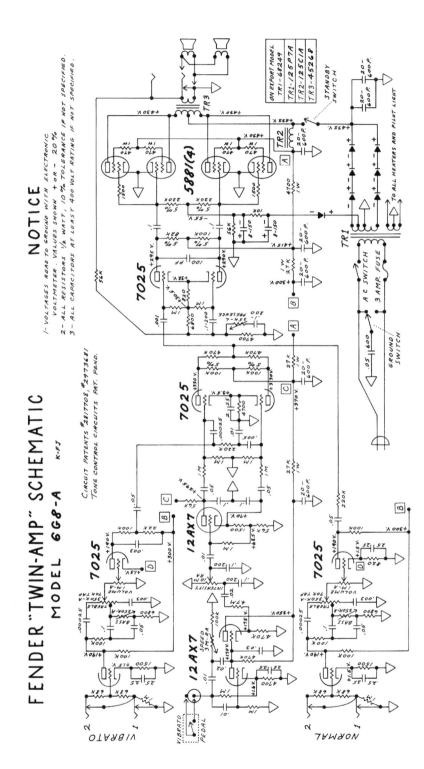

FENDER "TWIN-AMP" SCHEMATIC
MODEL 6G8-A   K-FJ

CIRCUIT PATENTS #2817708, #2973681
TONE CONTROL CIRCUITS PAT. PEND.

NOTICE

1 - VOLTAGES READ TO GROUND WITH ELECTRONIC
    VOLTMETER. VALUES SHOWN + OR - 20%
2 - ALL RESISTORS 1/2 WATT, 10% TOLERANCE IF NOT SPECIFIED.
3 - ALL CAPACITORS AT LEAST 400 VOLT RATING IF NOT SPECIFIED.

ON EXPORT MODEL
TR1-68249
TR1-125P7A
TR2-125C1A
TR3-45268

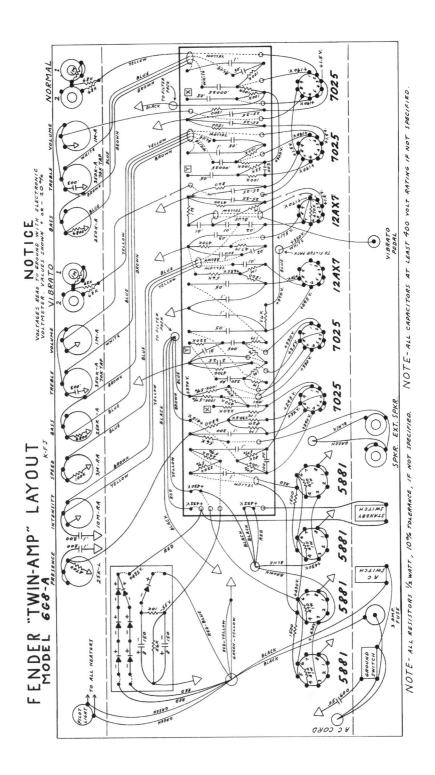

FENDER "TWIN REVERB-AMP AB763" SCHEMATIC NOTICE
MODEL

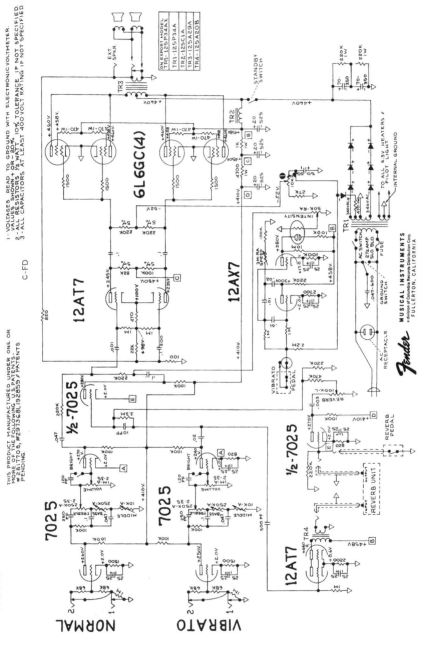

THIS PRODUCT MANUFACTURED UNDER ONE OR MORE OF THE FOLLOWING U.S. PATENTS #2,817,708, #2,973,681, 192,859 PATENTS PENDING.

NOTICE
1 - VOLTAGES READ TO GROUND WITH ELECTRONIC VOLTMETER.
2 - VALUES SHOWN ± 10% TOLERANCE IF NOT SPECIFIED.
    - ALL RESISTORS 1/2 WATT, 10% TOLERANCE IF NOT SPECIFIED.
3 - ALL CAPACITORS AT LEAST 400 VOLT RATING IF NOT SPECIFIED

MUSICAL INSTRUMENTS
a division of Columbia Records Distribution Corp.
FULLERTON, CALIFORNIA

ON EXPORT MODEL	TR1-125P34AX
TR1-125CIA	
TR2-125CIA	
TR3-125A29A	
TR4-125A20B	

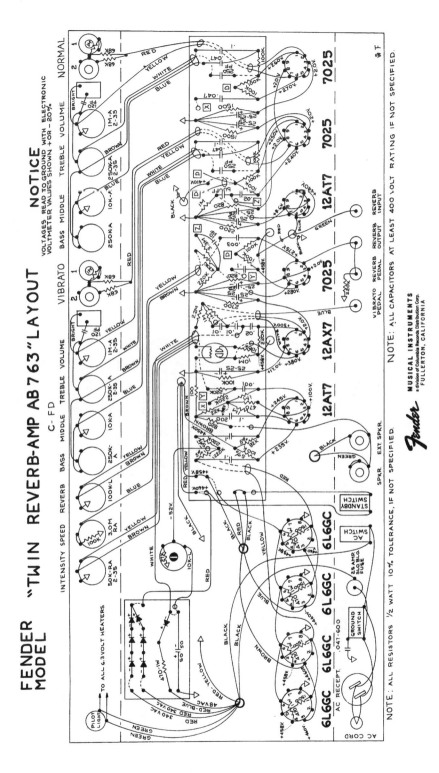

FENDER MODEL "TWIN REVERB-AMP AB763" LAYOUT

FENDER "TWIN REVERB-AMP AA769" SCHEMATIC NOTICE
MODEL

Kendricks

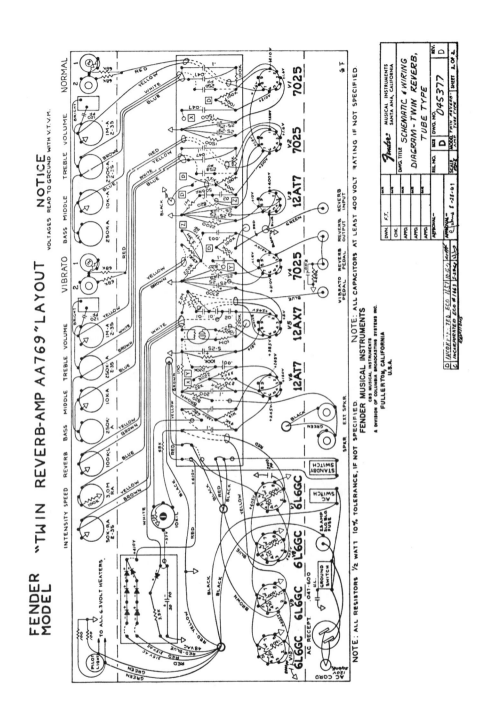

FENDER MODEL "TWIN REVERB-AMP AA270" SCHEMATIC NOTICE

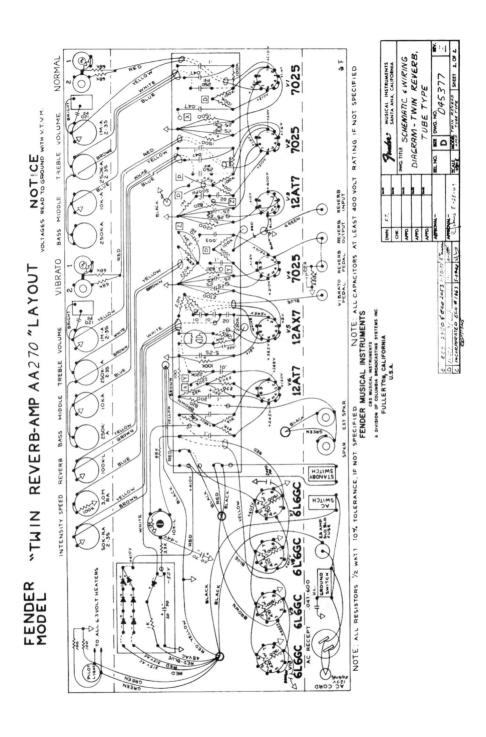

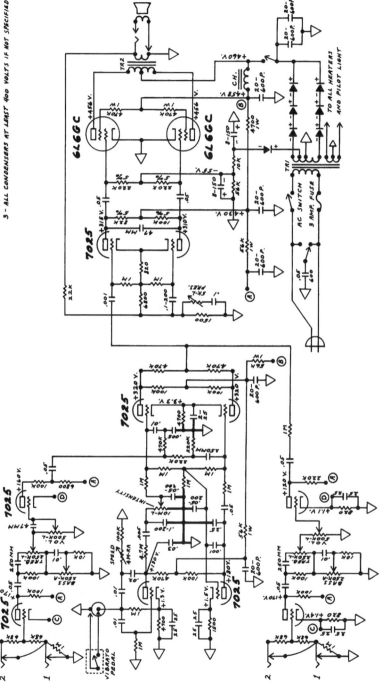

FENDER "VIBRASONIC" SCHEMATIC
MODEL 5G/3 A-FJ

NOTICE

1 – VOLTAGES READ TO GROUND WITH ELECTRONIC VOLTMETER. VALUES SHOWN + OR –

2 – ALL RESISTORS ½ WATT IF NOT SPECIFIED

3 – ALL CONDENSERS AT LEAST 400 VOLTS IF NOT SPECIFIED

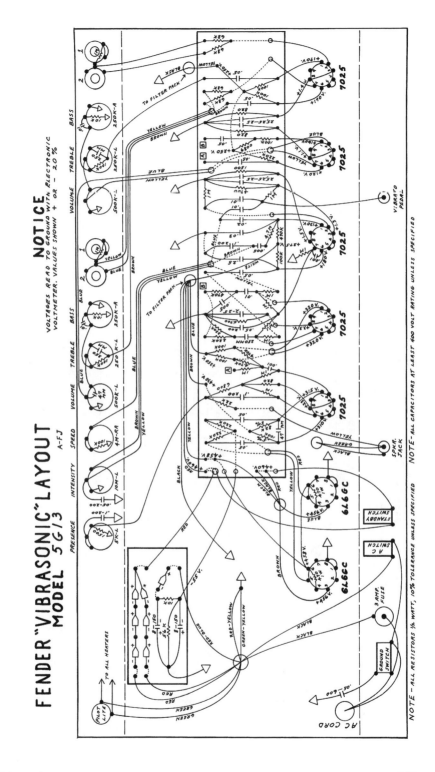

FENDER "VIBRASONIC" LAYOUT
MODEL 5G13
A-FJ

NOTICE

VOLTAGES READ TO GROUND WITH ELECTRONIC
VOLTMETER. VALUES SHOWN + OR - 20%

NOTE - ALL RESISTORS ¼ WATT, 10% TOLERANCE UNLESS SPECIFIED

NOTE - ALL CAPACITORS AT LEAST 400 VOLT RATING UNLESS SPECIFIED

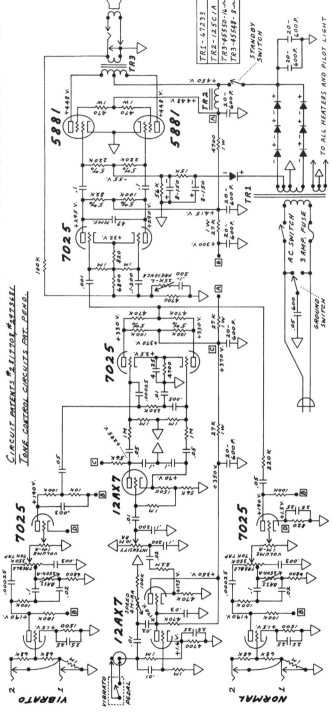

FENDER "VIBRASONIC" SCHEMATIC
MODEL 6G13-A   K-FJ

CIRCUIT PATENTS #2,817,708 #477368L
TONE CONTROL CIRCUITS PAT. PEND.

NOTICE

1 - VOLTAGES READ TO GROUND WITH ELECTRONIC
    VOLTMETER. VALUES SHOWN + OR - 20%
2 - ALL RESISTORS 1/2 WATT, 10% TOLERANCE IF NOT SPECIFIED
3 - ALL CAPACITORS AT LEAST 400 VOLT RATING IF NOT SPECIFIED

Kendricks

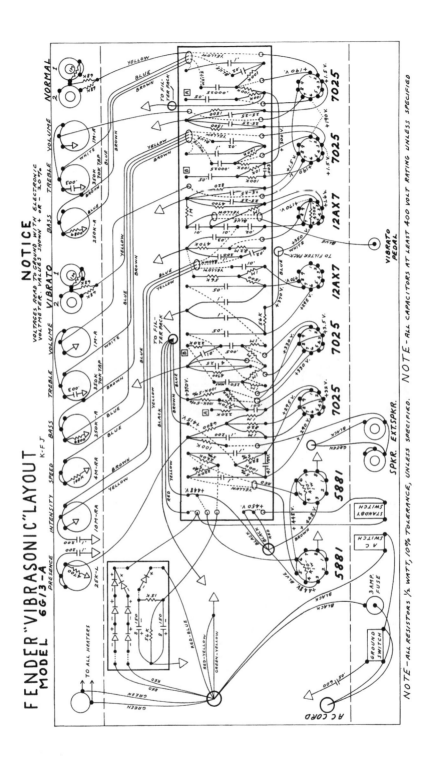

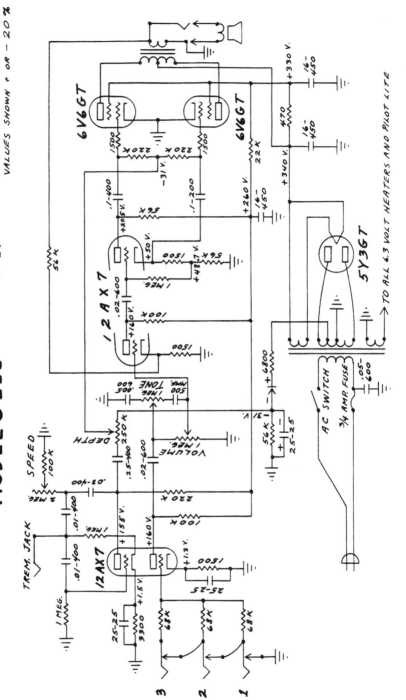

FENDER "VIBROLUX" SCHEMATIC
MODEL 5E11
G-EF

NOTICE

VOLTAGES READ TO GROUND WITH V.T.V.M. VALUES SHOWN + OR – 20%

Kendricks

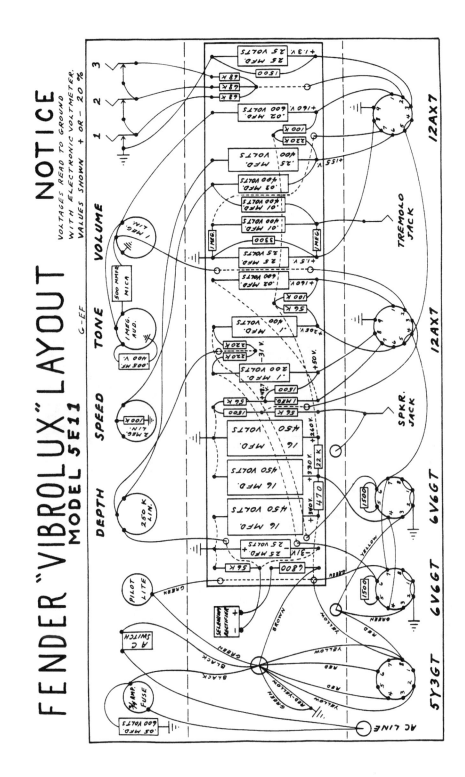

FENDER "VIBROLUX" LAYOUT
MODEL 5E11

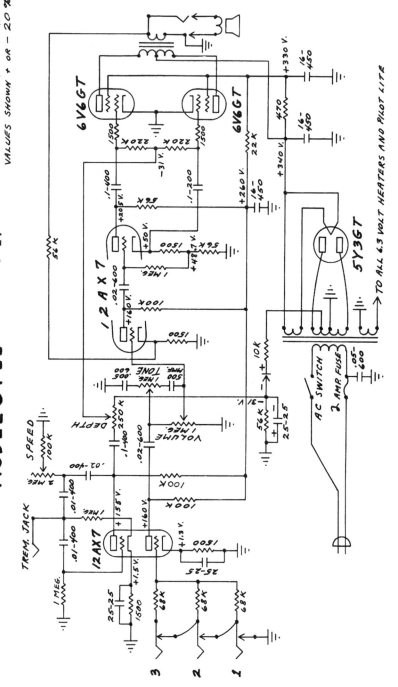

FENDER "VIBROLUX" SCHEMATIC
MODEL 5F11
G-EF

NOTICE

VOLTAGES READ TO
GROUND WITH V.T.V.M.
VALUES SHOWN + OR - 20 %

Kendricks

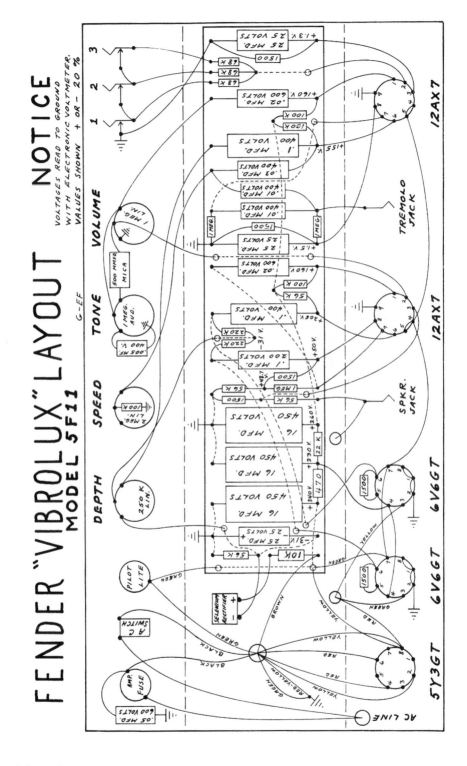

FENDER "VIBROLUX" LAYOUT
MODEL 5F11

NOTICE
VOLTAGES READ TO GROUND
WITH ELECTRONIC VOLTMETER.
VALUES SHOWN + OR - 20 %

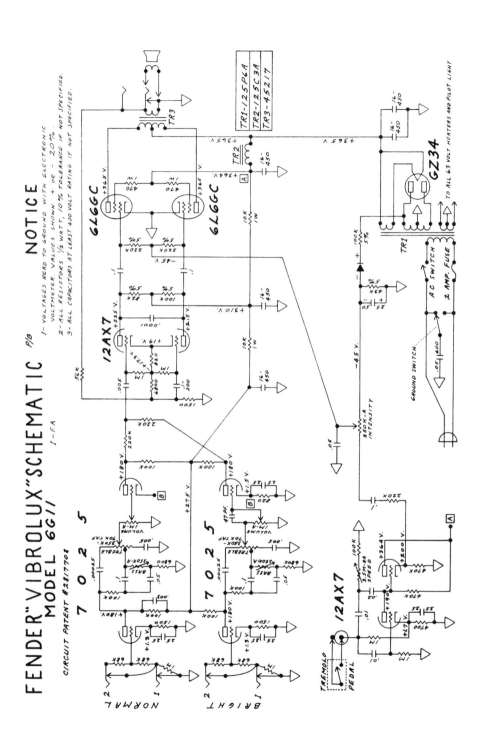

FENDER "VIBROLUX" SCHEMATIC P/B
MODEL 6G11
I-FA
CIRCUIT PATENT #2817704

NOTICE
1- VOLTAGES READ TO GROUND WITH ELECTRONIC
VOLTMETER. VALUES SHOWN + OR - 20%
2- ALL RESISTORS 1/2 WATT, 10% TOLERANCE IF NOT SPECIFIED.
3- ALL CAPACITORS AT LEAST 400 VOLT RATING IF NOT SPECIFIED.

Kendricks

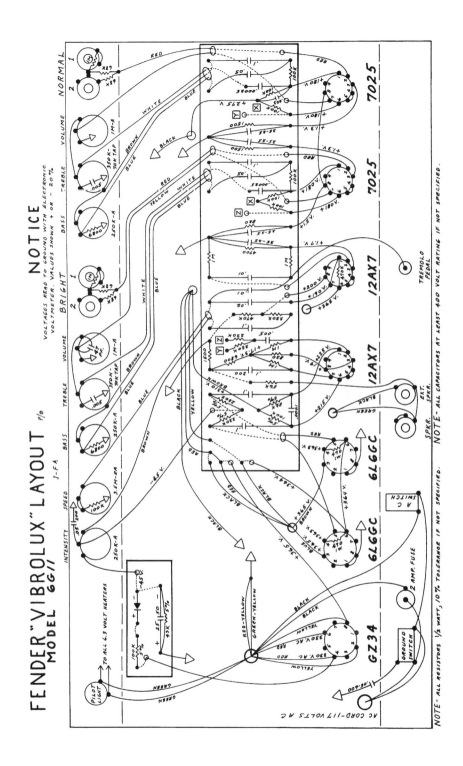

FENDER "VIBROLUX" LAYOUT P/B
MODEL 6G11

NOTICE
VOLTAGES READ TO GROUND WITH ELECTRONIC
VOLTMETER. VALUES SHOWN + OR - 20%

NOTE- ALL RESISTORS 1/2 WATT, 10% TOLERANCE IF NOT SPECIFIED.   NOTE- ALL CAPACITORS AT LEAST 400 VOLT RATING IF NOT SPECIFIED.

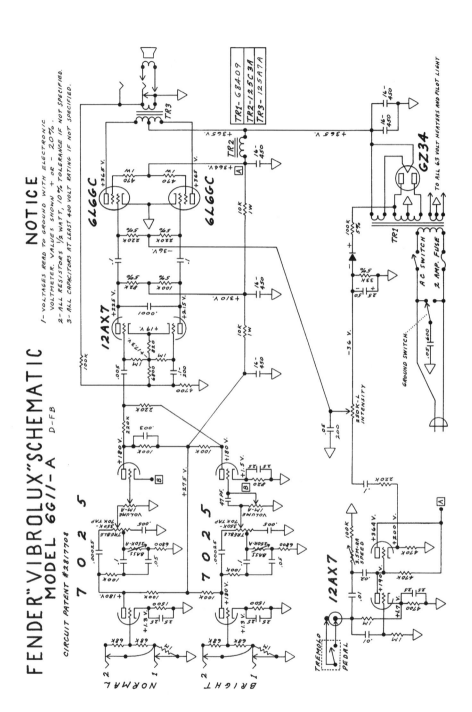

FENDER "VIBROLUX" SCHEMATIC
MODEL 6G11-A D-FB

CIRCUIT PATENT #2817708

NOTICE

1 - VOLTAGES READ TO GROUND WITH ELECTRONIC VOLTMETER. VALUES SHOWN + OR - 20%.
2 - ALL RESISTORS 1/2 WATT, 10% TOLERANCE IF NOT SPECIFIED.
3 - ALL CAPACITORS AT LEAST 400 VOLT RATING IF NOT SPECIFIED.

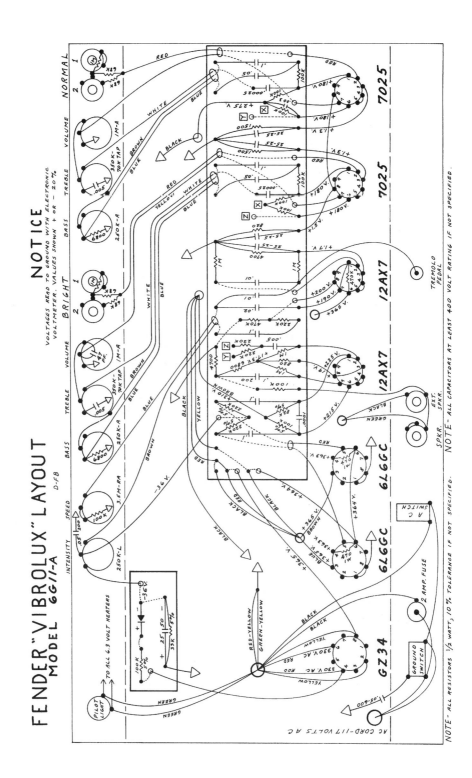

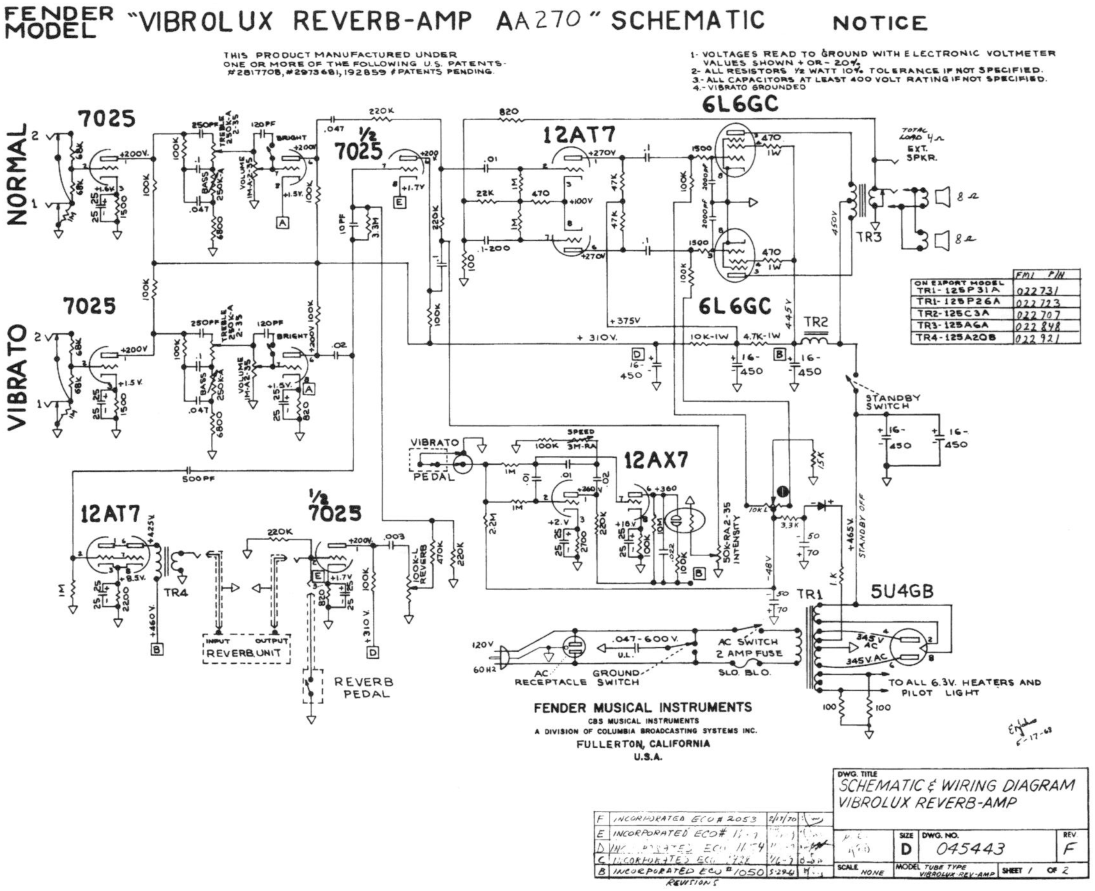
FENDER MODEL "VIBROLUX REVERB-AMP AA270" SCHEMATIC
NOTICE
THIS PRODUCT MANUFACTURED UNDER ONE OR MORE OF THE FOLLOWING U.S. PATENTS-#2817708, #2973681, 192859 & PATENTS PENDING.
1- VOLTAGES READ TO GROUND WITH ELECTRONIC VOLTMETER VALUES SHOWN + OR - 20%.
2- ALL RESISTORS ½ WATT 10% TOLERANCE IF NOT SPECIFIED.
3- ALL CAPACITORS AT LEAST 400 VOLT RATING IF NOT SPECIFIED.
4.- VIBRATO GROUNDED
NORMAL
VIBRATO
7025
½ 7025
12AT7
6L6GC
12AX7
5U4GB
TR1
TR2
TR3
TR4
BRIGHT
VOLUME
TREBLE
BASS
SPEED
INTENSITY
VIBRATO PEDAL
REVERB PEDAL
INPUT
OUTPUT
REVERB UNIT
STANDBY SWITCH
EXT. SPKR.
AC SWITCH
2 AMP FUSE
SLO. BLO.
AC RECEPTACLE
GROUND SWITCH
TO ALL 6.3V. HEATERS AND PILOT LIGHT
ON EXPORT MODEL TR1- 125P31A | FMI P/N 022731
TR1- 125P26A | 022723
TR2- 125C3A | 022707
TR3- 125A6A | 022848
TR4- 125A20B | 022921
FENDER MUSICAL INSTRUMENTS
CBS MUSICAL INSTRUMENTS
A DIVISION OF COLUMBIA BROADCASTING SYSTEMS INC.
FULLERTON, CALIFORNIA
U.S.A.
DWG. TITLE
SCHEMATIC & WIRING DIAGRAM
VIBROLUX REVERB-AMP
SIZE D
DWG. NO. 045443
REV F
SCALE NONE
SHEET 1 OF 2
REVISIONS

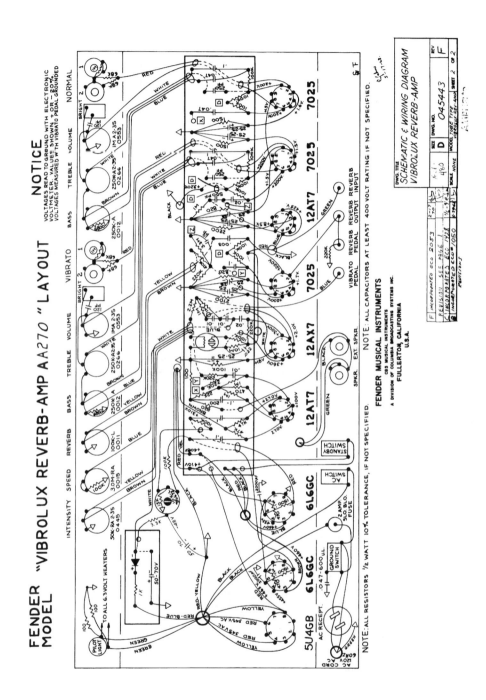

FENDER "VIBROLUX REVERB-AMP AA270 "LAYOUT
MODEL

NOTICE
VOLTAGES READ TO GROUND WITH ELECTRONIC
VOLTMETER. VALUES SHOWN MAY VARY 20%.
VOLTAGES MEASURED WITH VIBRATO PEDAL GROUNDED

NOTE: ALL RESISTORS ½ WATT 10% TOLERANCE, IF NOT SPECIFIED.   NOTE: ALL CAPACITORS AT LEAST 400 VOLT RATING IF NOT SPECIFIED.

FENDER MUSICAL INSTRUMENTS
CBS MUSICAL INSTRUMENTS
A DIVISION OF COLUMBIA BROADCASTING SYSTEMS INC.
FULLERTON, CALIFORNIA
U.S.A.

DWG. TITLE
SCHEMATIC & WIRING DIAGRAM
VIBROLUX REVERB-AMP

SIZE D   DWG. NO. 045443   REV F

MODEL TYPE   VIBROLUX REV. AMP   SHEET 2 OF 2
SCALE NONE

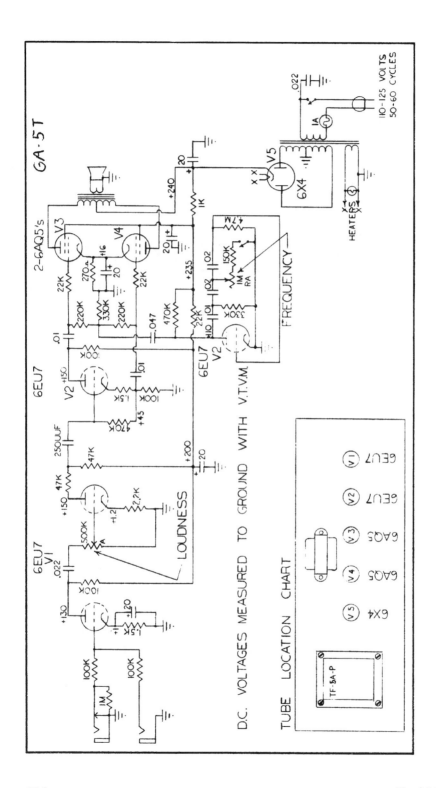

D.C. VOLTAGES MEASURED TO GROUND WITH V.T.V.M.

TUBE LOCATION CHART

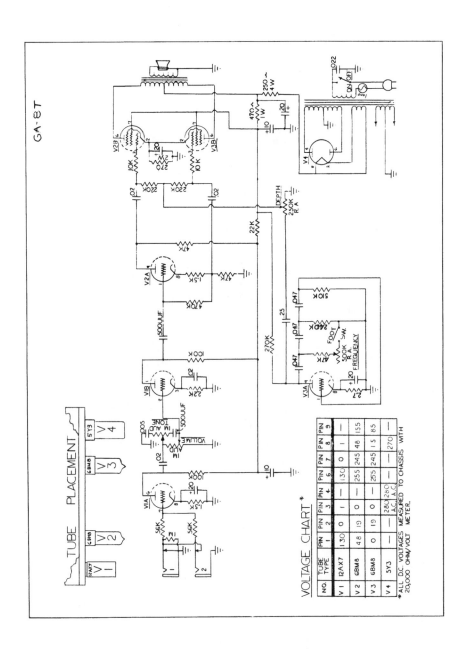

GA-8T

VOLTAGE CHART*

NO.	TUBE TYPE	PIN 1	PIN 2	PIN 3	PIN 4	PIN 6	PIN 7	PIN 8	PIN 9
V 1	12AX7	130	0	—	—	130	0	—	—
V 2	6BM8	48	19	0	—	255	245	48	155
V 3	6BM8	0	19	0	—	255	245	15	85
V 4	5Y3	—	—	280 / 280 A.C. / A.C.	—	—	—	270	—

*ALL D.C. VOLTAGES MEASURED TO CHASSIS WITH 20,000 OHM/VOLT METER.

TUBE PLACEMENT

12AX7	6BM8	6BM8	5Y3
V 1	V 2	V 3	V 4

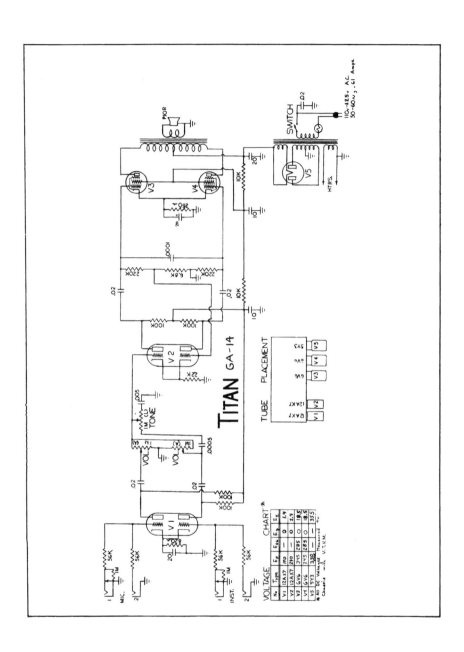

TITAN GA-14

TUBE PLACEMENT

12AX7	12AX7	6V6	6V6	5Y3
V1	V2	V3	V4	V5

VOLTAGE CHART *

No.	Type	Ep	Eg	Es	Ek
V1	12AX7	170	—	0	1.4
V2	12AX7	210	—	0	2.4
V3	6V6	345	285	285	18.5
V4	6V6	345	285	0	18.5
V5	5Y3	382	—	—	355

* All DC Voltages Measured to Chassis with V.T.V.M.

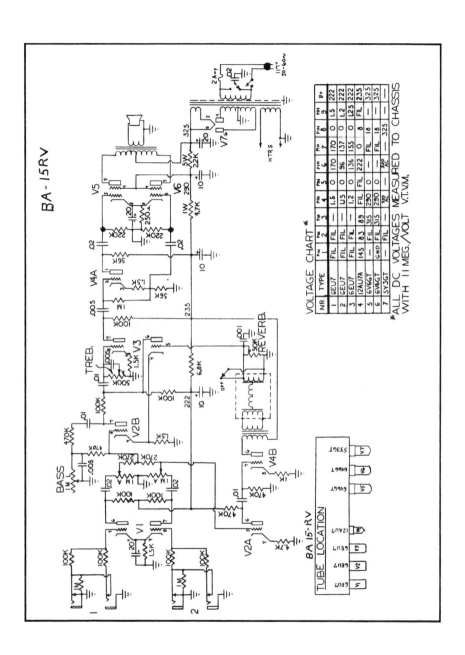

BA-15RV

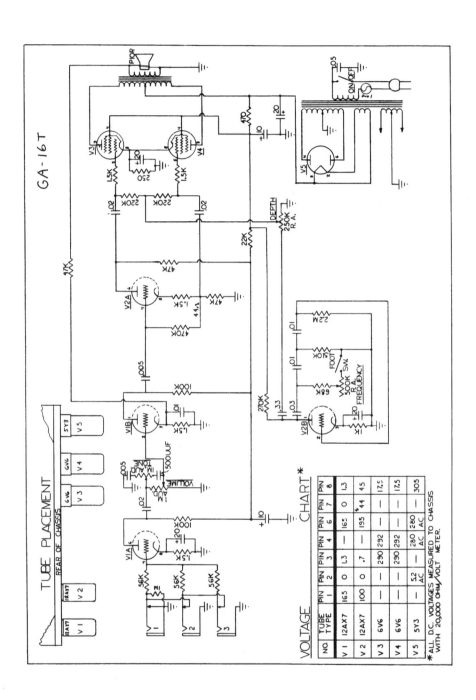

GA-16T

TUBE PLACEMENT

REAR OF CHASSIS

V 1	V 2	V 3	V 4	V 5
12AX7	12AX7	6V6	6V6	5Y3

VOLTAGE CHART *

NO.	TUBE TYPE	PIN 1	PIN 2	PIN 3	PIN 4	PIN 6	PIN 7	PIN 8
V 1	12AX7	165	0	1.3	—	165	0	1.3
V 2	12AX7	100	0	.7	—	195	4.4	4.5
V 3	6V6	—	—	290	292	—	—	17.5
V 4	6V6	—	—	290	292	—	—	17.5
V 5	5Y3	—	5.2 AC	—	280 AC	280 AC	—	305

* ALL D.C. VOLTAGES MEASURED TO CHASSIS WITH 20,000 OHM/VOLT METER.

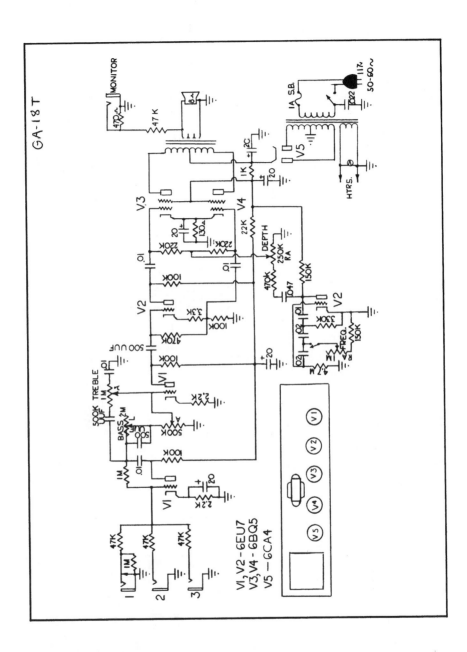

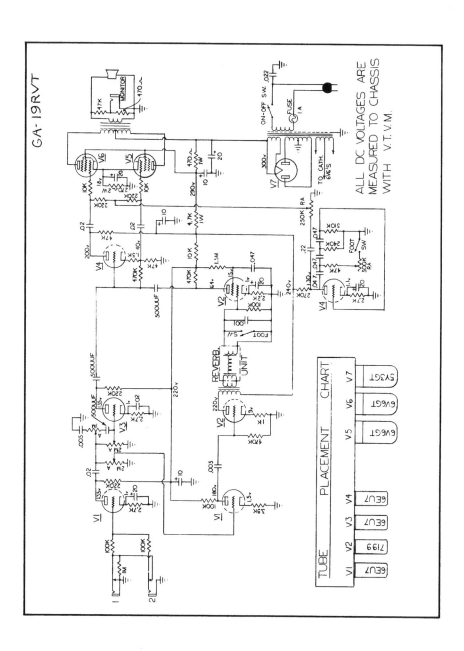

GA-19RVT

ALL DC VOLTAGES ARE
MEASURED TO CHASSIS
WITH V.T.V.M.

TUBE PLACEMENT CHART

V1	V2	V3	V4	V5	V6	V7
6EU7	7199	6EU7	6EU7	6V6GT	6V6GT	5Y3GT

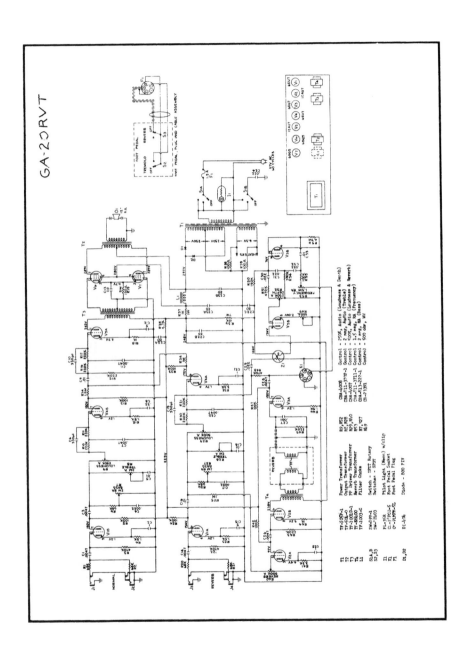

GA-20 RVT

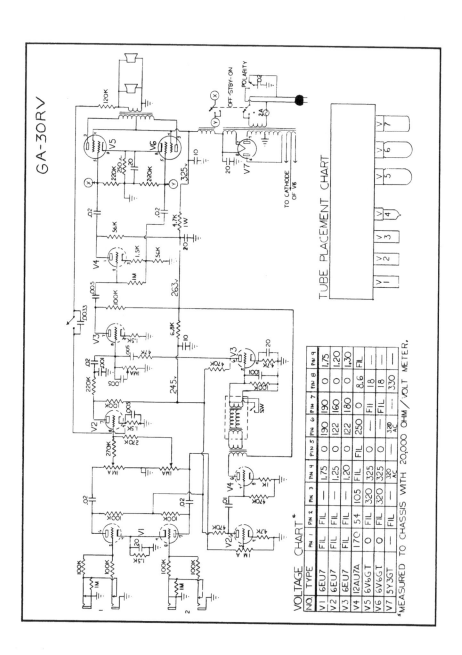

GA-30RV

TUBE PLACEMENT CHART

VOLTAGE CHART*

NO.	TYPE	PIN 1	PIN 2	PIN 3	PIN 4	PIN 5	PIN 6	PIN 7	PIN 8	PIN 9
V1	6EU7	FIL	FIL	—	1.75	0	190	190	0	1.75
V2	6EU7	FIL	FIL	—	1.25	0	122	160	0	1.20
V3	6EU7	FIL	FIL	—	1.20	0	122	180	0	1.30
V4	12AU7A	170	54	105	FIL	FIL	250	0	8.6	FIL
V5	6V6GT	0	FIL	320	325	—	—	FIL	18	—
V6	6V6GT	0	FIL	320	325	0	FIL	FIL	18	—
V7	5Y3GT	—	FIL	320 AC	320 AC	—	320 AC	—	330	—

*MEASURED TO CHASSIS WITH 20,000 OHM / VOLT METER.

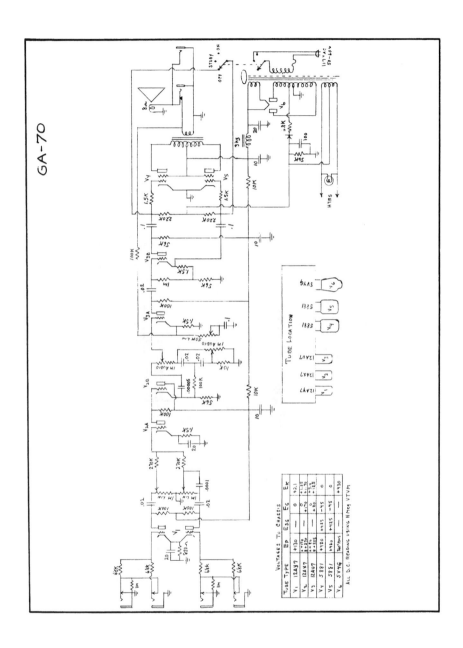

GA-70

GA 86

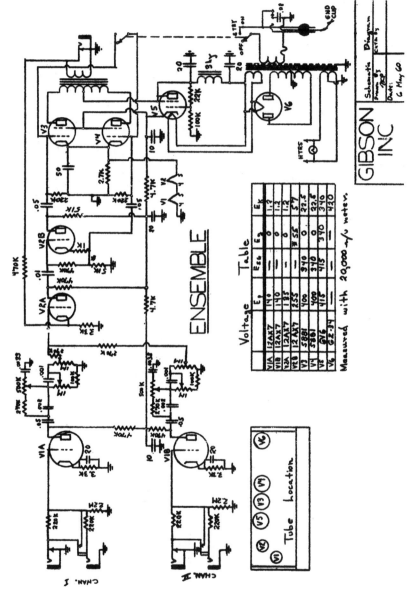

Kendricks

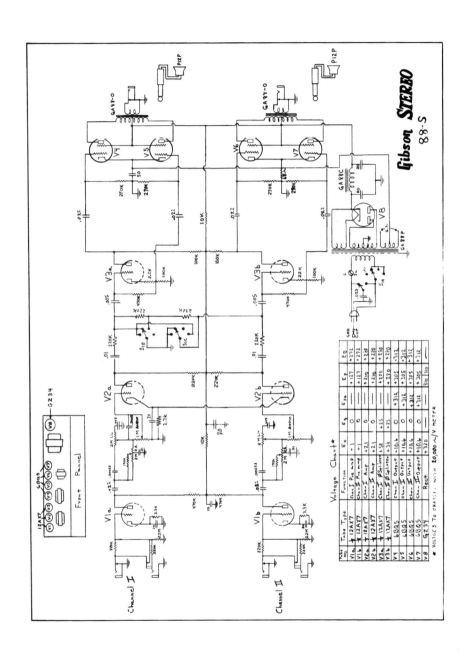

Gibson **STEREO** 88-S

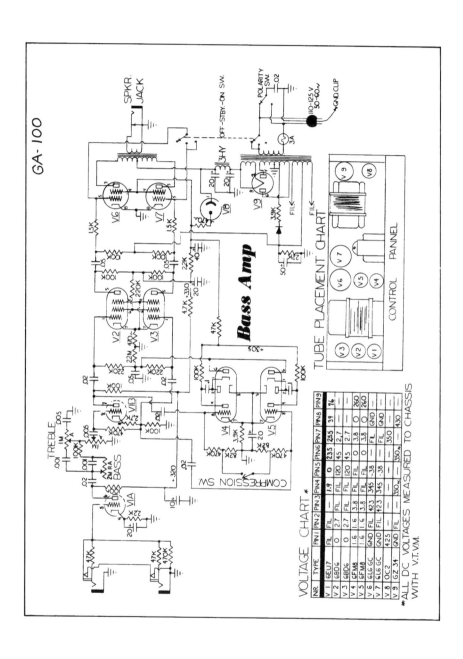

GA-100

Bass Amp

TUBE PLACEMENT CHART

CONTROL PANNEL

VOLTAGE CHART*

NR.	TYPE	PIN 1	PIN 2	PIN 3	PIN 4	PIN 5	PIN 6	PIN 7	PIN 8	PIN 9
V 1	6EU7	FIL	FIL	—	1.9	0	235	255	39	76
V 2	6BD6	0	2.7	FIL	FIL	120	45	2.7	—	—
V 3	6BD6	0	2.7	FIL	FIL	120	45	2.7	—	—
V 4	6FM8	1.6	1.6	3.8	FIL	FIL	0	3.8	0	260
V 5	6FM8	1.6	1.6	3.8	FIL	FIL	0	3.8	0	260
V 6	6LG GC	GND	FIL	423	345	-38	—	FIL	GND	—
V 7	6L6 GC	GND	FIL	423	345	-38	—	FIL	GND	—
V 8	OC2	425	—	—	—	—	—	350	—	—
V 9	GZ 34	GND	FIL	—	350~	350~	—	350~	430	—

*ALL DC VOLTAGES MEASURED TO CHASSIS
WITH V.T.V.M.

HIWATT CIRCUIT DIAGRAMS

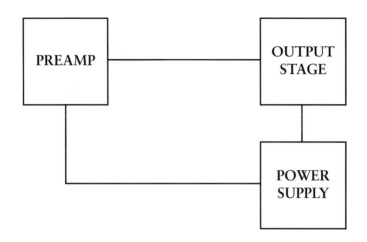

Pages:		Preamp	Output Stage	Power Supply
AP	DR504	410	412	414
	DR103	410	411	413
	DR201	410	418	415
	DR405	410/419	419	415
PA	DR112	417	411	413
	DR203	417	418	415
SLAVES	STA100	416	411	413
	STA200/R	416/420	418/420	415
	STA400	416/419	419	415
	STA200/D	416/420	418/420	415
COMBOS	SA112	410	412	414
	SA112FL	410	411	413
	SA115	410	412	414
	SA115FL	410	411	413
	SA212	410	412	414

SOURCE: HIWATT JULY 1979

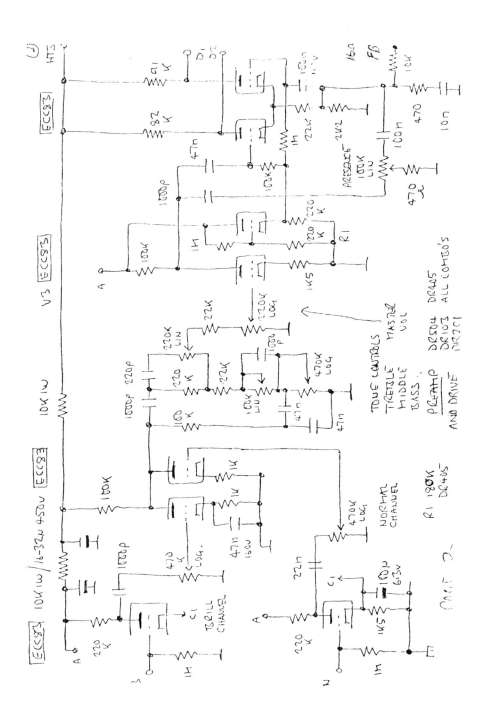

Kendricks

PAGE 3

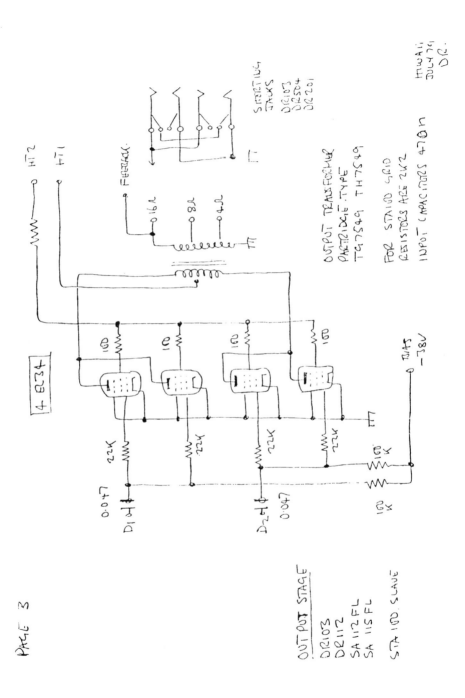

SMOOTHING
JACKS

DR103
D2504
DR201

HT2

HT1

FEEDBACK

.016Ω

8Ω

4Ω

OUTPUT TRANSFORMER
PARTRIDGE TYPE
TG7549 TH7549

FOR STA100 GRID
RESISTORS ARE 2K2
INPUT CAPACITORS 470n

HTWATT
JULY 76
D.C.

4 EL34

1Ω

1Ω

1Ω

1Ω

22K

22K

22K

22K

0.047

D1

D2

0.047

18K

18K

WATT
-38V

OUTPUT STAGE

DR103
DR112
SA112 FL
SA 115 FL

STA 100 SLAVE

Schematics   411

PAGE 4

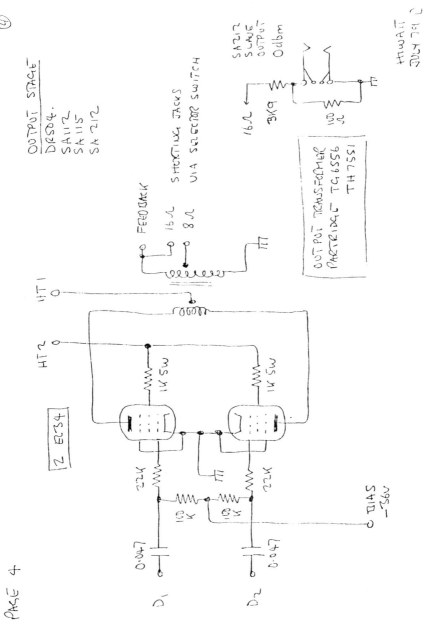

OUTPUT STAGE
DRSD4.
SA112
SA115
SA 212

FEEDBACK
16Ω
8Ω

SHORTING JACKS
VIA SELECTOR SWITCH

SA212 SLAVE OUTPUT 0dbm

16Ω
3KΩ
100Ω

4 WATT SLAVE O/P

OUTPUT TRANSFORMER
PARTRIDGE TG6556
TH7SSI

HT 1

HT 2

2 EL34

1K 5W
1K 5W

22K
22K

8K
8K

0.047
0.047

D1
D2

BIAS
−56V

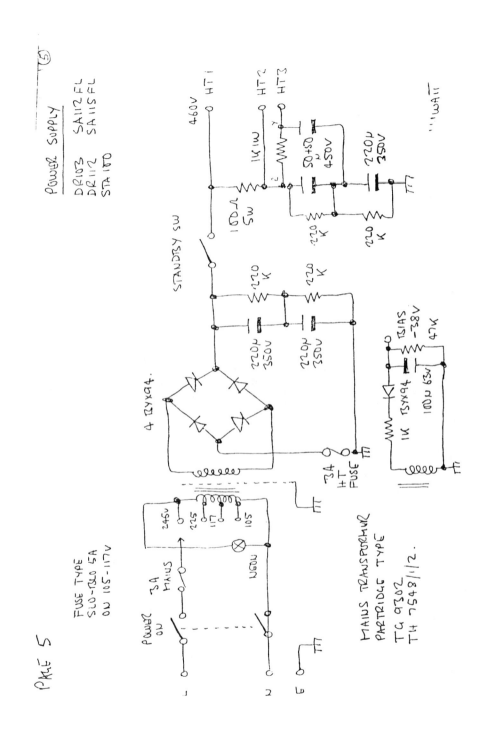

PAGE 5

Power Supply

DR103   SA112 FL
DR112   SA115 FL
STA 180

FUSE TYPE
S10-TSL0 5A
no 505-S01-117V

MAINS TRANSFORMER
PARTRIDGE TYPE
TC 9330Z
TH 7548/1/2.

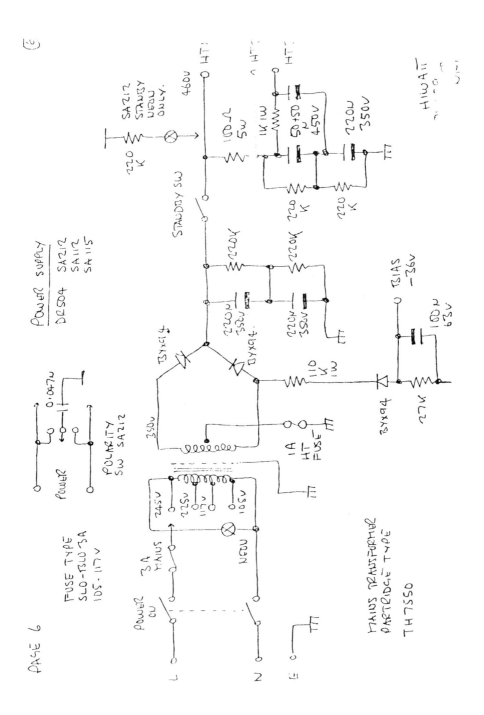

PAGE 6

FUSE TYPE
SLO-TSLO 3A
105 - 117V

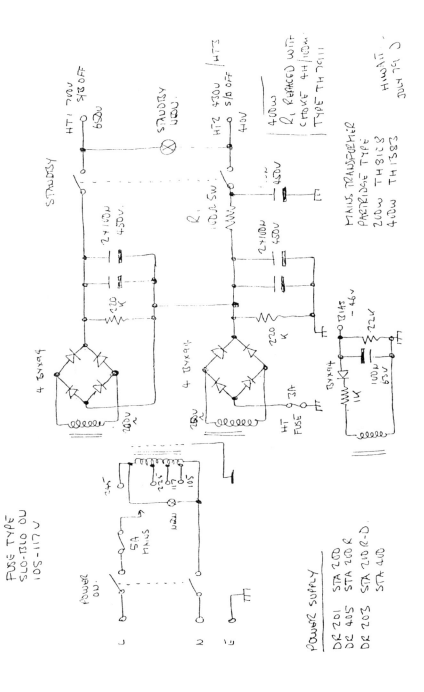

PAGE 7

FUSE TYPE
SLO-BLO OU
105-117 V

POWER SUPPLY

DR 201   STA 200
DR 405   STA 200 R
DR 203   STA 210 R-D
         STA 400

MAINS TRANSFORMER
PARTRIDGE TYPE
200w TH 8128
400w TH 15883

HIWATT
DR 103

Q₁ REPLACED WITH
CHOKE 4H/100m
TYPE TH 79111

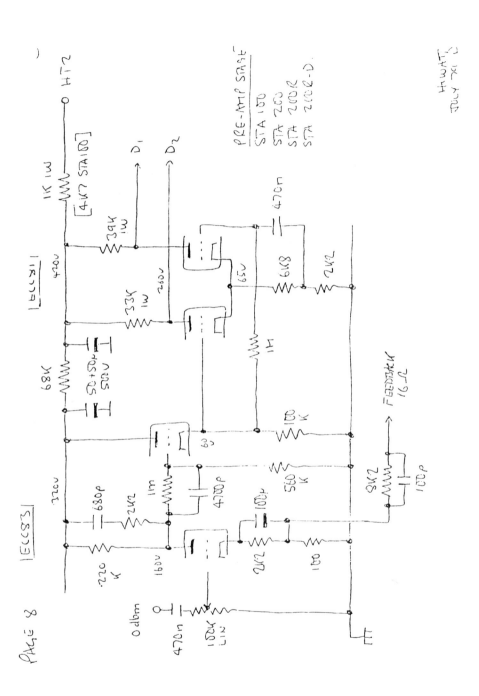

PAGE 8

416

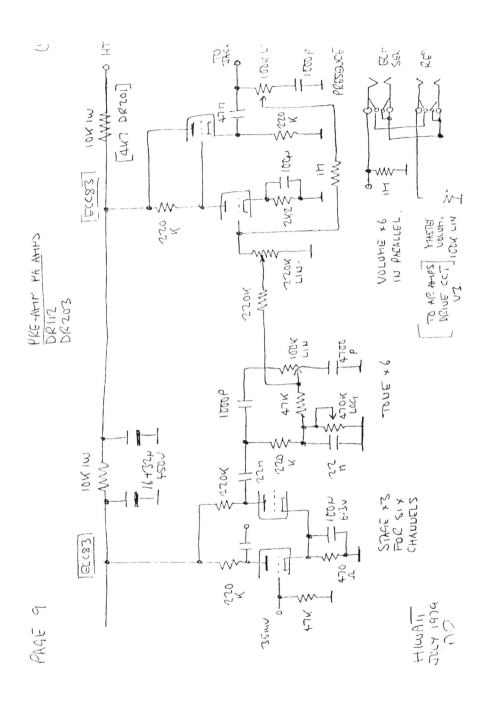

PRE-AMP PA AMPS
DR112
DR203

PAGE 9

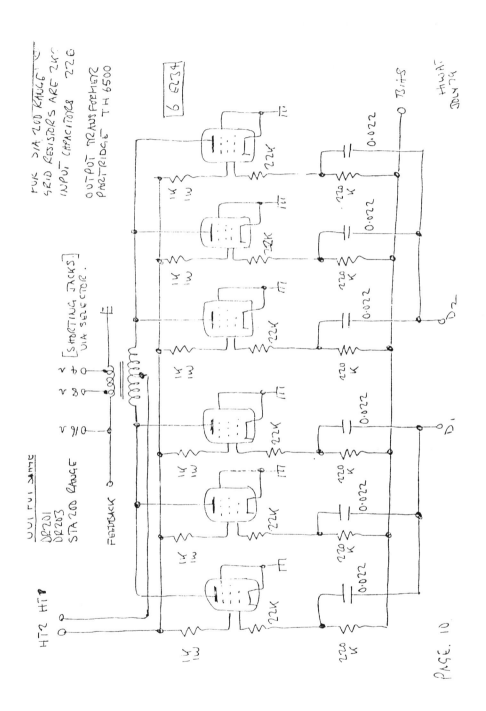

FOR S/A 700 RANGE
S2ID RESISTORS ARE 2K
INPUT CAPACITORS 22Ω

OUTPUT TRANSFORMER
PARTRIDGE TH 6500

FIG 9

OUTPUT STAGE
DR201
DR203
STA 700 RANGE

[SHORTING JACKS]
VIA SELECTOR.

PAGE. 10

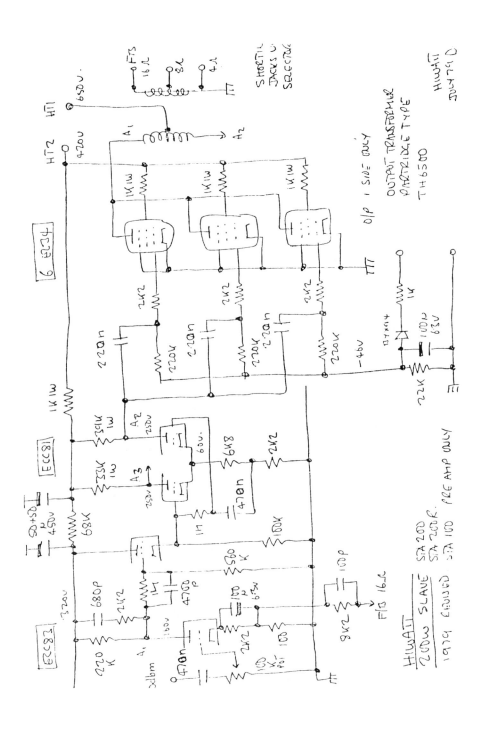

HIWATT
200W SLAVE
1979 ENCLOSED

STA 200
STA 200 R.
STA 100   PRE AMP ONLY

HIWATT
DW479 D

OUTPUT TRANSFORMER
PARTRIDGE TYPE
TH 6500

O/P (SIDE ONLY)

SHORTING
JACKS U
SELECTOR

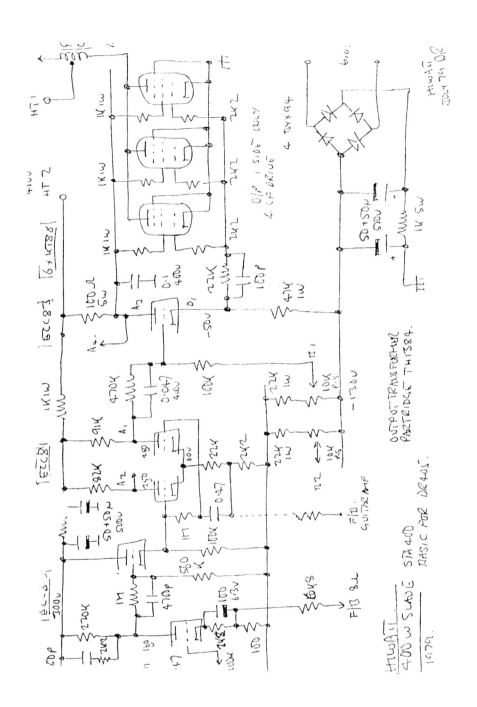

Kendricks

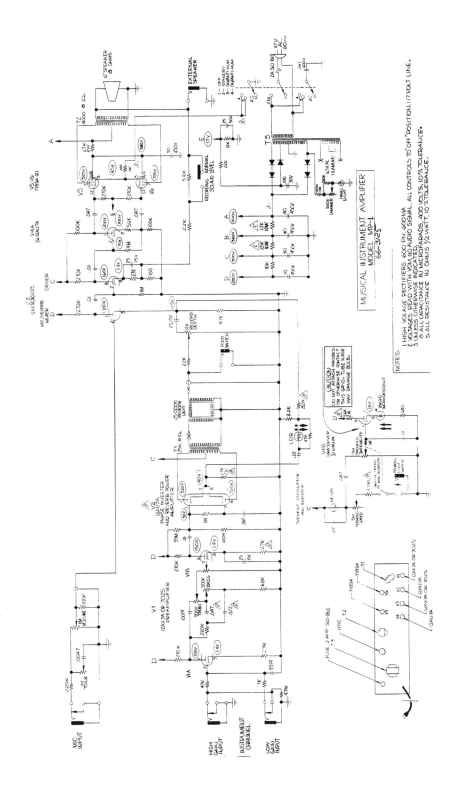

MUSICAL INSTRUMENT AMPLIFIER
MODEL MP-1
66-3/25

NOTES:
1. HIGH VOLTAGE RECTIFIERS 600 PIV, 600MA
2. VOLTAGES READ WITH VOM, NO AUDIO SIGNAL, ALL CONTROLS TO "OFF" POSITION, 117 VOLT LINE.
3. UNLESS OTHERWISE INDICATED, 400 VOLTS, 10% TOLERANCE.
   ALL CAPACITANCE IN MICROFARADS.
   ⚠ ALL CAPACITANCE IN MICROFARADS, 400 VOLTS, 10% TOLERANCE.
   ⚠ ALL RESISTANCE IN OHMS 1/2 WATT, 10% TOLERANCE.

CAUTION
DO NOT ATTACH PROBES
OR OTHERWISE CONTACT
THIS GRID, TUBE SURGE
MAY DAMAGE BULB.

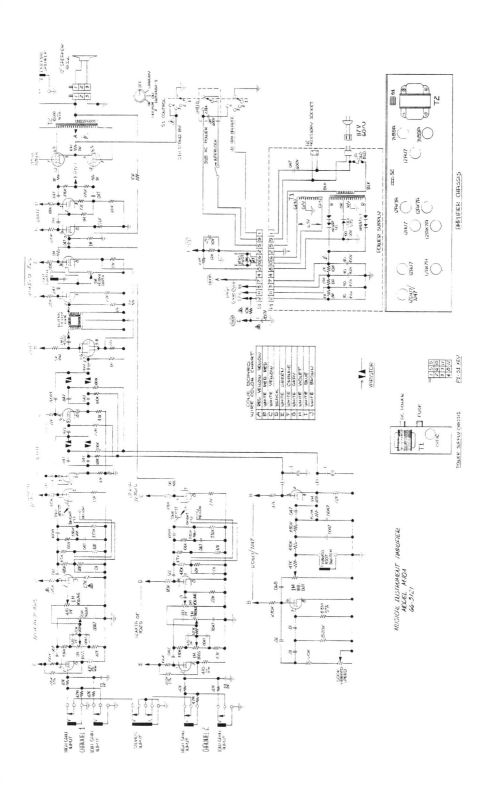

MUSICAL INSTRUMENT AMPLIFIER
MODEL M104
66-5121

Kendricks

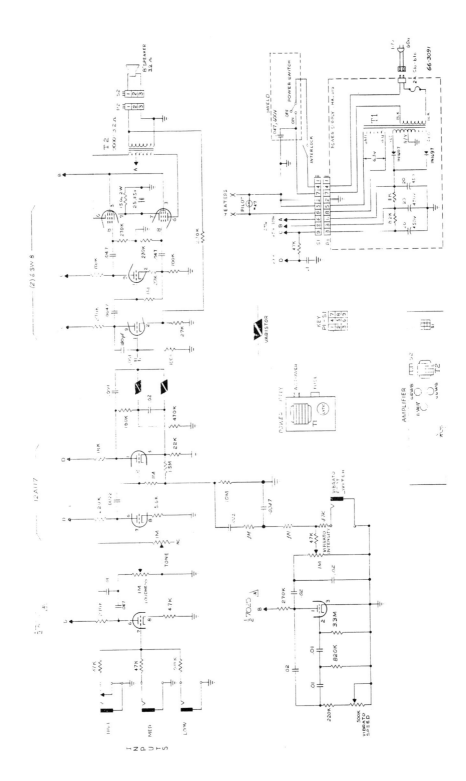

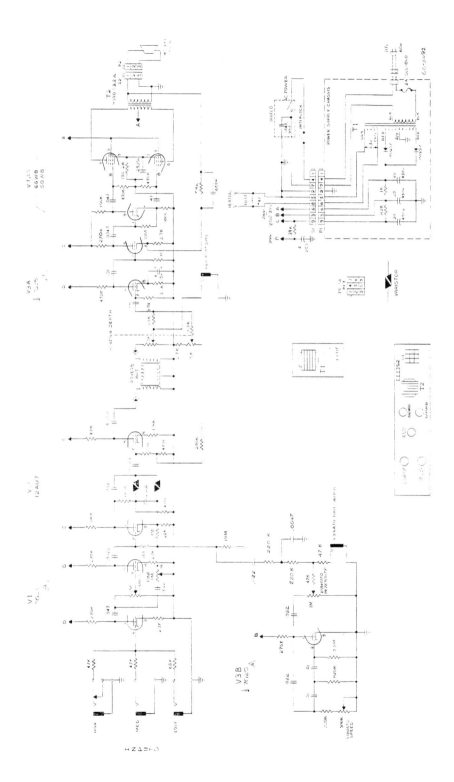

424   Kendricks

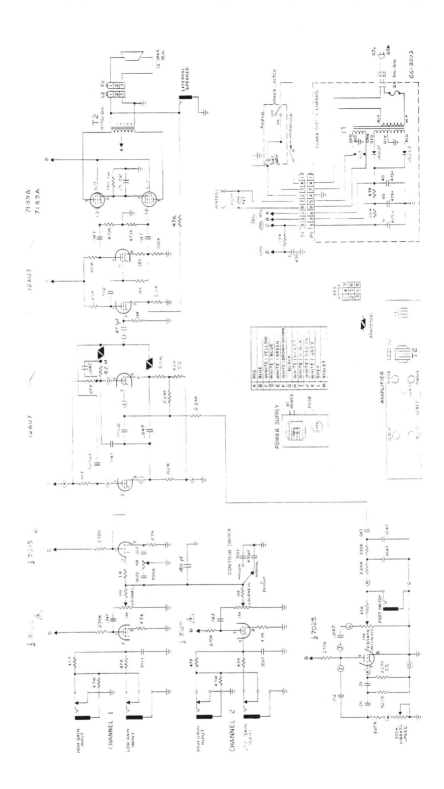

Schematics 425

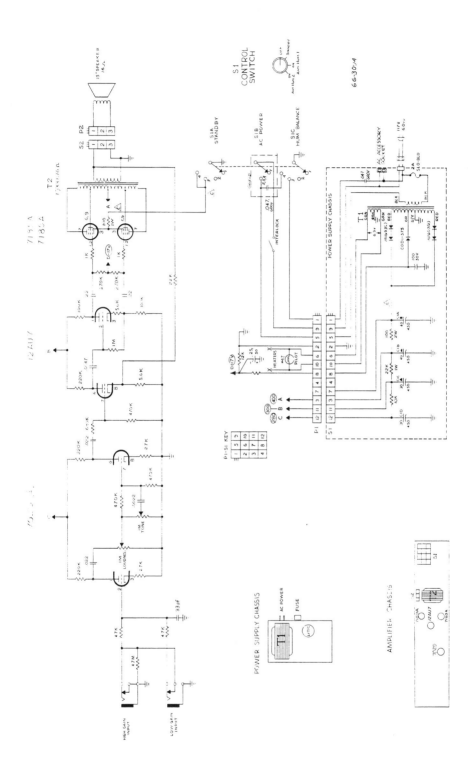

426   Kendricks

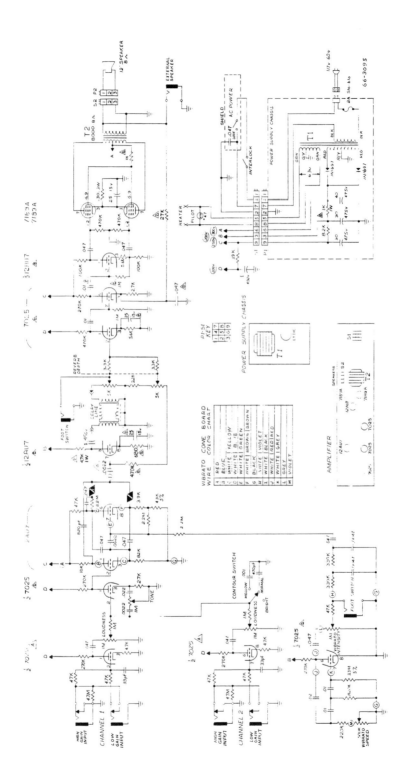

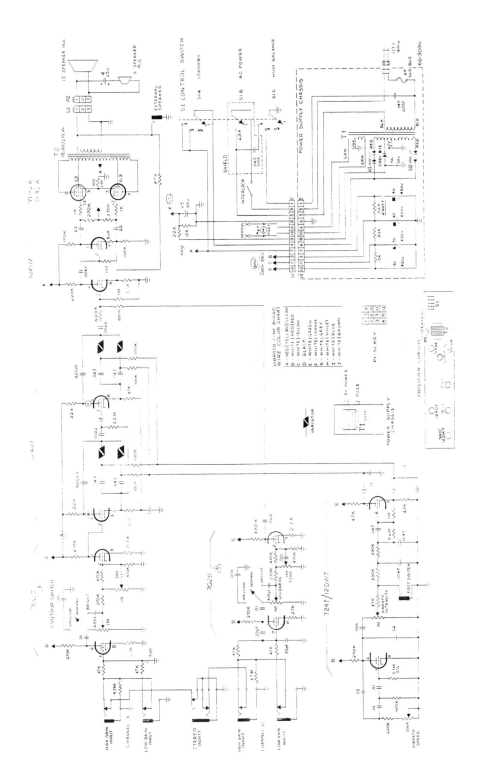

428   Kendricks

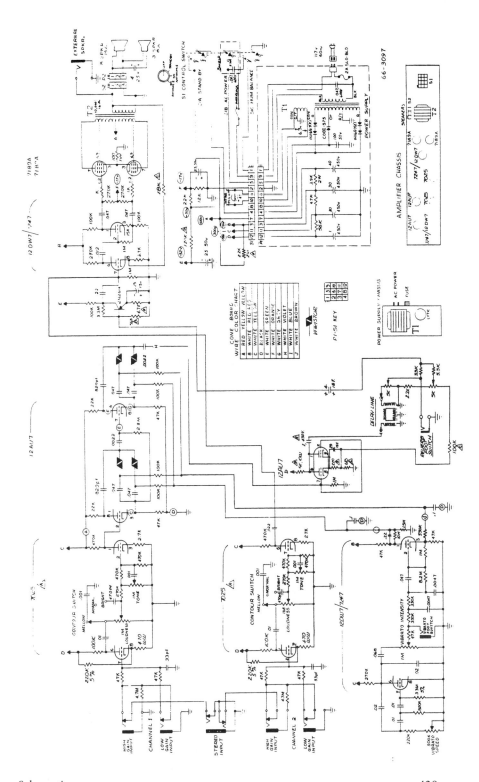

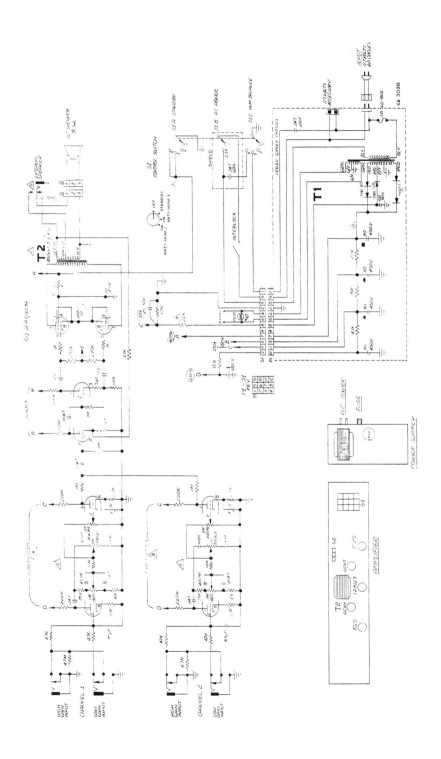

430   Kendricks

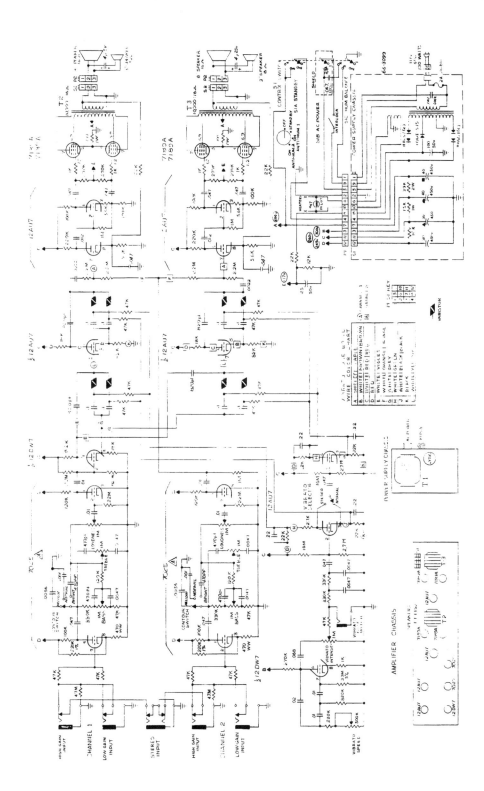

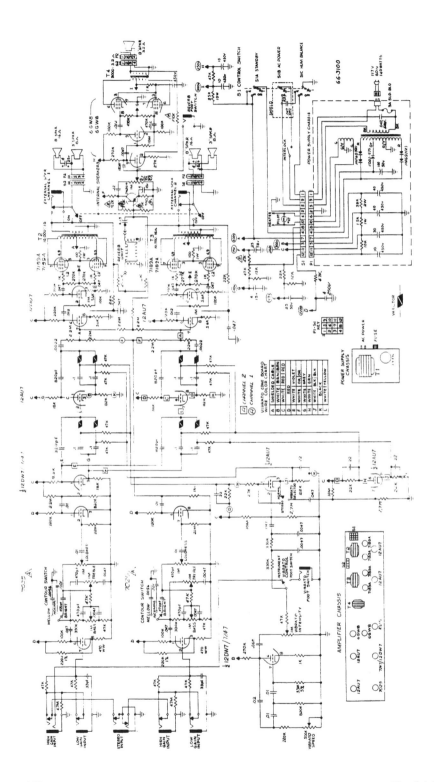

Kendricks

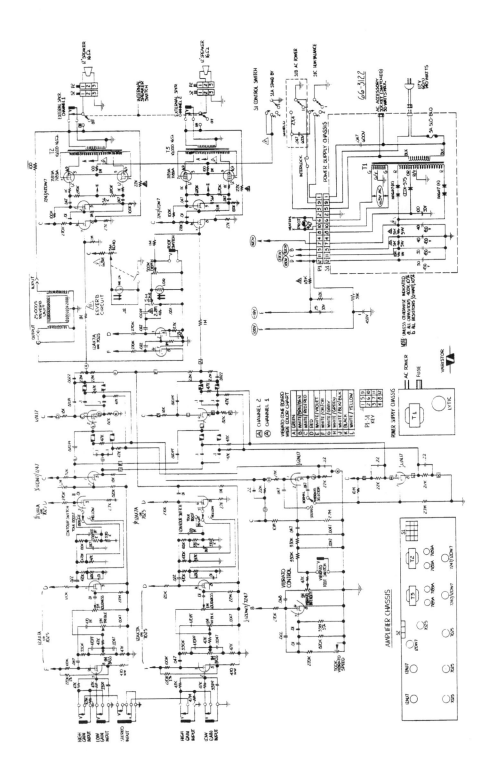

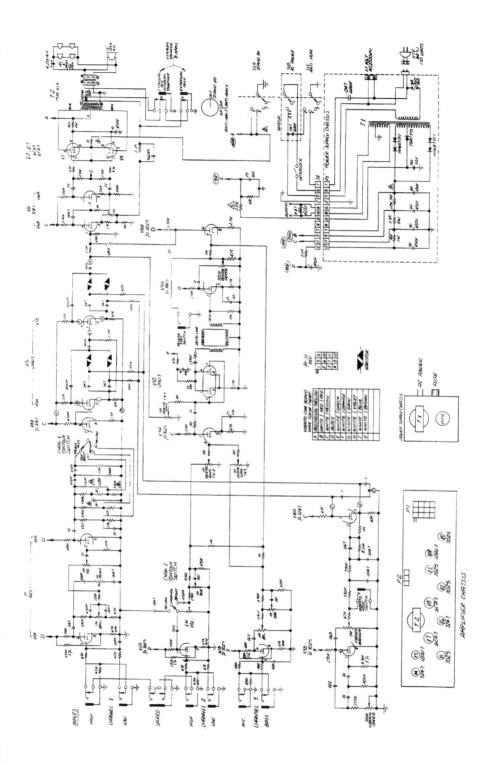

Kendricks

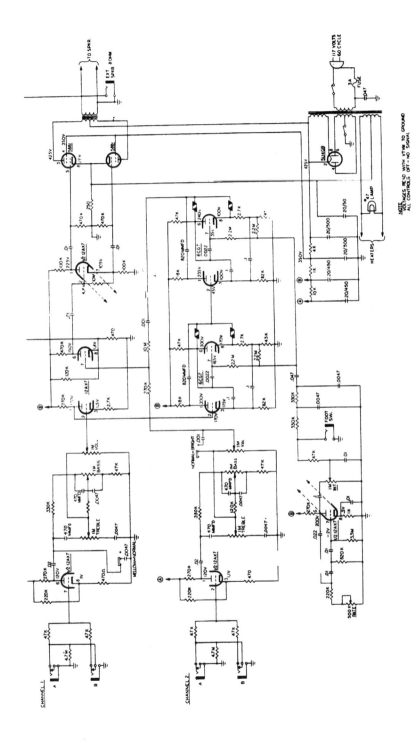

Schematic Diagram Courtesy MAGNA ELECTRONICS INC

MAGNATONE INSTRUMENT AMPLIFIER

MODEL 260-A

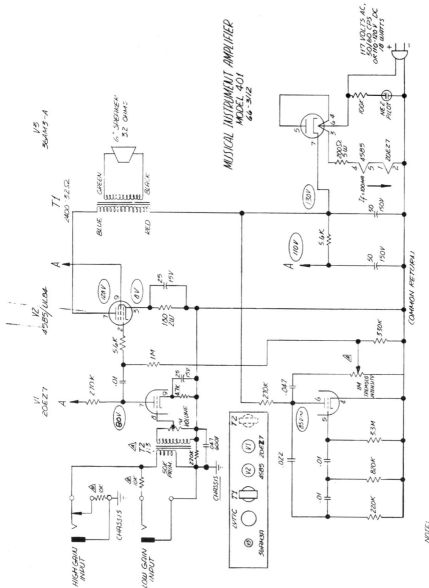

MUSICAL INSTRUMENT AMPLIFIER
MODEL 401
66-3/12

NOTE: VOLTAGES READ WITH VTVM FROM POINT INDICATED TO COMMON RETURN.

Kendricks

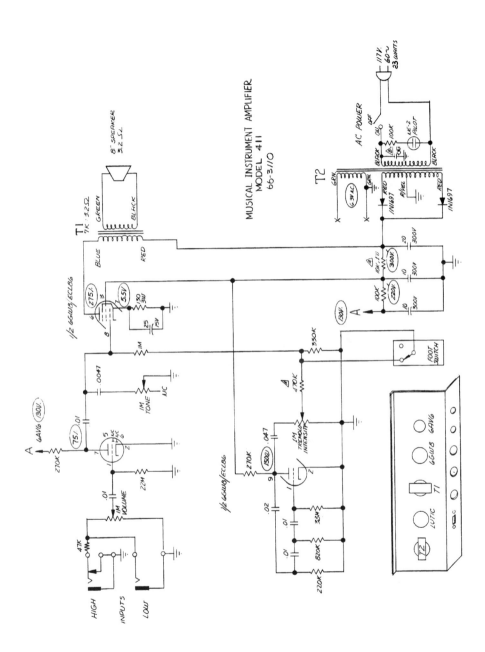

MUSICAL INSTRUMENT AMPLIFIER
MODEL 411
66-3/10

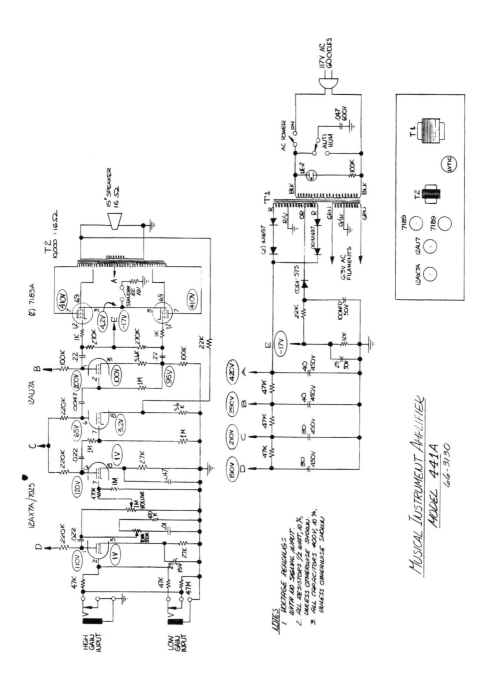

MUSICAL INSTRUMENT AMPLIFIER
MODEL 441A
66-3130

NOTES:
1. VOLTAGE READINGS WITH NO SIGNAL INPUT.
2. ALL RESISTORS ½ WATT, 10%, UNLESS OTHERWISE SHOWN.
3. ALL CAPACITORS 400V, 10%, UNLESS OTHERWISE SHOWN.

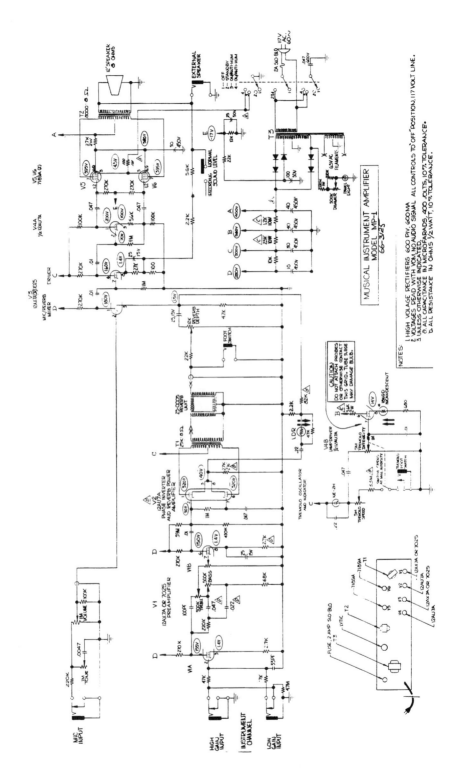

MUSICAL INSTRUMENT AMPLIFIER
MODEL MP-1
66-3/25

NOTES:
1. HIGH VOLTAGE RECTIFIERS 600 PIV, 600MA.
2. VOLTAGES READ WITH VOM, NO AUDIO SIGNAL. ALL CONTROLS TO "OFF" POSITION, 117 VOLT LINE.
3. UNLESS OTHERWISE INDICATED,
   A. ALL CAPACITANCE IN MICROFARADS, 400 VOLTS, 10% TOLERANCE.
   B. ALL RESISTANCE IN OHMS 1/2 WATT, 10% TOLERANCE.

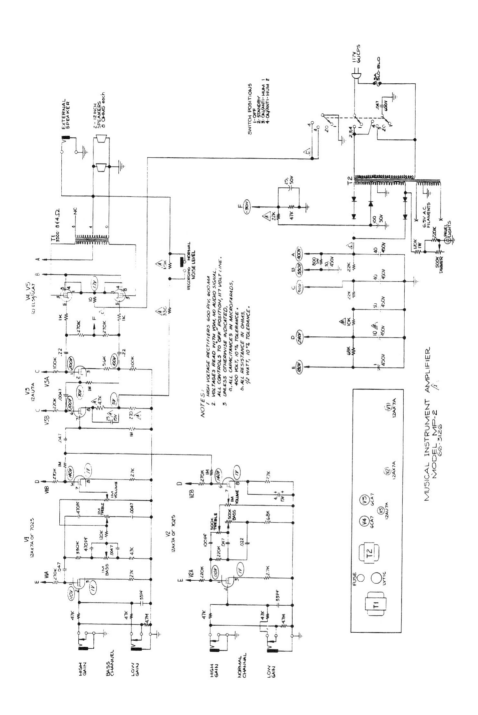

MUSICAL INSTRUMENT AMPLIFIER
MODEL MP-2
66-3126

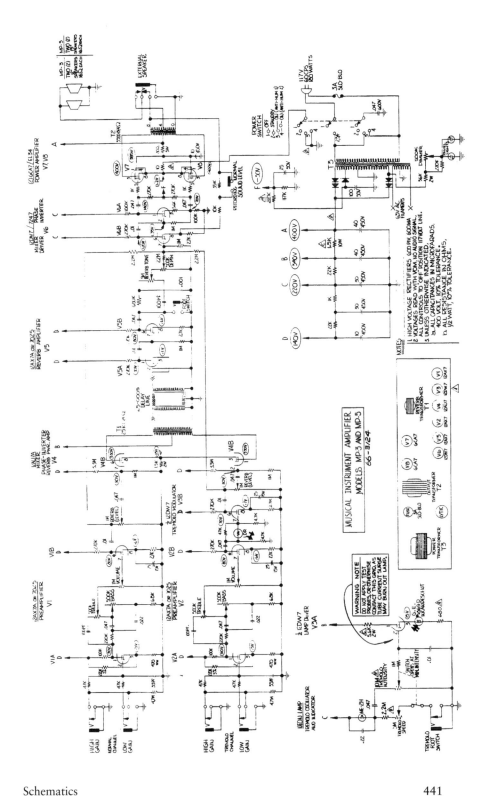

MUSICAL INSTRUMENT AMPLIFIER
MODELS MP-3 AND MP-5
66-3/24

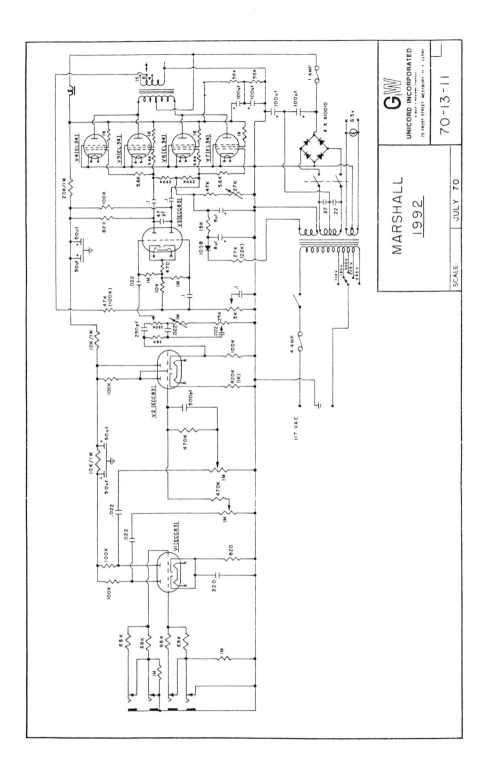

MARSHALL
1992

GW
UNICORD INCORPORATED
75 FROST STREET WESTBURY N Y 11590

70-13-11

SCALE: JULY 70

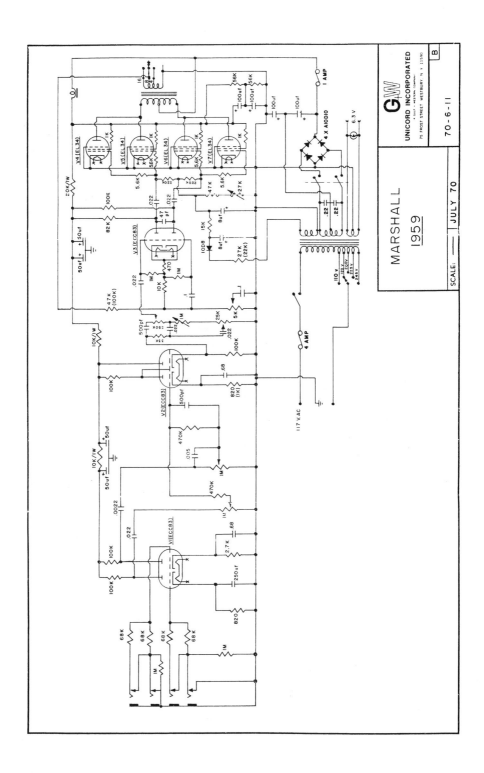

MARSHALL
1959

SCALE: ——— JULY 70

GW
UNICORD INCORPORATED
A GULF + WESTERN COMPANY
75 FROST STREET WESTBURY N Y 11590

70-6-11

B

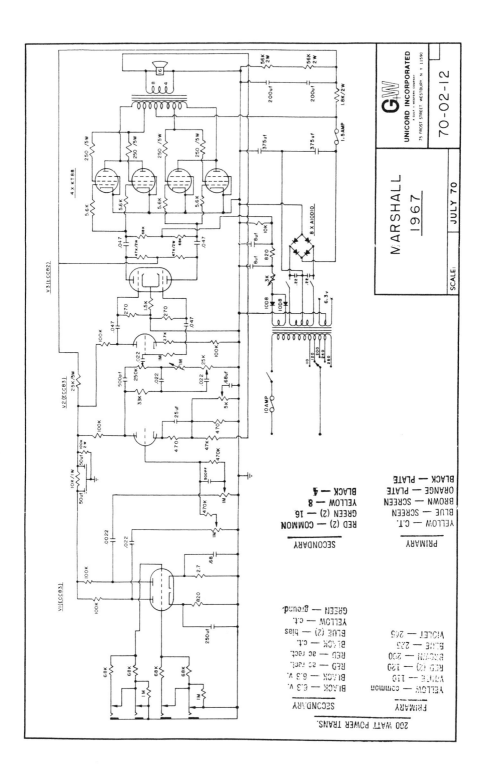

MARSHALL
1967

SCALE: JULY 70

70-02-12

G·W
UNICORD INCORPORATED
75 FROST STREET, WESTBURY, N.Y. 11590
A GULF + WESTERN COMPANY

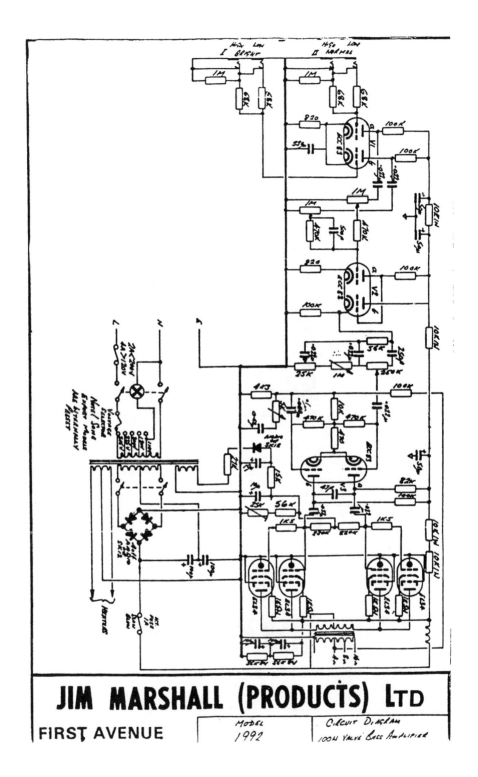

JIM MARSHALL (PRODUCTS) LTD

FIRST AVENUE

MODEL	CIRCUIT DIAGRAM	
1992	100W VALVE BASS AMPLIFIER	

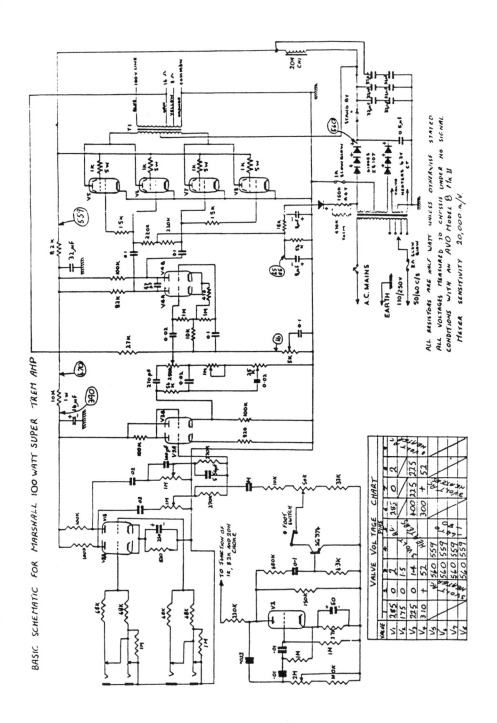

BASIC SCHEMATIC FOR MARSHALL 100 WATT SUPER TREM AMP

ALL RESISTORS ARE HALF WATT UNLESS OTHERWISE STATED
ALL VOLTAGES MEASURED TO CHASSIS UNDER NO SIGNAL
CONDITIONS WITH AN AVO MODEL 8 Mk II
METER SENSITIVITY 20,000 Ω/V.

VALVE	1	2	3	4	5	6	7	8	9
V1	285	0	2	52	560	559			
V2	175	0	1.5	52	560	559			
V3	225	0	1.4	52	560	559			
V4	310	+	52	300	+	400	225	52	
V5									
V6				285	0	2			

VALVE VOLTAGE CHART

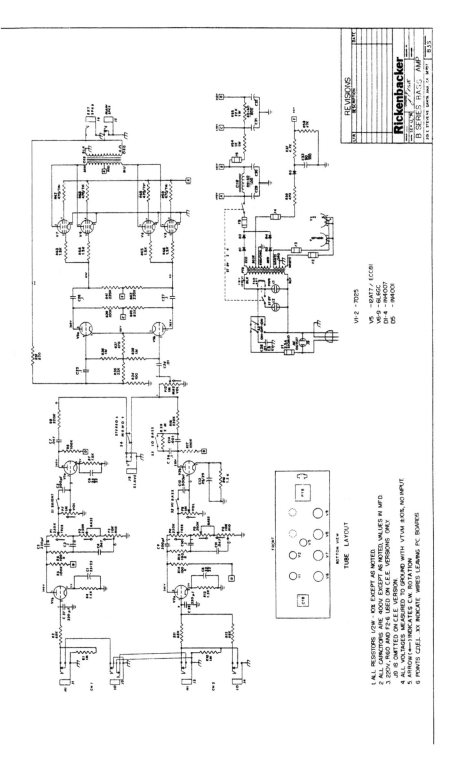

Rickenbacker B16, 16D,

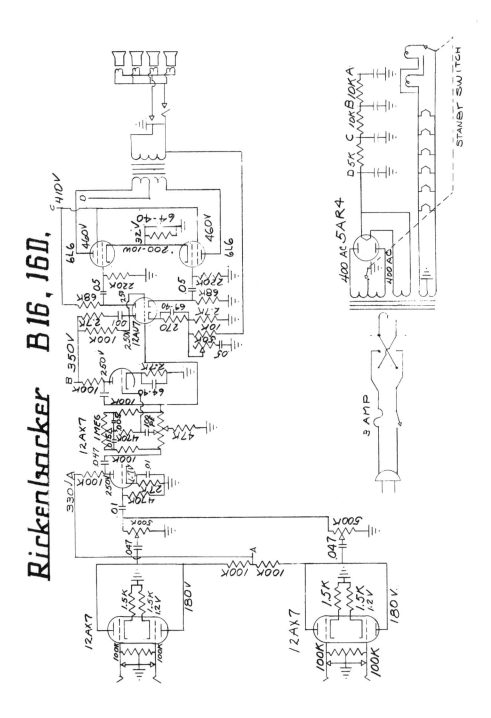

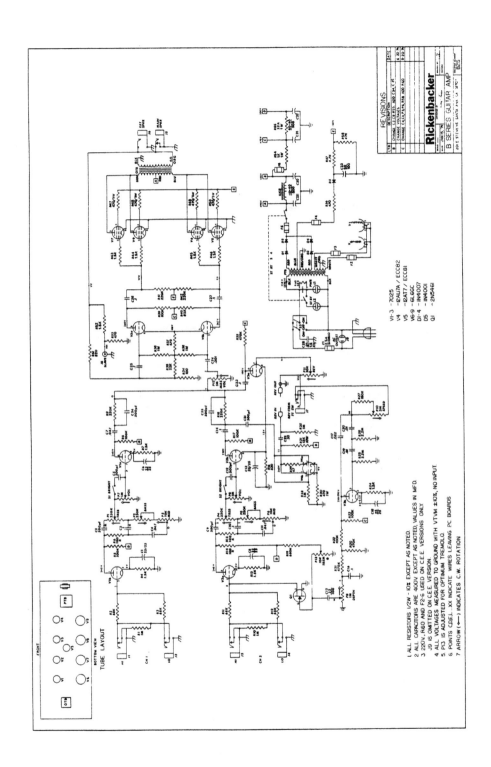

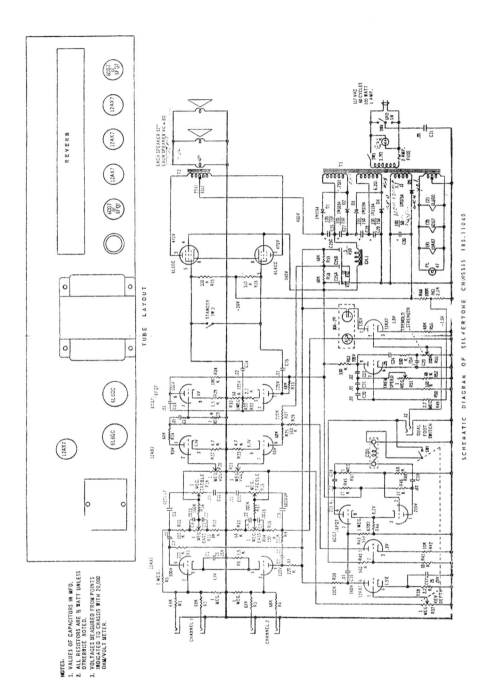

SCHEMATIC DIAGRAM OF SILVERTONE CHASSIS 185.11040

NOTES:
1. VALUES OF CAPACITORS IN MFD.
2. ALL RESISTORS ARE ½ WATT UNLESS OTHERWISE NOTED.
3. VOLTAGES MEASURED FROM POINTS INDICATED TO CHASSIS WITH 20,000 OHM/VOLT METER.

TUBE LAYOUT

REVERB

Kendricks

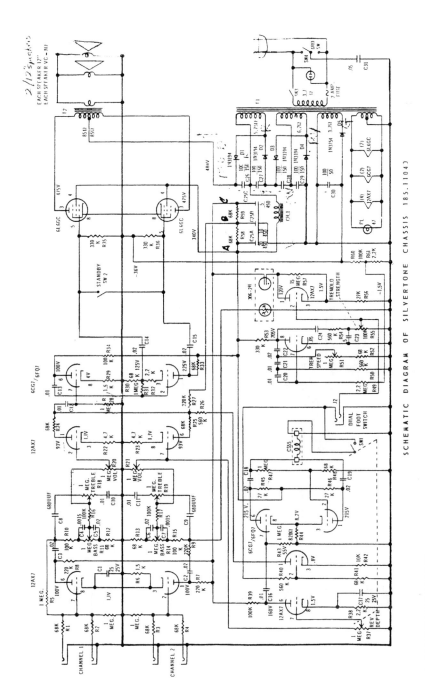

SCHEMATIC DIAGRAM OF SILVERTONE CHASSIS 185.11040)

SCHEMATIC DIAGRAM COURTESY OF SEARS, ROEBUCK

SILVERTONE MODEL
1484 (CH. 185. 11040)

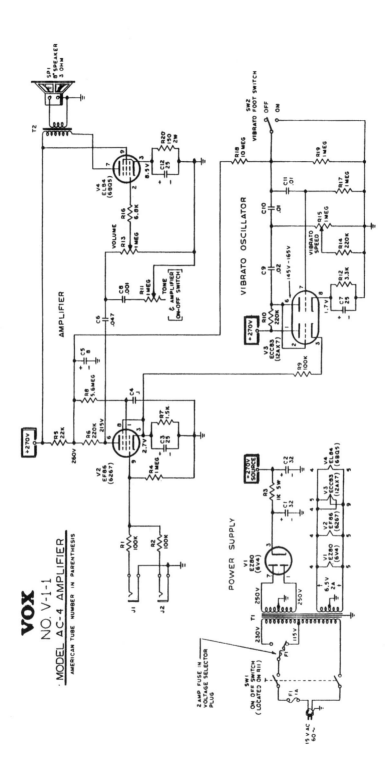

VOX

NO. V-1-1

MODEL AC-4 AMPLIFIER

AMERICAN TUBE NUMBER IN PARENTHESIS

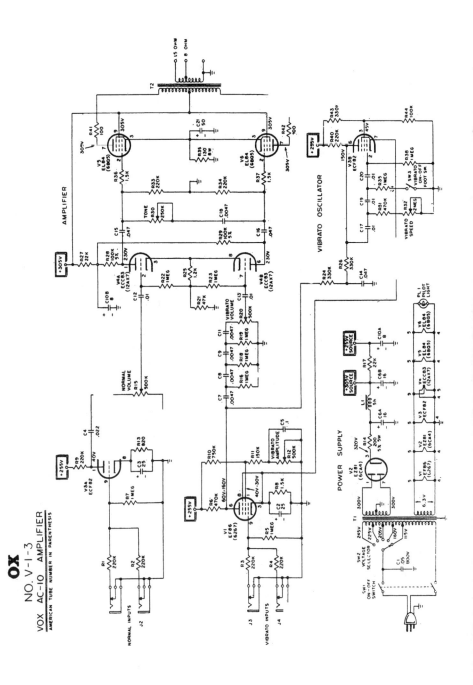

VOX

NO. V-1-3
VOX AC-10 AMPLIFIER
AMERICAN TUBE NUMBER IN PARENTHESIS

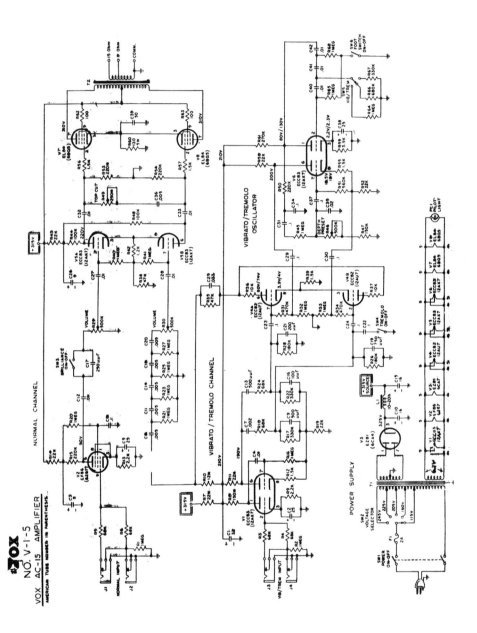

VOX
NO. V-1-5
VOX AC-15 AMPLIFIER
AMERICAN TUBE NUMBER IN PARENTHESIS.

Kendricks

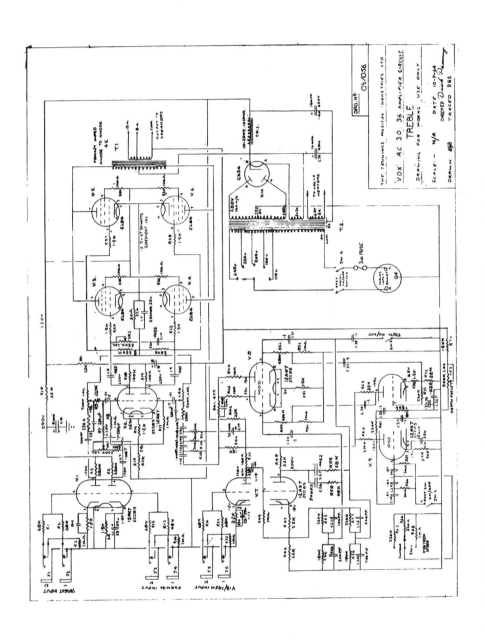

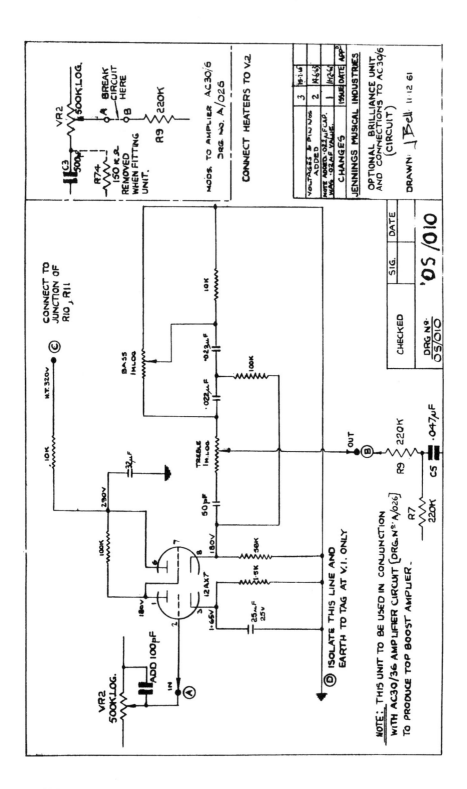

VR2
500K.LOG.

BREAK CIRCUIT HERE

R9 220K

C3 50pF

R74 150KΩ
REMOVED WHEN FITTING UNIT.

MODS. TO AMPLIER AC30/6
DRG. NO. A/026

CONNECT HEATERS TO V.2

				ISSUE
		3	19-2-62	
VOLTAGES & PIN NOS ADDED		2	14-6-63	
NOTE ADDED ·022µF CAP. WAS ·023µF VALUE.		1	14-2-62	
CHANGES		ISSUE	DATE	APP'D

JENNINGS MUSICAL INDUSTRIES

OPTIONAL BRILLIANCE UNIT AND CONNECTIONS TO AC30/6
(CIRCUIT)

DRAWN: J Bell 11·12·61

CHECKED	SIG.	DATE
DRG Nº. 05/010		'05/010

CONNECT TO JUNCTION OF R10, R11

M.T. 320v Ⓒ

10K

BASS 1M.LOG.

·023µF

10K

·022µF

100K

32µF

290V

100K

TREBLE 1M.LOG.

·047µF

OUT Ⓑ

R9 220K

50pF

180V

C5

7

8

6

180V

56K

12AX7

1·5K

R7 220K

180V

1·65V

25µF 25V

3

2

1

VR2 500K.LOG.

ADD 100pF

IN Ⓐ

Ⓓ ISOLATE THIS LINE AND EARTH TO TAG AT V.I. ONLY

NOTE: THIS UNIT TO BE USED IN CONJUNCTION WITH AC30/36 AMPLIFIER CIRCUIT [DRG.Nº A/026] TO PRODUCE TOP BOOST AMPLIER.

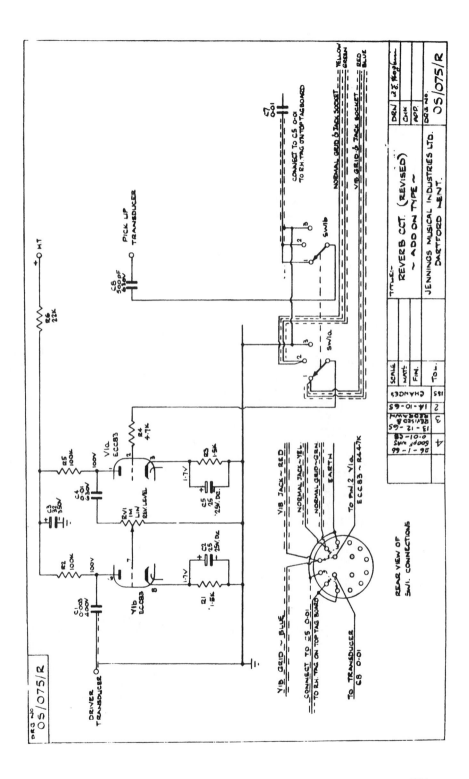

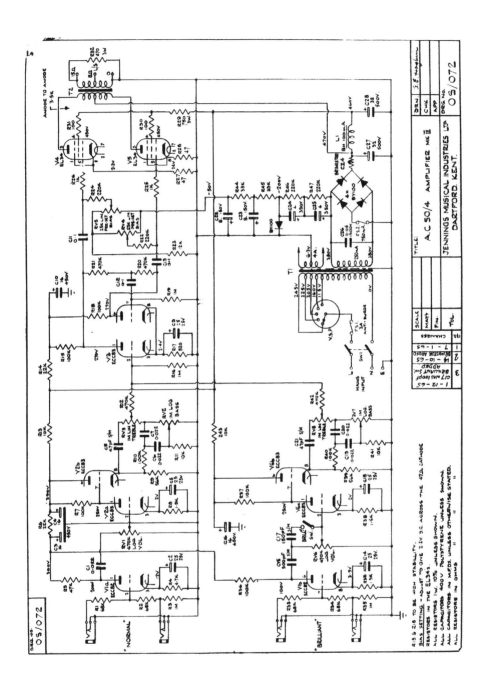

Kendricks

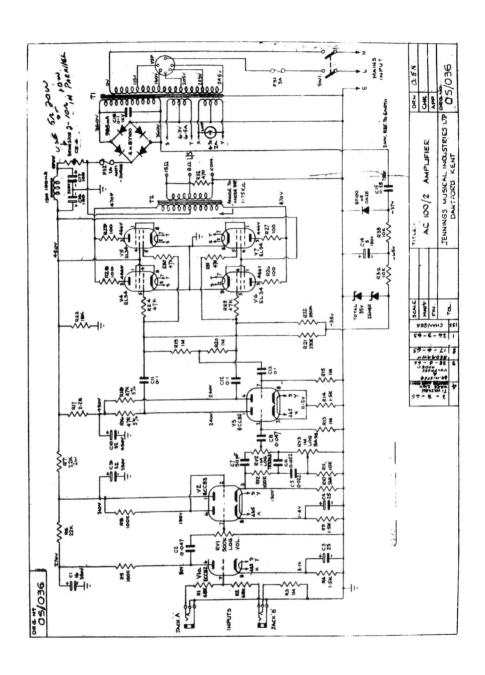

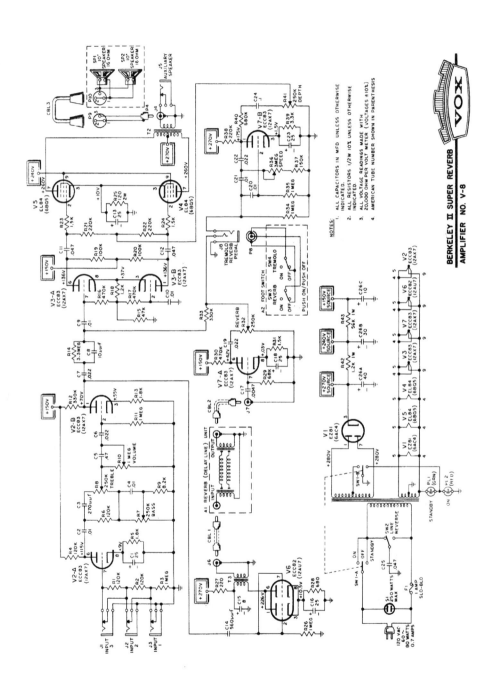

BERKELEY II SUPER REVERB
AMPLIFIER NO. V-8

VOX

NOTES:
1. ALL CAPACITORS IN MFD UNLESS OTHERWISE INDICATED.
2. ALL RESISTORS 1/2W 10% UNLESS OTHERWISE INDICATED
3. ALL VOLTAGE READINGS MADE WITH 20,000 OHM PER VOLT METER (VOLTAGES ±10%)
4. AMERICAN TUBE NUMBER SHOWN IN PARENTHESIS

Kendricks

REVIEWS

KENDRICK MODEL 1000 REVERB UNIT

"When all is said and done, only one important question remains: How does the Kendrick stack up against the original Fender unit?"

DESPITE RECENT ADVANCES in microchip technology, it remains the opinion of many guitarists that the best-sounding reverb comes from tubes and springs. One of the most sought-after outboard devices of this type is the early-Sixties Fender 6G15. Kendrick a firm known primarily for its tweed amplifier reproductions asserts that the company's model 1000 reverb is an exact copy of the in-demand Fender unit. So, to evaluate the Kendrick reverb, I tested it side by side with an original Fender 6G15 that was in fine shape.

The Kendrick reverb tested was covered in vintage tweed, with vintage oxblood grill-cloth, and a leather handle. While the

well-crafted tweed gave the amp the golden glow of a Fifties unit, it should be pointed out that Fender never used tweed on their reverb units.

The Kendrick's construction is first rate, a refreshing phenomenon in this era of short-cuts and limp facsimiles. The dwell control varies the strength of the signal sent to the full-size, two-spring reverb tank. With the dwell at low settings, the reverb effect is close and shallow, sort of like singing in the shower. With the dwell turned to higher settings, the effect sounds more like singing in the Grand Canyon. Anything between those two extremes can be easily programmed in.

Though the Fender unit uses just one, the Kendrick has two input jacks. The upper jack is guitar level, just like the Fender's, while the lower is effects level, a welcome

addition that makes it possible to use the Kendrick in the effects loop of any amp. This extra jack and the exclusion of an A.C. outlet on the Kendrick chassis are the only features different between the 6G15 and Model 1000.

The mixer control blends the amount of reverb added to the dry signal. The tone control affects only the tone of the reverb signal, not the dry signal. The output jack sends the final product to your amp's input or effects return.

When all is said and done, only one important question remains: How does the Kendrick stack up against the original Fender? I used both at gigs as well as in blind tests where I was unaware of which unit I was playing through. Several fellow guitarists performed the same tests. Though everyone agreed that both units sounded great, one emerged as the unanimous winner: The Kendrick Model 1000, which is a bit warmer than its ancestor and has a more even sound over the entire fingerboard.

If vintage is your thing, find a Fender 6G15. It sounds great and comes complete with 27 years of cool. But the Kendrick has a greater tonal range, works great—and comes with 27 extra years of unused life.

–KEN FISCHER

KENDRICK 4212

Originally printed in the November 1991 issue of Guitar World

By Luis Marcelo Fernandez

"Any fan of Clapton's tone on Live Cream Vol. 1 will be most impressed by the 4212's performance."

Ever wonder why tube amps don't sound like they used to? The Kendrick company obviously did and decided to do something about it.

The 4212 is a decidedly modern amp built the old-fashioned way. This 80 watt 2X12 open-back combo utilizes the Western Electric circuit that Leo Fender used in his 1959 tweed Twin amp. It also takes advantage of the same construction principles and materials used in late 50s and early 60s amplifiers. A peek inside the triple-plated, 16-gauge, cold-rolled steel chassis reveals point-to-point hand wiring with cloth-covered wire, ceramic tube sockets and hand-wound transformers.

The tube choices also reflect great attention to detail. The 4212 uses Tung-Sol 5881 beam power tubes, a Mullard GZ34 rectifier tube and selected preamp tubes. Tubes like these are difficult to score and, when found, they are expensive. However, they are well worth the effort and the price, as their tonal contribution is enormous. Their inclusion in this amp shows that Kendrick puts sound quality above everything else.

After voicing each 4212 for optimum performance, Kendrick removes the tubes and packs them separately, a practice usually seen only in hi-fi stereo tube amps. Add spike protection, transient power suppression circuits to extend tube wear, a circuit to reduce hum, and electronic components that are over-rated for long life, and you realize that these guys don't just care—they care a lot!

The Kendrick Blackframe 12" speakers are designed to duplicate the sound of a 30-year-old Alnico 5 Jensen. New Alnico 5s would not yield the same results, since the sound is extremely harsh and brittle. By using a voice coil bobbin made of heat-conducting aluminum foil instead of paper, Kendrick has provided cooling for the coil while eliminating the possibility of blown speakers—a very smooth move. And as if that weren't enough, they sound fantastic. The speakers' richness is emphasized by housing them inside a solid pine, finger-joined cabinet. Kendrick has also turned back the clock on style, with aged tweed covering, a leather handle, and chrome control panel, as well as vintage-correct grille cloth, knobs and pilot light jewel.

The control panel layout is the same as on early Fender and Marshall products: normal volume, bright volume, treble, bass, middle tone controls, presence, and two inputs (high and low gain) per channel. On the bottom of the chassis is the only concession to contemporary design: an effects loop. This can be activated by a slide switch located next to it, or via the supplied tweed-covered footswitch. There is an extra gain stage on the return side of the loop, controlled by a volume knob on the bottom of the chassis, to bring any weak return signal back up to unity. More importantly, this extra gain stage can also be used as a footswitch-controlled boost circuit. There is no external speaker jack, but there is a preamp out jack for driving slave power amps.

Since the Kendrick 4212 is designed to be played wide open, its tone is partially due to the tubes working hard, with much of the natural compression that occurs when power tubes are pushed. And what tone! The low end is thick and rich, while highs sing, bell-like, allowing notes to cut through effortlessly. Any fan of Clapton's tone on Live Cream Vol. 1 will feel at home; those floored by Stevie Ray's sounds will likewise be most impressed by the 4212's performance. The Kendrick Blackframe speakers really shine. They are superbly efficient and would greatly enhance the sound of any guitar amp.

The responsiveness of the 4212 is almost overwhelming, and with the extra gain stage engaged, dynamics become truly scary. This amp is extremely percussive. Pick softly, and the sound is sweet and clean; drive the strings hard, and the amp sings. It can also scream and growl, depending on your mood. From Bambi to Godzilla, it's all in your fingers. An amp like this one will undoubtedly make you a better player, since you'll learn to reach for tonal colors according to your attack. If you're used to, say, always picking hard and relying on effects (distortion, overdrive, puree, liquefy, or any other of the million blender flavors available) for dynamics, the Kendrick has a brave new (old?) tone world waiting. So what about our initial question? By using printed circuit boards, plastic bobbin transformers, and low-efficiency power tubes, manufacturers have cut their cost while increasing their profits, with tone coming in a distant second in the list of priorities. The 4212 is made the way they used to make 'em, and the result is an amp that won't make you search somewhere east of Java for your sound. No compromises have been made in construction or materials.

The only problem with making an amp like the Kendrick 4212 is that it's expensive to manufacture—and expensive to buy. The price for all the lust the 4212 can unleash is $2,495.00. Certainly hefty, but in the current back-to-the-future vintage reissue wars, nothing can touch the Kendrick. The craftsmanship is flawless and the amp is lovingly made, with a meticulousness rarely seen nowadays. Kendrick bills the 4212 as the best combo amp available anywhere; after auditioning it, it's hard for me to argue.

HEAD TO HEAD COMPARING 14 ALL TUBE COMBO AMPS

Reprinted by permission from the March 1992 issue of Guitar Player

By Stan Cotey

Kendrick 2410 ($1,799). Kendrick has gone out of its way to make the most authentic vintage tweed 4X10 Fender Bassman reproduction that money can buy. From the triple-plated (copper, nickel, and chrome) 18-gauge steel chassis to the finger corner joints to the faultless internal construction, they've done an amazing job. The original Marshall amps were inspired by the Bassman's astounding tone; the Kendrick faithfully replicates this sound.

Here's a twist: you can footswitch a tube-driven effects loop in and out of the signal path (when bypassed, the loop is totally out of the circuit). This loop has a return gain stage control; if you don't run effects, you can use the extra tube gain as a lead boost. In either mode, the loop works very well. The gain knob and loop jacks are on the bottom of the chassis. This retains the vintage look, but makes the loop awkward to access. According to Kendrick's Gerald Weber, some owners don't even realize it's there.

Kendrick uses a European rectifier tube. Its lower internal resistance is much closer to the original 50s design than most modern tube rectifiers. This makes the amp respond to pick transients faster and sound punchier; you can get beaucoup tonal variation by simply modifying your picking technique. So fine.

The 2410 comes with 5881 power tubes. Compared to 6L6s, 5881s sacrifice output for vintage tone. If you're after increased volume or a slightly more contemporary sound, you can replace the tube rectifier with a solid-state device and install 6L6s. A 25-turn precision trim pot lets your local amp doctor keep the bias voltage from drifting. Kendrick has designed their speakers to replicate the sound of 30-year-old Jensen Alnico 10s. In our opinion, they've succeeded. Kendrick 10s are available separately as Bassman replacement speakers.

This amp's distortion tones are definitely retro with a touch of Texas drawl—shredders won't dig this dirt the way blues freaks will. With the input volume cranked and the loop gain about halfway up, you can easily achieve a soulful "violin" lead tone. The clean tone, which sounds subtly compressed, is to die for. From twanging country to smoky jazz, this amp covers many bases. Kendrick has done a fine job of deciding where to stick to the 50s design (construction, parts, preamp, and power amp circuits) and where to modernize (footswitchable loop and bias circuits). A great amp.

COOL BLUES GEAR

Reprinted by permission from the August 1992 issue of Guitar Player

By Art Thompson

Texas' latest offering is the **Kendrick 4212** ($2,495). This 80 watt, 2X12 open-back combo is basically an updated and improved version of the old '59 Fender tweed Twin—the first guitar amp with four output tubes. The Kendrick features an all-tube circuit using NOS (new old stock), Tung-Sol 5881s (same as the original Twin), a Mullard GZ34 tube rectifier, and selected preamp tubes. We appreciate the effort and expense required to find these tubes; most are no longer made. Kendrick must literally scour the planet in search of ever-dwindling supplies. As if this isn't fanatical enough, after each

Stevie Ray spoken here:
The Kendrick 4212.

Kendricks

amp is fine-tuned for optimum tone, its tubes are then removed, packed separately, and shipped with precise placement instructions.

The Kendrick's construction shows equal attention to detail. The entire circuit is completely handwired on eyelet board with special cloth-covered wire (there's a Teflon jacket between the cloth and the wire) and NOS porcelain ceramic tube sockets. The cabinet is solid pine, finger jointed at the corners, and covered in lacquered tweed. The chassis is heavy triple-plated steel, with welded corners. We really like the Texas-size A.C. cord too—it's 20' long.

The 4212's top-mounted chrome control panel contains four input jacks, normal and bright volumes, tone, and presence controls. The combo's footswitchable effects loop can also double as an extra gain stage. The Kendrick Blackframe 12" speakers are specially designed for this amp and feature unusual trombone-bell-shaped cones. They sound mighty fine and could be a cool choice for other amps as well (yep, they're available separately). One niggle: the 4212 does not have an external speaker jack, a bummer for those who need to run extension speakers.

The Kendrick's tone is as clear and bright as a desert sky. With the extra gain stage activated, its dynamics are Herculean. With your guitar's volume control, you can dial in any level of distortion or long violin-like sustain and still have plenty of headroom for clean rhythm playing. The 4212, which just oozes Stevie Ray's soulful Texas vibe, sets a new standard for high-powered blues/rock combos and is going to be a tough act to follow.

THE BEST 100 WATT TUBE COMBO? A 13 AMP SHOOTOUT

Reprinted by permission from the December 1992 issue of Guitar Player

By Andy Widders-Ellis, Art Thompson, and Chris Gill

Kendrick 4212 ($2,495). If you're into warm and burnished tweed Fender sounds, you'll love the 4212. This latest Kendrick, an updated and improved version of the old '59 tweed Twin, pumps 80 watts into a pair of Blackframe Kendrick 12s. These speakers boast a unique, trombone-shaped cone.

From its solid pine cabinetry to its completely handwired electronics, the 4212 is a work of art. The amp features the fiber circuit board and construction techniques found in early Fender amps. Since no PC board traces are used, the cloth-covered wire must be cut to length and soldered to the components in point-to-point fashion. The result is an interior that looks like a brand-new vintage amp with outstanding workmanship. We encountered only one problem while probing the 4212's innards: a 12Ω resistor wire came loose at one end of the effects loop selector switch *after we poked it*. We quickly resoldered the part and were on our way. This underscores one of the benefits of handwired amps: they're easy to service. The 4212 features all American-made parts except for the imported Mouser pots. Kendrick also uses as many original 50s components as possible. The ceramic power tube sockets are NOS (new old stock), as are the Tung-Sol 5881s and Amperex 5AR4 rectifier. The preamp tubes included one Tung-Sol 12AY7 and Sovtek and Phillips 12AX7s. The 20' A.C. cord is a nice Texas touch.

Kendricks

Although we were vexed by a microphonic preamp tube, our tests showed the 4212 to be one hell of an amp. It sounds a lot like an old tweed Deluxe—it even breaks up the same way—but it's about 20 times as loud. It has incredible harmonic complexity and richness; we were impressed by how fat and chunky it sounds, even at low volume. Complex harmonics translate well in this amp, but we liked it best with single-coils, as humbuckers tended to mush out the low end. The 4212's extra gain stage adds a huge amount of boost that is controlled by a volume pot and an in/out switch on the underside of the chassis. (The gain boost is footswitchable; you can also use this control as a master volume.) When activated, the distortion quotient increases dramatically; we preferred the sound with gain boost off. Comments: "Strong, punchy midrange." "Tight, deep bottom." "Nice, rich harmonic complexity in lower midrange." "Tons of headroom and dynamic range." "Easy to get a good sound." "Beefier than a herd of Texas longhorns." "Begs to be goosed."

BENCH TESTS: KENDRICK BLACKFRAME SPEAKERS

Reprinted by permission from the January 1993 issue of Guitar Player

By Ken Fischer

When Kendrick decided to introduce a 12" version of their popular Blackframe 10" speaker, they wanted to improve upon, rather than simply clone, the original Jensen design. Accordingly, the new $130 Blackframe has a unique trombone-bell-shaped cone and boasts a very un-Jensen 70 watt power rating. With a tone signature all its own, it's touted as a sonic upgrade to a traditional Fender speaker.

For our tests, we mounted a pair of Blackframes into an open-back '64 Fender Bandmaster cabinet and wired them in parallel to provide a 4Ω load. Our test amps consisted of a blackface Twin with original Jensens, a '64 Super Reverb with stock ceramic-magnet 10" speakers, and a Trainwreck Rocket amp (a 30 watt head that sports four EL84 output tubes in class A configuration).

Through its original speakers, the Twin sounded very bright but was plagued by weak low end response. The distortion tones were crunchy with good note definition, yet the sound was small. Switching to the Blackframes was like experiencing the Twin through a 4X12 cabinet. The sound instantly became bigger and fuller, probably due to the Kendrick's larger magnets and higher power rating. The Jensens have more high end on tap, but the Blackframes don't razor your ears at high volume. Our stock Super Reverb sounded thicker and meatier than the Twin, with roughly the same amount of high end we heard from the Kendricks. (The difference in top end was like a 10" speaker versus a 12".) Running the Super into the Blackframe yielded considerably more punch, yet the amp retained its soulful trademark tone.

For our final comparison, we A/B'd the Kendricks against a pair of original blue Vox Bulldog speakers using the Trainwreck Rocket. With its thick midrange and ringing highs, this amp sounds 100% British through the Bulldogs. The Rocket into the Blackframes yielded a much more Fender-like tone with a groovy Vox-like chime to the top. Very cool indeed! Country players: if you use a Vox, Matchless, or Trainwreck amp, these speakers could provide you with the ultimate British-Fender crossover tone. They're also just the ticket to beef up a thin-sounding amp. Kendrick's unique Texas twist on vintage Fender tone makes this new 12" a very welcome addition to the guitar speaker scene.

Ken Fischer is a respected amp guru and president of Trainwreck Circuits.

GERALD WEBER
THE TWEED KING

Reprinted by permission from Vintage Guitar Magazine

By R.K. Watkins

When you ask most guitarists what, besides that '56 Strat or '59 sun-burst, they would like to own, the reply is usually a tweed Bassman or a '68 100 watt Marshall Super Lead. While most vintage guitars were cared for, a lot of amps weren't. They had the Tolex scraped off their sides while sliding into vans, speakers were replaced, master volumes were added and they were usually mishandled and mistreated. The at-titude towards them was more cavalier. That lack of concern has cost us many pieces that would be treasured today for their sound and beauty. Fortunately for most of us there is someone who understands our dilemma. Gerald Weber, the owner of Kendrick Amplifiers Inc., has been there. He understands the frustration of not getting the sound you want. Rather than settling for the status quo, he's doing some-thing about it. He's building amps and accessories that sit quite hand-somely alongside the best of the classics. Although his original inten-tions were singular in nature, he has since given the rest of the world the benefit of his knowledge. If you ever have the opportunity to try a Kendrick amp, do so and you'll understand what the fuss is about.

VG: So when and where were you born?

GW: I was born in the swamp, in Port Arthur, Texas, on November 4, 1952, the day Eisenhower was elected President.

VG: Did you play music?

GW: I was doing seven gigs a week when I was in the tenth grade. I was playing with the Carousels, a band from Port Arthur. We'd drive across the state line to Louisiana, and play the nightclubs. They had an unenforceable drinking age in Louisiana. Since we were right there on the line, everybody would go across the river and party. There were tons of clubs, maybe a dozen clubs and they all had live music. That's where I played.

VG: Did you do any recording with your early bands?

GW: We did some recording but nothing that anybody would recognize. Just local recordings.

VG: Did any of the guys you played with go on to become famous?

GW: Yes, as a matter of fact, the drummer who worked with us, Bobby Ramirez, went with Edgar Winter's White Trash. He was a real good drummer. Unfortunately he got murdered in Chicago after a concert, that's what broke up the band by the way. They were attacked in a bar and a couple of the guys in the band ended up in the hospital and Bobby lost his life. He's about the only one I've ever played with that ever got any national recognition. There were a lot of guys that played in the same clubs as I did, Johnny Winter, Billy Gibbons, all those guys played over at the Town House in Groves, Texas, where I played. The Texas Pelican Club which is in Louisiana, Janis Joplin played there.

VG: Did you ever get to jam with any of these people?

GW: Unfortunately no, they would be playing in one club and we'd be in another club. We would go see them during a break. I've played with Jerry LaCrois, who was in Rare Earth. His brother played in my band and we'd go jam with them during our break and he'd come over and jam with us during his break, because the clubs were just down the street from each other.

VG: What kind of guitar were you using?

GW: I played a Jaguar a lot back then. You've got to remember that we were playing soul music. The Jaguar was the top-of-the-line Fender at that time and that's what I played. That and a Pro Reverb amp which had a little mod later on. I couldn't get enough overdrive out of the Jaguar, I couldn't get the tone that I wanted. So what I used to do (and I wouldn't recommend anybody doing this because you can really damage your amp doing it, but at the time I didn't know any better and I liked the way it sounded, so I did it) was I plugged my Jaguar into a Magnatone 50 watt head and then ran the output of the head directly into the input of the Pro Reverb amp. No speaker load, no load box, no load resistor, nothing to bump it down, I just ran it straight through and I didn't run the Magnatone very loud, just bump it a little bit, but I'd get that extra gain out the Jaguar. It would give me this huge tone and it would sound more like a Les Paul.

VG: Do you still have that Pro?

GW: No, I sold it for $100 in 1972, traded it in on a transistor amp. That was before I was very hip about tubes.

VG: How long did you play and when did you quit?

GW: I guess I played pretty regular over there from 1967 to 1975.

VG: So do you still play?

GW: Yes, the name of my band is Red Hot Blue. We play around town. The people I play with are a bunch of old farts like myself. They've got kids and run businesses. We only play a few gigs a month. We rehearse twice a week. We don't like to do that many gigs because it's a hassle to move all that equipment. I have a C-3 organ and a Leslie plus all this massive P.A. equipment, it's just too much work.

VG: I take it everybody plays Kendrick amps?

GW: Right, all the amps are Kendrick amps. The bass player has two 180 watt power amps that I built and eight 10" speakers and four 15" speakers that he uses. I use a special Kendrick that I made for myself, it's the same head as our 4000 regular, the guts out of 4212 amp, basically a tweed Twin style circuit with a tube rectifier, a GZ34 tube rectifier, but then I've got a transformer to make it 8 ohms output and I've got a Kendrick 4X12 cabinet with four Blackframe speakers. It's a monster sound.

VG: How did you go from music to making amps?

GW: I had always tinkered with amplifiers. I did my first mod on an amp back in seventh grade in 1965. I had this little Silvertone, it had a single 7189 output tube and it was probably about 5 watts and it was not loud enough. This guy that I jammed with back then got a new amp and he gave me his old Silvertone amp that had one twelve in it, so what I did was hook the wire from my speaker on my 5 watt amp to the input of his amp and it gave me this really nice overdriven sound, a really good sounding rig. That was my first amp mod. Then we used to do crazy shit, I remember one time we had a cord broken at a gig and I wrapped a nail with some tape and jammed it in with the wire touching the tape, jerry-rigged it. We were always playing around doing stuff with amps back then. As far as actually building an amp, I didn't start building them until 1986 or so. I was in the meat business, and I wanted to buy a really good sounding amplifier, and I had plenty of money, so I could buy anything I wanted. I had meat companies in five states and the money was just rolling in. So I went around to all the music stores and started looking at all these amps and nothing sounded good. I was very disappointed and I thought, I know that there are a lot of classic circuits with tubes that do sound good. I'd heard them before and so I started experimenting with building some classic circuits.

VG: Did you have any training in electronics?

GW: None. I did some self training. I'd go the University of Texas here in Austin, Hook 'em Horns. They've got an engineering library over there that's just huge, there are racks and racks of books on tube technology. These are old books written in the 40s and 50s. What I did was I went over there and got me a non-resident library card and I'd just check out a bunch of books and read 'em. A lot of times I didn't really understand 'em but I'd read 'em anyway (laughing) and I just kept reading them and I'd get more and read those. Then I'd experiment, blow a few things up, shock the shit out of myself, fry a couple of transformers, that sort of thing. Pretty much that's how I learned about amps.

VG: What was the first amp that you built?

GW: The first amp that I built was a 100 watt head, using a tweed Twin basic circuit, but I altered it quite a bit, I was able to run the channels in series or parallel, and I put a master volume in it and an effects loop. I still have that amp and I'm using it as the power amp for the P.A. for my band.

VG: When you started was business just word of mouth or what?

GW: It was an accident really, I didn't actually start the company, what happened was I just wanted to have a good sounding amp, and I built this amp for myself. My son wanted an amp and I didn't want him messing around with my amp, and I thought it was fun building this amp, so I built one for him. His amp is a little different. He's more of a metal player so I put in some extra things he would like. Then his girl-friend's dad, who's an airline pilot, heard his amp, he had brought his amp over to show him, and then he wanted me to build him an amp, so I did. The next thing you know I was building amps. Actually what happened was, when I built that amp, a friend of mine who works in a music store in south Austin wanted to see it before I delivered it. I brought it over to show him and there were some guys in the store that saw it and they were knocked out and one of those guys ordered an amp, it was just kind of word of mouth and the next thing you know I was building amps, I got drafted. I was still in the meat business then, and I'd do my meat business in the day. At night I'd come home to my ranch, where I had this extra barn with a floor in it. At one time it was a recording studio. I just came home and worked on amps. When I wasn't building amps I was experimenting on circuits and doing listening tests and that sort of thing. I did it every night. That's how it all got started.

VG: So at that point did you realize that you had a cottage industry?

GW: No, I still hadn't even realized it at that point, it was more of a hobby. I wasn't even thinking about its being a business. It got to the point where I had more and more stuff to do, and then finally it got to the point where I couldn't keep doing it in my barn because we were getting a lot of equipment and tools. I ended up buying an eyelet press to press brass eyelets into fiberboard. At that time I thought if I'm going to keep doing this I'm going to need a bigger place. I had a building in Austin, where my meat company was and one of the buildings on that property was not being used. So I moved everything into it. Then I started hiring some people. I hired a Vietnamese fellow, Sanz Nguyen, who had worked for Texas Instruments for about 12 years, wiring for them, I hired him to wire stuff for me. It kinda grew from that.

VG: When did the shop open?

GW: January 1, 1989, formally. I used to work out of my ranch in Pflugerville. I worked out of my barn for several years just building stuff for myself and my son and friends, that sort of thing.

VG: How many people do you employ now?

GW: There's about a dozen of us altogether, counting me and my wife.

VG: So it's a family operation?

GW: Yes, my wife does the covering. She does that at home, because we have two kids and that gives her something to do while they're in school. We recently bought a glue spreader. We use the same type of glue that Fender used in the 50s and 60s: sugar animal glue, hot glue. We have the spreader for that.

VG: Where did the name Kendrick come from?

GW: Before there was Kendrick Amplifiers Inc., there was America's

Choice Meat Company. After I got through at the meat company I'd come home and fiddle around with amps till the wee hours of the morning. My wife would come in at midnight and ask, "When are you coming to bed?" I'd tell her I'd be there in another five minutes, just let me solder one last connection and I'd be there and then one thing would lead to another. About one o'clock she'd come back in and ask, "Well, when are you coming to bed?" "Well, let me finish putting in these capacitors. As soon as I've finished that I'll be there." Usually around two o'clock she would come in again and finally I'd go to bed, but she would be pissed by then. This was happening pretty much on a nightly basis. One night I had the idea of how much fun it is building amps and I'd sure like to go into the amplifier business, and we went through the same little scenario with her coming at midnight, and one o'clock. I'd been thinking about it all night, so when she walked in the door at two o'clock, I said "Let's get out of the meat business and start a amplifier company." She said "DO WHAT!" She had the woman scorned look on her face, and I said "Yeah we could call it Kendrick Amplifiers" (her middle name is Kendrick) and she smiled and said, "This sounds like a wonderful idea." (laughs) That's how the Kendrick name came about.

VG: So how many amps do you build in a month?

GW: Probably about thirty-five units per month.

VG: Are these built to order or do you have a stockpile?

GW: We couldn't keep a stockpile if we wanted to. We've been back ordered ever since we got started. We can't build them fast enough to get caught up. We just have never been able to catch up. Right now the wait's probably about twelve weeks. We build maybe thirty-five a month, but we take orders for about forty.

VG: What besides the tweed Twin and Bassman styles do you have?

GW: We also have those in head format. We have the 2000 which is the head style of the Bassman amp, and the 4000 which is the tweed Twin style, which is what I use in my band. We also have some other products. We have a reverb unit, in fact *Vintage Guitar* gave us a rave review. *Guitar World* and *Guitar Player* both gave us great reviews. *Guitar Player* said that we had tone to die for. I was pretty pleased that they put it that way. We make 10" and 12" speakers for our own amplifiers. We get a lot of restoration jobs where they'll want those as replacement speakers and we sell them for replacement purposes. We also do complete vintage restoration. I stock parts nobody else has. I have name plates for '59 Twins and early Fenders. We have the tweed and we do recovering. We do blackface amps, blond and brown amps. I had a Super Reverb that we had taken to the point of even chrome plating the legs and re-nickeling the bumper corners. We can carry 'em to the limit. We can go to the point of rewinding transformers. It just depends on how much somebody wants to get done. We can completely rebuild it. We get a lot of rebuilds like that. Right now we've got a '57 Twin, a '54 Twin, a couple of tweed Princetons. All of them are in for rebuilds. We get them in every day from all over the country, even from other countries.

VG: You also sell tubes?

GW: I've got to because nobody else has anything that's any good. There isn't anybody who's really going to take the time to track down these new old stock R.C.A.s and Tung-Sols and all this good stuff. Pretty much everybody is selling this cheap Chinese garbage that is made with recycled metal and it's just no good. So we sell tubes only because nobody else will do it. We do this because we want to sell something we would want ourselves. When it comes to tubes, an R.C.A. 6L6 or a Tung-Sol 5881, you've really got something that's going to give you good tone.

VG: You obviously spend a great deal of time tracking these down.

GW: A great deal of time. We do it every day. It's very consuming timewise, in postage and long-distance phone calls. We send out a weekly mailing list to 140 different places, requesting that they check their basements for tubes. We have a special tube matcher that I designed. We test tubes at about twenty percent higher voltage than they would normally be running at. That way if they're going to fail, they'll fail then. We also test them for gain, idling current, microphonics and noise. On any amp that has output of ten watts or more, there's a small phase-inverter tube in the preamp stage and it's important that it be balanced because it's like two tubes in one. Usually a 12AT7 or a 12AX7, it's like two little triodes in one, and we even test them for balance. It's important that they have the same amount of output. That's what we do with tubes. We think it really makes a difference or we wouldn't do it.

VG: Do you do other amps besides Fenders?

GW: Yes, we do other amps; we specialize in Fenders because we use standard Fender values on a lot of the stuff we build. We have all those parts here. We can completely rebuild a Fender amp real fast. A day or two, completely rebuilt. We also stock parts for other amps, we do Voxs, and we have a couple here right now. We do Marshalls too. I hate recovering Marshalls because they're very difficult to recover. We don't stock the Tolex for them, so it takes a lot longer to get a Marshall done. Fender stuff we keep in stock.

VG: Do you have any old amps yourself?

GW: Well, I used to, but the amps that I build sound so much better, I found that I never played them, so I just got rid of them. A couple of them I parted out. Right now at home I have about six or eight amps, just different designs. Some of them are pretty bizarre, in that they're designs that I'd work up and build a prototype, work out the bugs, then when I got it exactly the way I wanted it, I'd leave it around the office for people to listen to and see what they thought. Then I would bring it home. Then do something else and bring it home. I've got a whole bunch like that.

VG: How much of the amp is handbuilt?

GW: We build the whole amp ourselves. I have a cabinet shop that just does work for us. We don't actually weave the tweed, (laughing) there's a mill that does that. We have the wire made for us to our specifications. The parts we have made are made to our specs. We have control over 100 percent of it.

VG: I saw your booth at the Dallas show in March, and there seemed to be a lot of interest. Do the shows generate much business for you?

GW: When we do a show, we don't have anything to sell because all the stuff is backordered. So what we usually do is, a week before the show, we don't ship what's supposed to ship, (laughs) and we bring all that to the show. We get us a couple of coolers and put about three or four cases of beer in them. We slide them under the table and bring out some of our favorite guitars and play. We bullshit with the crowd and when we see our friends we offer them a beer so they don't have to pay those two dollar beer prices at the show. We just make a party out of it. We don't have anything to sell but we want to be there. It's fun to hang out at the booth and visit with people and play guitar all weekend. That's pretty much how we handle our shows. We pass out brochures, catalogs, and demo tapes.

VG: So what are some of your favorite guitars right now?

GW: One of my favorite guitars is a G & L Sky Hawk with Fralin pickups, they're like vintage Strat pickups. The guitar won't take them without special routing. It's got a fossilized ivory nut, I changed the tuners to non-graduated posts. It's a customized guitar. Light ash, real light ash, it was the lightest one out of 24 that the dealer had. He weighed all of them and this was the lightest one. The only thing I didn't like was the stock block. The endballs of the string go too far up the block so you end up with some string wrap coming up around the string saddles. That causes a buzz. All of the Sky Hawks are like that so you have to use G & L strings. I don't like G & L strings, I like Scalar strings which are pure nickel. Those are great sounding strings. Not only that, but because they're pure nickel they don't interact with your body oils and acid and they last a lot longer. I had to get that block filled in with brass rods and redrilled at a machine shop before I could play it. I like the guitar now. Another one is a '57 Strat reissue, American-made with a two piece body, also with Fralin pickups. I'm real big on Fralin pickups. They're the best as far as I'm concerned. I like SGs. I just sold my '65 SG and I'll probably end up getting another one. I'm remorseful about getting rid of it. I sold it to a Japanese guy who just kept offering me more and more money and I couldn't turn him down. I also have a Les Paul Recording, the first one shipped to Texas; I've had that since 1970.

VG: Since you're doing a thriving business, have you been approached by anyone to expand into a larger business?

GW: I wouldn't even consider it. I'm having too much fun doing what I'm doing now. Anyway, if I were doing it for the money, I wouldn't have gotten out of the meat business. This is something we're doing because it's fun and we enjoy doing it.

VG: Besides your amp business, you do a column for *Vintage Guitar*. You give away what seems to be a serious amount of hard-earned information. Why is that?

GW: It goes back to what I was saying earlier, that we're not doing this just for the money. Sure it's a business but I'm a musician first. I know what it's like to crawl up on stage and like your tone or not like your tone. I think if your tone is happening, then you're happening. It will show in your playing, your phrasing, your expression. It works both ways. It also shows when it's not happening, you're not happening. I'm a guitar player and I want to see other guitar players happy with their tone and sound. Another thing is that people have been very good to me. One person in particular is Ken Fischer, who designed and builds Trainwreck, Rocket and Liverpool amps. They're fabulous amps. When I first started, I'd be up against it about what to do or I'd run out of ideas and I'd call Ken and he'd give me some ideas or offer some food for thought and sometimes flat give me the answer to some things. He was always good to me and generous with his information, so I assume that's the way people should be.

VG: You've just mentioned Ken Fischer and Aspen Pittman also mentions him. You're not mentioned in the Pittman book. Do you know any reason why?

GW: I don't know about that. I've never actually met Aspen Pittman and I would like to because he was quite an influence in my life, with his tube amp book. The first time I really started to get interested in building tube amplifiers was after reading one of his books. I would love to meet the guy sometime. I think he has made a contribution to the music industry.

VG: Do you know of any famous musicians that play your amps?

GW: There's a lot of players that use our stuff, but I don't talk to the players. I'll talk to their techs, who'll order the stuff and then later someone will say "I saw Steve Vai using your reverb unit on David Letterman the other night." I hear these stories but I never talk to these guys. Let's see, Gary Moore uses our stuff, Kim Wilson (The Fabulous Thunderbirds) uses our speakers in his old Bassman. Ian Moore from Joe Ely's band. Tom Verlaine in New York uses our stuff. Robben Ford's tech called over here the other day and wanted an amp for his new album but he wanted it in three weeks and we couldn't do it. We don't give any of our stuff away so we don't have any product endorsement. Anybody who comes over here talking about endorsement or free equipment, we just about fall out of our chairs laughing.

VG: I understand that you're in the process of coming out with a book?

GW: Yes, we're looking forward to getting it out, we've had numerous requests from *Vintage Guitar* readers plus some sent directly to me. So we're going to go ahead and draft ourselves into the book publishing business.

VG: Well, that just about covers everything at this point. Any last thoughts?

GW: I really do appreciate Alan and Cleo over at *Vintage Guitar*. Without their vision for the magazine, this interview couldn't happen.

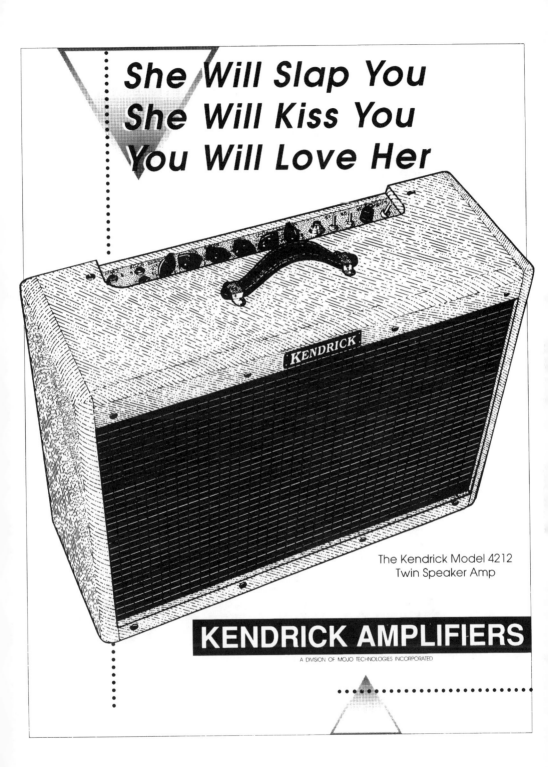

She Will Slap You
She Will Kiss You
You Will Love Her

The Kendrick Model 4212
Twin Speaker Amp

KENDRICK AMPLIFIERS

A DIVISION OF MOJO TECHNOLOGIES INCORPORATED

ABOUT KENDRICK AMPLIFIERS

Our purpose is to provide products and services in the field of tube amplifiers that allow musicians to experience their own musical expression as inspiration. We know from personal experience that a musician's ability to perform is somehow linked to the tone and dynamics of his amplifier. We believe that inspiration occurs when the amplifier is performing as well as the performer.

Inside our purpose, we produce amps that breathe with the player, speakers that can sing or whisper, and dynamic response not found in modern "Swiss army knife" amps. While other companies are mass-producing tone bleeding printed circuit boards, Kendrick is carefully individually hand wiring its amps, point to point style, to achieve maximum harmonic richness and warmth.

If you've ever asked yourself, "Why aren't tube amps made with raw tone and punch like they used to have in the 50's and 60's?" We can answer that question for you. It's because of money. Tone bleeding printed circuit boards, harmonic murdering plastic bobbin transformers, 50 cent - low efficiency Chinese power tubes, and unreliable push-on connectors are just some of the manufacturing cost cutters that can compromise your sound for someone's company profit.

At Kendrick, our concern is not what an amp cost us to make or even how long it takes to make. We are concerned with harmonic richness, tone, dynamic response, warmth, envelope, and reliability. This simple philosophy is what separates us from virtually all other amp manufacturers.

We feel that players who use a Kendrick amp have advantages over other players. Although our amps are considerably more expensive than virtually all other amps, they will sound better, last longer, and command higher resale value. They are however, priced within the reach of most players. The fact of the matter is that Kendrick amps just plain cost us more to build because our standards are so much higher. Your decision to own a Kendrick amplifier will be an easy decision to make when you realize that you care about your sound as much as we care about ours.

ABOUT OUR COMBO AMPS

All amps are hand wired point to point with cloth covered wire. There are never any printed circuit boards in anything we build. Printed circuit boards are co-planar, so the circuit would see small capacitances between traces even though they are not on the schematic. High frequencies would then leak out of the signal path which results in a dry tone. In a point to point layout, nothing is co-planar, therefore nothing gets lost. All of our transformers are hand wound directly on paper. Only the paper insulates the windings. This results in a rich tone and thick low end, and much greater efficiency. It is interesting to note that all transformers were wound this way in the 50's and early 60's. Kendrick amplifiers have special vacuum tubes, many of which are new old stock American military grade or new Russian military grade for optimum performance, reliability, and tonal characteristics. Of course, the combo amps are equipped with Kendrick Blackframe speakers. When you play a Kendrick for the first time, the first thing you are likely to notice is the dynamic response. Our amps can be very percussive. Cabinetry is solid pine with finger jointed corners and classic aged tweed covering and leather handle. All 40 watt and 80 watt amps feature the exclusive Kendrick footswitchable effects loop. In addition to the usual send and return jacks, the loop also provides a tube driven extra gain stage with volume control. The extra gain stage can be used three different ways. First, as a unity gain control, second, as an active master volume and third, as a pre-set volume boost for punching up solos. The extra gain stage does not color the sound in any way, but does provide the kind of flexibility not found in vintage amps.

80 WATT COMBO AMPS

MODEL 4212 TWIN SPEAKER COMBO AMP (pictured on front cover)

The 4212 utilizes the same Western Electric circuit used by Leo Fender in the 1959 Tweed Twin Amp(5F8A) with the addition of a footswitchable effects loop and extra gain stage. This was the first 4 output tube amp design and was also the circuit used in the original 100 watt plexi - Marshall.

Due to the deep clear bass response of the Kendrick 12" Blackframe speakers, the 4212 has the same broad, woody resonant tone of a classic 4 X 12. However, because of the open back cabinet design, the sound is more omni-directional, unlike a 4 X 12 closed back, which is more uni-directional. In other words, the 4212 combo has the presence and punch of a 100 watt half stack in a package half the size.
27"W x 20"H x 10"D   **Item #4212**

MODEL 4610 COMBO AMP ▶

This amplifier chassis is identical to the 4212 Amp above, however the speaker arrangement is six 10" speakers with the bottom two speakers in a closed back design and the top four speakers in an open back design., This amp moves a large wavefront of air (471inches) for the ultimate in fullness and low end. And because this combo uses Kendrick 10" speakers, the tone is a little browner and creamier.
231/2"W x 35 3/4"H x 11"D   **Item # 4610**

Model 4610

◄ MODEL 2410 COMBO AMP

After playing the 2410 Combo Amp, you will feel like you just had a conversation with someone. It will definitely affect you emotionally as you communicate with each other. This amp has all of the features of the 4212, except, it operates at 40 watts with four 10" speakers (in an open back design). Western Electric circuit as used in the 5F6A Fender 4 X 10 Bassman.
23 1/2"W x 22 3/4"H x 11"D **Item # 2410**

MODEL 2410B POWER CABINET ►

For use with the 2410 above or 2210 combo amp below, this unit has 40 watts of tube power and four 10" speakers, but no preamp. A Kendrick combo amp will stack on top of this unit and its preamp output jack will supply signal to the power cabinet. The 2410B power cabinet, with its powerful 40 watt chassis, actually doubles your power and doubles your wavefront of air. 23 1/2"W x 22 3/4"H x 12"D **Item # 2410B**

MODEL 2212 COMBO AMP

The broadness of the 2 X 12" speaker configuration married to the sweet compression of the 40 watt chassis makes this the choice of many club players. Grand piano bottom-end with singing lead tones. (not illustrated – looks and dimensions are identical to the 4212 pictured on the cover).
27"W x 20"H x 10"D **Item # 2212**

◄ MODEL 2210 COMBO AMP

Designed for studio use, small club gigs and living room picking. The 2210 has all the power and features of the 2410 but only has two 10" speakers. Since the power is split between two speakers instead of four, the amp will break-up at a lower volume. You will never hear a better tone in a small package—**never**. 23 1/2"W x 15"H x 10"D **Item # 2210**

MODEL 2210 BASS AMP - 60 WATTS

This special edition Kendrick amp, designed specifically for bass, sounds at least 3 times bigger than it looks. Built with a massive power supply, it provides a loud clear 60 watts with a tonal range that combines the broad woody resonance of an acoustic bass with the roundness, depth and definition of a concert grand piano. Perfect for recording and live performance. Two ten-inch Kendrick Bass Speakers, with massive 60 oz. magnets, deliver fullness and bottom end not usually associated with open back designs.

CATHODE BIASED COMBO AMPS

◀MODEL 2112 -25 WATT

Modeled after the 1958 Tweed Deluxe, the Kendrick 2112 has all of the tone, with none of the noise or service problems of an older vintage amp. A pair of cathode biased 6V6 output tubes produce honey-dripping tones that can sound like six violins playing in unison. Rich and woody, the amp is perfect for recording, rehearsal and gigging where lower volume is required.

The 2112 has two channels, with high gain and low gain inputs for each channel. All four inputs sound different. There are two volume controls (one for each channel) and a single tone control. All three controls are interactive. For instance, if you are plugged into channel one, turning the volume on channel two will affect both tone and volume of channel one and vice versa. Therefore, many variations of tone and gain are possible with only three control knobs.

With a loud 25 watt output and the efficient Kendrick 12" Bell Cone Blackframe speaker, the 2112 can easily handle small club gigs.

Here's the twist, there is a line level output that is wired from the output transformer. This output can go directly into a power amp, tape recorder, mixer, snake cable or effect device. Unlike a pre-amp output (which would not include the output stage), the line level output retains the sound of the output tube distortion, inductance of the output transformer, and kickback voltage of the speaker. 20"W x 15 3/4"H x 9 1/2"D   **Item # 2112**

MODEL 2112 - T.C. (Texas Crude) - 35 WATT ▶

With 35 watts of cathode biased output, this amp truly lives up to its name. The natural tube compression produces a gutsy, singing quality, without the need for multiple gain stages. Like the 2112, simplicity of design is the key to this amp's phenomenal tone. Line level output and Kendrick 12" Bell Cone speaker are standard.
22"W x 20"H x 10 1/4"D   **Item # 2112TC**

◀MODEL 118 - 5 WATT

Modeled after the 1959 Fender Champ, the model 118 pumps 5 watts into a 4 ohm 8" Kendrick speaker. The secret to the 118's pure, rich tone is its simplicity. With only a single volume control, this amp will produce the classic tweed overdrive heard on many historic blues/rock recordings. Like the 2112, the 118 comes stock with a line level output for direct injection.
13 1/2"W x 12"H x 7 1/2"D   **Item # 118**

HEADS

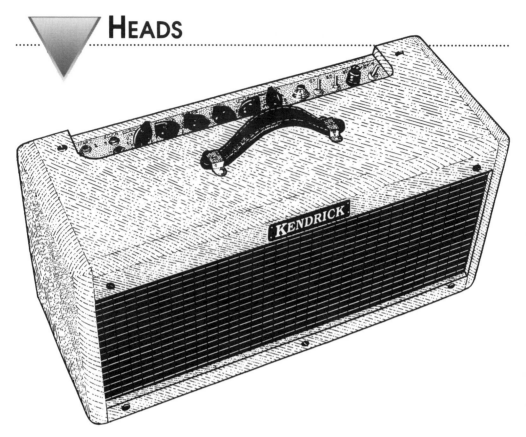

The circuitry of our 40 and 80 watt combo amps are available in head only versions. Classic aged tweed covering, with leather handle, is standard on all models. Like our combo amps, (cathode biased amps excluded), 20 ft. grounded A. C. Cord, tweed footswitch and footswitchable effects loop with extra gain stage are also featured. All of our heads use 5881 military grade power tubes (like all our combo amps).

MODEL 2000 HEAD — 40 WATTS

Identical circuitry to the 2410 combo amp, but without speakers (obviously). This amp has all the juice, punch and richness that you would expect from a Kendrick. Specify 2,4 or 8 ohm when ordering. 23 1/2"W x 10 1/2"H x 11"D   **Item # 2000**

MODEL 4000 HEAD — 80 WATTS

Identical circuitry to both the 4212 and the 4610, the Model 4000 gives a loud 80 watts of power. Although shipped with the higher fidelity 5881 power tubes, all 4000 series heads and combo amps can be converted to EL34, 6CA7, 6550A, KT66, KT77, KT88, EL37, 6L6GC or 7581A power tubes with only a minor bias adjustment. 4ohms — 23 1/2"W x 10 1/2"H x 11"D   **Item # 4000**

SPEAKER CABINETS

◄ MODEL 112 – 8 OHM

One 12" Kendrick speaker delivers clear bottom, airy dispersed midrange with chimey top end. Same size as 2112 combo amp. 80 watts maximum.
20"W x 15 3/4"H x 9 1/2"D   **Item # 112CAB**

MODEL 210 – 4 OHM►

Two 10" Kendrick speakers deliver defined harmonics with honey-dripping lead tones. Same size as 2210 combo amp. 40 watts maximum. 23 1/2"W x 15"H x 10"D **Item # 210CAB**

◄MODEL 212 – 4 OHM

Piano string bottom – end, with punch that is frightening — this cabinet could embarrass many 4 X 12 competitors. Same size as 4212 combo amp. 140 watts maximum.
27"W x 20"H x 10"D   **Item # 212CAB**

MODEL 410 - 2 OHM OR 8 OHM ►

Four Kendrick 10" Blackframe speakers in an open back design. Rich and full, this cabinet moves a huge 312 inch wave front of air. 80 watts maximum. Specify 2 ohm or 8 ohm when ordering. 23 1/2"W x 22 3/4"H x 11"D **Item # 410CAB-2**
Item # 410CAB-8

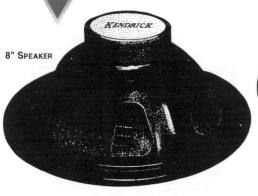

8" SPEAKER

10" SPEAKER

10 INCH KENDRICK SPEAKER

We originally developed the Kendrick Blackframe10" speakers for use in our combo amps, however we had so many requests for them we decided to sell them. These speakers are perfect replacement speakers for vintage amps because they are modeled after the old Jensen speakers. Our 10" speaker is a replication of a 30 year old P10-R Jensen Blue frame speaker. The P10-R was standard in the 4 X 10 Bassman. Our voice coils, seamed paper cones, and spiders are identical to the original Jensens, however, in order to duplicate the magnetism of a 30 year old Alnico 5 magnet we had to get creative. Alnico 5 has a half life of approximately 80 years. In other words, it loses about half of its magnetism every 80 years. New Alnico 5 will not work because it is extremely harsh and brittle sounding. we had to find a magnet that had the magnetism of 30 year old Alnico-5's. After months of exhaustive research, we developed a special cylindrical shaped Ferrite magnet. With this innovative design. the voice coil feels the same magnetic flux as a 30 year old Alnico-5 magnet; resulting in a virtually identical frequency response curve as the 30 year old Jensen speaker. Ferrite magnets have a half life of several hundred years, so your Kendrick Blackframe speaker will sound consistent for many centuries. Also since Jensen speakers were notorious for blowing, we chose to redesign the voice coil bobbin from paper which does not conduct heat, to aluminum foil which does conduct heat. This does not produce any audible change in the speaker, but it does provide cooling for the coil, thus eliminating the problem of blown speakers. Juice up your vintage amp with better sounding speakers.

Super Reverbs come to life with the Kendrick Blackframe10" speaker. In fact, Super Reverbs with the Kendrick 10's can be found as the house amps in many major recording studios. Harp players cannot live without this speaker.

8 INCH KENDRICK SPEAKER

When we developed the Kendrick Model 118 - 5 watt practice amplifier, we realized that there are 14 million Fender Champ amps that either had a bad speaker, a wrong speaker, or no speaker. That is why we were careful to make the speaker with 4 ohms impedance (3.2 ohms d.c. resistance). This speaker is obviously the best replacement speaker that money can buy for the Fender Tweed and Black-face Champ amps. With the original 3KSP paper and cones made by the original manufacturer, these speakers are as sweet as they are creamy.

KFRAME SPEAKERS

12 INCH BELL CONE SPEAKER

Our first 12" speaker was modeled after the P12-N Jensen (as used on the '59 Twin) but after 18 months of experimentation, we were proud to introduce a sonic upgrade of the popular P12-N style speaker. This is the 12" speaker we developed for use with our combo amps.

The bell-shaped cone is exponentially curved — like the bell of a trombone. This offers smoothness with punch. Extremely efficient, these speakers can make a small wattage amp sound huge, but are built to withstand the heat of higher wattage amps as well.

The Kendrick 12" Black-Frame speaker has a deep clear low end, an airy, diffused midrange and a well defined, chimey high end. The speaker has a very clear, transparent quality when using a clean setting. With the amp set for overdrive, the speaker takes on a woody resonance, much like the old Jensens, but, with a bigger, tighter low end and more focus.

Put the life back in your vintage amp with the Kendrick Blackframe 12" speaker. You will think you doubled your output. Power handling 80 watts.

WATTAGE OR EFFICIENCY?

I have noticed a lot of confusion about wattage and efficiency. Let's clear this up. Wattage is about **heat** dissipation. If a speaker is rated at a particular number of watts, then it can take the heat generated when that much power goes through the speaker. Efficiency has nothing to do with heat, but is actually how much **sound** comes out in relationship to how much power goes into the speaker.

Since low wattage speakers are usually very efficient, many otherwise knowledgeable players feel they must have a low wattage speaker to get a good tone. While Kendrick 12" Blackframe speakers are 80 watt speakers (this is how much heat they can take without burning up), they are also very efficient (SPL in excess of 100db). Highly efficient (lots of sound **out** in relation to power **in**), the speakers can easily be driven by a low wattage amp.

KENDRICK MODEL 1000 REVERB UNIT

You may have noticed that reverb occurs naturally in a large room and is affected by the size of the room (dwell), what the room is made from (tone), and the listener's placement in relationship to the source (mix). The **Kendrick Model 1000 Reverb** is the only reverb unit produced today that can control all three parameters.

▼ Exact vintage Western Electric circuit licensed to Leo Fender in the early 60's for Reverb.

▼ Enriches and thickens tone.

▼ Dwell, Tone, and Mix controls.

▼ Point to point handwired with cloth covered wire.

▼ Available in aged tweed/leather handle, or Tolex (Blonde, Brown or Black) with appropriate knobs and handles.

▼ Footswitchable Reverb kill.

▼ Works well with any quality amp.

19"W x 10"H x 7 1/2"D

Kendrick Model 1000 Reverb

Item # 1000

MODEL 100 REVERB ADD-ON MODULE

This 3 knob tube reverb module can easily be added on to any Kendrick amplifier (except the Model 118), as well as almost any other tube amplifier. Dwell, tone and reverb amount controls work nearly identically to the Model 1000 Reverb. Reverb tank and hookup wires included.
Uninstalled with instructions — order **Item # 100**.
Installation only — order **Item # 100 Install.**

Free installation when purchased with a Kendrick combo amplifier.

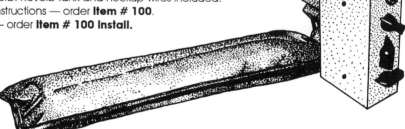

CLASS A OR CLASS AB - WHICH IS BETTER?

Much confusion exists about class of operation. Let's clear this up once and for all. An amplifier's class of operation is related to 1.) How much signal voltage is driving the tubes, and 2.) How those tubes are biased.

In a Class A design, the tubes are biased half way between cutoff and saturation and the signal swing voltage never exceeds cutoff or saturation. Since the signal voltage swing, plus the bias voltage never exceeds cutoff voltage, each tube is drawing current at all times. This sounds very good at low volume levels because the tubes are idling at significant current, and lots of current sounds rich and full. But high current generates much heat, and in order to keep the tubes from blowing up, the plate voltage must be significantly reduced. Reduced voltage means loss of power, efficiency, and dynamics.

With push pull Class A, the most current that the tubes conduct are when they are idling and here's where the problem lies. If you are playing and you want to accent a particular chord or note, the tubes cannot draw any more current than when they are idling, so the amp does not respond to the player's accents. In fact it will actually compress even more,(due to power supply sag), thus responding the opposite to the player's intention. This is the reason that Kendrick does not build pure Class A amplifiers. (The exception is the Kendrick Model 118 which is single-ended. All single-ended amplifiers must be Class A.)

On the other hand, in a Class AB design, the bias voltage is such that when the signal voltage peaks, one tube is cut off for a brief period while the other tube is **at or near saturation**. This sounds very sweet and musical. Not only will the tubes last longer, run cooler and ultimately be more dependable; but more power is available for accents. The result is an amplifier that does exactly what the player is doing.

For Kendrick Models	Soft Cover		Hardshell Flight Case	
	Order Item #	Price Code	Order Item #	Price Code
4212, 2212, 212CAB	4212SC	A	4212HFC	C
4610	N/A		4610HFC	C
2410, 410CAB	2410SC	A	2410HFC	C
2410B	2410BSC	A	2410BHFC	C
2210B, 2210, 210CAB	2210SC	A	2210HFC	C
2112, 112CAB	2112SC	A	2112HFC	C
2112 T.C.	TEXAS SC	A	TEXAS HFC	C
118	118SC	B	N/A	
2000, 4000	2000SC	B	2000HFC	D
1000	1000SC	B	1000HFC	D

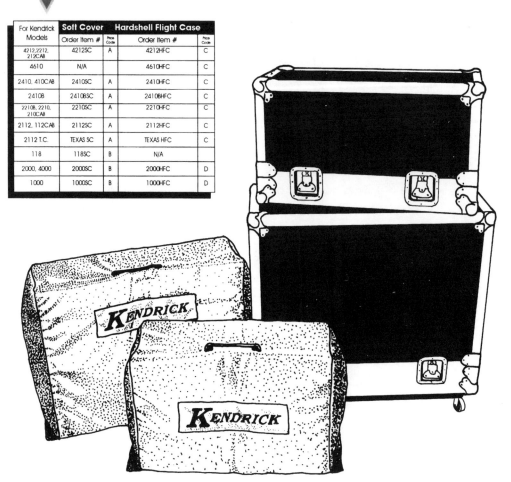

Would you bring your guitar to the gig without a hardshell case or at least a gig bag? Why not protect the investment your Kendrick amp represents and get yourself a soft case and/or a flight case? Use the soft cover for those times when you're transporting your amp or reverb in your own vehicle and want to avoid the dings and dangs of loading and unloading. When heavy duty protection is required, especially when someone other than yourself is the roadie, you can rest assured your rig will arrive safe and sound and in show room condition in a Kendrick flight case.

EXPERT REPAIRS & RESTORATIONS

Your tube amp may function, yet not perform! Electrolytic capacitors lose much of their effectiveness after 10 years, causing weak and mushy response and often times annoying hum. Resistor values drift, connections get corroded and components wear out. At Kendrick we are known for bringing life back to dead tube amps. We can make your tube amp sound better than it ever sounded. Also our recovering department can recover your amp in aged tweed, tolex or virtually anything you want. Speakers, grill cloth, handles, knobs, cabinet, hardware, logos — no problem. You tune your guitar every time you play, but when was the last time your amp was tuned? If you are like most people, it has been too long.

Here's how it works. Box up your tube amp with appropriate padding (remove the tubes and pack separately) and send it to us UPS. (Shipping is inexpensive - probably $10 - $20.00). Be sure to include your daytime phone number, shipping address and a letter stating what you want to accomplish with your amp. Upon receiving your amp, we will give your amp a thorough examination - checking all caps, resistors, transformers, voltages, tubes, etc. We will then call you with an itemized list of everything that is needed to bring your amp to optimum performance. There is no bench fee and our diagnosis is free! After you authorize the work to be completed, we will perform the work and ship your amp to you usually within 48 hours. Recovering or cabinet building will sometimes take a few more days depending on the job.

CUSTOM CIRCUIT DESIGN & MODS

I am frequently asked, "What kind of mods do you do?" My reply is always, "What do you want to accomplish?" There are many ways to alter tube amp circuitry, and when circuitry is altered, so is the sound. Do you want more sustain? Low end? Mid-boost? Dirtier? Cleaner? Hum reduction? Less noise? Browner tone? Dynamic response? Reverb? Gain? Punch? These are only a few of the possibilities!

We do not recommend any mod without knowing, "What result are you wanting to achieve?" Sure we do F/X loops, line-out, switch power tube types, etc. and we can do just about anything. However, when we know what you are wanting the amp to do, only then can we make recommendations to that end. Call us for a free consultation.

Ship to our factory address:

Kendrick Amplifiers
**110 W. Pflugerville Loop Unit C
Pflugerville, Texas 78660**

KENDRICK VACUUM TUBES

Kendrick Brand Tubes

5881	GZ34	7025A Grade 1	7025A Grade 2
Milky smooth distortion with creamy top end.	Punchy with character'	Toney, fat, with high gain, can be used in all 12AX7/7025 sockets	Toney, fat, with high gain for use in all 12AX7/7025 sockets except the 1st gain stage of a high gain amp
Item # KEN 5881	Item # KEN GZ34	Item # KEN 7025A1	Item # KEN 7025A2

OTHER POPULAR BRANDS

Mullard	EL34*	Item # MUL EL34
	EL84*	Item # MUL EL84
	GZ34	Item # MUL GZ34
Phillips	6L6GC*	Item # PHL 6L6GC
	6CA7*	Item # PHL 6CA7
	12AT7WC	Item # PHL 12AT7WC
	12AX7WA	Item # PHL 12AX7WA
RCA	6L6GC*	Item # RCA 6L6GC
	6V6GT*	Item # RCA 6V6GT
	6550*	Item # RCA 6550
	7027A*	Item # RCA 7027A
GE	7581A (20% upgraded 6L6GC)	Item # GE 7581A
Tung Sol	6550*	Item # TS 6550
	5881*	Item # TS 5881

AMERICAN MADE PREAMP TUBES & RECTIFIERS

12AX7	Item # AM 12AX7
12AT7	Item # AM 12AT7
12AU7	Item # AM 12AU7
6SC7	Item # AM 6SC7
6SJ7	Item # AM 6SJ7
6SL7	Item # AM 6SL7
6SN7	Item # AM 6SN7
5AR4/GZ34	Item # AM GZ34
5Y3GT	Item # AM 5Y3GT
5V4GT	Item # AM 5V4GT
5U4GA	Item # AM 5U4GA

* DUETS, QUARTETS AVAILABLE. PRICE PER TUBE IS THE SAME.

# OTHER KENDRICK GOODIES

▽ KENDRICK "T" SHIRTS

100% cotton, black "T" shirts with the Kendrick logo on the back and our slogan "She will slap you, She will kiss you, You will love her!", on the front. Specify size S, M, L, XL, XXL, XXXL. **Item # Shirt**

▽ KENDRICK SPEAKER STICKERS

Gold foil with the Kendrick Blackframe Speaker logo.

Specify size: for 8" speaker — **Item # Stick 8**
for 10" speaker — **Item # Stick 10**
for 12" speaker— **Item # Stick 12**

▽ KENDRICK DEMO TAPE

Cassette tape demonstrating the Kendrick combo amps and reverb. **Item # Tape**

▽ REPLACEMENT PARTS & TRANSFORMERS FOR VINTAGE AMPS

Complete line of replacement parts, components, transformers for the do-it-yourself repairman. Call for parts catalog and/or pricing. We can rewind any transformer. We stock most early tweed through 60's transformers.

▽ A DESKTOP REFERENCE OF HIP VINTAGE GUITAR AMPS

A 500+ page book written by Gerald Weber. This book covers the hip circuits of the 50's and 60's. Schematics of dozens of amps. Tricks, mods, tips, restoration ideas. **Item # Book**

A FINAL WORD

Dear Customer,

When you deal with Kendrick Amplifiers, you will find it is not the same as dealing with other amp companies. At Kendrick the president answers the phone. If you have a question or a problem, we are eager to help and will always make time to talk. Should you ever need a part, we will ship it to you that day. (Many other amp companies sell their parts only through a distributor which may take weeks or sometimes months.) All of our amps are guaranteed for one year. Tubes are guaranteed for six months. In the unlikely event that one of our amps should ever need service, they can almost always be repaired in just a few minutes because there are no printed circuit boards to cause inaccessibility of components. Occasionally our amp orders may be backlogged. This is to be expected when you consider both the demand for a perfect tube amplifier and the fact that our amps take 40 to 60 hours to hand assemble, and every amp is burned in, tested, and played an additional 50+ hours. We are pleased to offer our products and services to you. In ordering from us, you are supporting our company and what it stands for and for this I am grateful. I invite you to communicate with me.

Gerald J. Weber Jr.
President
(512) 990-5486

KENDRICK AMPLIFIERS

Mailing Address for orders and mail: P.O. Box 160, Pflugerville, Texas 78691-0160 U.S.A.
Factory Address: 110 West Pflugerville Loop Unit C, Pflugerville, Texas 78660 U.S.A.

Phone 512/990-5486

Fax 512/990-0548

www.kendrick-amplifiers.com

Kendricks

Other Works by Gerald Weber

"Tube Amp Talk for the Guitarist and Tech" with foreword by Billy F. Gibbons 500+ pages $29.95

"Tube Amp Basics for the Guitarist" - 60 minute video $29.95

Check your local dealer or contact Kendrick Books (512) 990 5486

NOTES

NOTES

NOTES

NOTES

NOTES

NOTES

NOTES